The Dangers of Ritual

The Dangers of Ritual

BETWEEN EARLY MEDIEVAL TEXTS
AND SOCIAL SCIENTIFIC THEORY

Philippe Buc

PRINCETON UNIVERSITY PRESS

PRINCETON AND OXFORD

Copyright © 2001 by Princeton University Press
Published by Princeton University Press, 41 William Street,
Princeton, New Jersey 08540
In the United Kingdom: Princeton University Press,
3 Market Place, Woodstock, Oxfordshire OX20 1SY
All Rights Reserved

Library of Congress Cataloging-in-Publication Data

Buc, Philippe, 1961–
The dangers of ritual : between early medieval texts and social
scientific theory / Philippe Buc.
p. cm.
Includes bibliographical references and index.

1. Ritual—History. 2. Europe—Religious life and customs. I. Title.
BL600. B76 2001
390′.094′0902—dc21   2001021156

British Library Cataloging-in-Publication Data is available

This book has been composed in Janson

Printed on acid-free paper.∞

www.pup.princeton.edu

Printed in the United States of America

3   5   7   9   10   8   6   4

ISBN 978-0-691-14442-9

CONTENTS

*The Bibliography for this book can be found in its entirety on the
Princeton University Press website, www.pup.princeton.edu/biblios/buc.*

PREFACE

THIS ESSAY was long in the making. I presented its first fruits starting in 1994, but I began working on it in 1990, as I was reading tenth-century sources in preparation of a lecture course comparing France and Germany between 800 and 1300. Noticing the high density of what one calls rituals in these documents, as well as the peculiar nature of the narrative patterns in which these rituals were embedded, I decided to explore further. Interest had much to do with intellectual biography. I had studied with Jacques Le Goff and Gerard Caspary, two men deeply interested in, widely cognizant of, and influenced by anthropology, especially of the structuralist sort. Among other mentors, Karl Leyser and Jean-Claude Schmitt utilized as well this social science, the one more Manchester school neo-Durkheimians, the other ethnology and literary studies of folklore. Close friends and contemporaries, then and later as the project evolved, drew effortlessly on anthropology. I think of Patrick Geary, Amy Remensnyder, and David Nirenberg. I too, I hoped, would come to understand what ritual was, and communicate this gnosis.

A seminar experiment convinced me that I had to investigate. I supplied my students with, on the one hand, several late antique and medieval texts containing what to some historians would have been rituals, and, on the other, several anthropological and sociological theories. The first set included coronation ordines, ordines for the ordeal, a chronicle featuring an ordeal, another depicting a royal accession, yet another with an imperial funeral and apotheosis, and a martyr's passion. The second set included Maurice Bloch, Emile Durkheim, Mary Douglas, Clifford Geertz, Victor Turner, and Max Gluckman, Renato Rosaldo, Georges Markus, and James Fernandez. There were two options for the written assignment. The one consisted in taking one primary source (or several from the same narrow era) and exploring it using a plurality of models, the other in using a single model to analyze a plurality of primary sources. The result was telling. Specific source-genres, and not all sources produced by a given culture, or not all sources bearing on a same sort of ritual, had a surface affinity with an individual theory. The literary texture of the source, that is, the mode in which it presented the ritual, led one to pick a social scientific model as opposed to another. A troubling conclusion, for it suggested that it is not the actual practice of the historical agents but the source genre that leads a scholar to employ a model. A priori, though, a given culture should be approachable through a single theory.

The inquiry now ends on a more destructive than constructive tone. No doubt, I shall be criticized for refusing to put forward a new theory of ritual. Friends have already done so privately. They have deplored as well the somewhat lachrymose tone (to use Nirenberg's term) with which I engage existing scholarship. Is it enough to overturn (or attempt to do so) a model that one thinks produces more confusions than positive results, and not to propose a fully constructed alternative? I think so. The absence of an alternative or rival does not entail that a model is true or logically sound. Why should one wait for a mature new thesis to invalidate the existing one?

The administration of Stanford University deserves my special thanks for having convinced me over the years, along with many other junior members of the faculty, that research is more important than teaching. Without its relentless pressure I might be a different human being.

Several other institutions have supported research and writing. I must thank the Netherlands Institute for Advanced Studies (Wassenaar), where I was a fellow for 1997–98, as well as the Max-Planck-Institut für Geschichte (Göttingen), where I finalized the introduction and the conclusion in July 1999. Stanford University Libraries and its staff (especially John Rawlings), the Leiden Royal University Library, and the Bibliothèque Nationale de France despite the dismal crisis that the hubris of Pharaoh François Mitterand (r. 1981–95) threw it in. My colleagues in the Department of History read drafts and commented on them, both owing to the tenure process and at the occasion of a faculty seminar in March 1999. No man being an island, I benefited greatly from many discussions and suggestions from individual colleagues across America, Western Europe, and the East. I acknowledge them in the relevant chapters, but want to give special mention to Alain Boureau and Mayke de Jong, as well as to Kathryn Miller and Brad Gregory. The latter named, as colleagues, have vastly enriched my self-awareness in this enterprise and provided fertile feedback. Some of Boureau's critiques of ritual anticipate my own; De Jong has been a valiant guide and sparring partner in my itinerary through the Carolingian world. No intellectual being self-made (contrary to the fictions of this age of individuals), I dedicate this book to my two old mentors, Jacques Le Goff in Paris and Gerard Caspary in Berkeley.

Paris, August 1999

ABBREVIATIONS

Journals and Serials

DA: Deutsches Archiv für Erforschung des Mittelalters.
EHR: English Historical Review
MIÖG: Mitteilungen des Instituts für Österreichische Geschichtsforschung
FMSt: Frühmittelalterliche Studien
HJ: Historisches Jahrbuch
HZ: Historische Zeitschrift
VuF: Vorträge und Forschungen
JEH: Journal of Ecclesiastical History
JRS: Journal of Roman Studies

Series of Edited Primary Sources

AASS: Acta Sanctorum. 50 vols. to date. Anvers-Bruxelles: 1643-- .
CCCM: Corpus Christianorum Continuatio Medievalis.
CCSL: Corpus Christianorum Series Latina.
CR: Corpus Reformatorum. Edited by Carl G. Breitschneider. 101 vols. Halle: 1834–1991.
CSEL: Corpus Scriptorum Ecclesiasticorum Latinorum.
MGH: Monumenta Germaniae Historica.
MGH Epp. Kar.: MGH Epistolae Karolini Aevi. Edited by Ernst Dümmler et al. 6 vols. Berlin: 1892–35. Equivalent to MGH Epistolae, vols. 3–8.
MGH Libelli de Lite: Monumenta Germaniae Historica, Libelli de Lite imperatorum et pontificum saeculis XI. et XII. conscripti. Edited by Ernst Dümmler. 3 vols. Hannover: 1891–97.
MGH SS: Monumenta Germaniae Historica, Scriptores. 34 vols. to date. Hannover: 1826–.
MGH SS rer. Germ. in u.s.: Monumenta Germaniae Historica, Scriptores rerum Germanicarum in usum scholarum.
MGH SS rer. Germ., n.s.: Monumenta Germaniae Historica, Scriptores rerum Germanicarum, nova series.
MGH SS rer. Lang.: Monumenta Germaniae Historica, Scriptores rerum Langobardicarum. Edited by Georg Waitz. Hannover: 1878.

MGH SS rer. Merov.: Monumenta Germaniae Historica, Scriptores
   rerum Merovingicarum. 7 vols. Hannover: 1884–69.
PG: Patrologia Graeca. Edited by Jean-Paul Migne.
PL: Patrologia Latina. Edited by Jean-Paul Migne.

Individual Primary Sources

AB: *Annales Bertiniani*. Edited by Félix Grat, Jeanne Vielliard, and
   Suzanne Clémencet, with an introduction and notes by Léon
   Levillain. *Les annales de Saint-Bertin*. Paris: 1964. Translated by
   Janet L. Nelson as *Ninth-Century Histories: The Annales of St.
   Bertin* (Manchester: 1991).
AF: *Annales Fuldenses, sive Annales regni Francorum Orientalis*. Edited
   by Friedrich Kurze. MGH SS rer. Germ. in u.s. 7. Hannover:
   1891. Translated by Timothy Reuter as *The Annals of Fulda*
   (Manchester: 1992).
Antapodosis: Liudprand of Cremona, *Antapodosis*. Edited by Paolo
   Chiesa, *Liudprandi Cremonensis Opera Omnia*. CCCM 156, 1–
   50. Turnhout: 1998.
CA: Fustel de Coulanges, Numa-Denys. *La Cité antique. Etude sur le
   culte, le droit, les institutions de la Grèce et de Rome*. Paris: 1864.
   Reprint, Paris: 1984, with a preface by François Hartog.
De civitate Dei: Augustine of Hippo. *De civitate dei*. Edited by
   B. Dombart and A. Kalb. 2 vols. CCSL 47. Turnhout:
   1955. Translated by Henry Bettenson as *The City of God*
   (Harmondsworth: 1972).
FE: Emile Durkheim. *Les formes élémentaires de la vie religieuse: Le sy-
   stème totémique en Australie*. 2d ed. Paris: 1912. Translated by
   Karen E. Fields as *The Elementary Forms of the Religious Life*
   (New York: 1995).
GC: *Liber in Gloria Confessorum*. Edited by Bruno Krusch and Wil-
   helm Arndt, corrected by Gottfrid Opitz. MGH SS rer. Merov.
   1:2. Hannover: 1969. Translated by Raymond Van Dam as *Glory
   of the Confessors* (Liverpool: 1988).
GM: *Liber in Gloria Martyrum*. Edited by Bruno Krusch and Wilhelm
   Arndt, corrected by Gottfrid Opitz. MGH SS rer. Merov. 1:2.
   Hannover: 1969. Translated by Raymond Van Dam as *Glory of
   the Martyrs* (Liverpool: 1988).
HIPAF: Fustel de Coulanges, Numa-Denys. *Histoire des institutions
   politiques de l'ancienne France*. T. 1, *L'empire romain—les Ger-
   mains —la royauté mérovingienne*. 1st. ed. Paris: 1875; 2nd. ed.
   Paris: 1877; 3rd. ed. as *La Gaule romaine*. Paris: 1891.

LH: Libri Historiarum Decem. Reedited by Bruno Krusch and Wilhelm
  Levison. MGH SS rer. Merov. 1:1, ed. altera, Hannover: 1951.
LP: Liber Pontificalis. Edited by Louis Duchesne. Reprint, 3 vols. Paris:
  1955.
Mansi: *Nova Conciliorum omnium collectio*. Edited by Johannes Domini-
  cus Mansi et al. 53 vols. Venice-Arnhem-Leipzig, 1760–1927.
Reallexikon: Reallexikon für Antike und Christentum. Edited by Theodor
  Klauser et al. 18 vols. to date. Stuttgart: 1950–.
ST: Thomas Aquinas. *Summa Theologica*. Edited in Thomas Aquinas.
  Opera Omnia. Vols. 4–12. Rome: 1888–1906.
TPPR: Bonald, Louis G. A., Vicomte de. *Théorie du pouvoir politique
  et religieux*. In *Oeuvres complètes*. Vols. 13–15. Paris: 1843. Reprint, Geneva: 1982.
VP: Vita Patrum. Edited by Bruno Krusch and Wilhelm Arndt, cor-
  rected by Gottfrid Opitz. MGH SS rer. Merov. 1:2. Hannover:
  1969. Translated by Edward James as *Lives of the Fathers* (Liverpool: 1985).

CONVENTIONS

ad an.: for the year

The Dangers of Ritual

INTRODUCTION

> Nous avons déplacé les notions et confondu leurs
> vêtements avec leurs noms
>   aveugles sont les mots qui ne savent retrouver que
> leur place dès leur naissance
>   leur rang grammatical dans l'universelle sécurité
>   bien maigre est le feu que nous crûmes voir couver
> en eux dans nos poumons
>   et terne est la lueur prédestinée de ce qu'ils disent
>   —Tristan Tzara, *L'homme approximatif*

THIS BOOK is an essay. Its surface object is political ritual in the early Middle Ages. By necessity, this object must be vague, because historians have, collectively at least, piled a vast array of motley practices into the category. In the process, no doubt, splendid studies have vastly enlarged the historical discipline's map of early medieval political culture.[1] We are indebted for many stimulating insights to the crossbreeding of history and anthropology—an encounter that began before World War II and picked up speed in the 1970s. From late antiquity to the early modern era, from Peter Brown to Richard Trexler, it revolutionized our ways of looking at the past. In this meeting, ritual loomed large.[2]

Yet from the start, it should be said that the present essay ends up cautioning against the use of the concept of ritual for the historiography of the Middle Ages. It joins those voices that have underscored how social-scientific models should be employed with extreme caution, without eclecticism, and with full and constant awareness of their intellectual genealogies.[3] In the pages that follow, then, the use of the term "ritual" is provisional and heuristic (the ultimate aim being to suggest other modes of

---

[1] See, e.g., Gerd Althoff, *Spielregeln der Politik im Mittelalter. Kommunikation in Frieden und Fehde* (Darmstadt: 1997); Geoffrey G. Koziol, *Begging Pardon and Favor: Ritual and Political Order in Early Medieval France* (Ithaca: 1992); Hagen Keller, "Die Investitur. Ein Beitrag zum Problem der 'Staatssymbolik' im Hochmittelalter," *FMSt* 27 (1993): 51–86.

[2] I provide an incomplete panorama in Buc, "Political ritual: medieval and modern interpretations," in Hans-Werner Goetz, ed., *Die Aktualität des Mittelalters* (Bochum: 2000), 255–272. Paradigmatic is Jacques Le Goff, "Le rituel symbolique de la vassalité," trans. as "the Symbolic Ritual of Vassalage," in Le Goff, *Time, Work and Culture* (Chicago: 1980), 237–87.

[3] See Hildred Geertz, "An Anthropology of Religion and Magic—1" *Journal of Interdisciplinary History* 6,1 (1975): 71–89. Cp. Natalie Zemon Davis, "The Possibilities of the Past," *Journal of Interdisciplinary History* 12,2 (1981): 267–75, at 275, 273, and Edward P. Thompson,

interpretation more fitted to the documents). Consequently, in the first part of this book, the word "ritual" will be shorthand for "a practice twentieth-century historians have identified as ritual." Throughout, the term stands implicitly between quotation marks.

More than medieval political ritual, thus, the essay's final object is the relationship between medieval documents and twentieth-century theories of ritual. More precisely, these chapters explore the fit (or lack thereof) between, on the one hand, the late antique and early medieval sources that contain depictions of rituals, and, on the other hand, the social-scientific (especially anthropological) models that twentieth-century historians have employed to analyze medieval rituals. The sources were produced in a political culture with specific traits and specific agents.[4] It had a highly developed "native" understanding of rite that "in turn reacted on symbolic practices". A status-group, the clergy, claimed a monopoly of legitimate interpretation (even if nonclergy could appropriate clerical methods and challenge clerical exclusivity).[5] Arguably, the exegesis of the (Holy) Book, the Bible, conditioned premodern Christian production and reception of texts in general. Critical in these clerical hermeneutics (and hence critical for our modern reconstructions of medieval political culture) were the relationship of letter to spirit and the notion of *Heilsgeschichte*, providential history.

As for the social-scientific models that twentieth-century historians use, they also emerged from a specific political culture. Or rather, from a plurality of cultures. From at least the Reformation onward, successive historical moments impressed their mark on the elements that ultimately coalesced, circa 1900, in the concept of "ritual." Like many concepts, then, ritual is the multilayered product of a *longue-durée* diachronic stratification. As such, it carries within itself the baggage of its early geological history. It is one of the main theses of this essay that the roots of our contemporary concept(s) reach down, with complicated subterranean trajectories, into the humus of the Middle Ages, and that this engenders methodological problems when one wants to apply these concepts to medieval sources.[6]

"History and Anthropology," repr. in Thompson, *Making History: Writings on History and Culture* (New York: 1994), 199–225, pleading for methodological eclecticism.

[4] For the concept of political culture, see Keith Michael Baker, "Introduction" to *The Political Culture of the Old Regime* (Oxford: 1987), xii.

[5] See Dan Sperber, *Du symbolisme en général* (Paris: 1974), 29–32, 60–61. The most visible usurpers (always helped in this by individual clergy) include kings and members of the high aristocracy. For the High Middle Ages, see Buc, *L'ambiguïté du Livre: Prince, pouvoir, et peuple dans les commentaires de la Bible au Moyen Age* (Paris: 1994), 173–97, whose erroneous assumption (173 n. 2) that Carolingian kings lacked interest in exegetical wisdom should be corrected in the light of, e.g., Nikolaus Staubach, *Rex christianus* (Cologne: 1993).

[6] See as well the controversial study by John Milbank, *Theology and Social Theory: Beyond Secular Reason* (Oxford: 1990), criticizing, on the grounds of such a genealogy, the application of social-scientific models to religion.

The intellectual tradition of hermeneutics would see in such a continuum an inviting chance to shuttle progressively back and forth between past and present categories. (And indeed, when reading the sources through the lenses it favors, those of exegesis, this study shall also avail itself of hermeneutic *Verstehen*.) But in the case of the relation between the social sciences and the medieval document, this chance is simultaneously a danger. One can lose one's way on the paths of pseudounderstanding. The risk lies in too fast an appropriation of the other, in a shortened, truncated hermeneutic spiral. Medieval modes of authorship and current social scientific habits do share one trait: Both purport to reveal the truth, spiritual or social, hidden behind the "letter" or data.[7] This commonality does not facilitate the match between the document and theory, to the contrary. It sets up a potential rivalry between the medieval author and the scholar, since the latter's data is provided and shaped by the former. Both are interpreters, and make same-order claims that their interpretation goes to the heart of reality—religious *mysterium* for the one, society's sinews for the other. Furthermore, as recent discussions of forgery have shown, these two "truths" differ profoundly in the way in which they find their expression in writing. An illustration of this can be found in Augustine's discussion of lies. For the Church father, a "fact" in the visible world can be true despite its seeming mendaciousness when it signifies a transcendental truth.[8]

The essay, then, aims at three things. First, it seeks to explicate what late antique and early medieval authors thought happened when events that historians have identified as ritual occurred. What did they assume rituals did or ought to do? In other words, what was the medieval native's implicit anthropology (as opposed to that, explicit, of the twentieth-century social scientist)? The mastery of the thought-world that informs the documents is an absolutely necessary precondition to any speculation about social

---

[7] As underlined in a pioneering essay by Talal Asad, "Towards a Genealogy of the Concept of Ritual", reed. in his *Genealogies of Religion* (Baltimore: 1993), 60.

[8] Horst Fuhrmann, "Die Fälschungen im Mittelalter. Überlegungen zum mittelalterlichen Wahrheitsbegriff," *HZ* 197 (1963): 537–38, discussing Augustine's reading of Gen. 27.19f., where Jacob dresses up as his brother Esau to obtain his blind father's benediction. See Augustine of Hippo, *Contra mendacium* 10.24, ed. Joseph Zycha, CSEL 41 (Prague: 1900), 467–528, at 499:7–13: "If we consider carefully and with a view to the faith what Jacob did at the instigation of his mother, with the result that he seems to have deceived his father, it is not a lie but a *mysterium*. Were we to call his deeds lies, then one would call lies all the figures that are meant to signify some realities (*res*), which figures are not to be taken literally but in which one should understand some other, dissimilar thing. This should by no means be done." (*Iacob autem quod matre fecit auctore, ut patrem fallere videretur, si diligenter et fideliter adtentatur, non est mendacium sed mysterium. quae si mendacia dixerimus, omnes etiam figurae significandarum quarumque rerum, quae non ad proprietatem accipiendae sunt, sed in eis aliud ex alio est intelligendum, dicentur esse mendacia: quod absit omnino*). And ibidem, 501:6–7: "These things are called true, not false, because, either in word or in deed they signify truths, not falsehoods" (*tamen vera non falsa dicuntur, quoniam vera, non falsa significantur seu verbo seu facto*).

agents' mentalities and practices. But authorial intentions and methods are
no less critical. The second aim, consequently, is to understand why authors wrote about these rituals, and how.[9] What was the role of a ritual in
the economy of a late antique or early medieval narrative? In a pointed
critique of Robert Darnton's *Great Cat Massacre*, Roger Chartier underlined that the historian must take seriously the textuality of the sources
(especially authorial intention and literary genre) and refrain from immediately applying anthropology to what is not raw data.[10] The same rules obtain when dealing with early medieval "evidence" on rituals.[11] One might
be tempted to employ a two-step approach to address Chartier's critique.
The first step is to reconstruct from the source, taking into account authorial intention, the ceremonies as they actually happened. The second step is
to process the resulting data through anthropology to come to conclusions
concerning society or culture. But as much as Darnton's approach, this
two-step operation results in an ultimately direct relationship between text
and the sought-after deeper social realities.[12] The authors, and the texts
with which they sought to influence the world around them, vanish; they
are lost as agents. Ultimately, there can be no anthropological readings of
rituals depicted in medieval texts. There can only be anthropological readings of (1) medieval textual practices or perhaps (2) medieval practices that
the historian has reconstructed using texts, with full and *constant* sensitivity
of their status as texts. The latter is nonetheless much more difficult (especially for data-poor eras), less reliable, and allows only a circumscribed
realm of appropriate questions and possible results.

[9] For a first attempt at a typology of narrative style in relation to authorial aims, see Philippe Buc, "Ritual and interpretation: the medieval case," *Early Medieval Europe* 9,2 (2000): 1–
28. The crafted nature of early medieval annals has been emphasized in recent years, most
noteworthily by Rosamond McKitterick. See also Paul Antony Hayward, "Demystifying the
role of sanctity in Western Christendom," in *The Cult of Saints in Late Antiquity and the Middle
Ages: Essays on the Contribution of Peter Brown*, ed. by James Howard-Johnston and Paul Antony
Hayward (Oxford: 1999), 115–42, at 124.

[10] See Roger Chartier, "Text, Symbols, and Frenchness," *Journal of Modern History* 57,4
(1985): 682–94, esp. 694.

[11] See also the caveat in Jacques Chiffoleau, Lauro Martines, and Agostino Paravicini Bagliani, introduction to *Riti e rituali nelle società medievali* (Spoleto: 1994), i–xiv, at xiii, but this
collection offers scant realization of the promised "attention scrupuleuse aux sources ... [aux]
limites spécifiques des sources qu'ils [the authors of the articles] utilisaient." Many historians
are well aware of the problem, but it is more common to invoke it and then forget it.

[12] For it is the product of two linear equations, (1) of deciphering, from text to historical
data, (2) of explanation, from historical data to the social or cultural processes subjacent to
this data. In the language of algebra, $ax + b = y$ and $cy + d = z$ resolves in $ex + f = z$. See
Kathleen Ashley and Pamela Sheingorn, "An Unsentimental View of Ritual in the Middle
Ages," *Journal of Ritual Studies* 6,1 (1992): 63–85. Despite an initial caveat (that the text is a
complicated filter), the authors move on to read the *Liber miraculorum sanctae Fidis* positivistically—the filter is, at best, linear.

The third and final agenda takes us into an analysis of concepts. For the essay's ultimate aim is to examine the fit between, on the one hand, medieval narratives and their implicit anthropology, and, on the other hand, the theories of ritual that twentieth-century historians have employed. When, where, and how are there continuities between the two? When, where, and how do we note breaks? In what ways does the combination of commonalities and ruptures produce misinterpretations of the medieval evidence? While German-style *Begriffsgeschichte*, like hermeneutics, helps link past and present, it can also serve to underline the disjunctions between them. Reinhart Koselleck's *Begriffsgeschichte*, while covering the immediate present and the deep past, ultimately concentrates on the eighteenth century. For this era constitutes the temporal locus of the *Sattelzeit*, the moment in German History when the concepts then emergent were "Janus-faced," that is, when they still allowed apprehension of the past but were already such as to make our present world intelligible.[13] Like Otto Brunner, whose approach Koselleck adopted and modified, I am more interested in the Middle Ages and the present than in the periods that mediated between them.[14] In Koselleck's enterprise, the subject of conceptual history looks like a bell curve, with its apex in the eighteenth century; this essay considers it, rather, like an inverted bell curve, with twin apices in the early Middle Ages and the twentieth century.

Given the essay's agendas, it is pointless to attempt to survey all the practices that historians have labeled "ritual." This hazy laundry list includes: the baptism of rulers; coronations and crown-wearings; princely funerals; entries in cities (or churches) and other processions or parades; civic games; banquets; the hunt; relic-translations and elevations; oath-takings; acclamations or laudes; knightings; ordeals; public penances; and acts of submission or commendation. More important for this study are early medieval categories and vocabulary. Occasionally, authors did group together a plurality of solemnities—here we get a glimpse of "native" classifications that do not quite dovetail with our own. For example, Thegan, one of the biographers of the Frankish emperor Louis the Pious (r. 813–40), took care to signal, in a single breath, his ruler's proper demeanor in hunting, wearing royal ornaments, participating at Christian high feasts (such as Christmas and Easter), and feeding the poor. Another author active under Louis, Ermold the Black, recounting the conversion at the emperor's

---

[13] See below, introduction to part 2, 162–63.

[14] I am indebted to Martial Staub for the (perhaps flattering) comparison. See Otto Brunner, *Land und Herrschaft*, 3d ed. (Brunn: 1943), 187–88 and 504 (*quellengemasse Begriffssprache*), 5th ed. (Vienna: 1959), 163–64 and 440, with Howard Kaminsky and James Van Horn Mellon, "Introduction" to Brunner, *Land and Lordship* (Philadelphia: 1992), xix–xxi; and Reinhart Koselleck, introduction to *Geschichtliche Grundbegriffe*, ed. Otto Brunner, Werner Conze, and Reinhart Koselleck, 8 vols. (Stuttgart: 1972–97), 1.i–xxvii.

court of the Danish prince Harald Klak (826), made it part of a series of solemnities. First, Louis sponsored the baptism of the Viking and acted as his godfather at the baptismal font, then Franks and northerners moved on together to banquet, hunt, mass, and gift-giving. It is noteworthy, however, that Thegan placed the solemnities just listed within a wider set of characteristics, which he called "sacred virtues" (*sacrae virtutes*). He did not mean to isolate the right performance of practices, which we might label "rituals," from other qualities of the ruler.[15] The sources' vocabulary also underlines a concern with right conduct, custom, pomp, and honor. Medieval writers, in order to indicate patterned behavior, might employ shorthand verbal markers such as *rite* or *secundum morem*,[16] or, with more descriptive valence, *solemniter, honorifice, humiliter*.[17] We are told, for instance, that Louis the Pious's son Charles the Bald celebrated Christmas 861 "festively, as is customary" and Christmas 862 "with the highest reverence."[18] This may or may not indicate that a bishop placed on the king's head, in the sight of all, a crown, which Charles then wore during the whole celebration of the Lord's Nativity.[19] At the minimum, the caption means to say that the ruler did what he was supposed to do on such a liturgical occasion.

Finally, early medieval authors had at their disposal a notion imperfectly approximating that of ritual. Fundamental for late antique and early medieval structures of thought (and especially for exegesis) is the relation between the Old Testament and the New. The Jewish Law, now superseded

[15] Thegan, *Gesta Hludowici Imperatoris* 19, ed. Ernst Tremp, MGH SS rer. Germ. in u.s. 64 (Hannover: 1995), 200:4–204:10; Ermold Nigellus, *Poème sur Louis le Pieux* vv. 2164–2529, ed. Edmond Faral (Paris: 1932), 166–91, with Janet L. Nelson, "Carolingian royal ritual," in *Rituals of Royalty*, ed. Simon F. R. Price and David Cannadine (Cambridge [UK]: 1987), 167–69.

[16] On the near equivalency of *ritus* and *mos*, see Andreas Alföldi, *Die monarchische Repräsentation im römischen Kaiserreiche*, reed. (Darmstadt: 1970), 7 and 10 n. 6.

[17] See Keller, "Investitur," 59; Koziol, *Begging Pardon*, 45, 60. Ingrid Voss, *Herrschertreffen im frühen und hohen Mittelalter. Untersuchungen zu den Begegnungen der ostfränkischen und westfränkischen Herrscher im 9. und 10. Jahrhundert sowie der deutschen und französischen Könige vom 11. bis 13. Jahrhundert*, Beihefte zum Archiv für Kulturgeschichte 26 (Cologne-Vienna: 1987), 123, 134–37, 198. Thietmar of Merseburg, for example, opposed one bishop's reception of a would-be king *honorifice* to a second prelate's "caritative" acceptance of the pretender at his table. See Thietmar, *Chronicon* 5.4–5, ed. Robert Holtzmann, MGH SS rer. Germ. n.s. 9. (Berlin: 1935), 224, with the excellent study by David A. Warner, "Thietmar of Merseburg on Rituals of Kingship," *Viator* 26 (1995), 53–76. But see Susan Reynolds, *Fiefs and Vassals: The Medieval Evidence Reinterpreted* (Cambridge: 1994), passim, who doubts that such expressions as *in hominagium* always imply that a ritual was performed.

[18] Hincmar of Reims, *Annals of Saint-Bertin ad an.* 861 and 862, ed. Felix Grat et al., *Les annales de Saint-Bertin*, 87 and 95.

[19] Carlrichard Brühl and others have assumed that Carolingian annalists mentioned where the ruler spent Easter and Christmas *because* rulers "wore their crown" festively on such occasions. See Carlrichard Brühl, "Fränkischer Krönungsbrauch und das Problem der 'Festkrönungen,'" *HZ* 194,2 (1962): 319.

by the New Dispensation of the Gospel, had mandated the performance of a great number of religious practices. Before the Coming of Christ, these Jewish rites had prefigured darkly Christian truths, and especially the Lord's Incarnation, life, and Passion. These *caerimonialia*, as they were called, were par excellence the letter to be read according to the spirit. With the Incarnation and Passion, their prefigurative role disappeared, since the truths that they had foreshadowed were realized in Christ. Consequently, the New Dispensation abolished for Christians Jewish ceremonial observances now emptied of meaning. The "blind" Jews still performed them, but, according to the logic of (Christian) providential history, to no real purpose. The early modern (and still current) expression, "vain ceremony," as well as the correlated idea that some or all rituals are "empty," harkens back to this assertion of superiority over Judaism. The opposition between practices empty of any true spirit and practices with a transcendental content or referent was highly appealing because it drew on the foundational opposition between the Old and the New Law. That it always implied superiority should be kept in mind throughout this essay.[20]

I shall *not*, then, aim at collecting all the descriptions of ritual that can be found throughout early medieval sources. Nor shall I draw up the histories of particular practices, e.g., the royal funeral or the king's civic entry (*adventus*), unless they serve the contextualization of a specific text. A number of monographs providing histories of this kind already exist.[21] Instead, the first part of the essay will explore fairly coherent documentary bodies, that is, either whole works or clusters of texts produced in an identifiable milieu. Symmetrically, the second part will *not* consider every anthropological theory that a historian might use to explain the Middle Ages, but focus on the social scientific traditions that twentieth-century historians have most commonly employed.[22]

[20] Cf., e.g., Jacques Chiffoleau, "Analyse d'un rituel flamboyant. Paris, mai–août 1412," *Riti e rituali nelle società medievali*, ed. Jacques Chiffoleau, Lauro Martines, and Agostino Paravicini Bagliani (Spoleto: 1994), 215–44, at 241–44, who suggests in neo-Protestant fashion, if admittedly "sur le mode hypothétique," a transformation of ritual into ceremonial. Cf. below, ch. 5:1, for the Reformation origins of the dichotomy ceremonial-ritual.

[21] E.g., Richard A. Jackson, *"Vive le Roi": A History of the French Coronation from Charles V to Charles X* (Chapel Hill: 1984); Lawrence Bryant, *The King and the City in the Parisian Royal Entry Ceremony* (Geneva: 1986); Ralph Giesey, *The Royal Funeral Ceremony in Renaissance France*, 2d ed. (Geneva: 1983).

[22] Hence such models as those proposed by the anthropologists Rosaldo and Fernandez, for example, will remain beyond the scope of this essay. See James W. Fernandez, "Symbolic Consensus in a Fang Reformatory Cult," *American Anthropologist* 67 (1965): 902–29; idem, *Persuasions and Performances: The Play of Tropes in Culture* (Bloomington: 1986), esp. "The Mission of Metaphor in an Expressive Culture," 28–70; Renato Rosaldo, *Culture and Truth: The Remaking of Social Analysis*, 2d ed. (London: 1993). While Miri Rubin, *Corpus Christi* (Cambridge: 1991), invokes these two authors in her preface, it is unclear to me whether she utilizes them.

As just argued, the medieval notion of *caerimonialia* is not identical with modern "ceremony." Another phenomenon that highlights the distance between medieval conceptions and social scientific models is that of "bad ritual." By this shorthand I mean rituals that social agents manipulate or rituals that break down. In strict method, these bad rituals should first be approached as elements belonging to narratives and not immediately (if at all) as actual events. But since modern analysts have taken rituals that work ("good rituals") as *eigentlich gewesen*, it is legitimate, heuristically, to place bad rituals on the same positivistic plane. Read naively as evidence for the real, the abundance of depictions of manipulated or failed rituals suggests that far from creating consensus or order, rituals could be positively dangerous. To perform a ritual, then, must in many cases have been positively a gamble, because one's enemies might manipulate it or disrupt it. Such is the first, surface meaning of this essay's title, *Dangers of Ritual*. Far from providing an unambiguous system of communication among the aristocracy, and hence a lubricant for the political system, the "rules of the game of politics" invited cheating and manipulation.[23] And far from automatically legitimizing the this-worldly hierarchy, ritual references to the exemplary heavenly order never stood beyond the challenge of the disaffected.[24]

Studies of political ritual probably trust the letter of medieval documents more than method warrants. Yet they have not always failed to notice how authors could heighten or deemphasize the rituality of historical events.[25] This insight should be an essential part of any model that takes ritual as its object. For challenges and manipulations happen in texts, and, in some political cultures at least, it may be ritual-in-text rather than ritual-in-performance that best legitimizes or delegitimizes. This is a second meaning of the title, *Dangers of Ritual*. In many a political culture, any performance can be the object of divergent interpretations through oral discussion (which, in the medieval case, we have lost) and through writings (which is all that we have).[26] This is especially the case in an early medieval world

---

[23] As demonstrated in one of Althoff's earliest studies on ritual, Gerd Althoff, "Das Bett des Königs in Magdeburg," in *Festschrift für Berent Schwineköper*, ed. Helmut Maurer and Hans Patze (Sigmaringen: 1982), 141–53. See the critique of ritual as creating order in Boureau, "Ritualité politique et modernité monarchique," in *L'Etat ou le roi*, ed. Neithard Bulst et al (Paris: 1996), 13–14.

[24] Cf. Koziol, *Begging Pardon*. Contrast his later study, "England, France, and the Problem of Sacrality in Twelfth-Century Ritual," in *Cultures of Power: Lordship, Status and Process in Twelfth-Century Europe*, ed. Thomas N. Bisson (Philadelphia: 1995), 124–48.

[25] Koziol, *Begging Pardon*, 110–12, 119 ("recorded or invented"), 146, on Flodoard and Richer of Reims. See as well Richard Trexler, *Public Life in Renaissance Florence* (New York: 1980), 229, 312.

[26] For pagan Rome and misinterpretation of kneeling before the ruler, see the remarks of Alföldi, *Die Monarchische Repräsentation*, 49–50. Stephen D. White, "Proposing the Ordeal

informed by exegesis. One must suppose, then, that to perform a ritual with an end in mind was to gamble that one's desired interpretation would ultimately triumph. A majority of our sources, and especially the narrative ones, are the product of interpretation or of attempts to channel interpretation. Even the earliest liturgical *ordines* for the royal coronation may have owed their production to ninth-century conflicts—the need to have a fixed blueprint to reinstate Louis the Pious as king after his 833 deposition and the desire to solemnize the highly irregular annexation of Lotharingia by Charles the Bald in 869.[27]

Rituals, then, are a complicated point of entry into early medieval political culture, precisely because of the importance this culture attached to solemnities.[28] They were too momentous for their depictions *not* to be highly crafted. To the specific techniques at play in this crafting we shall return. But while important, rituals did not constitute the sole foci of meaning in texts, and probably not in medieval political culture either. In a preface to his collected essays, Max Gluckman, an author often cited by historians, warned his readers that the early anthropologists, being missionaries, had focused mostly, in collecting data, on the religion of the natives and especially on ritual—"witchcraft trials, fertility ceremonies, masked dancers, wedding ceremonies, myths." This slant in the documentation, he cautioned, risked influencing reconstructions of cultures to the detriment of their more prosaic components—for example the family, the economy, and warfare.[29] The same applies to the era that medievalists study. And indeed, as the following chapters will show, authors concentrated also on efficient and God-willed warfare as well as on the behavior, especially but not exclusively sexual, of females of the ruling families.

That sources owe their being to purpose and circumstance means that the historian cannot establish a linear relationship between ritual and political order. Were the documents to restitute, positivistically, the events, he

---

and Avoiding It: Strategy and Power in Western French Litigation, 1050–1110," in *Cultures of Power: Lordship, Status and Process in Twelfth-Century Europe*, ed. by Thomas N. Bisson (Philadelphia: 1995), 89–123, at 98–99, 100 n. 53, 104–105, underlines how ordeals, pace Peter Brown, could intensify disputes, and be subject to divergent interpretations. Here his conclusions, based on a praxeological approach, dovetail with my own, grounded in textual criticism and medieval hermeneutics.

[27] Richard A. Jackson, "Who Wrote Hincmar's Ordines?" *Viator* 25 (1994): 31–52; *AB* ad an. 869–70, 156–78 with *AF* ad an. 869–70, 69–71. Admittedly, the *Ordo of Judith* cannot be placed in a conflictual context.

[28] For the importance the Latin West's Byzantine neighbors attached to solemnities, see Michael McCormick, "Analyzing imperial ceremonies," *Jahrbuch der österreichischen Byzantinistik* 35 (1985): 1–20. For the determining importance of historiography over ceremonial, see Gilbert Dagron, *Empereur et prêtre. Etude sur le "césaropapisme" byzantin* (Paris: 1996), esp. 129.

[29] Max Gluckman, *Politics, law and ritual in tribal society* (Oxford: 1965), 20–23.

or she might use good ritual as an indicator of order or social consensus
and bad ritual as an indicator of disorder or social dissent.[30] The lazy dream
of contemporary historiography could come true: The analysis of a single
phenomenon would grant access to society's essence. We would be as
blessed as stock-image Roman sacrificers, who could divine by reading a
single victim's liver the order (or disorder) of cosmos and polis.[31] However,
like good rituals, the bad rituals that the medievalist encounters do occur
in texts. They do not reveal necessarily so much the existence of disorder
in society or polity as point to authorial dissent. Whether authorial dissent
is itself symptomatic of actual social disorder is another matter altogether,
to be explored with other parameters factored in.[32]

Bad rituals, then, cannot be fitted in the putative linear relationship between actual performance and actual order. They belong to another evi-
dential realm. They should lead the historian to reevaluate recent reconstructions of medieval political culture, which have been distorted by
explicit or implicit functionalism. At the simplest level, bad rituals constitute evidence for authorial practice. More fundamentally, they betray a
sometimes radical (but in any century of the Middle Ages always present)
distrust for any simple relationship between the appearances and the reality
of *potestas*. Signs often deceived. Augustine distinguished between the miracles performed by good Christians, by bad Christians, and by magicians.
The phenomena looked the same; the powers called upon and intentions
of the agents differed radically.[33] He warned also that the fortune and mis-
fortune of an emperor did not correspond in any way, either as cause or as
effect, to his standing before God.[34] Likewise, a ruler's ability to present in
ritual his power as an image of God's *potestas* did not stand beyond suspicion. It could be attributed to a carnal spirit of ambition, rather than to the
spirit of God that should animate the liturgy and point to a *mysterium*.

---

[30] The linear equation attempted by Koziol, "England, France," using, especially, disrupted
royal funerals and coronations. Cf. his *Begging Pardon*, 305, where rituals are "indicators of
whether a political system is legitimate". Compare, on an Indonesian funeral, Clifford Geertz,
"Ritual and Social Change: A Javanese Example," repr. in Geertz, *The Interpretation of Cultures*
(N.p.: 1973), 143–69.

[31] Carlo Ginzburg, "Traces. Racines d'un paradigme indiciaire," repr. in Ginzburg, *Mythes,
emblèmes, traces. Morphologie et Histoire* (Paris: 1989), 139–180, at 149–51, speaks of a "paradigme indiciaire ou divinatoire."

[32] Such as the genre to which the source belongs, the author's spatial and temporal distance
to the event, and his or her importance in (or isolation from) political or social networks.

[33] *De diversis quaestionibus* 79.4, ed. Almut Mutzenbecher, CCSL 44A (Turnhout: 1975),
229:98–101: "*Quapropter aliter magi faciunt miracula, aliter boni christiani, aliter mali christiani:
magi per privatos contractus, boni christiani per publicam iustitiam, mali christiani per signa publicae
iustitiae*" (incidentally a possible ancestor of early anthropology's coordination between the
pairs private-public and magic-religion).

[34] *De civitate Dei* 4.33 & 5.24–25, 1.126–27 & 160–61.

These issues lead us to the third sense in which rituals are dangerous, that is, in terms of the scholarly risks that the use of the concept entails. The implicit or explicit functionalist bent of the historiography is not purely accidental. As part two of the essay will show, this propensity or affinity owes much to the history of the concept itself. The readiness with which medievalists have embraced anthropology is also a factor of *longue-durée* intellectual history. A quarter of a century ago, in his classic study of the cult of the saints, Peter Brown, with characteristic eloquence, explained the pregnance of the two-tiered model of religion by its rootedness in Western intellectual culture:

> Such models [positing a sharp divide between popular and elite religion] have entered the cultural bloodstream . . . Plainly, some solid and seemingly unmovable cultural furniture has piled up somewhere in that capacious lumber room, the back of our mind. If we can identify and shift some of it, we may find ourselves able to approach the Christian cult of saints from a different direction.[35]

Brown then went on to comment on the enormous "subliminal" force of this model. It was in no small part a factor of its "armchair quality," drawing on high-culture commonplace evidence that the educated could only recognize as authoritative.

Mutatis mutandis, the post-Reformation concept of ritual, with its increasing emphasis on the social function of religion, has worked in similarly "subliminal" ways. Certainly, the attractiveness of anthropology for medievalists owes something to the descriptions of poison ordeals and political ceremonies harvested in ethnographic fieldwork. In these African or Pacific Islands materials, historians identified materials cognate to, and as such likely to help explain, European trials by fire and monarchic rituals.[36] But the willingness to recognize, rightly or wrongly, this datum as relevant to the analysis of the premodern West has been favorably overdetermined (and the analytical results twisted) by the social-scientific analytical framework in which fieldwork was conducted—through and through Western in lineage. In the mirror of the other, we have been seduced primarily by the self.

The bipartite structure of the essay is a function of these three agendas. The first part concentrates on medieval understandings of "ritual," and narrative purposes and techniques. I have chosen to look at four moments of late antique and medieval political culture—backward, from the tenth to the first century c.e., in order to suggest simultaneously historical deri-

---

[35] Peter Brown, *The Cult of the Saints. Its Rise and Function in Late Antiquity* (Chicago: 1981), 12–13.

[36] As pointed out by one of the anonymous readers for Princeton University Press.

vation and limited determinism. The first chapter opens with the tenth century. It analyses how Liudprand of Cremona constructed the superiority of the Ottonian kings of Germany over their rivals for the Italian crown through a contrast between the two parties' rituals—sacral and consensual for the Saxons, ideological and deceitful for the others. The second chapter takes us backward to the ninth century. In a manner consonant with its increasing political fragmentation, the Carolingian world produced a plurality of sources. Taken together, they allow one to demonstrate the inadequacy of the functionalist approach to political ritual: It is as much the outcome of the struggle to control a ritual's interpretation as its actual performance that give it its efficacy. The third chapter centers again on the strategies of a single author, Gregory of Tours; here too rituals are mustered to demonstrate a superiority, this time that of saintly bishops over kings. The fourth chapter, devoted to martyrdom as a (narrated) ritual, underlines and explains dissent and opposition within rituals. Medieval political culture owes to the remembrance of martyrdom an idea: Patterned action within and against an enemy's ritual prevents this solemnity from manifesting and creating the order one opposes. In this first part of the essay, the reader may sometimes lose sight of ritual, precisely because the sources have to be dissected lengthwise and crosswise if one is to understand authorial intention and the place of this or that depiction of a solemnity in the economy of a text.

Comprising two chapters, the second part of the essay traces the formation of the concept of "ritual" out of an originally medieval theological matrix. It highlights the simultaneous co-construction of the ancestors of, respectively, Marxist and functionalist anthropology, starting with the Reformation and Counter-Reformation. The French Revolution provides the caesura between the fifth and sixth chapters. The organizational choice is somewhat arbitrary, but the event is not. Revolutionary disruptions, like World War I's aftermath a century later, provoked the crystallization of a new sociology.[37] It is well known that nineteenth-century and early twentieth-century thinkers often used the premodern era, especially the Middle Ages, to think about the problem of order. This role of the distant past explains to some degree why and how historians are prone to match anthropology with medieval documents. The sixth chapter ends with a confrontation between the logic of medieval documents and that of the social sciences. The idiosyncrasies of the social-scientific models relative to their medieval ancestors serve in turn to underscore anew the specificities of early medieval political culture—those traits that anthropological readings of the sources tend to misapprehend or leave aside.

---

[37] For the centrality of conservative (and often Catholic) categories to nascent sociology, see Robert Nisbet, *The sociological Tradition* (New York: 1966).

PART I

Late Antique and Early
Medieval Narratives

Chapter One

WRITING OTTONIAN HEGEMONY:
GOOD RITUALS AND BAD RITUALS
IN LIUDPRAND OF CREMONA

RELATIVE TO its competitors and neighbors, the Ottonian dynasty (919–1024) enjoyed remarkable success. Ruling Germany from an initially Saxon power base, Ottonian kings managed to capture and monopolize the imperial office; to exercise hegemony over northern Italy, Burgundy, and West Francia; and to foster the integration into Latin Christendom of their northern and eastern neighbors. This positive balance sheet, however, has not blinded historians to the real limitations of royal power, to the crises that repeatedly shook the *regnum*, and to the Ottonians' difficult beginnings.[1]

Recently, this last issue—Ottonian beginnings—has been hotly debated. Was the first Ottonian ruler, Henry I (r. 919–36), widely accepted as king in Germany in the first decade of his rule? Slightly posterior historiography, that is, sources produced during the reign of Henry's son, King Otto I (r. 936–73), would present Henry as the orderly successor of the Franconian King Conrad (r. 911–18). The most volubile of these sources— the continuator of Regino of Prüm's *Chronicle* (probably to be identified with Adalbert of Magdeburg), Widukind of Corvey's *Deeds of the Saxons*, and Liudprand of Cremona's *Antapodosis*—all recount Conrad's deathbed wish that Duke Henry should succeed him, and how Conrad's brother transmitted the royal insignia to the Saxon leader. But, remarkably, Ger-

I would like to thank here G. Caspary, M. de Jong, P.J. Geary, J. Glenn, I. Gorevich, G. I. Langmuir, M. MacCormick, A. G. Remensnyder, B. Rosenwein, as well as the Utrecht medievalists to whom I presented these materials in May 1995 and the participants at the November 1995 Majestas conference (Houston). This is a slightly reworked version of the text published in *Majestas* 4 (1996). All references to the *Antapodosis* will be to the new edition by Paolo Chiesa, *Liudprandi Cremonensis Opera Omnia*, CCCM 156 (Turnhout: 1998). It supersedes Joseph Becker, *Die Werke Liudprands von Cremona*, MGH SS rer. Germ. in u. s. 41 (Hannover: 1915), but Becker is still very useful for the historical apparatus. Chiesa has proven that Liutprand/Liudprand himself corrected one of the manuscripts; given that in one of these autograph corrections spells the author's name *Liudprand* with a "d," I have adopted, against my earlier usage, the latter spelling.

[1] See Karl J. Leyser, *Rule and Conflict in an Early Medieval Society: Ottonian Saxony* (Oxford: 1979), 25–26. A good master narrative is Timothy Reuter, *Germany in the early Middle Ages, c. 800–1056* (London: 1991), 113–74.

man annals produced during the first third of the tenth century (as opposed
to entries written later into annalistic manuscripts) do not mention the
accession of Henry I. Johannes Fried concludes from this silence that the
Saxon duke acquired recognition without any defining ceremony, and
probably only gradually.[2] This hypothesis receives support from West-
Frankish historiography. Flodoard of Reims (d. 966), a well-informed historian, called Henry "king" (*rex*) only once in his *Annals* (unlike Henry's
son and successor Otto, who was consistently *rex* from 936 on). The annalist did not deny the Saxon's strong reach into West-Frankish affairs. Henry
was a real presence whose help was sought by many parties in the semi-
permanent civil wars west of the Rhine. But when Flodoard gave him a
title, it was that of "*princeps*," like Hugh the Great, William Longsword the
Norman, Raymond-Pons III and Ermengaud *principes Gothiae*, Charles-
Constantine of Provence, William II of Aquitaine (d. 927), or the ambitious
margrave of Ivrea Berengar II.[3] Flodoard's use of titles is far from arbitrary.
He did not shy away from calling rulers *reges*, starting with the Carolingian
and non-Carolingian kings who governed, often feebly, West Francia. *Reges*
were as well, and consistently, kings over foreign lands and people, such as
Rudolf II of Burgundy (r. 912–37) or the rulers of Italy Hugh of Arles (r.
926–47) and his son Lothar. And after 936, Otto I became *rex Otto*. For
Flodoard, then, there was a strict difference between *princeps* and *rex*. A
passage in the *Annals* brings it home: "*Rex* Lothar, Hugh's son, having been
poisoned . . . a certain *princeps* Berengar is made *rex* of Italy."[4] The only
time Flodoard granted Henry the name of king was at the Saxon ruler's
death, to follow immediately on a dispute concerning the *regnum* between
his sons.[5] Clearly, while Flodoard did not deny Henry's effective power, he
recoiled from accepting him as a king.[6]

---

[2] Johannes Fried, "Die Königserhebung Heinrichs I.", in *Mittelalterforschung nach der
Wende 1989*, ed. Michael Borgolte (Munich: 1995), 267–318. See the rejoinder by Hagen
Keller, "Widukinds Bericht über die Aachener Wahl und Krönung Ottos I.," *FMSt* 29 (1995):
406–10 esp. nn. Keller rightly underlines the factor of intentionality in post-Henrician reconstructions of the past as opposed to the reception of formless oral histories.

[3] E.g., Flodoard, *Annales ad an.* 920, 921, ed. Philippe Lauer, *Les annales de Flodoard* (Paris:
1905), 3, 6: *Heinricus princeps Transrhenensis*; *ad an.* 928, 42: *Heinricus Germaniae princeps*. He
is otherwise simply *princeps*, or nothing.

[4] Flodoard, *Annales ad an.* 950, ed. Lauer, 128.

[5] Flodoard, *Annales ad an.* 936, ed. Lauer, 64: "*Heinrico rege sub isdem diebus obeunte, contentio
de regno inter filios ipsius agitatur; rerum tandem summa natu maiori, nomine Othoni, obvenit.*"

[6] Flodoard may have refused to call a "king" an unanointed ruler. See Carl Erdmann, "Der
ungesalbte König," repr. in *Ottonische Studien*, ed. Helmut Beumann (Darmstadt: 1968), 1–
30; summary of recent historiography in Reuter, *Germany*, 139–41, following Gerd Althoff
and Hagen Keller, *Heinrich I. und Otto der Grosse. Neubeginn und karolingisches Erbe*, 2 vols.
(Göttingen: 1985), 1.61–65.

Even the Ottonians' "pathway to the imperial office" did not proceed without severe bumps.[7] Germany did not constitute a secure basis. Before Otto I obtained the emperorship in 962, his half-brother Thankmar, his brother Henry, his son Liudolf, as well as his relatives by marriage fought against the king in a series of rebellions that flared up all the way into the mid-950s.[8] The Lotharingian princes used these dissensions, and played several times the card of alliance with the West-Frankish Carolingians to gain some autonomy between the two kingdoms. While starting in the 940s Otto's kingship took imperial trappings, the Saxons' access to, and control of, Italy was not a foregone conclusion. Northern Italy, where the imperial crown was to be obtained, was even more perhaps than Germany an extremely fractious political arena. The South-German dukes of Swabia and Bavaria had traditionally intervened in peninsular affairs, in forays both caused and facilitated by transalpine familial bonds.[9] Similar connections had led West-Frankish princes, such as Rudolf II king of Burgundy or the Carolingian Hugh of Arles, to seek and obtain control (however frail) over northern Italy.[10] Local peninsular ambitions mattered. Tuscan and Friulese margraves enjoyed quasi-royal influence and might reach the crown; I have mentioned Berengar II, king from 950 on, who with his son and co-king Adalbert was Otto's most immediate rival. Shortly after Otto's accession, the constellation of power altered itself, without however immediately simplifying the Saxon king's position. His brother Henry married into the Bavarian ducal family in a form of peace pact. Swabia was no longer an obstacle after Liudolf's 947 marriage to Ida, the only child of Duke Hermann, and his 950 accession to the Swabian ducal office immediately after his father-in-law's death (949). But, as Liudolf's 953–54 rebellion shows, marital alliances that placed a relative in a quasi-royal position in a duchy did not constitute fail-safe insurance for Otto. In this last major crisis of

---

[7] Master narrative in Heinrich Büttner, "Der Weg Ottos des Grossen zum Kaisertum," repr. in an amplified version in Helmut Beumann and Heinrich Büttner, *Das Kaisertum Ottos des Grossen. Zwei Vorträge*, VuF Sonderband 1 (Sigmaringen: 1963). For a recent reconstruction that marvelously interweaves the factors of tradition and circumstances, see Hagen Keller, "Entscheidungssituationen und Lernprozesse in den 'Anfängen der deutschen Geschichte.' Die 'Italien—und Kaiserpolitik' Ottos des Grossen," *FMSt* 33 (1999): 20–48.

[8] On all this, see Leyser, *Rule and Conflict*.

[9] See Gunter Wolf, "Über die Hintergründe der Erhebung Liudolfs von Schwaben," reed. in *Otto der Grosse*, Wege der Forschung 450, ed. Harald Zimmermann (Darmstadt: 1976), 56–69. E.g., the *Annales Iuvavenses maximi* (Annals of Salzburg) *Continuatio ad an.* 934, ed. Harry Bresslau, MGH SS 30:2 (Hannover: 1934), 734:4–6: "*Longobardi Epahardum filium Arnolfi ducis in dominum acceperunt. Eodem anno Arnolfus dux et Udalpertus archiepiscopus cum Baiowariis iter hostile in Italiam fecerunt.*"

[10] See Eduard Hlawitschka, *Franken, Alemannen, Bayern und Burgunder in Oberitalien, 774–962. Zum Verständnis der fränkischen Königsherrschaft in Italien* (Freiburg im Breisgau: 1960).

his governance, traditional regional interests compounded intrafamilial rivalries.[11] Finally, no matter how distant, Byzantine emperors still maintained an interest in Italian affairs: Liudprand's friend Emperor Constantine VII Porphyrogenitus evidences a fair knowledge of the Carolingian world and of peninsular politics in his *On the Governance of the Empire*.[12] Bavarians, Swabians, Burgundians, Hugonides—all these were hefty rivals for the Ottonians. And no matter who the key contenders for the kingdom of Italy and the imperial office were in any given decade, they had to take into account local aristocrats of lesser rank.[13] Like everywhere else in tenth-century Western Europe, loyalties had to be bought and maintained. Both stability in Germany and hegemony over Italy, then, were far from evident before 962.[14]

Furthermore, they were connected. Before 962, in the first decades of Saxon expansionism, hegemony had had to be justified, and more perhaps to the German aristocracy than to the non-German victims of expansion. The German magnates had looked upon Otto's father, Henry, as a prestigious partner, fundamentally as a first among aristocratic equals. Aristocratic groups shared in what one will anachronistically call "foreign policy": They were accustomed to swearing pacts whose membership transcended the borders of the *regna*. At Augsburg, in 952, the German magnates had guaranteed a pact between Otto I and the Italian ruler Berengar II. It defined Berengar's position in Italy: that of a semi-autonomous king subject only to Otto's distant overlordship. Yet within a few years, Otto had chosen to tighten his hold on Italy. In 956/7, he sent his son Liudolf across the Alps, probably in preparation for what came soon after. In 961/2, Otto himself struck south, finally to obtain the imperial coronation.[15]

The earliest surviving narrative of some length dealing with these Ottonian "beginnings," Liudprand of Cremona's *Antapodosis*, served two purposes. First, before 961/2, the new turn in policies had to be explained to

---

[11] See Odilo Engels, "Überlegungen zur ottonischen Herrchaftsstruktur," in *Otto III.—Heinrich II. Eine Wende?* ed. Bernd Schneidmüller and Stefan Weinfurter (Sigmaringen: 1997), 267–325, at 268–84.

[12] See Constantine VII, *De administrando imperio* 26–27, G. Moravcsik and R. J. H. Jenkins, 2d ed., Corpus Fontium Historiae Byzantinae 1 (Washington: 1967), 109–19.

[13] Roland Pauler, *Das Regnum Italiae in ottonischer Zeit* (Tübingen: 1982), is too cursory on the lay aristocracy to be helpful.

[14] Historiography in Philippe Buc, "Italian Hussies and German Matrons: Liutprand of Cremona on Dynastic Legitimacy," *FMSt* 29 (1995): 207–12 nn. 3–21.

[15] See Reuter, *Germany*, 166–74, building on Gerd Althoff, *Amicitiae und pacta. Bündniss, Einung, Politik und Gebetsgedenken im beginnenden 10. Jahrhundert* (Hannover: 1992), but compare the recent reconstruction by Keller, "Entscheidungssituationen." On the other side of the Rhine, and thus able to eschew Ottonian hagiology, Flodoard of Reims, *Annales ad an.* 951–52, 962, ed. Philippe Lauer (Paris: 1905), 132–33, 151, gives a sense of the pact and of Berengar's indignation at its rupture.

the aristocratic warrantors of the Augsburg pact, whose help the German king no doubt needed to conquer the imperial crown.[16] As Gerd Althoff has convincingly shown, mediators engaged their social esteem in the pacts they brought to existence.[17] By painting a dysfunctional Italian polity, Liudprand helped them save face. Second, the *Antapodosis* participated in the historiographic sublimation of the incipient Saxon dynasty's difficulties.[18] More precisely, the *Antapodosis* elided some of them, but transmuted others into character-testing crises on the upward trajectory of providential history. This rendition of recent events may as well have helped to rally necessary aristocratic helpers behind Otto I.

In this task, Liudprand employed a plurality of methods. Historiographers in the service of the Carolingians' ninth-century neighbors and rivals had often omitted mentioning the Frankish imperial office.[19] Liudprand similarly "forgot" the emperorship of Italian princes' ancestors. But primarily, his justification of Saxon destiny took the form of an exaltation of the Ottonian dispensation and a denigration of all of the actual or potential contenders in Italy. Liudprand besmirched the memory of the last Carolingian rulers of East Frankland to have intervened in Italy, in the person of Arnulf of Carinthia, and the Ottonians' rivals for hegemony in the 920s, the leading Bavarians and Swabians. But he especially aimed at the Byzantine emperors as well as at two rival royal kindreds: those of Berengar II of Friuli (d. 966) and of Hugh of Arles (r. 926–45).[20]

Leaving aside Byzantium, this chapter will examine the dichotomous opposition between Saxon and Italian rulers. Liudprand constructs it by drawing sharp oppositions between the two realms in key registers of ruler legitimacy: blood purity, war, and rituals. While the subject of this essay dictates a focus on the last of these, all three registers are equally important. But it would be wrong to isolate "rituals" from other principal markers of legitimacy and illegitimacy in the *Antapodosis*. "Rituals" did not constitute

---

[16] Their identity is not evident, given that we do not have an actual written pact. A necessarily hazy approximation of this circle may be found, however, by looking at the participants of the synod of Augsburg, the religious gremium within which or in the course of which the pact was struck. See Ernst-Dieter Hehl, MGH Concilia 6:1, *Concilia Aevi Saxonici DCCCCXVI-MI* (Hannover: 1987), 189–91.

[17] Gerd Althoff, *Spielregeln der Politik. Kommunikation in Frieden und Fehde* (Darmstadt: 1997), 126–53.

[18] On Liudprand's techniques as applied to Byzantium, see Karl J. Leyser, "Ends and Means in Liudprand of Cremona," repr. in Leyser, *Communications and Power in Medieval Europe*, 2 vols., (London: 1994), 1.125–42.

[19] See Heinz Löwe, "Von den Grenzen des Kaisergedankens in der Karolingerzeit," *DA* 14 (1958): 345–74, repr. in his *Von Cassiodor zu Dante* (Berlin: 1973), 206–30, esp. 216–17.

[20] Recent historiography in Buc, "Italian Hussies," 207–12. Robert Levine, "Liutprand of Cremona: History and Debasement in the Tenth Century," *Mittellateinisches Jahrbuch* 26 (1991): 70–84, has rightly noticed the attacks on Otto's enemies.

the center of this text (and, one may assume, of actual tenth-century political culture in the Ottonian world); they were only one among several narrative focal points. Indeed, it has been shown elsewhere how Liudprand systematically besmirches the virtue of Italian princesses in order to obfuscate the royal (and in some cases imperial Carolingian) blood of their male offspring. Misogyny, however, stops at the Alps: A woman associated with the Ottonian house such as Queen Mathilda will avoid sexual temptations and quietly retreat to a nunnery after her husband's death.[21] The issue was not simply one of purity or of the symbolic capital that accrued to a dynasty when it donated its women to God.[22] A man in thrall to women could hardly lead other men. This idea Liudprand expressed most graphically in a passage in which the sexually voracious Willa, wife of Hugh's brother Boso, mother of Berengar II's wife, Willa, and grandmother of Berengar's son and co-ruler Adalbert, hid in her vagina Boso's *cingulum militare*—the baldric that symbolized honor, office, and military leadership. Not only did the grotesque story dishonor the king's mother and hint at disorderly sexuality (and perhaps even at the illegitimacy of her children); it smothered manly warring abilities in a female womb.[23] For leadership in war, especially against the pagans, provided Liudprand with a second axis along which to differentiate the two polities. While Henry and Otto wage battles for Christendom against the Hungarians, Berengar I (r. 888–924) and Berengar II pay these same heathens to fight against their own Christian rivals. Furthermore, Ottonian warfare is "liturgified." Liudprand clothes battles fought against the pagans north of the Alps with the trappings of the Christian liturgy of war; south of the Alps, similar encounters tend to belong to the realm of the secular.[24] Like Augustine, who had withdrawn

[21] Buc, "Italian Hussies." See below, n. 79, for two non-German exceptions to this rule.

[22] See Patrick Corbet, *Les saints ottoniens. Sainteté dynastique, sainteté royale et sainteté féminine autour de l'an mil* (Sigmaringen: 1986); the key text linking dynasty and female sanctity is the *Primordia coenobii Gandersheimensis*, ed. Helene Homeyer, *Hrotsvithae opera. Mit Einleitung und Kommentar* (Munich and Paderborn: 1970).

[23] *Antapodosis* 4.12, 103–104, with Buc, "Italian Hussies," 214–15. On the *cingulum militare*, see below, n. 101.

[24] On the importance of providential war leadership in Ottonian circles, see most recently Hagen Keller, "*Machabaeorum pugnae.* Zum Stellenwert eines biblischen Vorbilds in Widukinds Deutung der ottonischen Königsherrschaft," in Hagen Keller and Nikolaus Staubach, eds., *Iconologia sacra . . . Festschrift für Karl Hauck zum 75. Geburtstag* (Berlin 1994), 417–37. Michael McCormick, *Eternal Victory: Triumphal Rulership in Late Antiquity, Byzantium, and the Medieval West* (Cambridge-Paris: 1986), is a magnificent study of the ideology of victory, to be complemented for liturgified warfare by his "Liturgie et guerre des Carolingiens à la première croisade," in *'Militia Christi' e Crociata nei secoli XI–XIII*, Miscellanea del Centro di studi medioevali 13 (Milan: 1992), 209–40. For a good example of ninth-century holy war, see Louis II against the Saracens near Bari in Andreas of Bergamo, *Historiola* 13, ed. Georg Waitz, MGH SS rer. Lang., 228:3–20, esp. 7–16: "*Tunc moniti, ut gallotinnio matutinis et summo diluculo episcopis et sacerdotibus missarum sollemnia celebrarent et populus communionem vel benedic*

"the history of the Roman Empire from the dimension of sacred history," Liudprand wrote up the deeds of Otto's enemies as if they had not any positive connection to God's plan.[25]

The liturgy of war (or its absence) leads us back to the theme of this essay, political ritual. To use Johannes Fried's felicitous expression, the first surviving generation of Ottonian historiography was "Ritualgeleitete Vergangenheitskonstruktion": Depictions of past rituals served to crystallize very presentist considerations.[26] Under Liudprand's quill, Ottonian rituals verify the Augustinian understanding of *religiones*: They are ceremonies that happen to manifest the presence of a consensual community of human beings because they demonstrate the existence of a vertical bond tying these humans to God. Such is the purpose of the prayer and vow to renounce simony King Henry proposes to his warriors before joining battle against the pagan Magyars: "Love and unity (*unitatis caritas*) will bind together those whom the Devil's cunning may have divided [from one another]."[27] Saxon rituality thus justifies Saxon centrality in the *imperium christianum*. On the other hand, the *Antapodosis* depicts the North-Italian and Byzantine attitude toward rituals in a wholly negative light. Rituals constitute the objects for, or occasions of, manipulations that serve not the community but segmentary interests. The political culture in which Otto's rivals partake seems nothing else but a latter-day version of Augustine's pagan Roman order, where the great manipulate religious rites to stay in power.[28] Illuminating dissimulation, however, requires adequate rhetorical tactics. I shall thus first comment on the *Antapodosis*'s style before moving on to rituals proper.

If Italian bloodlines are anything but clear, Italian political rituals are everything but transparent. Liudprand paints them as faction-serving shams; for their *metteurs-en-scène*, the dissimulation of their manipulative purpose is essential. This is not without consequences for the style of the *Antapodosis*. Liudprand will sometimes allow himself an artful tactic: to delude us into believing the seeming, before revealing the being of these rituals. The au-

---

tionem acciperent, sicuti et fecerunt. Et exierunt querentes Sarracini, et illis querentes Franci iuncti sunt in loco [lacuna]. *Factum est sonitus magnus clangore bucine, innita equorum, strepitus populorum. Cumque prope se coniungerent, fideles Christi oraverunt, dicentes:* Domine Ihesu Christe, tu dixisti: *Qui manducat carnem meam et bibit sanguinem meum, in me manet, et ego in eum;* ergo si tu nobiscum, quid contra nos? *Statim commissum est prelium. Cumque forti intencione pugnantes, arma celestis confortavit christianos. Pagani vero terga vertentes fugire ceperunt."*

[25] See Robert A. Markus, *"Saeculum": History and society in the theology of St. Augustine,* 2d ed. (Cambridge [UK]: 1988), esp. 15–17, quotation at 32.

[26] Fried, "Königserhebung,' 302–303.

[27] *Antapodosis* 2.27, 47:545–46.

[28] See below, ch. 4, 143–47.

thor thus allows himself the technique that he counsels his political actors:
"In certain circumstances, the highest wisdom is to simulate stupidity."[29]
Ironic reversals and an ironic, sometimes sardonic, tone characterize the
sections devoted to Italy (and Byzantium). Liudprand turns Lombard political practices into a systematic exercise in deception: Crown-wearings, the
liturgical care of the poor, political friendship, and the king's advent are
shown in the most cruel light—literally. In other words, Liudprand reads
Italian rituals with a vulgar Marxist or conflict-theory grid *avant la lettre*.
But the other half of the diptych presents their Ottonian counterparts according to what one may perhaps call a proto-Durkheimian model: Saxon
political rituals breathe consensus and sacrality. We shall see in chapter 4
how Augustine's *City of God* already paired these two interpretive options.
Granted, the *Antapodosis* develops fewer Ottonian ceremonies and tends to
dwell on these at lesser length: Unlike Paradise, Hell has a story. But the
main ritual event in the Saxon tier of the *Antapodosis*, the battle of Birten—
ritual because it encompasses Otto's Moses-like prayer for victory at the
foot of the Holy Lance—elicits major stylistic hypertrophy. It is first connected to Saxon dynastic continuity and hegemony by a lengthy history
and description of the Lance. It is then lifted out of historical time into
theology by an extraordinary excursus into the Apostle Thomas's doubt. It
is removed from the sphere of human pettiness by being framed in the
providential: Liudprand attributes the rebellion of Otto's brother Henry to
the Devil's inspiration—a face-saving grace denied to actors in the Italian
political game. For now, let us turn to Lombardy, after a short detour
through Constantinople.

Nomen-Potestas

Among other presents from King Hugh to Emperor Romanos (r. 920–44),
[my father, Hugh's ambassador] had brought along two dogs of a kind never
seen in that country. When they were brought before the emperor, if the arms
of many men had not restrained them, they would have immediately bitten
him and torn him [to pieces]. Indeed, I believe that when they saw this man
[Romanos] wearing (according to the custom of the Greeks) a handkerchief
over his head and a strange dress, they believed he was not a human being but
some kind of prodigy (*monstrum*).[30]

---

[29] *Antapodosis* 4.10, 102:215–16, citing Cato, *Distichs* 2.18: "*stultitiam simulare loco prudentia
summa est.*"

[30] *Antapodosis* 3.23, 76:358–365, with Michael Rentschler, *Liudprand von Cremona. Eine Stu-
die zum ost-westlichen Kulturgefälle im Mittelalter* (Frankfurt: 1981), 11, and Carl Dändliker
and Johannes Müller, *Liudprand von Cremona und seine Quellen*, Untersuchungen zur mittleren
Geschichte, ed. Max Büdinger, no. 1 (Leipzig: 1871), 157–58: Liudprand makes Romanos a
usurper.

It was one of the myths of Late Roman and Byzantine political theory that even mindless animals recognized the emperor. An old myth: "O Caesar, sang Martial, the pious elephant worships you, groveling"; "Groveling at Caesar's feet, the antelope, akin to a petitioner, stands still." "Believe, the poet went on, that Cesar has something divine (*numen habet Caesar*); indeed, wild animals (*ferae*) do not learn to lie."[31] Belief or unbelief, this led Roman rulers and their barbarian imitators and successors to establish parks and collect beasts.[32] Presents of wild animals became tokens of alliance or subjection. But clearly Hugh's gifts, the Italian mastiffs ("wild animals do not learn to lie") did not acknowledge Romanos's legitimacy. They should have groveled; instead, they almost shredded Byzantium's myths about its own ceremonials. They did not see the emperor under the mask of the imperial robe; they saw—and Liudprand suggests that they saw rightly—through his vestments a monster.

The theme of appearances and reality runs as a red thread through the *Antapodosis*. Byzantine emperors disguise themselves as drunkards to test the mettle of their Constantinopolitan night watch.[33] An aristocratic spy dons the humble garb of a poor pilgrim to penetrate the secrets of an enemy court.[34] After the coup that brings him control of Constantinople, but without de jure legitimation, Romanos argues that "some token of imperial attire on his body should point to him as worthy of" the imperial acclamations that people already sang to honor him.[35]

A skillful courtier-ambassador, Liudprand is obsessed with the disjunctions between the appearances and the reality of power. Since at least Carolingian apologetics for the deposition of the last Merovingian king (who had had the *nomen* without the *potestas*), the correspondence between *nomen* (title or "name") and *potestas* (effective power) served as an index of rightful rule.[36] But in the *Antapodosis* rulers rarely achieve this match: "The Italians considered Berengar to be in title (*nomine*) a margrave but in power (*potestate*) a king, while these men [Hugh and Lothar] they saw as kings only in

---

[31] Martial, *De Spectaculis*, 17 and 30, ed. Walter C. A. Ker, 2 vols. (Cambridge, Mass. and London: 1968), 1.14 and 22–24, with Andreas Alföldi, *Die monarchische Repräsentation im römischen Kaiserreiche*, reed. (Darmstadt: 1970), 51, 55. See as well Igor Gorevich, *O Kritike Antropologii Zhivotnikh* (Towards a critique of animal anthropology) vol. 2: *Zvyeri i Anektoti* (Kaboul-Kishinev: 1987), 301–303, whom I thank for the reference.

[32] Karl Hauck, "Tiergarten im Pfalzbereich," *Deutsche Königspfalzen*, 3 vols. (Göttingen: 1963–75), 1.30–74.

[33] *Antapodosis* 1.11, 10–14, see also 1.12, 14–16.

[34] See below, 28–30.

[35] *Antapodosis* 3.35, 84:566–68.

[36] Heinrich Fichtenau, "Karl der Grosse und das Kaisertum", *MIÖG* 61 (1953): 257–334; Arno Borst, "Kaisertum und Namentheorie im Jahre 800," reed. in *Zum Kaisertum Karls des Grossen*, ed. Gunther Wolf (Darmstadt: 1972), 216–39; Edward Peters, *The Shadow King: Rex Inutilis in Medieval Law and Literature*, 751–1327 (New Haven: 1970), 47f.

name (*vocabulo reges*) and, as far as actions were concerned (*actu*), considered them to be even less than counts."[37] As Alcuin had told Charlemagne, "names" can lie and be used to lie.[38] In dissimulating his wickedness and desire to rule prior to Hugh and Lothar's death, Berengar was the arch-hypocrite.[39] Liudprand pretends to be scandalized by this long-lasting mismatch. Only Ottonian power transparently evidenced the fit between *nomen* and *potestas*. This correspondence grounded the Saxon dynasty's legitimacy and expressed itself in its political rituals. In Italy, on the other hand, ceremonies served to obfuscate the realities of power. Liudprand's *Antapodosis* plays vis-à-vis Lombard rituals the role his father's mastiffs had in Byzantium, that of the barking revelator of a monstrous ceremonial dispensation.

AMICITIA

For the political generation following the breakup of the Carolingian empire, sealed in its tripartite division among Louis the Pious's sons at the treaty of Verdun (843), few terms carried a burden comparable to that of *amicitia*, "friendship." Frankish thinkers sought to compensate for a now dismantled unity through the fiction of an imaginary "body of the brothers." This *corpus fratrum* was held together by the exoskeleton of *amicitia*-pacts entailing faith, charity, and unity of purpose to the exclusion of conflicts.[40] The tragic chasm between these sworn (and theoretically insoluble) friendships[41] and the downward, centrifugal whirlwind of late Carolingian

---

[37] *Antapodosis* 5.30, 141:628–30; see also 6.2, 146:31–32: "[Berengar] was prince over all the Italians by his strength (*virtute*), King Lothar solely by his title (*nomine*)"; see Ernst Karpf, *Herrscherlegitimation und Reichsbegriff in der ottonischen Geschichtsschreibung des 10. Jahrhunderts* (Stuttgart: 1985), 37–41.

[38] Borst, "Kaisertum," 41. Liudprand makes a number of comments on appearances and reality; see *Antapodosis* 2.31, 49:592–93: "[*picturam*] *rem veram potius quam verisimilem videas*"; ibidem 6.8, 148:108–109: "*quod nomen non ab re sed ex apparentibus causis sortita est*."

[39] Hans Jessen, *Die Wirkungen der augustinischen Geschichtsphilosophie auf die Weltanschauung und Geschichtsschreibung Liutprands von Cremona* (Ph.D. diss. Greifswald, Bamberg: 1921), 13–19, pointing out what *Antapodosis* 5.30 owes to Gregory the Great's *Moralia*.

[40] Reinhard Schneider, *Brüdergemeine und Schwurfreundschaft. Der Auflösungsprozess des Karlingerreiches im Spiegel der caritas-Terminologie* (Lübeck: 1964), esp. 84–99. For a tenth-century example, Karl Schmid, "Unerforschte Quellen aus quellenarmer Zeit. Zur amicitia zwischen Heinrich I. und dem westfränkischen König Robert im Jahre 923," *Francia* 12 (1984): 119–47. See now Althoff, *Amicitiae und pacta*, and Régine Le Jan, *Famille et pouvoir dans le monde franc* (Paris: 1995), 83–85.

[41] See Nicephorus's complaint in Liudprand, *Legatio* 6, ed. Paolo Chiesa, CCCM 156, 190:107–10, "Explain why you assaulted the frontiers of our empire with war and arson. We were friends (*amici*) and had considered to strike an indissoluble association (*societatem*) through marriage," and Liudprand's retort, ibidem 7, ed. Chiesa, 190:123–25: "That associa-

politics rendered these pacts all the more momentous and desperate. *Amicitiae* were not unknown in the Italian political world; in 898, Berengar I swore to Angiltrud, widow of his rival Wido (d. 894), that "from now on and henceforth I am your friend, just as a friend must be to his friend." The material bases and grounds of friendship were not nonexistent, far from it; Berengar promised to respect the privileges that Angiltrude's husband and her son Lambert (d. 898) had conceded her.[42] It is on this theme of *amicitia* that the Italian tier of the *Antapodosis* opens. Ominously:

> Two very powerful nobles had served [King] Charles [the Fat] during his lifetime. One was called Wido, the other Berengar. They became glued to one another by such a pact of friendship (*amicitiarum foedere*) that they promised to one another that if they survived King Charles, they would each conspire to one another's appointment, that is, that Wido would obtain the Francia they call Romance, and Berengar, Italy.

Liudprand follows immediately with a lengthy indictment of political friendships. Its rhetoric draws on the theological antithesis between true and false *amicitia*. It harks back as well to the long-standing Carolingian distrust vis-à-vis horizontal sworn pacts (*coniurationes*). In 866/76, Wulfad archbishop of Bourges had denounced such sworn *amicitiae* as the antithesis of one's (vertical) oath to one's lord. They were necessarily broken, hence necessarily sinful.[43] Liudprand, agent of a hegemonistic king, argued no differently:

> But many of these kinds of friendships, which bind humankind through an associative attraction, are uncertain and unstable. A previous commendation induces some to enter in the commerce of friendship; for others, it is a similarity in business, military service, craft or pursuit. But just as these friendships are brought about through diverse associations aiming at gain, desire, or various necessities, so they are dissolved whenever any occasion for separation arises. But this [friendship between these two men] belonged, I say, to the kind of friendship that has most often been tested by experience; it shows that those who enter a sworn pact of political friendship (*amicitiarum foedus coniurationis*) never preserve an unruptured concord.

And indeed, the vicissitudes of Charles the Fat's succession soon pitted the two friends against one another. The compact broke down; Wido and

---

tion in friendship (*societatem . . . amicitiae*) which you say you wanted to strike through parentage, we hold to be a fraud and a trick."

[42] MGH Capitularia 2:1 n. 231, ed. Alfred Boretius and Victor Krause (Hannover: 1897), 126:35–39; Schneider, *Brüdergemeine*, 86.

[43] MGH Ep. 6 = Ep. Karolini Aevi 4, ed. Ernst Perels (Berlin: 1925), 190:31–33, see Schneider, *Brüdergemeine*, 76.

Berengar fought a number of pitched battles, opening up—within the *Antapodosis*—the age of civil wars in Lombardy. Liudprand, deliberately or owing to actual ignorance, does not mention the antagonism that had existed earlier between Wido and Berengar: Already in Charles' latter years both men were on their way to quasi-royal status in northern Italy.[44] Thus in the economy of the *Antapodosis*, Wido and Berengar's *amicitia* stands as the original sin of Italian politics, from which only the pure—and the author has probably in mind the Saxon monarchs—can escape.[45] In the light of recent historiography, it may not be fortuitous that Liudprand, Otto's man in Italy, criticized *amicitiae*. Gerd Althoff has underlined how Henry of Saxony's rise to the royal office in Germany had been secured by such horizontal pacts between quasi-royal stem-dukes and himself, a former duke risen to the royal office. These *amicitiae* demonstrated, as it were, the king's willingness to respect his partners' *potestas*.[46] To the south, in the multipolar Lombard system, multiple friendships were the necessary small change of political life. But Henry's son Otto was bent on rolling back this dispensation as far as he could. His conception of kingship implied a reduction in the component of equality between lord and aristocratic followers, and such horizontal pacts, when they did not include the king, could form the backbone of conspiracies.[47]

Italian friends, like Italian women, were fickle. That both King Lambert and King Berengar I should have been assassinated by retainers of theirs would have seemed already bad enough to the readers of the *Antapodosis*. Liudprand himself, being a chanter of royal authority, could not but admit Lambert and Berengar into the category Frantisek Graus has defined as that of "martyrs owing to a remarkable death." Both assassinations explic-

---

[44] Adolf Hofmeister, *Markgrafen und Markgrafschaften im italischen Königreich in der Zeit von Karl dem Grossen bis auf Otto den Grossen 774–962, MIÖG Ergänzungsband 7:1* (Vienna: 1907), 215–435, at 367 and n.1; Eduard Hlawitschka, *Franken, Alemannen*, 73; see *Annalium Fuldensium Continuatio Ratisbonnensis, ad an.* 883, ed. Friedrich Kurze, MGH SS rer. Germ. in usum scholarum 7 (Hannover: 1895), 110.

[45] *Antapodosis* 1.14, 17:455–18:479. I detect here possibly an echo of Leo I, *tractatus* 26.3–5, ed. Antoine Chavasse, CCSL 138 (Turnhout: 1973) 127–31, as well as a clear one of Augustine, *De civitate dei* 12.23 and 28, 380–81 and 384. See as well Heiric of Auxerre, *Homiliae* 2.15, 2.50, CCCM 116B (Turnhout: 1994), 129:228–130:245, 471:181—93, contrasting carnal and spiritual *amicitiae* and *pax*. Liudprand goes on: "Indeed, he [the devil], that most cunning enemy of the human race, labors with great speed and sagacity to break friendship so that human beings may betray their oaths. But should someone less learned interrogate us on the true kind of friendship, we shall answer that concord and true friendship can stand only between men of pure mores and sharing the same purpose and virtue." *Antapodosis* 1.13, 17:434–50, leads the reader to this theme: Among human beings, the Fall has brought about a war of all against all.

[46] Gerd Althoff, "Zur Frage nach der Organisation sächsischer *coniurationes* in der Ottonenzeit," *FMSt* 16 (1982): 129–42; and especially Althoff, *Amicitiae und pacta*, 88–96.

[47] Althoff, *Amicitiae*.

itly refer to Judas's betrayal of Christ the King. Lambert, second and last king of the Widonide dynasty, had made Hugo, son of the justly executed rebel Meginfred, his sworn *familiaris* and had covered him with benefices. Hugo murdered him during a royal hunt. "O, if only this hunt had caught wild animals and not kings!" laments Liudprand. Lambert's aura died with him: He was safely childless. Flambert killed King Berengar, his *compater*, after having consented to drink from, and take as a gift, the golden cup the king presented to him "for the sake of love and my safety" (*amoris salutisque mei causa*). The murder took place as Berengar stepped out of the church, where he had attended morning mass and sung hymns to the Lord; in front of the church doors, an indelible bloodstain still testified to the crime.[48] If, after an ambiguous reign characterized by mercy but also by *calliditas* and a willingness to ally with the pagan Hungarians, the crime finally endowed Berengar with some sanctity, it was as a murdered king: His christomimetic death served to highlight the dysfunctionality of Italian loyalties. But could Liudprand allow Berengar II, the martyred king's grandson, any "blood holiness"? Along with the desire to deny Otto's competitors any Carolingian ancestry, this risk explains Liudprand's efforts to smear the sexual reputation of Berengar's wife, Willa, mother of Berengar's son and co-ruler King Adalbert. Any potential *Geblütsheiligkeit* stood little chance of being transmitted to her son Adalbert, co-ruler with her husband Berengar II.[49]

Even bishops were not beyond using the smokescreen of *amicitia* for murderous games. When in 926 Burchard duke of Swabia—a rival of Henry I—descended upon Italy to advance the fortunes of his son-in-law Rudolf II of Burgundy, he made his way to Milan in order to spy on the locals. Unbeknownst to the Swabian, his aggressive intentions were revealed to Lambert, the city's archbishop. This prince of the Church consequently decided to play on the irresistible aristocratic love for animal slaughter in order to gain time and helpers to butcher the unsuspecting duke. He led him into his city:

> Being cunning and tricky, [Lambert archbishop of Milan] did not spurn Burchard [duke of Swabia]. To the contrary, with evil intent, he received him and

---

[48] *Antapodosis* 1.42, 28–29; *Antapodosis* 2.68–72, 62–64. For the concept of *merkwürdiger Martyr*, see Frantisek Graus, *Volk, Herrscher, und Heiliger im Reich der Merowinger: Studien zur Hagiographie der Merowingerzeit* (Prague: 1965). Landenolfus of Capua (d. 993), murdered right after mass outside the church, is another such martyr, see the *Catalogum comitum Capuae* (Montecassino), MGH SS rer. Lang., 500:12–27.

[49] For Willa's promiscuity, see Buc, "Italian Hussies," 214–15. That Adalbert was fully king in the 950s is suggested by the *Annals of Einsiedeln, ad an.* 956, ed. Georg Pertz, MGH SS 3 (Hannover: 1839), 142: 35–11: "*Liutolfus in Italiam hostiliter fugato Peringario et filio eius, Papiam intravit*"; and *ad an.* 957: "*Bellum inter Liutolfum, et Adalbertum, victoque Adalberto, regnum optinuit, omnesque sibi subiugavit . . .*"

honored him wonderfully. Indeed, among other privileges, as if out of love, he granted him the following privilege: that he would hunt deer in his park (*brolium*), which privilege is never conceded unless to the dearest and greatest of friends.[50]

This was to be the Swabian's last cigarette. Lambert's delaying tactics allowed the Italians to fall on the duke's retinue near Novara. Burchard's horse stumbled into a pit and its rider was killed;[51] Lambert's allies massacred the duke's men in the holiest part of the church (*sub ipso etiam altari*) where they had sought asylum. Desecration of holy grounds thus followed the debauching of the rites of friendship. It also echoed Burchard's earlier sacrilege. The duke had visited the church of Saint-Lambert outside Milan "not so much in order to beseech [the saint] but for another reason": to reconnoiter it with a view to transform it into a fortress from which he would pressurize the Italians.[52] Deceit thus echoed deceit; the Ottonians' rivals in Italy shared in a single willingness to abuse rites of friendship and the sacred.

PAUPERES IN PRESENTIA REGIS

By the late tenth century, kings had adopted a clerical and monastic ritual, the liturgical care of the poor.[53] Most historians are familiar with the portrait of King Robert II the Pious (d. 1032) produced by his biographer Helgaud. According to his *Life*, the king fed *pauperes* by the hundred during Lent and gave them special treatment on Holy Thursday. Robert had twelve household poor, official recipients of regular charity, who always went where he went. In the economy of Robert's *Vita*, the presence of the poor and care for the "holy poor"—images of Christ—turn the king him-

---

[50] *Antapodosis* 3.14, 74:289–94. The words *suscipiens* and *honoravit* suggest an *adventus*.

[51] See *Annales Alamanici ad an.* 926 (an entry contemporary to the fact), ed. Walter Lendi, *Untersuchungen zur frühalemannischen Annalistik* (Freiburg: 1971), 192: "*Purchardus in italia fugiens Langobardos de equo lapsus brevi momento vitam finivit.*"

[52] *Antapodosis* 3.15, 74:298–311. Ibid., 3.14, 73:271–79.

[53] On the *matriculatio*, see Michel Rouche, "La matricule des pauvres. . ." in Michel Mollat, ed., *Etudes sur l'histoire de la pauvreté*, 2 vols. (Paris: 1974), 1.83–110; Egon Boshof, "Untersuchungen zur Armenfürsorge im fränkischen Reich des 9. Jhs.," *Archiv für Kulturgeschichte* 58:2 (1976): 265–339; Heinrich Fichtenau, *Lebensordnungen des 10. Jahrhunderts. Studien über Denkart und Existenz im einstigen Karolingerreich*, 2 vols. Monographien zur Geschichte des Mittelalters 30:1–2 2 vols. (Stuttgart: 1984), 1.61–63, tr. Patrick Geary, *Living in the Tenth Century* (Chicago: 1991), 40–41. See as well the *AF ad an.* 850, ed. Kurze, 40, where archbishop Hrabanus Maurus of Mainz feeds during a famine more than three hundred poor per day, not counting those *qui in praesentia illius assidue vescebantur*. Ritual charity was well established and codified by the eleventh and twelfth centuries. Pierre-André Sigal, "Pauvreté et charité aux XIe et XIIe siècles d'après quelques textes hagiographiques," in Mollat, *Etudes*, 1.141–62, at 151–53.

self into a penitent pauper, make him into a saint.[54] Closer to Liudprand's own period, in Widukind of Corvey's *Deeds of the Saxons*, by the time of Otto I's death (973), the Saxon emperor's well-regulated liturgical day included care for the poor between morning mass and breakfast—probably a distribution of alms, if he or his biographer followed the Carolingian model of Thegan and Notker of Saint-Gall's Louis the Pious. Indeed, as Egon Boshof has shown, royal solicitude for the poor was part and parcel of the Carolingian language of legitimacy. This is best attested in a diploma of 851 for the royal abbey of Saint-Denis, in which Charles the Bald delegated to the monks, *vice nostra*, "the reception, feeding, clothing, and footwashing" of Christ's poor (not quite already Helgaud's *sancti pauperes*, but almost). The details suggest that the king felt it was incumbent on him to perform this task at least at Easter on Maundy Thursday.[55] Thus, well before the turn of the millennium, the feeding of the *pauperes* contributed to the sacral aura surrounding the ruler. The liturgical redistribution of food and wealth (Robert allowed himself to be the knowing victim of thefts on the part of his household poor) rectified the this-worldly imbalance between the powerful (*potentes*) and the powerless (*pauperes*). It took place in the locus of consensus par excellence, the banquet table, image of Christ's holy sacrificial table.[56]

[54] Helgaud de Fleury, *Epitoma vitae regis Rotberti pii* 21, ed. Robert-Henri Bautier and Gilette Labory, *Vie de Robert le Pieux*, Sources d'histoire médiévale 1 (Paris: 1965), 102–104.

[55] Widukind, *Rerum gestarum saxonicarum* 3.75, ed. Paul Hirsch and H.-E. Lohmann, MGH SS rer. Germ. in u.s. 60 (Hannover: 1935), 152:19–25: "*Proxima nocte iuxta morem diluculo de lecto consurgens nocturnis et matutinibus laudibus intererat. Post haec paululum requievit; missarum deinde officiis celebratis* pauperibus iuxta morem manus porrexit, *paululum gustavit iterumque in lecto requievit. Cum autem hora esset, processit, laetus et hilaris ad mensam requievit. Peracto ministerio vespertinis laudibus interfuit; peracto cantico evangelii . . .* [emphasis mine]." The paratactic structure (*post haec, deinde . . .*) conveys the sense of a unitary complex of liturgical actions. Thegan, *Vita Hludowici imperatoris* 19, ed. Ernst Tremp, MGH SS rer. Germ. in u.s. 64 (Hannover: 1995), 204:4–6: "*Cottidie ante cibum aelemosinarum largitionem pauperibus exhibuit, et ubicumque erat, semper xenodochia secum habebat.*" Notker, *Gesta Karoli* 2.21, ed. G. H. Pertz, MGH SS 2 (Hannover: 1824), 762:36–763:17, seems to widen the circle of *pauperes* to include ordinary warriors and bath attendants. See Boshof, "Armenfürsorge," 265–67, for this care as *administratio regni*. D.Ch.II.135 (16 Jan. 851), ed. Georges Tessier, *Recueil des actes de Charles le Chauve*, vol. 1 (Paris: 1943), 357–59, here 358:13–27: ". . . *ut, quod secundum dei praeceptum, in pauperibus suscipiendis atque alendis sive etiam vestiendis ac pedibus eorum lavandis, occupationibus praepediti . . . minus inservire valeremus . . . inibi a fratribus huic studio mancipatis vice nostra cotidie ageretur.*" Cf. further, 359:1–5: "*et in cena domini duodecim collecti ac pedibus abluti . . .*" Charles became abbot of Saint-Denis only in 867, which means that in 851 the monks cared vicariously for the king, not for the king as abbot.

[56] *Epitoma vitae regis Rotberti* 5, ed. Bautier, 62–64; where one of the "holy poor," whom the king fed at his feet, steals with Robert's knowledge one of his golden ornaments. On the pair *potens-pauper* (the latter term meaning both economic "poor" and social "powerless"), see Karl Bosl, "*Potens* und *Pauper*," Begriffsgeschichtliche Studien zur gesellschaftlichen Differenzierung im frühen Mittelalter und zum 'Pauperismus' des Hochmittelalters," in *Alteuropa*

Liudprand's narrative shows that royal household poor were known in Lombardy. But he is quite unwilling to dress the local dynasts in the robes of sacrality. The institution, when one meets it in the *Antapodosis*, is not enveloped in the aura of holiness produced around Louis the Pious, Otto and Robert. Rather, it is being abused by the unscrupulous Amedeus, agent of Berengar II. Amedeus left Germany (where Berengar had found refuge) for Italy in the guise of a poor pilgrim. His mission was to see whether it would be possible to foment an aristocratic conspiracy calling his master into Lombardy against King Hugh. Amedeus was a skillful chameleon. He soiled with pitch his aristocratically fluffy beard, darkened his golden hair, made his face ugly, and faked physical disability. Thus vilified, Amadeus was able to "show himself to Hugh, naked, among the poor who ate in the king's presence, and receive clothing . . . from Hugh's hand, as well as listen to everything that the king said concerning Berengar and himself."[57] Liudprand indicts Berengar II through his agent Amedeus: The exiled contender for the throne does not shy from taking advantage of the most hallowed forms of royal piety, essentially "religious" because practiced also by the monks. But neither does the author seek to develop for King Hugh's praise the potential sacrality inherent in the institution of the *pauperes in presentia regis*. The *Antapodosis* neutralizes it both stylistically and narratively. The description is brief; in no sense is it liturgified. The author of the *Antapodosis* could not have read Helgaud's *Life of Robert*. Yet, as it were, Amedeus plays the role of one of Robert's poor, fed by the ruler, clothed by the ruler. But the banquet at Hugh's court is not the occasion for the ritual despoiling of a willing king by his holy poor. It provides the setting for the theft of secrets by a powerful man on behalf of another *potens* and to the detriment of the king. In the Lombard courts that the *Antapodosis* depicts, nothing is sacred enough not to be manipulated—not even, as we shall now see, a coronation.

Coronamentum Fallax

In 945 the ever-fickle Italian magnates trickled away from Hugh and Lothar, his son and co-ruler; they streamed to the kings' not fully declared rival, Berengar of Frioul:

---

und die moderne Gesellschaft. Festschrift für Otto Brunner (Göttingen: 1963), 60–73. I draw here on Claude Carozzi's fine analyses, "La vie du roi Robert par Helgaud de Fleury: historiographie et hagiographie," in *Annales de Bretagne et des pays de l'Ouest* 87, 2 (1980): 219–35, esp. 227–30, and "Le roi et la liturgie chez Helgaud de Fleury," Evelyne Patlagean and Pierre Riché, eds., *Hagiographie, cultures et sociétés, IVe–XIIe siècles* (Paris: 1981), 417–32. Banquets: see Fichtenau, *Lebensordnungen*, 1.82f., tr. Geary, 58f.; and Gerd Althoff, *Verwandte, Freunde und Getreue. Zum politischen Stellenwert der Gruppenbindungen im früheren Mittelalter* (Darmstadt: 1990), 202f.

[57] *Antapodosis* 5.18, 133–34, quotation at 133:383–134:386.

As [Berengar II] resided in Milan and distributed the honors of Italy to his partisans, King Hugh sent his son Lothar to the audience (*ad praesentiam*) not simply of Berengar, but also of the whole people (*totius populi*). Hugh requested that since they had rejected one who was not pleasing to them (*eis non morigerum abdicant*) they would at least, for the love of God, receive his son, who had committed no crime against them, and that they would reform him (*morigerum reddant*) according to their desires. Thus, as Lothar made his way to Milan, King Hugh, leaving Pavia, considered abandoning Italy and going to Burgundy with all his treasury. But something retained him here. Indeed, when Lothar prostrated himself (*prostratum*) in front of the Cross in the church of the blessed confessor Ambrose and of the blessed martyrs Gervasius and Protasius, they [the *populus*], yielding to mercy, raised (*erigerent*) him up and constituted him their king. Soon after this, they sent a messenger to Hugh, promising that he would reign again over them.[58]

The scene is sacral and consensual. Exaltation follows humiliation. The royal child's submission to Christ the King restores the Italian aristocracy's subjection to Hugh's dynasty. The complex humiliation-exaltation, well studied by Lothar Bornscheuer and more recently by Patrick Corbet and Geoffrey Koziol, belonged to the basic architectonic features of tenth-century political ritual (at least as presented in contemporary texts); it was especially well developed in Ottonian Saxony, where Gerd Althoff has shown it underpinned reconciliations and acts of royal mercy.[59] Princely diplomata utilized it. A great magnate might appear titled in his charters now *humilis*, now count, margrave, or prince by the grace of God (*gratia dei*), oftentimes both:[60] self-humiliation brought on one the uplifting *gratia dei*. Coronations specifically referred to Christ's humiliation on the Cross and the subsequent exaltation of His human nature to kingship in Heaven, the "name (*nomen*) above all names" (cf. Matt. 23.12; Phil. 2.9).

One will recognize in Lothar's prostration the opening segment of a tenth-century coronation order. Liudprand the ex-chaplain evidences here masterful knowledge of contemporary royal rituals. It is not clear whether

---

[58] *Antapodosis* 5.28, 140:593–605; see Gina Fasoli, *I re d'Italia* (Florence: 1949), 159–60. The Latin description of the ritual is fast-paced: ". . . *dum misericordia inclinati Lotharium . . . ante crucem prostratum erigerent regemque sibi constituerent . . .*"

[59] Lothar Bornscheuer, *Miseriae regum. Untersuchungen zum Krisen- und Todesgedanken in der herrschaftstheologischen Vorstellung der ottonisch-salischen Zeit* (Berlin: 1968); Corbet, *Les saints ottoniens*; Geoffrey G. Koziol, *Begging Pardon and Favor* (Ithaca [NY]: 1992); Gerd Althoff, "Königsherrschaft und Konfliktsbewältigung im 10. und 11. Jahrhundert," repr. in Althoff, *Spielregeln*, 22–56. For art, see Bornscheuer (op. cit.); Robert Deshman, "The Exalted Servant: The Ruler Theology of the Prayer Book of Charles the Bald," *Viator* 11 (1980): 385–417; and Henry Mayr-Harting, *Ottonian Book Illumination*, 2 vols. (London: 1991), 1.135–38.

[60] Karl Brunner, "Fränkische Fürstentitel," in *Intitulatio II. Lateinische Herrscher- und Fürstentitel im neunten und zehnten Jahrhundert*, MIÖG Ergänzungsband 24, ed. Herwig Wolfram (Vienna: 1973), 203–207.

he paraphrases a German or a Lombard *ordo*. We have no witnesses to Italian *ordines* before the turn of the millennium, and if Liudprand drew on the knowledge acquired in Pavia rather than on that acquired in Germany, his testimony would indicate that Italy contributed to the pan-European elaboration of the coronation liturgy.[61] Be this as it may, I paraphrase the liturgical document closest in time to Liudprand, the Frühdeutsche Ordo (before 960): Let the future ruler prostrate himself (*prosternat*) before the altar, and await for the *Te deum laudamus* or the Litanies of the saints to be sung; he shall then be picked up (*erigatur*) and elected king after or before having sworn the famous triple promise.[62] Liudprand does not explicitly mention an oath for what seems to have been a recoronation or less probably a crown-wearing.[63] Yet it is implicit. To the reader of the *Antapodosis*, Hugh's proposal to let the *populus* (that is, the magnates as representatives of the political totality) reform the young king (*morigerum reddere*), might have suggested that Lothar swore a humiliating promise similar to the one his relative Boso had sworn in 879 to his Burgundian electors:

> Concerning my *mores* (even though I know myself to be a sinner more than anyone else) I claim that it is my will to show myself docile (*morigerum*) in all things to the good and in no way to the bad. Yet should I (given that I am a

[61] The question is thus: Should one assume that the complex prostration-elevation was in use in Lombardy ca. 947? or that Liudprand, familiar with Ottonian practice, used it for his narrative? Carl Erdmann, "Konigs- und Kaiserskrönung im ottonischen Pontifikale," in his posthumous *Forschungen zur Ideenwelt des Frühmittelalters*, ed. Friedrich Baethgen (Berlin: 1951), 63, insists on the German origins of the Frühdeutsche Ordo; let us note, though, that the earliest manuscript—the Sacramentary of Warmund of Ivrea (1001/2)—is Lombard. Fried, "Königserhebung," 299, suggests that Liudprand reconstructed the solemnities of Henry's 919 accession on the basis of Otto II's 961 royal coronation, a hypothesis that might account as well for these echoes.

[62] "Early German Ordo," ed. Erdmann, *Forschungen*, 84: "*ad altaris gradus . . . humiliter totus in cruce prostratus iaceat . . . Finita autem letania erigant se* [rex et episcopi]." See C. A. Bouman, *Sacring and Crowning*, Bijdragen van het Instituut voor Middeleeuwse Geschiedenis der Rijks-Universiteit te Utrecht 30 (Groningen: 1957), 147–48. The Frühdeutsche Ordo is also accessible in Cyrille Vogel and Reinhard Elze, *Le pontifical romano-germanique*, 3 vols., Studi e testi 226–27, 269 (Vatican: 1963–72), here 1.260:5–8. Prostration-elevation seems first attested in *ordines* for the Queen's coronation, see the Westfränkische Ordo (or "Erdmann") ca 900, in Richard A. Jackson, *Ordines coronationis Franciae I* (Philadelphia: 1995), 151: "*Veniente ea in ecclesia, prosternat se ante altare ad agendam orationem. Expleta vero oratione, producatur ab episcopis ad altare.*" A contemporary Anglo-Saxon ritual may also have been influential: the so-called Ratold ordo, which Janet L. Nelson, "The Second English Ordo," *Politics and Ritual*, 361–74, at 361–67, dates to ca. 900; see ms. BN Latin 12052 (A.D. 973/86), f. 22r, ed. Paul L. Ward, "An Early Version of the Anglo-Saxon Coronation Ceremony," *EHR* 57 (1942): 345–61, at 351. Edith daughter of the West-Saxon ruler Aelfflaed was consecrated with Otto I in 936 (Nelson, 367); the ceremony possibly brought prostration to Germany.

[63] Carlrichard Brühl, "Fränkischer Krönungsbrauch und das Problem der Festkrönungen," *HZ* 194 (1962): 265–326; Kurt-Ulrich Jäschke, "Frühmittelalterliche Festkrönungen? Überlegungen zur Terminologie und Methode," *HZ* 211,3 (1970): 556–88.

human being) transgress . . . against anyone, I shall strive to rectify (*corrigere*) [this transgression] according to your counsel (*consilium*).[64]

We can thus imagine the scene in Saint-Ambrose, ceremonially amplified in Liudprand's narrative by the enunciation of the names and ranks of the saints as well as by the presence of the cross. It is further amplified (but in the mind of the modern historian) by the setting. Saint-Ambrose was already earmarked to be the Hugonides' necropolis. Hugh and Lothar had endowed the monastery in 942 to be their future resting place, and it already celebrated their ancestors' *memoria*.[65] One can speculate that Liudprand's intended audience included some of the magnates who, having accompanied Otto I south of the Alps in 951–52, had witnessed the king's festive and highly political confirmation of diplomata for that church— one at least to commemorate his bond to the Hugonides.[66] The *Antapodosis* fashions an atmosphere of consensus to package the ceremonially correct proceedings. Lothar arrives *ad praesentiam totius populi*, to the audience or presence of the whole aristocracy (the term *praesentia* suggests the sovereign and judicial nature of this body).[67] It is an indeterminate (and hence encompassing) "they" who raises him up from his prostration and makes him king again. Boso too had presented himself to his electors humbly, as *humilis vernaculus Boso*; and their unanimity had proven similarly decisive in the economy of the ceremony; consensus stood as a divine sign that the elect had to accept the royal office (*per dei nutum cor unum datum et animam unam in unum consensum*) despite his awareness of his natural human frailty.[68]

Yet the hieratic image of reconciliation in Saint-Ambrose is a narrative trick Liudprand plays on his reader.[69] It parallels Berengar's own trick (*deceptio*). The author now reveals the being behind the seeming and tears the veil of apparent sacrality he (and Berengar) had woven out of the religiously charged threads of consensus and humiliation-exaltation:

---

[64] *Bosonis regis electi ad synodum [et fideles] responsio* (Mantailles, 10/15/879), MGH Capitularia II:2 n. 284, ed. Alfred Boretius and Victor Krause (Hannover: 1890), 387; see Schramm, *Kaiser, Könige und Päpste*, 2.257–64. In the Early German Ordo, the future king promises to rule *iuxta morem patrum suorum*. See Brunner, "Fränkische Fürstentitel", 205.

[65] See Buc, "Italian Hussies," 217–18, 222–23.

[66] Ibid., 218, 222 n. 68 (D.O.I 138 and 145).

[67] See Marc Reydellet, *La royauté dans la littérature latine de Sidoine Apollinaire à Isidore de Séville* (Rome: 1981), 376–81. For the contemporary meaning of *praesentia*, see Cesare Manaresi, ed., *I placiti del "Regnum Italiae"* (Rome: 1955), e.g. (among many but the closest in time to 945), 139 (Milan, 941), 521:1–522:5: "*Dum . . . in iuditio resideret Berengarius marchio . . . residentibus cum eo . . . vicecomes . . . iudices dominorum regum . . . notarii et reliqui multis. Ibique eorum veniens presencia Petrus . . .*"

[68] *Bosonis . . . responsio*, as n. 64, 367:13–15.

[69] Germana Gandino, *Il vocabolario politico e sociale di Liutprando di Cremona* (Rome: 1995), 69–70, also remarked this falsification.

But this counsel (*consilium*), no, I should say, this trick, was devised not by all (*omnes*) but rather by Berengar, who was filled with cunning. He did not intend these two to reign, but (as it became evident later) he wanted to avoid that Hugh should leave [Italy] and use his immense monies to call against him [Berengar] the Burgundians or other peoples.[70]

Lothar's elevation is not the (consensual) act of the all-encompassing "all" (*omnes*); it is not "consiliar." As the word play on *consilium* (meaning both counsel and plan) makes clear, it is one man's trick. Lothar's *coronamentum* has been engineered to serve the segmentary interests of a faction in the Italian civil wars.

Contrast Henry of Saxony's accession to the royal office at Conrad I's death. Liudprand's narrative uses the same legitimizing motifs but describes a truly sacral and consensual event. We are dealing with being, not seeming. In tenth- and eleventh-century Saxony, the last rites for a ruler could be framed in the same liturgical complex, humiliation-exaltation, that Liudprand manipulates to expose Berengar's manipulation. Dying on earth, reborn to reign in Heaven—kingship had adopted the paradoxical triumphal ideology of Christian martyrdom.[71] But humiliation-exaltation structured more than the personal fate of the deceased king; writ large, it gave rhythm, emotion, and meaningfulness to the whole royal succession— that is, to the demise and rebirth of kingship. Indeed, the royal death rites could be presented as the first act of the creation of a new king. A good royal funeral projected a sense of crisis, finally overcome by the restoration of order with the successor's accession.[72]

The description that the *Antapodosis* gives of Henry of Saxony's accession contradicts much of what we know from other contemporary sources.[73] On his deathbed, Conrad I calls all the *principes* (except for Arnulf of Bavaria and Henry), preaches peace, concord, and rejection of lust for power (*regnandi cupiditas*), and orders them to elect Henry as his successor. Conrad then signals for the crown and other royal ornaments to be brought *in medium*, to the center of the group formed by the dukes. Liudprand lingers

---

[70] *Antapodosis* 5.28, 141:606–10.

[71] This at least since Ambrose's *De obitu Theodosii* 56, ed. Otto Faller, *Sancti Ambrosii Opera* 7, CSEL 73:7 (Vienna: 1955), 400–401; see Sabine MacCormack, *Art and Ceremony in Late Antiquity* (Berkeley: 1981), 145–47.

[72] Thietmar of Merseburg, *Chronicon* 4.50–53, ed. Robert Holtzmann, MGH SS rer. Germ., n.s. 9 (Berlin: 1935), 188–94, with Bornscheuer, *Miseriae*, 208–11. But see the perceptive comments of David A. Warner, "Thietmar of Merseburg on Rituals of Kingship," *Viator* 26 (1995): 53–76, esp. 70f., on the constructed nature of rituals in this document. Cp. Charles the Bald's funeral, ch. 2 below, 85–87.

[73] Dändliker-Müller, 140–41; Karpf, *Herrscherlegitimation*, 14–23.

at length on the objects; the hypertrophy is designed to heighten the ceremonial charge of the moment:

> He ordered that should be brought *in medium* his own crown—which was decorated (I should say, weighed down) with gems and not simply of gold (since almost all *principes*, no matter which order they belong to, wear such [crowns])—and the scepter as well as all the royal vestments. And, as he could, he poured out these words: "Through these ornaments I constitute Henry heir and vicar to the royal dignity; I not only order but pray that you should obey him."[74]

And so it is done. Henry humbly refuses, then accepts the *dignitas regia*. Not all the princes, however, bow immediately before him. Arnulf of Bavaria's own ambition for the royal office, and the subsequent armed confrontation between the two men, serve to highlight and explain Henry's legitimacy. Here again, Liudprand is in no hurry to conclude and crafts two long speeches. Presenting himself as the elect of the aristocracy (*populus*) by the will of God, Creator of the world, Who quashes the proud and exalts those who pray Him, the king exhorts the rebel. Arnulf's men then themselves give a Gregorian and Augustinian apology for submission to the powers ordained by God. Clearly, "in his election the whole people could not have been of one mind, if the Highest Trinity, Who is the One God, had not elected him before the creation of the world." And so Arnulf submits.[75] *Totus populus, animus unus*: An aura of consensus descends on Henry's accession, sealed in the dignified agony of the previous king. As in the Holy Lance episode, politics is uplifted by theological discourse into the sphere of *Heilsgeschichte*, and its outcome becomes providential.

Orderly succession characterizes the German dispensation. At Henry's death, "his body was carried to the monastery of most noble and religious girls [Quedlinburg] . . . where it was, with immense veneration, deposited within the church." Mathilda retired chastely to a nunnery and (so Liudprand tells us, but probably not in accordance with the facts) did not seek to influence the kingdom's governance. Her Italian counterparts understood widowhood differently and played politics through intrigues and the use of her charms.[76] After having established what we might call funerary and sexual legitimacy, Liudprand pens a poem on Henry's designated successor, Otto: "The multitude, widowed of its dear king, now stops shedding tears,

---

[74] *Antapodosis* 2.18–20, 43–44, citation at 43:422–44:428. Dändliker-Müller surmise that Liudprand may have projected into Conrad's reign Gislebert and Eberhardt's plot of 938 against Otto.

[75] *Antapodosis* 2.21–23, 44–46, citation at 45:474–77.

[76] *Antapodosis* 4.15, 105:337–41. For Mathilda's activities, see Buc, "Italian Hussies," 217–19.

when another surges up to be worshipped by the world, a son image of the father who called him, Otto King"[77]

By contrast, hardly anywhere in the Italian tier of the *Antapodosis* can one find orderly succession. The sole exception is Hugh of Arles, "whom God wanted to rule in Italy." Pushed by favorable winds, he came to Pisa, then traveled to Italy, where he received the kingship "with the agreement of all (*cunctis coniventibus*)," and then struck an alliance with the pope. Clearly, Liudprand viewed Hugh with greater indulgence than Berengar, even if Hugh's many qualities had been sullied by his love for women.[78] Otto, after all, derived his claim to peninsular kingship in part through Hugh, through his marital alliance with Hugh's daughter-in-law Adelheid.[79] Still, the *Antapodosis* does not tarry to describe any ceremonial for Hugh's king-making. Liudprand pays much more attention to, and depicts in much more detail and with much more theological density, the Germanic accessions of 919–36 than comparable Italian events.[80] South of the Alps, power seems to be transmitted without ceremony, as magnates fall away from a king and go over to his rival—sometimes owing to feminine plotting or charms—or through violence.[81] Could this reflect an actual difference in the royal liturgy? I think not. Liudprand's apparent lack of interest in Italian ceremonies owes everything to his unwillingness to see cisalpine royalty as sacred. And it is only a relative lack of interest: As we have seen above with Lothar's *coronamentum*, and as we shall see below with

[77] *Antapodosis* 4.16, 106:368–72; cf. Karpf, *Herrscherlegitimation*, 25–27.

[78] *Antapodosis* 3.16–19, 75.

[79] This connection may explain as well Liudprand's praiseful words for the still-living Waldrada sister of Rodulf of Burgundy (hence Adelheid's aunt) "a matron honored with both shapeliness and wisdom" (*Antapodosis* 2.66, 61:984–87). Another good woman, Hugh's mistress "the most noble Wandelmoda" (*Antapodosis* 3.20, 75:339–76:342) was related to Waldrada through the marriage of her son Hubert to Waldrada's daughter. Liudprand may have praised Wandelmoda and Hubert, who was "still alive and powerful prince of the province of Tuscany," because the latter ended up siding with Otto. See Hofmeister, *Markgrafen*, 407–409, 421–24; and Robert Davidsohn, *Geschichte von Florenz*, vol. 1 (Berlin: 1896), 102f., 111f. I had not dealt with these two women in "Italian Hussies."

[80] Karpf, *Herrscherlegitimation*, 36–37, who also (37–38) asserts that Liudprand is generally uninterested in formal acts, even "*weltliche Formalakte*," with the exception of *Antapodosis* 2.19–20. Gandino, *Il vocabolario*, 72–76, demonstrates how Liudprand's terminology creates a German continuity: German accessions from Arnulf on happen in usually consensual and always orderly fashion (*principari, constitui, ordinari*).

[81] Dändliker-Müller, 57: "Beachtenswerth ist ferner, wie die unnationalen [*sic*] Herrscher, besonders Rudolf und Hugo, hauptsächlich durch Buhlerinnen sollen berufen worden sein." Gandino, *Il vocabolario*, 75–76: In Italy, with the exception of Hugh, kings come to power by force, fraud, or violence (*potenter, viriliter, auferre, subiugare*). This dovetails with the spectrum for means of accessions developed by Liudprand's contemporary Atto of Vercelli, from God's will and "the acclamation of all (*omnium vox*)" to battles, savagery, conjuration, and rebellions, *Polipticum* 2, ed. Georg Goetz, Abhandlungen der philologisch-historischen Klasse der sächsischer Akademie der Wissenschaften 37:2 (Leipzig: 1922), 14:30–35.

Hugh's murderous advent, the *Antapodosis* does not shy from describing rituals if it can help to expose the corrupt nature of Italian politics.

ADVENTUS CARNIFICIS

Liudprand destroys the consensus-building functionality of yet another political ritual, the royal advent.[82] We should first examine, synthetically and from a diachronic standpoint, its meaning in early medieval political culture. Not only will this allow us to understand better Liudprand's strategic use of it; it will as well inform the analysis of similar processional rituals in the following chapter. The advent had allowed late antique urban communities to demonstrate their allegiance to a ruler. When he made his way toward the city (*adventus*), the citizens would come out of the gates in orderly fashion (*occursus*) and meet him and his retinue some distance away from the walls (*susceptio*). From the age of the Dominate on, in fact as well as fiction, the late antique and medieval ruler owed his legitimacy to military force. Furthermore, he was supposed to be not quite simply human, but a friend of God or the gods. As such, he manifested this otherness by outstanding pomp. It was therefore as a quasi god, different from the citizens, and as a military lord, in arms and leading an army, that the prince proceeded toward the city—a self-representation of rulership still current in the late medieval ceremonial language of politics, as miniatures well attest.[83] This apparatus signified in a thinly veiled fashion the violence he could unleash if the townspeople did not recognize his authority. Indeed, nonrecognition could be depicted as an *adventus* turned upside down, metamorphosed into the conflict it was supposed to forestall. Bonizo of Sutri, a partisan of Pope Gregory VII, could thus deride Henry IV's failure to enter Rome in 1081 as an inversion of the ceremonial order: "How honorifically was he received (*suscipiebatur*) by the Romans! For one could see lances instead of tapers, armored men instead of clerical choirs, jeers instead of lauds, howls instead of applauses."[84] Or more soberly, in Hrotsvitha

---

[82] Fundamental studies: Erik Peterson, "Die Einholung des Kyrios," *Zeitschrift für systematische Theologie* 7 (1930): 682–702; Ernst H. Kantorowicz, "The King's Advent and the Enigmatic Panels in the Doors of Santa Sabina," repr. in Kantorowicz, *Selected Studies* (Locust Valley [NY]: 1965), 37–75; O. Nussbaum, art. "Geleit," ibidem, vol. 9 (Stuttgart: 1976), 908–1049, at 963–79 and 1024–36.

[83] Bernard Guenée et Françoise Lehoux, *Les entrées royales françaises de 1328 à 1515* (Paris: 1968); Lawrence M. Bryant, *The King and the City in the Parisian Royal Entry Ceremony* (Geneva: 1986); idem, "The Medieval Entry Ceremony at Paris," in *Coronations*, ed. Janos Bák (Berkeley: 1990), 88–118.

[84] Bonizo of Sutri, *Liber ad amicum*, ix, ed. Ernst Dümmler, *MGH Libelli de lite* I (Hannover: 1891), 568–620 at 613:31-2; Dümmler quotes (613 n. 3) Henry's indignant letter to the Romans: "We are amazed that, even though you had learned of our adventus, no embassy came from you to perform an occursus in the customary, solemn way (*sollempni more occurit*)"; see

of Gandersheim's *Gesta Ottonis*, the normal alternative was between waging war and coming out to meet the king.[85] Medieval historians wrote with the assumption that there existed an array of graduated signals that allowed agents to convey differentiated messages ranging from full recognition to outright refusal of honor.[86] Thus, in 1002, one of the candidates to Otto III's succession, Ekkehard, margrave of Meissen, was met differently in cities according to whether they favored or opposed him: He entered Hildesheim as a king (*ut rex suscipitur*) and was treated with honor (*honorifice*), but found Paderborn's doors closed against him. This initial reluctance already conveyed Bishop Rethar's unwillingness to recognize the pretender, even if the prelate finally allowed him in. After having prayed in the cathedral, Ekkehard went to the house where Rethar was dining, and there "was received owing to charity (*caritative susceptus*)"—meaning, not in recognition of the royal honor the margrave claimed.[87] Recognition could be complete only if it involved all the politically meaningful members of the city; therefore, in the *occursus*, all important groups of the urban social imaginary were represented—the youth, accepted foreign minorities, people, and magistrates, categories to which Christian late antiquity added clergy and monks. As a sermon attributed to John Chrysostom makes clear, marginal groups, being worthy of the ruler's severity rather than of his clement friendliness, were excluded from the *occursus*, even though once in the town the prince might choose to grant mercy, instead of strict punishment, to criminals.[88] In the Middle Ages a mock battle sometimes would pit the urban youth, vanguard of the *occursus*, against the princely train. This both hinted at the city's own strength and justified a dignified, pactlike, mutual recognition within subjection (as opposed to an abject, servile, and unconditional surrender to the prince).[89] Once the two

---

Carlrichard Brühl, *Fodrum, gistum, servitium regis. Studien zu den wirtschaftlichen Grundlagen des Königtums im Frankenreich und in den fränkischen Nachfolgestaaten*, 2 vols., Kölner historische Abhandlungen 14:1–2 (Cologne: 1968), 1.522–23 n. 408.

[85] "*Beringarius . . . non bellum movit, regi non obvius exit*": *Gesta Ottonis*, v. 622, ed. Homeyer, *Hrotsvithae opera*, 430.

[86] Cf. processions, which I examine in ch. 2.

[87] Thietmar, *Chronicon* 5.4–5, ed. Holtzmann, 224. Cf. Warner, "Thietmar," 73.

[88] *Homilia* viii *in Ep. I ad Thessalonicenses* 4, 16, *PG* 62, 440, quoted and translated by Kantorowicz, "King's Advent," 225: "Why, if Christ is about to descend, are we going to be taken up [in the clouds]? For honor's sake. For when the Basileus enters a city, those who are in the state of honor go out to meet him; the criminals, however, remain in the city and there expect their judge."

[89] See Karl Hauck, "Zur Genealogie und Gestalt des staufischen *Ludus de Antechristo*," *Germanische-Romanische Monatsschrift*, n.f. 2,1 (1951): 11, 16, and *The Murder of Charles the Good*, ch. 66, trans. James B. Ross (New York: 1959), 227–30. Lawrence Bryant, "Medieval Entry," 94, draws attention to the motif of the raised drawbridge or closed church door prior to princely acceptance of the urban (or churchly) escort.

ensembles, ruler and people, had met, the townspeople festively led the prince and his followers into the city (*ingressus*). There, he disarmed and manifested his humanity, that is, his willingness to be a friend to the community and not its enemy.[90] As in Republican times, the *imperator*, once within the civic perimeter (in Rome, the *poemerium*, in walled cities, the main gate that iconographically represented the town), abdicated violence and some of its trappings. I have mentioned how it might entail mercy for condemned criminals or opponents. For the citizens, it often meant confirmation of certain privileges.[91] Finally (as a description of Louis the Pious's ceremonial *ingressus* into Barcelona after its 809 surrender demonstrates), an *adventus* could publicly erase an initial refusal to recognize a ruler.[92]

This ritual was alive and well in the tenth century. It had long since been christianized thanks to the cross-fertilization between Christ's advent and imperial *adventus*, and rendered common thanks to a process of devolution that granted *adventus* to relics, bishops, and royal officials (and in western Francia or Italy, to quasi-independent potentates).[93] Not only towns, but also churches and monasteries (being heavenly cities) received public figures into their walls with a processional *occursus*. Hence its liturgification and codification in *ordines*, probably already in our tenth century;[94] hence the composition of hymns the clergy chanted during its outward procession. A whole collection of such chants produced by the monks of Saint-

---

[90] For the stages of the advent and the terms denoting them, see Martin Heinzelmann, *Translationsberichte und andere Quellen des Reliquienkultes*, Typologie des sources du Moyen Age occidental 33 (Turnhout: 1979), 72–74. For the Late Antique transformations of the advent and their significance, MacCormack, *Art and Ceremony*, especially 40–42, on the emperor's transformation from potential conqueror to quasi citizen, from being remote to being friendly, from being an alien savior to being a fellow human.

[91] Gate: see Kantorowicz, "King's Advent," 214–15 with plates 8, 10, and 21, who also notes the triumphal arch's function as gate; MacCormack, *Art and Ceremony*, 28–29, 51f. with plates 9 and 10. Privileges: E.g., the boys who had feigned a fight against the new count of Flanders negotiated the right to hunt small game (above, n. 89).

[92] As Brühl, *Fodrum*, 1.106 n. 419, suggests. See also closer to Liudprand the *AF ad an.* 896, ed. Kurze, 127–28.

[93] Heinzelmann, *Translationsberichte*, 66–77; Nikolaus Gussone, "Adventus-Zeremoniell und Translation von Reliquien. Vitricius von Rouen, *De laude sanctorum*," FMSt 10 (1976): 125–33; Karl Hauck, "Von einer spätantiker Randkultur zum karolingischen Europa," FMSt 1 (1967): 30–43; Walther Bulst, "*Susceptacula regum*. Zur Kunde deutscher Reichsaltertümer," in *Corona Quernea, Festgabe K. Strecker*, Schriften der MGH (then Schriften des Reichsinstituts für ältere deutsche Geschichtskunde) 6 (Stuttgart: 1941), 97–135; Peter Willmes, *Der Herrscher-"Adventus" im Kloster des Frühmittelalters*, Münstersche Mittelalter-Schriften 22 (Munich: 1976). McCormick, *Eternal Victory*, has studied the permanence and transformations through the year 1000 of the Late Antique *profectio ad bellum* and triumphal entry.

[94] Kantorowicz, "King's Advent," 208–09. The eleventh-century Cluniac *consuetudines of Farfa* seem to attest to the tenth-century existence of *ordines* regulating *adventus* into monasteries; see Heinzelmann, *Translationsberichte*, 74.

Gall has survived; it insists on the mercy of the ruler, on the cosmic peace
he will bring, as well as on the return of the golden age, *saeculum aureum*.[95]
This multiplication could only render the ceremonial form more intelligible; it had become a common idiom.

Liudprand (whom King Hugh had made a member of his royal chapel
owing to the quality of his voice) may well have sung hymnic *laudes* to his
prince upon one or another of Hugh's returns to the capital city of Pavia.
By his time, the *adventus* had become such ritual small change that he could
make it the subject of political jokes. Liudprand could thus snicker ironically at hymns sung to Berengar II that proclaimed the coming of the
golden age.[96] The biggest joke of all was the advent of a deposed ruler.
Emperor Romanos had been thrown into a monastery by his rebellious
sons. The two men in turn were exiled to the same place by Constantine
VII. They were met in a mock *occursus* by their father, who congratulated
them for having sent him ahead to teach the monks how to receive emperors (*imperatores suscipere*).[97] The ceremony had been vulgarized to such a
point that it allowed a play within the (in this case, narrative) play.

Yet the two main descriptions the Lombard historian gives of an *adventus*
ceremony must have left his readers with a less playful, more sinister impression. In the first case, the citizens deny an *occursus* to a ruler, triggering
bloodshed that culminates in an inverted use of the advent's very idioms.
In the second case, the advent is manipulated for the sake of a vendetta,
leading to gruesome mutilations and deaths—another play within the (in
this case, political) play. Insofar as their message and meaning's intelligibility hang on Liudprand's careful utilization of the symbols, forms, and vocabulary conveyed by the ceremonial tradition, the two stories deserve full
analysis and quotation.

The East Carolingian Arnulf of Carinthia, then hegemon over most of
the rulers created in 887–88, had been siphoned into Italian politics owing

---

[95] *Sylloga codocis Sangallensis* 331, ed. MGH Poetae IV:1, e.g., n° xvi (Versus Hartmanni ad
suscipiendum regem), v. 1 and 9, "*Suscipe clementem, plebs devotissima, regem . . . Te nobis
blandum dederat dilectio Christi*" [327], or xviii, v. 4, *Rex, miserere.* Notker of Saint-Gall's hymn,
n° x, v. 1–5 [324], contains a great number of characteristic themes and expressions, among
others: "*omnis tibi militia occurat . . . tibi procedat obviam . . . omnesque sancti ordines semper vocent
te laudibus . . . Nos . . . pio domino occurimus in omnibus . . .*" On the monastic entries, see Bulst,
"*susceptacula regum,*" and Willmes, *Herrscher-"Adventus."* A study of the political context of
the rediscovery in two ninth-century monasteries, Saint-Germain d'Auxerre and Saint-Gall,
of Victricius of Rouen's fourth-century treatise on the advent of relics, is in progress.

[96] *Antapodosis* 5.27, 140:590–92: "In his advent all promised a Golden age, and proclaimed
the times which had brought him forth felicitous."

[97] *Antapodosis* 5.23, 137:497–505: "*Quorum pater Romanós adventum ut audivit, graciarum
actiones Deo exhibuit eisque extra fores monasterii obvians laeta fatie,* 'Festivum tempus,' *inquit,*
'*quod humilitatem nostram imperium vestrum visitare coegit. . . . O factum bene, quod me quam
dudum praemisistis! Confratres enim et commilitones mei* [monachi] *supernae tantum phylosophyae*

to the civil war between the margraves Wido of Spoleto and Berengar of Friuli, both contenders for the *regnum Italicum*. He was making his way through the kingdom and decided to seize Bergamo, a city Jörg Jarnut has identified as a key point in Wido's territorial concentration of power:[98]

> Arnulf, having been received (*susceptus*) by the men of Verona, made his departure (*proficicistur*) to Bergamo. There, as they trusted in the extremely strong fortifications of the place (or rather, were deceived by them), the men refused to grant him an *occursus*. He encamped himself, then seized the city by the force of arms, killed, massacred. Furthermore, he had the count of the city, Ambrosius by name, hanged in front of the gate's door, with his sword, baldric, armbands (*armillae*), and his other most precious clothes. This fact terrorized in no small fashion all the other cities and all princes. And whomsoever heard it, it set both of his ears ringing. Therefore, the Milanese and the Pavese, terrorized by this rumor, did not dare to wait for his [Arnulf's] *adventus* but rather sent ahead an embassy and promised to comply with his orders.[99]

Here, the gates of the city do not "curve inward and flanked by twin towers . . . receive in a kind of embrace" the ruler, as in the Latin panegyric of 312 to Constantine.[100] They embrace one of the most honorable members of the community, its count, hanged like a common criminal, with the full ornaments pertaining to his office and honor—the *armillae* marking Germanic nobility as well as the baldric and sword associated with the public *militia* since late antiquity.[101] The citizens are slaughtered. Everybody

---

incunbentes, qualiter imperatores susciperent *ignorarent, si non me iam dudum imperialibus institutis attritum haberent* [emphases mine; compare with texts cited in preceding note].'"

[98] Jörg Jarnut, "Die Eroberung Bergamos (894). Eine Entscheidungsschlacht zwischen Kaiser Wido und König Arnulf," *DA* 30,1 (1974): 208–15, at 211, and the same's *Bergamo 568–1098*, Beihefte der Vierteljahrschrift für Sozial- und Wirtschaftsgeschichte 67 (Wiesbaden: 1979), 247, for Ambrosius count of Bergamo, and 252 for Gislebert.

[99] Liudprand, *Antapodosis* 1.23–24, 20:569–21:580.

[100] *Panegyrici latini*, n. 8, 7, 4–6, translated by MacCormack, *Art and Ceremony*, 28.

[101] See *Antapodosis* 2.62, 59:927–29, where Adalbert of Ivrea throws away *balteum, armillasque aureas, omnem preciosum apparatum* and puts on *vilibusque . . . militis sui . . . indumentis* to escape recognition. Mathilda gives two *armillae* to the priest who celebrates the first mass for the dead for her husband Henry, *Vita Mahthildis posterior*, cap. 8, ed. Bernd Schütte, *Die Lebensbeschreibungen der Königin Mathilde*, MGH SS rer. Germ. in u.s. 66 (Hannover: 1994), 159:16–160:7. Thankmar, Otto I's half-brother, wore a *torquis aurea*, which he laid on the altar of the Eresburg church as a sign of surrender of his royal claims, see Widukind, *Rerum gestarum Saxonicarum* 2.11, ed. Hirsch-Lohmann, 77:1–2, with Karl Hauck in P. E. Schramm, *Herrschaftszeichen und Staatssymbolik*, 3 vols., Schriften der MGH 13:2 (Stuttgart: 1955), 1.180. For the *cingulum*, see Karl Ferdinand Werner, "Du nouveau sur un vieux thème. Les origines de la 'noblesse' et de la 'chevalerie,' " in Académie des inscriptions et belles-lettres, *Comptes-Rendus des séances de l'année 1985* (Janvier–Mars 1985), 186–200, building on Karl J. Leyser, "Early Medieval Canon Law and the Beginnings of Knighthood," reprint in Leyser, *Communications and Power*, 51–71. See most recently Carine van Rhijn's 1996 Utrecht University master's thesis.

would have understood this violence: Refusing to honor the ruler with an *occursus*, the citizens of Bergamo could expect Arnulf's bloody vengeance. The saints too punished those who neglected to meet them in procession *de more*—thus in Bernard of Angers's eleventh-century *Miracula sanctae Fidis*, a girl, insensible either to fear or to the delectable sound of the hymns that accompanied the procession, "began to be tortured (*distorqueri*) throughout all her limbs."[102] Terror leads other Italian cities not to wait for the Carolingian's "*adventus*"—here Liudprand may have intended a double-entendre (simple "arrival" but also given the earlier passages, "advent"). They submit without further negotiation. Sources closer to the event such as Regino of Prüm confirm that urban communities were struck by fear but not that they avoided recognizing the ruler in festive form: "[N]one dared to speak against him, but all went out in procession to meet him as he came (*obviam procederent venienti*)."[103]

The main *adventus*-story in the *Antapodosis* is equally, if not more, bloody. It may have been prefigured by Arnulf's 896 *adventus* into Rome, during which the king had a number of Roman nobles, who were coming to meet him, beheaded.[104] It involves two *iudices* of the royal city of Pavia, Gezo and Walpert. Walpert we know to have been the father-in-law of the then count of the palace Gislebert. In the *Antapodosis*, the two judges have turned against Hugh of Provence and made an attempt against his royal life. The king manages a narrow escape, but despairs of avenging himself against the rebels because they are solidly entrenched in Pavia—as *iudices*, they belonged to a literate class of powerful local magnates, who represented in political matters the civic community.[105] One count, Samson, whom we

---

[102] *Libri miraculorum* 1.15, ed. A. Bouillet (Paris: 1897), 51.

[103] Regino, *Chronicon*, ad. an. 894, ed. Friedrich Kurze, *Reginonis abbatis Prumiensis Chronicon cum continuatione Treverensi*, MGH SS rer. Germ. in u.s. 47 (Hannover: 1890), 142. The source closest to the event is the Regensburg continuation of the *AF*, ed. Kurze, 124: "Such a great terror filled Italy, that the greatest cities, that is Milan and Pavia, came spontaneously to the king and subjected themselves to him."

[104] *Antapodosis* 1.28, 22:619–23: "*Hoc in tempore Formosus papa religiosissimus a Romanis vehementer aflictabatur, cuius et hortatu Romam rex Arnulfus advenerat. In cuius ingressu ulciscendo papae iniuriam multos Romanorum principes* obviam sibi properantes *decollare praecepit*" [emphases mine]. One learns in the three preceding chapters that the Romans had denied entry to Arnulf (*a Romanis* ingrediendi urbem huic [Arnulfo] *fidutia negaretur*) and that the king had had to storm "the queen of cities" (1.25–27). See below, ch. 2, 53–54.

[105] On Walpert, see Donald A. Bullough, "Urban Change in Early Medieval Italy: The Example of Pavia," *Papers of the British School at Rome* 34, n.s. 21 (Rome: 1966): 82–130, at 113–14 and 130. According to Bullough, Gislebert's wife Roza-Rotruda (Walpert's daughter) became Hugh's mistress. The sexual alliance can be interpreted as a way to save the fortunes of Gislebert's sons. It may testify as well to the importance for Hugh of the political power Rotruda wielded, either personally or in her sons' name: Hugh chose to tap it through concubinage. On the *iudices*, see Guido Mohr, "Gouvernés et gouvernants en Italie du VIe au XIIe siècle," *Gouvernés et gouvernants. Antiquité et Haut Moyen Age*, vol. 2, Recueils de la Société

shall meet in another context, is a personal enemy of Gezo. A future count of the palace, he is probably already intriguing for this office. That Hugh called, in his diplomata, Samson his *consiliarius* testifies to the count's standing in Italian politics—such men were often more "partners and opponents of the king" than royal servants.[106] Samson offers his advice to Hugh, conditionally. He is willing to reveal to him the means to catch the two men if the king promises to hand over Gezo to his vengeance. The bargain is struck, and the count profers his *consilium*:

> He went on: "Leo, bishop of the city of Pavia, is no friend of Gezo and Walpert; these indeed oppose him in all ways wherever they can. Further, you know it is customary that the strongest citizens run out of the city to meet the king (*regi . . . occurere*) when he makes way to Pavia from other places. Therefore, secretly order the bishop that, when on an agreed upon date you will come toward Pavia and these men will come to meet you outside the city, he should shut all the doors of the city and keep the keys himself. This way, when we shall begin to capture them, they should neither be able to flee to the city nor hope for help from it." And so it was done. Indeed, as on the set date the king made his way toward Pavia and the aforementioned went out to meet him, the bishop willingly did what he had been ordered to do. Therefore, the king ordered that they should all be captured. And thus without delay Gezo was handed over to Samson. He was deprived of sight in both his eyes; his tongue, which had blasphemed against the king, was cut off. . . . Once he had been disfigured in his members, his wealth was snatched away from him. Many others are imprisoned. Walpert is beheaded in the morning; his wife Cristina is captured, and torn into pieces by various torments to force her to hand over hidden treasures.

After these lengthy and gruesome details, the final caption echoes the closure of the Bergamo story:

> Fear of the king grew from this incident not only in Pavia, but also in all parts of Italy; neither did she hold him for naught as she had other kings, but she strove to honor him in every way.[107]

Jean Bodin pour l'histoire comparée des institutions 23:2 (Brussels: 1968), 395–420, at 402, 405–406, 413: "la classe dominante, mais aussi celle qui représente la ville."

[106] See Hlawitschka, *Franken*, 260, with Hagen Keller, "Zur Struktur der Königsherrschaft im karolingischen und nachkarolingischen Italien. Der *consiliarius regis*," *Quellen und Forschungen aus italienischen Archiven und Bibliotheken* 47 (1967): 123–223, at 218, who surmises Samson became *comes palatii* in relation to the demise of Walpert and Gezo and the disgrace, if not the death, of Gislebert. Quotation at 189.

[107] Compare *Antapodosis* 3.41, 88–89, with Dio Cassius, *Epitoma* 78.22.1–2, tr. E. Cary, 9.332–35, on Commodus's deceptive advent into Alexandria: ". . . concealing his wrath and pretending that he longed to see them. So when he reached the suburbs, wither the leading citizens had come with certain mystic and sacred symbols, he first greeted them cordially,

What has Liudprand (or Samson) done here? The narrative is not value neutral, as earlier historiography would have one believe. Liudprand does not need to utter explicit disapproval of the king's behavior.[108] In a nutshell, the author of the *Antapodosis* has revealed a rite of consensus building to be a tool of power-politics; he has turned it into the means for the king to sanction *maiestas* and for Samson to pursue his personal vendetta. Let us recall how the ceremony suggests the potential violence the king could exercise against the citizens (in the much later *Murder of Charles the Good* it even incorporates a mock battle pitting the ruler's retinue against his subjects). In the *Antapodosis, adventus* becomes pure slaughter, and the show of force, from being theatrical, becomes the essence of the action. Let us recall as well how the ruler was expected to grace the criminals and favor the citizens. Our narrative ends with the punishments meted out to those who, from Hugh's standpoint, were criminals, and, at least in Gezo's case, were treated as *humiliores*. Gezo and Walpert, in their own eyes, had been worthy of honor—which is why they, as *cives fortiores*, had come out to meet the king. The consensus between ruler and ruled reveals itself to be just as fractious as this *adventus*.

RITUAL AND SACRED HISTORY: THE HOLY LANCE

God plays a fairly limited but highly selective role in Liudprand's *Antapodosis*. Rare are the narrative moments that bring into play the divine will and providence.[109] Almost without exception, these passages center on a member of the Ottonian dynasty. Henry I's victory against the Hungarians at Riade is one such moment.[110] The chapters devoted to the Holy Lance form another. They provide the centerpiece of the second half of the *Antapodosis*'s fourth book. The first half of the fourth book of the *Antapodosis* is devoted to Hugh of Italy. It opens on a brief mention of young Lothar's elevation to the throne as co-king, *cunctis coniventibus*, but quickly moves on to a fully negative register. Liudprand mocks the king's inability to take

---

even making them his guests at a banquet, and then put them to death. Then, having arrayed his whole army, he marched into the city." Manipulated processions and advents were a feature of ninth-century historiography; see ch. 2, 72ff. For other Italian examples, see the *Chronicon Salernitanum* 147b, ed. Ulla Westerbergh, Studia Latina Stockholmiensia 3 (Stockholm: 1956), 154–56 (assassination attempt using deceitful *occursus*), or Erchempert, *Historia Langobardorum* 50, MGH SS rer. Long., 256:3–14.

[108] Ludo Hartmann, *Geschichte Italiens* (Gotha; 1911), 3.2, 200: "So berichtet wenigstens der Geschichtschreiber jener Zeit ohne ein Wort des Tadels über das Vorgehen seines Königs."

[109] Most allusions to the divine will are extremely brief, e.g. *Antapodosis* 3.46, 92:791–93: Hugh is expelled from Rome by divine dispensation; or 2.46, 54: The Saracens provide salvific *terrores* until they are beaten in a God-given victory, 2.49–54, 54–57.

[110] *Antapodosis* 2.31, 49:581 and 586–88: "*Fitque divini muneris pietate . . . omnipotens deus, qui pugnandi eis* [Hungariis] *audatiam tulerat, fugiendi etiam copiam omnino negabat.*"

Rome, criticizes indignantly his illegal gift to his relative Manasses of the churches of Verona, Trent, and Mantua, and describes the fraternal conflict between Hugh and his full brother Boso (provoked by wicked Willa) to close on the king's shameful polygamy (*Antapodosis* 4.2–14).

With Henry I's death, the second half of the book opens with another transmission of power. It is principally devoted to a drama, the rebellion of Henry's second-born Henry against his older brother King Otto (*Antapodosis* 4.18–35).[111] The event could have embarrassed the propagandist of the Saxon dynasty—wasn't it a clear northern equivalent to the civil wars Liudprand loved to insist upon in Italy? Liudprand attenuates Henry's responsibility: He attributes the initial impulse to rebel to Gislebert of Lotharingia and Eberhardt of Bavaria, who then seduce the young man; he does not mention what he probably knew, that Henry briefly renewed his rebellion after Otto had first pardoned him. Liudprand thus erases Henry's frightful attempt against Otto's life at Easter 941.[112] This is systematic forgetfulness: Nowhere in the *Antapodosis* does Liudprand allude either to Otto's half-brother Thankmar's rebellion, or to that of the Saxon king's first-born son Liudolf.[113] In Henry's case, the author evades the potential problem by interpreting the rebellion within the framework of providential history. Not unlike Arnulf of Bavaria's challenge to Henry I, this episode reveals the new Saxon king's sacral aura and election. Like Hrotswitha of Gandersheim, Liudprand exculpates Henry by invoking a rare and remarkable player, Satan, Satan whom the author excoriates in a direct address:[114] Despite his original defeat, the impious Leviathan seeks to renew his challenge (*duellum*) to God and drag down to Hell Christians whom baptism had cleansed from sin. But the first rebel in sacred history is unaware that God's grace, which saved mankind once by the Cross, can intervene again. Liudprand here points to Henry's ultimate salvation, a theme he amplifies with an idea borrowed from Gregory the Great: "[C]arelessness often provokes the fall not only of those who are addicted to worldly things but also of those who devote themselves to eternal things

[111] On this episode, see, besides Leyser, *Rule and Conflict*, the studies cited in Buc, "Italian Hussies," 219.

[112] Liudprand conflates the two rebellions of 939 and 941, see Dändliker-Müller, 98–99; compare with Adalbert, *Continuatio Reginonis*, ad an. 941, 942, ed. Kurze, 161–62, and Widukind, *Rerum gestarum saxonicarum* 2.29, 31, 36, ed. Hirsch-Lohmann, 91, 92, 95.

[113] A silence he shares with the contemporary author who most seeks to downplay the tensions within the royal family, Hrotsvitha of Gandersheim, see Dändliker-Müller, *Liudprand*, 90, 98–99, 298–99.

[114] *Antapodosis* 4.19, 108, esp. 108:412–23, see also 4.18, 107:391–402, and 4.28, 118:719–27, with Dändliker-Müller, 86–90, and Karpf, *Herrscherlegitimation*, 33–34. See *Gesta Ottonis*, e.g., vv. 214f., 220, 318f., ed. Homeyer, 418–19. Satan also appears in *Antapodosis* 1.14 (the devil always seeks to break oaths of *amicitia*) and (fully rhetorically for the already discredited Manasses: *quo impellente diabolo*) in *Antapodosis* 4.6.

and are steady in the very vision of internal contemplation." Otto's brother is an elect whom God mercifully tests, finds wanting, and purges through the devil and his human agents.[115]

If Henry is an elect who is tried, found lacking, and ultimately graced (by God and the king), the rebellion reveals Otto's higher election. The true New David is not Berengar, whom sycophantic Italians address in their lauds as "another David," but Saint Otto I.[116] As in Gregory the Great, the holy man's trial has a function: "Indeed, holy men, unless they test it, ignore how much virtue they have and how much they stand in the sight of divine justice."[117] Lothar Bornscheuer has shown how later Ottonian narratives were structured by the concept of "Krise"—a severe trial leading to a restoration of right order that is simultaneously a demonstration of this order's legitimacy.[118] We have a crisis here as well. Otto demonstrates his faith in the face of adversity by refusing to give the abbey of Lorsch to a greedy supporter—this, for Liudprand, is fighting back the "invisible enemies" (a possible reference to the function of anointing in contemporary pontificals).[119] This refusal may have served as a counterpoint to Hugh's *contra ius fasque* grant of three bishoprics to his relative Manasses; it patently causes the loyalists' victory at Andernach (939)—a repeat of Henry I's victory over the Hungarians, insofar as Otto's followers obtain it thanks to their king's promise to renounce simony.[120]

---

[115] *Antapodosis* 4.20, 108:427–30. See Carol Straw, *Gregory the Great: Perfection in Imperfection* (Berkeley: 1988), passim. See Jessen, *Wirkungen*, for Liudprand's use of Gregorian themes.

[116] Compare *Antapodosis* 5.30, 141:625–27, "*Quam inmensum tunc Italis gaudium! Alterum David venisse latrabant, sed et magno Karolo caeca hunc mente praeferebant ...*" with 4.28–29, 118:727–35: "*... rex sanctus ob temptationis huius constantiam Deo pro se pugnante creverit ... David sanctus ex persona Domini dicit, Si populus meus audisset me, Israhel si in viis meis ambulasset, pro nichilo forsitan inimicos eorum humiliassem et super tribulantes eos misissem manum meam* [Ps. 80, 14]. *Quod in hoc rege Dominum audiente atque in viis eius ambulante esse completum, quam prompturus sum ratio declarabit*"—the deaths of the rebellious dukes Eberhardt and Gislebert follow. Berengar II is the tyran par excellence, and "Liutprando utilizza '*sanctus*,' '*sanctissimus*' in relazione sopratutto a Ottone I"—Gandino, *Il vocabolario*, 79–80, 36–37.

[117] *Antapodosis* 4.26, 114:612–14.

[118] Bornscheuer, *Miseriae regum*, 16f.

[119] As pointed out by Karpf, *Herrscherlegitimation*, 34, comparing the German Ordo of Mainz, ed. Vogel-Elze 1.251:6f. with *Antapodosis* 4.28, 719–20. The original redaction probably read *abbatiam quandam*; Liudprand himself seems to have added the identification *Laresheim dictam* to the manuscript Munich Clm 6388 f. 68v, see Paolo Chiesa, *Liutprando di Cremona e il codice di Frisinga Clm 6388*, Corpus Christianorum Autographa Medii Aevi 1 (Turnhout: 1994), 39 and T. xxiv. Interesting, for Bruno, Otto's brother, was abbot of Lorsch from 948 or 950 to 951, and the abbey received Otto's favor and protection in a series of diplomata from 940 on, with DD.O.I 24, 166, 176–77, 252 falling within the years of the *Antapodosis*'s composition. See Hans-Peter Wehlt, *Reichsabtei und König, dargestellt am Beispiel der Abtei Lorsch mit Ausblicken auf Hersfeld, Stablo und Fulda*, Veröffentlichungen des Max-Planck-Instituts für Geschichte 28 (Göttingen: 1970), 39–43.

[120] See above, n. 27, *Antapodosis* 2.27.

But the greatest success of Otto's outnumbered troops comes earlier, at Birten (939). As Germana Gandino recently pointed out, the episode comes exactly midway in the section of Book IV devoted to the Ottonians: chapter 25.[121] A river separates the king and the bulk of his army from his small vanguard, which has to fight alone on the other bank. Otto, confiding in the Lord, enacts a New Dispensation type of an Old Testament miracle (*renovatum antiquum miraculum*).[122] The king descends from his horse and, along with all his people, tearfully prays before the "victory-bringing nails [once] affixed to the hands of our Lord and Savior Jesus Christ and [now] placed on his lance."[123] Liudprand calls this object the "Holy Lance." It had once, he asserts, been a possession of Constantine, calling on the legend that saw in the first Christian emperor the owner of the nails. Enshrined, not yet in a lance, but in a horse bridle and a helmet, they were already in the fourth and sixth centuries victory-bringing relics.[124]

Prayer before the Lance is a ritual, a consensual ritual against the fractious rebels: Otto "remembers God's people" and prays "with all his people." This ritual acts out an exemplar, the "Old Testament miracle," Moses' victory-bringing prayer against the Amalechites (Exod. 17.12). Incidentally, it acts it out with a twist on the earlier, Carolingian reading: For Charlemagne, in a clear division of labor between priesthood and kingship, the pope was to stand and pray like Moses while the king fought. King Otto has borrowed a type the previous century attached to the *sacerdotium*.[125] There is also an innovation in the ritual itself. Collective prayers before (or after) a battle belonged to the stock and trade of early

---

[121] Gandino, *Il vocabolario*, 33. For earlier cases of history writing where a "central" chapter obtains "central" meaningfulness, see Martin Heinzelmann, *Gregor von Tours (538–594)*. *"Zehn Bücher Geschichte". Historiographie und Gesellschaftskonzept im 6. Jahrhundert* (Darmstadt: 1994), 131–32.

[122] Hraban Maur uses the same expression in his sermon on Heraclius' return of the true cross to Jerusalem, *renovante domino antiqua miracula*, PL 110, 134c.

[123] *Antapodosis* 4.24, 111:501–506: "*Recordatus populi domini, qui repugnantes sibi Amalechitas orationibus Moysi servi dei devicerat, protinus de equo descendit seseque cum omni populo lacrimas fundens ante victoriferos clavos, manibus domini et salvatoris nostri Iesu Christi adfixos suaeque lanceae impositos, in orationem dedit . . .*" Cf. Widukind, *Rerum gestarum saxonicarum*, 2.17, ed. Hirsch-Lohmann, 82:11: *ad deum supplices expandens manus*. See Martin Lintzel, "Mathildenviten," repr. in his *Augewählte Schriften*, 2 vols. (Berlin: 1961), 2.414.

[124] Since Ambrose's *De obitu Theodosii* 47, ed. Otto Faller, CSEL 73 (Vienna: 1955), 396, mediated in the Frankish West by Gregory of Tours, *GM*, 491; tr. Raymond Van Dam, *Glory of the Martyrs* (Liverpool: 1988), 24–25.

[125] See Albert Michael Koeniger, *Die Militärseelsorge der Karolingerzeit: Ihr Rechht und Praxis*, Veröffentlichungen aus dem Kirchenhistorischen Seminar München 4:7 (Munich: 1918), 57; see, e.g., Charlemagne to Leo III, MGHEpp. Kar. 2, ed. Ernst Dümmler (Berlin: 1895), 137, n. 93. See also, later, the Regensburg Sacramentary (MS Munich Clm 4456): Henry II's arms are supported in prayer by two bishops-saints, Emmeram and Udalrich. This miniature is built on the model of Moses' arms being supported in prayer by Joshua and Aaron.

medieval military piety—one will think of Fontenoy, but also, in the *Anta-podosis* itself, of Otto's similarly phrased reaction to his dukes' victory at Andernach sometime later: "[H]earing this the king immediately descended from his horse and tearfully gave himself to prayer, thanking God."[126] At Birten, in an innovation created either by Liudprand's pen or by circumstances (Otto had not anticipated a clash), battle and prayer have been conflated in time.[127]

This specific avatar of the liturgy of war has a meaning beyond itself. It is typology—the actuation in Christian times (*renovatio*) of an Old Testament miracle (*antiquum miraculum*)—that makes the event liturgical. Henry I had also inscribed his prayer and vow before battle in the exemplarity of the biblical past.[128] As the structure of the narrative demonstrates, the significance of Birten is twofold—the prayer at the foot of the Lance is followed, first, by a disgression on the Italian and Burgundian origins of the relic, second, by a theological excursus. First, it points to Ottonian claims on Italy; second, it manifests the dynasty's sanctity.[129]

That surviving Saxon historiography never states that the Holy Lance gave a title to Italy[130] is no proof that Liudprand did not attempt to present it as such to Otto I. It may simply be that the *Antapodosis* did not impose its reading of the object lastingly. Liudprand himself connects the Lance

---

[126] *Antapodosis* 4.30, 120:781–83: "*rex . . . mox de equo descendit seseque cum lacrimis deo gratias agens in orationem dedit*" (he then goes to mass). On fasts, penances, and prayers before or after a battle, Koeniger, *Militärseelsorge*, 56. Nithard, *Histoire des fils de Louis le Pieux*, 2.10 (before Fontenoy: "*primum . . . ieiuniis ac votis deum invocent*"), 3.1 (after: a three-day purgative fast), ed. Philippe Lauer, Classiques de l'Histoire de France au Moyen Age 7 (Paris: 1926), 70, 82. See McCormick, "Liturgie et guerre," at 220–33. Prayer before battle (with fasting and mortification) enjoyed an exemplary pedigree; see the first Christian emperor in Eusebius, *Life of Constantine* 2.12 and 2.14, rev. ed. Friedhelm Winkelmann, in *Eusebius Werke*, vol. 1:1 (Berlin: 1991), 53:12–26 and 54:13–17; E. tr. by Averil Cameron and Stuart G. Hall (Oxford: 1999), 99 and 100..

[127] By the early eleventh century, the king's prostrate prayer belonged to the liturgy of war, in text or reality. See Thietmar, *Chronicon* 2.10, ed. Holtzmann, 48:24–33, Otto I before the battle of the Lech "*postera die . . . rex, solum se pre caeteris culpabilem deo professus atque prostratus, hoc fecit lacrimis votum profusis . . . Nec mora, erectus a terra, post missae celebrationem sacramque communionem . . . sumpsit rex clipeum lancea cum sacra.*" Or Bern of Reichenau, *Letter* 27, on Henry III after the battle of Menfö, *Die Briefe des Abtes Bern von Reichenau*, ed. Franz-Josef Schmale, Veröffentlichungen der Kommission für geschichtliche Landeskunde in Baden-Wurttemberg A:6 (Stuttgart: 1961), 60, with Carl Erdmann, "Bern von Reichenau und Heinrich III.," in Erdmann, *Forschungen* (as n. 61), 110–12.

[128] See *Antapodosis* 2.27, 47:534–35: "Touched again by the gift of divine prophecy, he added: 'The deeds of the kings of yore and the writings of the holy fathers teach us what we should do.' "

[129] Or, as Gandino, *Vocabolario*, 33, aptly puts it, the episode's function is "di materializare di rendere fisicamente concreto il motivo ideologico che sta emergendo nell' *Antapodosis* a proposito di Ottone, quello della sua connotazione insieme come re guerriero e come re santo."

[130] Historiography in Buc, "Italian Hussies," n. 6.

to the *regnum Italiae* only implicitly, but the unwillingness to be explicit is characteristic of his style of argument. We have seen throughout that he uses words with great care. It is therefore far from fortuitous that Liudprand presents the former owner of the Lance, Rudolf of Burgundy, as one who had reigned over Italy for a number of years.[131] It may not be coincidental either that Rudolf was Adelheid's father, Adelheid who transmitted (what Liudprand never states explicitly either) to her second husband Otto a claim to Italy. Otto's father, Henry, learning that Rudolf had in his possession Constantine's lance, tries to buy it from the Burgundian king, then threatens war against him. Christ and the Holy Lance itself reconcile the two men, and Rudolf, becoming Henry's man (*dantem se*), hands over the Lance, receiving the countergift of part of Swabia.[132] Conflict over the relic underlines its value, reconciliation its power.

The victory at Birten serves to demonstrate, to the king as well as to others, his election. It is the central piece of the *Antapodosis*: Liudprand joins it to his only theological excursus, a one-folio discussion of Thomas's doubt, brought (like Conrad I's royal insignia) *in medium*.[133] Why did the apostle Thomas have to touch Christ's wounds after the Resurrection? He did so not so much for himself as for heretics who might doubt that the Lord had risen in the flesh. Similarly, the miraculous triumph underlines Otto's sanctity. Stylistic and lexical parallels further the explicit comparison between Thomas and Otto. Both events happen "by God's disposition";[134] in both, the actors are addressed personally (*inquam, sic itaque sic*) as well as directly in the second person singular and the vocative: King and saints are on a narrative par (*sancte Thoma, O sancte Petre, rex piissime, bone rex*).[135] This lengthy digression, juxtaposed to and connected with the battle, reveals how the seemingly worldly event belongs actually to the supramundane level of the meaningful and truly real. To use Stephen Nichols's terminology, the Thomas excursus provides Gospel *theoria* for the Saxon *historia*, integrating both into providential history.[136] It also indicates to the reader that the battle, and perhaps the whole *Antapodosis*, should be read with an eye to the spirit hidden behind the letter. Thomas's doubt constituted a key pericope to reflect on the relationship between levels of reality. On its

---

[131] *Antapodosis* 4.25, 111:520–21: "*Burgundionum rex Rodulfus, qui nonnullis annis Italicis imperavit, lanceam illam a Samson comite dono accepit.*"

[132] See Heinrich Büttner, "Henrichs I. Südwest- und Westpolitik," VuF Sitzungberichte 2 (Constance: 1964), 52–53. For Adelheid and Italy, see most recently Keller, "Entscheidungssituationen," 42 and n. 99.

[133] *Antapodosis* 4.26, 113–15, here 113:567. See Karl J. Leyser, "Liudprand of Cremona: Preacher and Homilist," repr. in Leyser, *Communications and Power*, 1.111–124 at 122–23.

[134] *Antapodosis* 4.26, 113:564, 114:606, 608.

[135] *Antapodosis* 4.26, 113:573–74, 115:626, 114:607, 115:637.

[136] Stephen Nichols, *Romanesque Signs* (New Haven: 1982), ch. 2.

basis, the Apostle Paul had linked a series of complementary oppositions: between the Ancient Law and the New Law, between letter and spirit, between truth written obscurely on stone and truth written on flesh (2 Corinthians 3.3–8). It is illustrated in a stark late tenth-century ivory plaque now in Trier, contrasting Moses receiving the Tables of the Law, engraved on stone, and Thomas touching Christ's wound.[137] In the ninth century, Hincmar, archbishop of Reims had picked up the Pauline exegesis, mediated by Gregory the Great, as an argument in favor of the ordeal (*divinum iudicium*). While Hincmar's use of the pericope does not seem to have had any tenth-century posterity, it is worth developing it here, for it points to what Liudprand was trying to do.[138] Trial by the elements made visible the normally invisible justice of God; like Thomas's touch, it allowed humans to see with the eyes of faith what they had not perceived through carnal eyes.[139] Thus, in the economy of the *Antapodosis*, Birten served as a revelation of both Otto's election and of Liudprand's hermeneutics. Rightly interpreted, the paraliturgical prayer before the Holy Lance made manifest a vertical axis connecting simultaneously letter to spirit and the king to God.

Ottonian rituals and Lombard rituals thus stand as contrasting tests of opposite political dispensations. On the one hand, the sacrality of orderly funerals, transmission of power, and victory-bringing prayer, on the other, manipulations of friendship, advent, coronation, and care of the poor. That good rituals characterize Saxony and bad rituals, Lombardy, does not reflect the actual practice of these areas. Nor can this narrative opposition tell us anything, directly, about the respective degree of cohesiveness of these two polities. We are not dealing here with the contrast between an old, eroded southern rituality and a younger, still confident northern one. As we shall see in the next chapter, the late Carolingian political culture in which Saxony participated evidences actors manipulating ceremonies with as much skill and self-servingness as Liudprand's Italian dynasts.

[137] See the catalogue *Bernward von Hildesheim und das Zeitalter der Ottonen*, 2 vols. (Hildesheim: 1993), 2.191–93, fig. IV–35.

[138] While Liudprand read and used Gregory, I see no direct connection between Hincmar and Liudprand, and as far as I can count, all the formulas for the ordeal collected in Karl Zeumer, *Formulae merowingici et karolini aevi*, MGH Leges 5 (Hannover: 1886), invoke Thomas only once.

[139] Hincmar of Reims, *De divorcio Lotharii*, ed. Lehta Böhringer, MGH Concilia 4, suppl. 1 (Berlin: 1992), 159:20–28, excerpted in the same's *Letter 25 to Hildegar of Meaux*, PL 126, 161c–71d, at 171, drawing on Gregory the Great, *Homiliae in Evangelia* 2.6.9, PL 76, 1202a.

Chapter Two

RITUAL CONSENSUS AND RITUAL VIOLENCE: TEXTS AND EVENTS IN NINTH-CENTURY CAROLINGIAN POLITICAL CULTURE

Transition: Two Faces of Arnulf of Carinthia

We saw how the last decades of the ninth century delineated the farthest past horizon of Liudprand of Cremona's *Antapodosis*. One of its main villains was King Arnulf, the next-to-last Carolingian to have governed the eastern part of Charlemagne's empire (887–99), the last Carolingian to have intervened in Italy, and the last Carolingian in a direct male line to have obtained the imperial office. Why did Liudprand besmirch the man's memory? Arnulf stood for two rivals of the bishop's Saxon patrons, the Carolingians and the Bavarians. Charlemagne's line, as we saw, still lived in the veins of his Italian descendents south of the Alps—especially Berengar II and his son Adalbert—and still sat on the West Frankish throne across the Rhine. Bavarian dukes had recently competed with the Saxons for hegemony north and south of the Alps, and Bavaria, still in the 950s and 960s, had not been integrated fully into Ottonian governance.[1] Liudprand sought to counter a memory that was not quite dead yet. The Bavarian continuation of the *Annals of Fulda* as well as Bavarian conciliar records preserved this positive image of King Arnulf. It is to this contrast that we now turn, in order to introduce a main theme in this chapter: contending textual renditions of the same ceremonial events.

The Bavarian sources developed fully the themes of Christian liturgical kingship so dear to Liudprand's own portrayal of Henry I and Otto I—but in Arnulf's favor. They projected, to paraphrase the acts of the Council of Tribur (895), a mutually reenforcing relationship between "divine reli-

Parts of this chapter were published in *Medieval Concepts of the Past: Rituals, Memory, Historiography*, ed. Gerd Althoff, Johannes Fried, and Patrick Geary (Cambridge: 2001), 123–38, and in "Ritual and interpretation: the early medieval case," *Early Medieval Europe* 9,2 (2000), at 196–99. I presented other parts at King's College, London, in March 1995. My thanks for comments to Catherine de Firmas, Mayke de Jong, Tom Head, Patrick Geary, Janet Nelson, and Catherine Peyroux.

[1] See Timothy Reuter, *Germany in the early Middle Ages, c. 800–1056* (London: 1991), 151–52 for the gradual whittling away of Bavarian autonomy over the course of the century.

gion's sacrosanct mysteries" and "the palace's secrets."[2] As seen from Bavaria, the Carolingian used churches to celebrate orderly councils, not—as in Liudprand's tendentious misrepresentation—banquets (*simbola*) with shameful gestures, theatrical chants (*cantus ludicres*), bacchanalia, and open fornication.[3] The lengthiest surviving version of the acts of the council (the so-called Vulgate) was tellingly preserved in a Bavarian tradition and possibly reworked close to or even in the tenth century. All versions (but with greater theological amplification and denser scriptural referencing in the Bavarian tradition) describe at length a conciliar ceremonial designed to exalt the king's leadership of the Christian commonwealth.[4] It is not only collective singing of the Laudes Regiae that operates the liturgical fusion between earthly and heavenly.[5] The narrative itself engenders the same effect. Like Liudprand's disquisition on Otto I's kingship, the Acts bring together the two levels of letter and spirit in such a way that the reader cannot fully tell this-worldly reality from anagogical mystery. Arnulf, after having enjoined a three-day fast, makes forth for the royal palace and sits on his throne "dressed in a most splendid vestment (*vestis*) that wisdom had woven, filled with prudence, exalted by power . . . dealing PRAKTIKE with the state of the kingdom and THEORETIKE with the order and stability of Christ's Church."[6] Like this *vestis*, which may denote both the material dress

---

[2] Council of Tribur (895), prologue, MGH Capitularia 2:1–2, ed. Victor Krause and Alfred Boretius (Berlin: 1897), 2.196–249, at 2.213:39–40: "*Post haec prudentissimus rex regnorum sacrosanctis divinae religionis interfuit mysteriis et sancti patres secretis palatinis.*" "Mysteries of state" as well in the *Chronicle of Moissac ad an.* 817, ed. Georg Pertz, MGH SS 1 (Hannover: 1826), 280–313, at 312:23, diplomatic transcription in Buc, "Ritual and interpretation," 201–209. The text probably does not postdate by much 818. There, Louis, having convoked the great, *manifestavit eis mysterium consilii sui*: his decision to make Lothar co-emperor.

[3] See *Antapodosis* 1.33, 24:691–25:699: "*Credo autem Arnulfum regem iusta severi iudicis huiusmodi pestem incurrisse censura. Secundae enim res dum imperium huius ubiubi magni fecerent, virtuti suae cuncta tribuit, non debitum omnipotenti deo honorem reddidit. Sacerdotes dei vincti trahebantur, sacrae virgines vi obprimebantur, coniugatae violabantur. Neque enim ecclesiae confugientibus poterant esse asylum. In his namque simbolam faciebat, gestus turpis, cantus ludicres, dibachationes; sed et mulieres eodem publice—pro nefas!—prostituebantur.*"

[4] MGH Capitularia 2.211–13. Critical to this interpretation is Rudolf Pokorny, "Die drei Versionen der Triburer Synodalakten von 895," DA 48,2 (1992): 429–551, esp. 481–91.

[5] Both versions, MGH *Capitularia* 2.213:30–36 and 212:22–31 recount the same ceremonial: ". . . *ter quaterque proclamantes et divinae maiestati supplicantes, 'Exaudi Christe! Arnolfo magno regi vita!' et sonantibus campanis 'Te Deum Laudamus' concinentibus cunctis, glorificantes et Iesum Christum conlaudantes, qui in servis suis consolabitur, qui ecclesiae suae sanctae tam pium et mitem consolatorem tamque strenuum adiutorem ad honorem nominis sui condonare dignatus est, et peractis divinae maiestati precibus inclinantes se coram piis principis asstantibus missis, gratificantes et magno principi laudes debitas persolventes* . . ." and ". . . *in venerationem regis se humilians per alta voce 'Te Deum Laudamus' sonantibus campanis, lacrimantibus quam plurimis in finem usque decantavit; dictaque oratione, tam pro serenissimi regis incolomitate quam eciam pro fratribus gloriosam maiestatem trinitatis conlaudabant qui eis tam mitem et strenuum contulit regni tutorem* . . ."

[6] Vulgata, prologue. MGH Capitularia 2 211:28–35: ". . . *regale sedit solium iundutus veste splendissima, quam texit sapientia, repletus est prudentia, erectus et potentia, pro sua magnitudine*

worn by, and the balance of virtues in Arnulf's soul, the physical throne fuses with its allegorical meaning. When the king, answering clerical delegates who "expound theology as if from Heavens," prophetically "reveals his mystery's secret," it is "from his mind's imperial seat."[7]

If one now returns to the *Antapodosis*, one is struck by the absence of any positive use of the liturgy in Liudprand's portrait of the northern hegemon. As for divine providence, it appears only in a consideration of punishment: The Lombard author muses whether Arnulf's painful death allowed him to expiate in this world his critical sin, to have been the first ruler to call in against fellow Christians pagan Hungarian auxiliaries.[8] Liudprand's erasure of the vertical axis especially becomes apparent when one contrasts the last chapters devoted to Arnulf in the *Antapodosis* with the Regensburg continuation of the *Annals of Fulda*. Liudprand details Arnulf's ultimate journey to Italy and conquest of Rome, avoids mentioning his imperial coronation, and collapses the disease he caught there with his death (actually three years later). The two sources agree on at least one thing: The faction following a rival king, Lambert, had shut Rome's doors against Arnulf; Arnulf besieged the City and stormed it. But they completely diverge on about everything else, with one source insisting on chance, disorder, and plain cunning, the other, on providence, liturgy, and piety. In the *Antapodosis*, sheer luck, not God's will, allowed Arnulf to take Rome; the sudden panic of a smallish hare, which ran toward the walls, triggered a battle that allowed his troops to take over the Leonine City around Saint-Peter. The defenders on the other side of the Tiber, stricken by fear, "submitted their necks (*colla*) to his lordship." Liudprand's choice of images felicitously conveys how unfelicitous this submission was. For Arnulf "in his entry (*ingressu*), in order to avenge insults to the pope, ordered to behead (*decollare*) many Roman princes who were hastening out to meet him (*obviam sibi properantes*)."[9]

The tone is completely different in the Regensburg continuation of the *Annals of Fulda*.[10] Arnulf, whom Pope Formosus has called to Rome, finds

---

stipatus multitudine, tractans PRAKTIKE de statu regni et THEORETIKE de ordine et stabilitate ecclesiarum Christi, et qualiter boni quiete viverent, et mali inulti non peccarent." On "theoretike-practike," see Nikolaus Staubach, *Rex christianus. Hofkultur und Herrschaftspropaganda im Reich Karls des Kahlen*, vol. 2, *Die Grundlegung der "religion royale*," Pictura et Poesis 2:2 (Cologne: 1993), 9. The editor of the conciliar acts surmises that they draw here on a poetic model. Court poetry often merged two levels of reality to exalt its patrons, Staubach, *Rex christianus*, 28–29, 46f.

[7] Vulgata, prologue. MGH Capitularia 2.213:1–7: "*Quibus rex theologiam quasi ab alto disserentibus ab augusta mentis suae sede . . . archanum mysterii sui revelans in haec verba prorupit . . .*"

[8] See *Antapodosis* 1.33 (above n. 3) and 1.13, 16–17.

[9] See *Antapodosis* 1.25–28, 21:591–22:623, and ch. 1 at 104.

[10] On the *Annals of Fulda*, see Heinz Löwe, "Geschichtsschreibung der ausgehenden Karolingerzeit," repr. in his *Von Cassiodor zu Dante. Ausgewählte Aufsätze* (Berlin: 1973), 180–205

all the doors blocked at the order of Angiltrud, Lambert of Spoleto's mother, "so that all would be equally denied entry to Saint-Peter's church." The king takes counsel—a liturgified assembly that proposes a liturgical solution: "All came together (*conveniunt*), tearfully swore fidelity and confessed themselves publicly before the priests. Unanimously (*in commune*) they proclaimed (*acclamatum est*) that they would fast for one day and then attack in warlike fashion the city." As we saw, liturgified warfare, unless under Ottonian leadership, is wholly absent from the *Antapodosis*.[11] At this point, God (not a small animal's chance fright) provokes a skirmish, which escalates into a full-scale battle and leads to Rome's "liberation" (without any victims in Arnulf's sizable army). An *occursus*, mobilizing the whole senate and the Greek *scola*, banners, crosses, hymns, and *laudes*, brings the victorious emperor into Rome;[12] Formosus meets him at Saint-Peter's steps, crowns him emperor in the basilica; the Roman people swear an oath of fidelity rejecting Lambert and his mother.

The opposition between the narratives Liudprand and the Regensburg continuator propose jumps to the eye:

	Siege	*Occursus*	Coronation
AF:	Liturgified	Liturgified	Liturgified
Ant.:	Nonliturgified	Abused	[*deest*]

Arnulf's image owes its two-facedness to the historical geography of his rule. While he would enjoy a relatively long-lasting popularity in Bavaria,[13] other areas, Italy, which soon fell in his rivals' hands, or Saxony, whose main rival in the Germanic ensemble was Bavaria, had less reason to preserve anecdotes presenting him positively. As we saw for Otto I, an author's opinion of a king guides his or her pen in describing that king's rituals. Consequently, a divided opinion tends to make for contradictory descriptions. Reconstructions of Carolingian politics from the sources have often had to

---

at 183–88; idem, *Deutschlands Geschichtsquellen im Mittelalter. Vorzeit und Karolinger*, vol. 6 (Weimar: 1990), 671–87; and Timothy Reuter, *The Annals of Fulda* (Manchester: 1992), 1–9.

[11] *Annals of Fulda* (henceforth *AF*), *Continuatio Ratisponensis ad an.* 896, ed. Friedrich Kurze, *Annales Fuldenses, sive Annales regni Francorum orientalis*, MGH SS rer. Germ. in u.s. 7 (Hannover: 1891), 127. Arnulf is the agent in other instances of liturgified warfare in the *AF*, e.g., the battle of the Dyle against pagan Northmen, *ad an.* 891, 120–21, and against fellow Christians at the storming of Bergamo, *ad an.* 894, 123, which occurs *missarum solemnitate completa* and *Dei nutu*. The latter episode is also recounted in Liudprand, but without war liturgy, cf. chapter 1, 40–42.

[12] *AF ad an.* 896, 128: "*Omnis namque senatus Romanorum necnon Grecorum scola cum vexillis et crucibus ad pontem Malvium venientes regem honorifice cum ymnis et laudibus suscipientes ad urbem perduxerunt.*" See below, 76.

[13] See Patrick J. Geary, *Phantoms of Remembrance: Memory and Oblivion at the End of the First Millenium* (Princeton: 1994), 171–72.

face such apparently unresolvable documentary contradictions.[14] And as we shall see, rituals, and especially liturgical processions such as the *occursus*, play an important role in the texts' narrative structure.

THE NINTH-CENTURY FIELD

The competition between Arnulf and Lambert of Spoleto over Rome was a late act in a long and apparently chaotic play: the series of disputes that rent the Carolingian world during the ninth century. For this reason, the century's last two-thirds provide an especially fertile field in which to harvest manipulations of ritual. The disputes themselves conditioned and were conditioned by descriptions of ceremonies. A plurality of interests and a plurality of authors recounting the same events allow, in some cases, the historian to reconstruct political strategies and their means.[15] A first set of conflicts opposed members of the Carolingian family to one another; after 840, one can view them through the contrasting lenses provided by East Frankish and West Frankish sources—especially the *Annals of Fulda* with their continuations and the so-called *Annals of Saint-Bertin*. Other tensions coexisted with these intrafamilial disputes. Relationships could be difficult between bishops and their lay rulers, between archbishops and their bishops, between bishops and the pope, and (last but not least) between pope and the kings. They condition as well the surviving evidence.

Starting with the second third of the ninth century, several such tensions came to intersect one another. One first issue was the progressive political partition of Charlemagne's empire. The standard master narrative will help to situate the medieval sources. The empire's dissolution began with the first major disputes between Louis the Pious and his sons. A main highlight was the emperor's forced penance and coerced withdrawal from power for a few months in 833. After Louis's death (840), the bloody battle of Fontenoy, pitting the two brothers Charles the Bald (d. 877) and Louis the German (d. 876) against their eldest sibling Lothar I and their nephew Pippin II, led to the treaty of Verdun (843). This sworn pact provided for a tripartition of the empire's territory. Shifting alliances kept the Carolingian world dangling between war and peace. Lothar's death in 855 complicated the game but did not change its nature insofar as his three sons and heirs, Lothar II in Lotharingia, Charles in Provence, and Emperor Louis II in Italy, inserted themselves as weaker pieces on the existing chessboard.[16]

---

[14] See e.g., Thomas F. X. Noble, *The Republic of St. Peter: The Birth of the Papal State, 680–825* (Philadelphia: 1984), 80–81 (below, n. 80).

[15] On Hincmar's manipulative silences, see Carlrichard Brühl, "Hincmariana," *DA* 20 (1964): 49–77, esp. 76, repr. in his *Aus Mittelalter und Diplomatik. Gesammelte Aufsätze*, 2 vols. (Berlin: 1989), 2.292–322, esp. 320.

[16] See most recently Janet L. Nelson, *Charles the Bald* (London: 1992), who provides an up-to-date bibliography.

The relationship between the papacy and the Carolingians constituted a second major issue. Dependent on Charlemagne's help against the Lombards, the popes, and more precisely the shifting Roman factions that supported them, found Frankish tutelage inconvenient whenever they did not need it against their local rivals.[17] Italian coteries, while primarily fighting for local stakes, identified themselves in terms of hostility to, or alliance with, this or that northern hegemon. Repeatedly, the Carolingians intervened in Rome, seeking to assert a right to oversee papal elections and even local administration. An older imperial idea, according to which political virtue, not anointing by the pope, made the emperor, survived into the tenth century. Yet over the course of the century, through assertion and practice, the popes managed to impose the idea that the imperial coronation (for any male member of the divided Carolingian family a sign of supremacy over his royal relatives) had to be performed in Rome and by the Roman pontiff. Furthermore, starting with the sixth decade of the century, another question, the so-called divorce of Lothar II, gave some churchmen, including the great popes Nicholas I (r. 858–67) and Hadrian II (r. 867–72), another handle on Carolingian politics.[18] Was Waldrada as beautiful as some French scholars would have had her be? Turn-of-the-century Gallic historiography could debate whether "elle le tenait par les sens plutôt que par le coeur,"[19] being blind to the fact that in her the young king could conciliate passion and politics. Had they read the German Thietmar, the French would have learned that one can love because of power combined with good looks: Henry I of Saxony would kidnap and marry the nun Hatheburg, his love having been inflamed "because of her beauty and the profit of her inherited wealth."[20]

Be that as it may, Waldrada, who was probably an early love of Lothar, had been put aside in favor of the better-connected Theutberga. Impelled by what contemporaries called passion or (as hard-nosed modern historians surmise) some reversal in political alliances, the young king sought to obtain a canonical separation from that queen in order to marry Waldrada. First, Theutberga was accused of sodomitic incest with her brother Huc-

---

[17] On the early phase of the relationship, see Noble, *Republic*.

[18] I follow here Lehta Böhringer, introduction to her edition of the *De divortio Lotharii regis et Theutbergae reginae*, MGH Concilia 4, suppl. 1 (Berlin: 1992), 5–20. Peter McKeon, *Hincmar of Laon and Carolingian Politics* (Urbana: 1978), 39–56, provides an English-language narrative of Lothar II's divorce, but see now Karl Heidecker, *Kerk, huwelijk en politieke macht: de zaak Lotharius II, 855–869* (Amsterdam: 1997), with German summary, and Stuart Airlie, "Private bodies and the body politic in the divorce case of Lothar II," *Past and Present* 161 (1998): 3–38.

[19] See Robert Parisot, *Le royaume de Lorraine sous les Carolingiens* (Paris: 1898, repr. Geneva: 1975), 87 n. 1.

[20] Thietmar, *Chronicon* 1.5, ed. Robert Holtzmann, MGH SS Rer. Germ., n.s. 9, 8:20–29.

bert, and Lothar's partisans forced her to undergo a judicial ordeal by proxy, from which she emerged cleared (858). After this initial failure, the king sought his bishops' help. Under the leadership of Theutgaud of Trier, Gunthar of Cologne, and Adventius of Metz, and in four successive councils (860–63), the Lotharingian episcopate stage-managed the queen's spontaneous confession of sin and her request to be allowed to retire to a nunnery. The bishops also allowed the king to remarry, and sent the two archbishops, Gunthar and Theutgaud, to Rome, in the hope that Nicholas I would rubber-stamp proceedings that his legates, perhaps bribed, had approved of. But the converging forces of the pope's disapproval and of the hostility of the king's royal uncles Charles the Bald and Louis the German forced Lothar into an increasingly desperate corner. Nicholas compelled the Lotharingian bishops to back down; he even excommunicated and deposed Gunthar and Theutgaud. For this specific issue, the pope found help in the skillful quill of Hincmar of Reims, an archbishop who did not shy from confronting, at least on vellum, kings and Roman pontiffs whenever they threatened his interests. The two senior Carolingians gave shelter to Lothar's enemies, especially to Theutberga and her brother. By the dispute's latter years, they certainly hoped that the Church's sanctions would help them conquer Lotharingia. Theutberga was childless; were Waldrada, then, to be denied the name of rightful wife, her and Lothar's children (his only progeny) might be considered bastards and despoiled of their father's inheritance. The young king's sole hope lay in his brother, Emperor Louis II, king of Italy. In retrospect, given this formidable opposition, Lothar II seems to have been fated to lose from the tragedy's very onset. Yet in all probability, more than anything else, it was principally his early death that determined historiography's image of the quarrel as well as Lotharingia's immediate destiny: to be partitioned between the eastern and western Frankish kingdoms.

THE AVAILABLE RITUAL LANGUAGE

The case of Lothar II brings home how, in the Carolingian ninth century, like later in Liudprand of Cremona's world, a ruler's relationship to women crafted, and was crafted by, his legitimation and defamation. So did solemnities of all sorts, solemnities that following current historiographic convention we shall provisorily call "rituals." This and the following two sections explore how ninth-century conflict could express itself in ritual, and be fought or imagined through texts recounting rituals. They move from the obvious to the more fundamental, from the repertoire of rituals that the documentation enables us to see existed generically, to the use of specific rituals for specific conflicts. But just as the modern reader will not assume that Waldrada and Theutberga's images correspond to their reality, so should he or she question the transparency of the narratives recounting rituals. It is a thesis of this chapter that struggles within Carolingian political culture occurred more through depictions of ceremonies than through their actual performance. It is only heuristically, then, that we turn first to the ninth-century ritual repertoire, with full awareness that each individual datum employed to establish this repertoire probably owes its being to authorial craft and would be as such worthy of individual analysis.

By the ninth century, the great political rituals that historians of the High Middle Ages study were well established. Looked at from the standpoint of Carolingian culture, the eleventh-century repertoire that Helgaud of Fleury employs in his *Life of Robert the Pious* seems hardly innovative. One has advanced institutional reasons for rituals' vigor and centrality in that era. The conjunction of anointing and coronation created vested ecclesiastical interest in the resulting ceremony.[21] Self-appointed Christian rulers, the Carolingians understandably emphasized what could demonstrate their bond with the holy—the verticality so critical in Liudprand. Competition and ritualization fed one another. Before the 820s, rivalry, first with other princely kindreds for hegemony within Latin Europe and then with East Rome for imperial legitimacy, impelled the new dynasty to underline this dimension of its authority. Starting with the crises in Louis the Pious's reign, divisions within the ruling family maintained and even heightened this phenomenon.[22]

In the period we are concentrating on, there existed both well-established staples and newer ones. Some forms seem to have been already fairly routinized, such as the ruler's participation in the Christian liturgical year's major feasts. If rituals are a good index of consensus, then the early years of Archbishop Hincmar of Reims's activity as continuator of the so-called *Annals of Saint-Bertin* seem to testify to harmony between king and bishop. Charles the Bald celebrated Christmas 861 "festively, as is customary" and Christmas 862 "with the highest reverence." In between, he lent his presence to Hincmar's dedication of Saint-Mary in Reims, the archdiocesan cathedral church. After Christmas 862, and for a number of years, the notations become terser, lean, and monotonous: "[I]n this place the king celebrated the Lord's Easter" or "in this place the king celebrated the Lord's Birth." Yet year after year, the archbishop kept noting the king's presence

---

[21] See, e.g., Walter Ullmann, *The Carolingian Renaissance and the Idea of Kingship* (London: 1969).

[22] See for example the effects of Louis the Pious's Compiègne penance in Mayke de Jong, "Power and humility in Carolingian society: the public penance of Louis the Pious," *Early Medieval Europe* 1,1 (1992): 29–52, and their effects on Charles the Bald, compounded by the same king's redefinition of his propaganda in the context of the controversies over Lothar II's divorce, Nikolaus Staubach, *Rex Christianus*, 15 and passim. Nelson, *Charles the Bald*, 17, speaks of that king's "taste for ritual."

at holy feasts and where he had attended them. From 861 to Charles's death in 877, with the sole exception of 866, Hincmar indicates where the king celebrated the Nativity. Out of eighteen Easters, he locates eleven. And he tells six times of the king's location during Lent—for three of which he explicitly says that the king fasted. These notations last all the way into Charles's final years, when (owing to the king's favor for newer councillors, property disputes, and the Carolingian's desire for the imperial office), Hincmar had come to severely dislike the ruler he had for so long hoped to guide. The mere mention by a medieval writer of a specific ruler's attendance at yearly Church rituals, then, is not necessarily a positive index of the author's liking for him. It could be that Hincmar felt it incumbent upon him as an annalist to give this information when he had it. It could be that he felt that attendance at these feasts did not endow a king with a halo that he, as annalist, might have wanted to deny to a bad ruler. It could be that he respected the royal office regardless of the incumbent—it was the king's presence, not Charles's, that he noted. And finally, it could be that in the case of Hincmar, these notations reflect the conservatism of a cleric trained under the archchaplain Hilduin.[23]

Indeed, mention of the ruler's place in space for the Christian calendar's two highest points had been a constant staple of the *Royal Frankish Annals* since 757 or 759.[24] It was only in 806 and 808 that they first noted the Lenten fast. Until 798, the ninth-century annalist almost always gathered together at the end of the year's entries the information concerning Nativity and Easter, unless either of these moments was so wrapped up with a major political event that it had to be separated from the other and put in its sequential context.[25] The *Royal Annals*, then, were interested not so much in locating the prince's geographical position through liturgical time markers for March–April and late December, as in identifying where he had participated in the commemoration of Christ's birth and Passion. In the tenth century still, in some Easter tables, a good share of the terse notations jutted there would focus on the location of the ruler at Chrismas.[26]

Thus, while the Christian high feasts remained meaningful, it was other liturgical or liturgified practices that princes used for distinction (or that

[23] Janet L. Nelson, "The Annals of St. Bertin," repr. in J. Nelson, *Politics and Ritual*, 174–94, at 185; the best guide to Hincmar remains Jean Devisse, *Hincmar archevêque de Reims 845–882*, 3 vols. (Geneva: 1974–76).

[24] For these notations, see Carlrichard Brühl, "Fränkischer Krönungsbrauch und das Problem der 'Festkrönungen,' " *HZ* 194,2 (1962): 319–20 (with earlier bibliography).

[25] E.g., *Annales regni Francorum ad an.* 775–76, 780–81, 784–85, 793–94.

[26] See, e.g., the so-called *Annals of Einsiedlen*, in Manuscript Eisiedlen 29, partial facsimile plate in Reginald L. Poole, *Chronicles and Annals* (Oxford: 1926), 4; ed. Georg Pertz, MGH SS 3 (Hannover: 1839), 142, or the mid-century *Annals of Mainz*, Paris Bibliothèque Nationale de France MS Latin 4860, 154r–v, ed. Etienne Baluze, *Miscellanea novo ordine digesta*, reed. J.-D. Mansi (Lucca: 1761), 1.121.

authors employed to distinguish their princes). Among royalty and at a
lesser social level, the institution conveniently but imprecisely labeled "lay
abbacy" gave a dual identity to a number of aristocrats;[27] accordingly, they
learned to communicate in the monastic language of service to the holy.
Other magnates acquired this ability owing simply to their being closely
related to an abbot.[28] This made available and intelligible a relatively new
repertoire of forms—how new is open to debate. The giving of alms and
the ostentatious care for the poor constitute an essential part of Thegan's
portrait of Louis the Pious and continue to inform the royal image all the
way to the Monk of Saint-Gall.[29] Royal penance, studied by Rudolf Schieffer and Mayke de Jong, as well as penitential begging for pardon, explored
by Koziol, had been part and parcel of the clerical ruler representation
since the fourth century. They were reactualized and redefined with Louis
the Pious's two public humiliations at Attigny and Compiègne, Lothar's
surrenders to his father, as well as Nicholas I and Hadrian II's demands
on Lothar II and Waldrada.[30] Secular rulers involved themselves in the
solemnities surrounding relic elevations and translations. The practice was
not novel; Emperor Constantius II had inaugurated it, and it had been
maintained in political culture by fully legendary or semilegendary events
such as Helena's invention of the Cross or Heraclius's entry into Jerusalem.[31] But we have striking ninth-century examples: In 838, Lothar I car-

---

[27] Franz Felten, "Laienäbte in der Karolingerzeit. Ein Beitrag zum Problem der Adelsherrschaft über die Kirche," in *Mönchtum, Episkopat und Adel zur Gründungszeit des Klosters
Reichenau*, VuF 20, ed. Arno Borst (Sigmaringen: 1974), 397–431; and (up to Louis the Pious),
Felten, *Äebte und Laienäbte im Frankenreich*, Monographien zur Geschichte des Mittelalters
20 (Stuttgart: 1980).

[28] See Geoffrey Koziol, *Begging Pardon and Favor: Ritual and Political Order in Early Medieval France* (Ithaca [NY]: 1992), 38–39, 90–91. E.g., Count Conrad at Saint-Germain of Auxerre, in Heiric of Auxerre, *Miracula sancti Germani* 2.1.84–98, ed. L.-M. Duru, *Bibliothèque
historique de l'Yonne*, 2 vols. (Auxerre and Paris: 1850–64), 2.158–66, or PL 124, 1247–54.
Heiric justifies the Welf's festive restoration of the crypt through closeness to royalty (*Kön-
igsnähe*), not through an abbacy he may not have held: "*Chuonradus, princeps famosissimus,
collega regum, et inter primates aulicos apprime inclytus . . .*" (2.1.84, 158; PL 124, 1247c). See
Yves Sassier, "Les Carolingiens et Auxerre," in *L'école Carolingienne d'Auxerre, de Murethach à
Rémi, 840–908*, ed. Dominique Iogna-Prat, Colette Jeudy, and Guy Lobrichon (Paris: 1991),
at 29–32.

[29] Boshof, "Untersuchungen" (see ch. 1 n. 29); but see the Merovingian evidence below,
ch. 3, 109, 111.

[30] Koziol, *Begging Pardon*; Rudolf Schieffer, "Von Mailand nach Canossa. Ein Beitrag
zur Geschichte der christlichen Herrscherbusse von Theodosius d. Gr. bis zu Heinrich IV.,"
DA 28 (1972): 333–70; De Jong, "Power and humility." Lothar's surrender in Thegan, *Gesta
Hludowici imperatoris* 55, ed. Ernst Tremp, MGH SS rer. Germ. in u.s. 64 (Hannover: 1995),
250.

[31] Constantius II: see Kantorowicz, "King's Advent," 44 n. 28. Helena: Jan Willem Drij-
vers, *Helena Augusta. The Mother of Constantine the Great and the Legend of Her Finding of the
True Cross* (Leiden: 1992); E. D. Hunt, *Holy Land Pilgrimage in the Later Roman Empire* (Ox-

ried on his shoulders the "holy bones" of Januarius, a saint worshiped in the monastery of Reichenau;[32] his half-brother and rival Charles the Bald effected translations of relics in Saint-Médard of Soissons (841) and Auxerre (859).[33] There are hints that Carolingian audiences had come to expect that their rulers would physically participate in such rituals to manifest their piety. The ninth-century *Life of Ambrose of Milan* sandwiched, between the bishop's two confrontations with Theodosius I over Callinicum and Thessaloniki, the following detail. At Ambrose's prompting, the emperor and his son had carried on their shoulders the just-discovered relics of Nazarius.[34] It may not be fully coincidental that the two earliest surviving copies of Bishop Victricius's sermon describing the arrival of relics into his city of Rouen, and justifying theologically both the solemnity and the holy bones' power, date from the ninth century and come from two monasteries closely associated with Carolingian kings, Auxerre and Saint-Gall. The two manuscripts containing them were exact twins; one of them, at least, was dedicated to a ruler, Louis the German. The coincidence suggests the importance of relic translations for Carolingian rulership, east and west of the Rhine.[35] The *Annals of Saint-Vaast* for the year 985 superbly illustrate

---

ford: 1982), 28–49. Heraclius: A. Frolow, "La vraie croix et les expéditions d'Héraclius en Perse," *Revue des études byzantines* 11 (1953): 88–105. In the Carolingian world, Heraclius provided a model for royal humility within pomp; see Hrabanus Maurus, *Homilia* 70, *De reversione sanctae crucis*, PL 110, 131d–34d, especially 133c–34d.

[32] Lothar I in Walahfrid Strabo, "De sancto Ianuario martyre," ed. Ernst Dümmler, MGH Poetae 2 (Berlin: 1884), no 77.11, 416: "For he went by foot, surrounded by many throngs, and put his shoulders under the sacred bier, to carry the precious bones of the illustrious martyr." The poem ends on prayers for Lothar, his wife, children, the kingdom's prosperity, and his faithful subjects. See Peter Willmes, *Der Herrscher-"Adventus" im Kloster des Frühmittelalters*, Münstersche Mittelalter-Schriften 22 (Munich: 1976), 89 n. 334, 136–41.

[33] Charles at Saint-Médard de Soissons *beatorum corpora propriis humeribus cum omni veneratione transtulit*, Nithard, *Historia* 3.2, ed. Philippe Lauer (Paris: 1926), 86–88 with n. 4 (right after Fontenoy); Charles in Auxerre, Heiric, *Miracula sancti Germani* 2.2.99–102, ed. Duru, 2.167–68 or PL 124, 1254–55c (thanksgiving for help in the critical situation of the 858–59 East Frankish invasion). Both events are not beyond suspicion (Nithard's text may have been interpolated), but see the evidence gathered by Baudoin de Gaiffier, "Le Calendrier D'Héric d'Auxerre du manuscrit de Melk 412," *Analecta Bollandiana* 77 (1959): 392–425.

[34] Ed. Pierre Courcelle, *Recherches sur saint Ambroise. Vies anciennes, culture, iconographie* (Paris: 1973), 49–121, here 83: ". . . *in lectica reverenter composuit sacrisque imperatoribus, patri videlicet ac filio, propriis humeris ferendum contradidit ad basilicam apostolorum quae est in Romana . . .*" Angelo Paredi, *Vita e Meriti di S. Ambrogio*, Fontes Ambrosiani 37 (Milan: 1964), 11, dates on the strength of Bernard Bishoff's expertise the MS St. Gall Stiftbibliothek 569 to 860/80 and attributes it to a Milanese scriptorium.

[35] See the introduction to my translation of Victricius, *In Praise of the Saints*, in Thomas Head, ed., *Medieval Hagiography* (New York: 2000), 31–51. Eric J. Goldberg, "Frontier Kingship, Martial Ritual, and Early Knighthood at the Court of Louis the German," *Viator* 30 (1999): 41–78, proposes an interesting contrast between the East and West Frankish monarchies' practice of ritual but reads his evidence literally.

another stock-in-trade of later "liturgical kingship," tearful prayer before the saints. During his siege of Arras, King Odo I, taking advantage of a truce, had visited the monastery and dissolved in lachrymose piety before the saint's tomb. Odo may have imitated higher example in what was possibly an attempt to assert suitability for rulership in a disputed province: Two years earlier, his overlord King Arnulf had toured the episcopal churches of Lotharingia "in order to pray." Our source, Regino of Prüm, did not impugn the ruler's piety, but made it clear that the peregrination had a political tack: On the king's tour, the bishops showered on him huge gifts— probably manifesting their obedience through the donatives normally owed to a recognized ruler.[36] Like personal translation of relics and like care for the poor, this form of territorial pilgrimage or *Umritt* to the saints would survive the Carolingian dynasty in the West: In the 1030s, Robert the Pious tried to assert paramountcy in semi-autonomous Aquitaine by visiting the region's major shrines.[37]

The phenomenon did not limit itself to the *regna*. The ninth-century strata of the *Liber pontificalis* abound in descriptions of ceremonies. After the catalogue of popes' building and renovating activities and of their gifts of ornaments to various churches, ceremonies occupy the bulk of papal biographies. In Rome, solemnities provided the best shorthand for office. Witness the godsent visions foretelling Hadrian II's accession to the papal dignity:

> Among [these visions] . . . some saw Hadrian reclining on the papal throne, his shoulders covered with the pallium (*palleum*). Others saw him celebrating

---

[36] *Annales Vedastini ad an.* 895, ed. Bernhard de Simson, *Annales Xantenses et Vedastini*, MGH SS rer. Germ. in u.s. 12 (1909; reprint, Hannover: 1979), 76–77: "[Odo] *miseratus Christianitati noluit eum* [monasterium seu castellum] *bellando capere . . . Et . . . rex iussit sibi aperiri portas, ingressusque monasterium seu castellum ad limina perrexit sancti Vedasti coramque eius sepulchro humi prostratus devotissime oravit ac uberrime flevit, inibi etiam missam audivit, gratias agens deo.*" For Arnulf, see the *AF ad an.* 893, 122: "*Ante quadragesimam rex per totam occidentalium Francorum provintiam monasteria, episcopatus causa orationis obibat,*" and Regino, *Chronicon ad an.* 893, ed. Friedrich Kurze, MGH SS rer. Germ. in u.s. 50 (Hannover: 1890), 141: "*Rhenum transiens civitates, quae in regno Lotharii sunt, ex maxima parte circuivit; in quo itinere ingentia dona illi ab episcopis oblata sunt.*" See already the *Chronicle of Moissac ad an.* 800, MGH SS 1, 304:22–25: "*Karolus rex circa quadragesimae tempus circuit corpora sanctorum quae sunt in Francia*" (in the text's economy, apparently to prepare for a major assembly on a *dispositio regni* between his sons). See as well the putative source, *Annales Laureshamenses ad an.* 800, MGH SS 1, 38: "*circa quadragesimae tempore circuivit villas suas seu etiam corpora sanctorum.*" Cf. Ermold, *In honorem Hludowici* 2, vv. 790–801, ed. Edmond Faral, *Poème sur Louis le Pieux et Epitre au roi Pépin* (Paris: 1932), 62 (Louis tours the churches of Orléans and Paris before taking power in 814), with Willmes, *Herrscher-Adventus*, 77–80, who also reports yet other cases.

[37] Helgaud of Fleury, *Epitoma vitae regis Rotberti pii* 22 (relics borne by king's shoulders), 5, 9, 11, 21 (poor) 27 (pilgrimage), ed. Robert-Henri Bautier and Gilette Labory, *Helgaud de*

masses in papal ornaments. Many saw him distributing gold coins according to the papal custom (*more apostolico*) in the Lateran basilicas. Quite a few saw him, wearing the pontifical pallium, with the *axiomatici* preceding him and the other colleges following him, return to the city (on the horse Pope Nicholas used to ride when Nicholas went to Saint-Peter), and [then] receive the patriarchate.[38]

The papal dignity seems coterminous with the deeds and gestures of the pope at his installation.[39]

Yet (and probably correlatively) the utilization of rituals for naked partisan purposes seems a staple of ninth-century sources' denunciations of rivals and enemies. Gunthar, the deposed archbishop of Cologne, was twice accused of having forced his cathedral clergy, or deceived them to receive him as if he had still had episcopal power (*potestas*)—with a procession and to the sound of ringing bells.[40] Theutberga's enemies insinuated that the hot water ordeal through which she had cleared herself might have been rigged, a claim most forcefully asserted in the acts of the second Aachen council, which call it a *falsum iudicium* as opposed to a *verifica examinatio*. The ordeal's outcome, it was suggested, had been swayed in either of two ways. Either Theutberga had cleansed herself beforehand vis-à-vis God through a secret confession, or she had deceptively twisted the oath's meaning with a trick that nicely anticipates Isolde's in *Tristan*: When she swore that Hucbert had not known her, Theutberga placed in her mind

---

Fleury, Vie de Robert le Pieux. Sources d'histoire médiévale 1 (Paris: 1965), 110, 62–64, 70–72, 76, 126. See chapter 1, 28–30.

[38] *Vita Hadriani II* 5, in *Liber pontificalis*, ed. Louis Duchesne [henceforth *LP*], 3 vols. (Paris: 1955), 2.174:9–14. For a good insight on this source's crafted character (the *LP* begins recording or inventing manifestations of ritual consensus at papal elections only when the papacy begins its drive for autonomy vis-à-vis Constantinople's emperors), see Philip Daileader, "One Will, One Voice, and Equal Love: Papal Elections and the *Liber Pontificalis* in the Early Middle Ages," *Archivum historiae pontificiae* 31 (1993): 11–31.

[39] Some of the visions' rituals can be recognized in the Ordo IX, ca. 800–50, closest in time to the *Life*, ed. Eduard Eichmann, *Weihe und Krönung des Papstes im Mittelalter*, Münchener Theologische Studien 3, Kan. Abt. 1 (Munich: 1951), 9–18, or the Roman Ordo 36 (probably used for Leo IV in 847), ed. Michel Andrieu, *Les Ordines Romani du haut moyen age*, 5 vols. (Louvain and Paris: 1931–51), 4.204–205 ("*sella apostolica . . . equus praedecessoris pontificis . . . vallatur a iudicibus . . . praecedente eum clero*"). See Klemens Richter, *Die Ordination des Bischofs von Rom*, Liturgiewissenschafliche Quellen und Forschungen 60 (Münster: 1976).

[40] Reported in the *Annales Xantenses ad an.* 867, ed. Bernhard de Simson, MGH SS rer. Germ. in u.s. 12, 24: . . . "*officio episcopali interdicto, ipse tamen cum magna elatione, clangentibus signis, occurenti clero cum evangeliis et turribulis, aecclesias adiit.*" Similarly *ad an.* 870, 29: "*Coloniam venit et misso legato signa aecclesiae pulsare precepit et sibi honorifice occurrere iussit, dicens se potestatem habere quam non habuit . . .*" Cologne circles, responsible for this source's redaction, express hostility to the bishop's nepotism and use of the cathedral treasury *ad an.* 865, 22. See as well how Ebbo of Reims, deposed, then ephemerally reinstated, was met at Reims' cathedral, in MGH Concilia 2.2, 808–809.

(*intentio*) another Hucbert than her corruptor.[41] Many of the ceremonies described in the *Liber pontificalis* are recounted to expose rivals' nefarious manipulations of established *mos*.[42] Popes and others knew how to use rituals for their own purposes. If we trust Hincmar's pen, in 870, Hadrian II (r. 867–72) sent envoys to Charles the Bald. They reached him in the monastery of Saint-Denis, whose abbot he was, on the saint's very feast day, while the king was attending the saint's mass. The envoys presented there and then the pope's letters. In them, Hadrian denounced the West Frankish ruler's coronation as king over Lotharingia. Charles "received them grudgingly." Was it because the legates' message was already known to him or because they chose to arrive and reveal the pope's fulminations at the central moment of the liturgical cycle in Charles' own abbey?[43] Time and space lent weight and drama to the prospect and the performance of a confrontation.

Such demonstrations could sometimes be countered if one possessed advance knowledge of them. The chance survival of a Lotharingian letter meant to be kept secret sheds light on a political culture of maneuvers and countermaneuvers. Some years before the Saint-Denis episode, through messages sent to neighboring kingdoms, Hadrian's predecessor Nicholas I had let it be known that he would smite Lothar II with excommunication unless the king repudiated Waldrada on the eve of the feast of the Virgin's Purification. The pope had prepared a letter to this effect; it was probably in his legates' hands. While our source, Bishop Adventius of Metz, does not explain why Nicholas had chosen this specific deadline, it is suggestive to the cultural historian. Mary's purity signified the Church's own, soiled by Lothar's illegitimate union. Either the king cleansed himself before the feast, or the Christian body would have to cut him off from itself on the Purification day to preserve its collective sanctity. Another source

[41] Ed. Böhringer, 101, 146:16–19, 161–63. The antithesis at 122:2, from what the editor, introduction, 10, calls the *Tomus Prolixus*, that is, the (lost) proceedings of the second Aachen council, February 860. For *Tristan* and related twelfth-century ordeals in literature, see most recently John W. Baldwin, "The Crisis of the Ordeal: Literature, Law, and Religion around 1200," *Journal of Medieval and Renaissance Studies* 24,3 (1994): 327–53, and Stephen D. White, "Imaginary Justice: The End of the Ordeal and the Survival of the Duel," *Medieval Perspectives* 13 (1998): 32–55.

[42] See e.g., Leo III, captured (if we trust the *Vita Leonis III* 11–12, in *LP*, ed. Duchesne, 2.4:10–30), while celebrating processionally the major litanies, *ubi sibi populus obviam sacra religione occurrere deberet*.

[43] *Annales Bertiniani* [henceforth *AB*], *ad an.* 870, ed. Félix Grat et al., 177: "*ipsa die inter missarum sollemnia praefatos apostolici missos cum epistolis ad se et ad episcopos regni sui directos terribiliter sibi regnum quondam Hlotharii, quod fratri suo imperatori debebatur, interdicentibus moleste suscepit.*" Did they read the letters during the mass, or did Charles already know their contents? For the date's significance, see Janet L. Nelson, "La mort de Charles le Chauve," *Médiévales* 31 (1996): 63.

lends its weight to this hypothesis. Hincmar recounts how the legate Arsenius, after having forced Lothar to take back under oath Theutberga as wife and queen, met them again in Gondreville near Toul and celebrated there, on the Day of Mary's Assumption, a mass at which the pair wore their crowns. In these years, the Virgin's feast cycle provided the richest setting for a discourse on marriage and purity.[44]

The deadline was to be met in Saint-Arnulf of Metz, a church named after the Carolingian dynasty's holy founder and a focus of the dynasty's liturgical and historical *memoria*.[45] The pope had probably ordered his legates to stage a row in this most meaningful of spaces if the king did not accede to his demands. We should imagine that they would have publicly denounced Lothar and hedged him away from the sacraments. Yet Adventius believed he could trump Nicholas's hand of cards. Through Hatto of Mainz, he advised Lothar to confess his marital mistakes to three bishops, "in secret." The king was to humbly request pardon and promise to mend his ways "amid tearful sighs." While the suggested pose was penitential, it was still not public penance. If we turn again to Hincmar's account of the forced reconciliation Arsenius effected in 865, we see that the archbishop of Reims bewailed a settlement that did not involve "the performance according to the sacred canons of an ecclesiastical *satisfactio* for the public adultery."[46] Adventius, then, offered his king a way out of a public humiliation of this sort. If Lothar followed his advice, he would enter Saint-Arnulf to celebrate Mary's feast without fearing for his soul or kingship.[47] This was a culture in which one could advise hypocrisy in rituals and accuse one's opponents of precisely that: According to Hincmar, Lothar II had feigned compassion at the Aachen councils that had received Theutberga's confession. Lothar's sadness (*tristitia*), like Herod's at John the Baptist's execution, was affected not real. Here the archbishop indicted the king for more than perverse feelings of a "private" nature. *Tristitia* and

---

[44] *AB ad an.* 865, 119–122: "*Hlothario et Theotberga regio cultu paratis et coronatis, in die assumptionis sancte Marie missas celebrat.*" Nikolaus Staubach, *Das Herrscherbild Karls des Kahlen*, Ph.D. diss. Münster (Münster: 1981), 492–94, well demonstrates the importance of the Virgin's feast throughout the ninth century for such penitential occasions. See Hans Martin Schaller, "Der heilige Tag als Termin mittelalterlicher Staatsakte," *DA* 30:1 (1974): 1–24, at 8 n. 23, and Airlie, "Bodies," 34–35.

[45] See Otto-Gerhardt Oexle, "Die Karolinger und die Stadt des heiligen Arnulf," *FMSt* 1 (1967) at 351f., for Metz's (temporary) importance in the ninth century.

[46] *AB ad an.* 865, 119. On Adventius's letter collection, Staubach, *Herrscherbild*, 153–214, and 188–92 for the letter to Hatto.

[47] See now Mayke de Jong, "What was public about Carolingian public penance?" *La giustizia nell'alto medioevo (secoli IX–XI)*, 2 vols., Centro italiano di studi sull'alto medioevo, Settimane 44 (Spoleto: 1997), 2.863–904, on the nature of *poenitentia publica*, its potentially severe consequences, and its politicized uses.

laetitia were public bodily postures intended to manifest respectively political hostility and friendship.[48]

Thus we have every indication that actors and observers paid extreme
attention to actual performance. But remembered or recounted performance mattered at least as much. Like Liudprand, a crafty Carolingian
polemicist knew how to juxtapose and contrast rituals. Witness Hincmar
of Reims, this same annalist who placidly mentioned his king's participation in the Christian calendar's main feasts. For 862, Hincmar the annalist
chose to place next to one another two events, and stylized them. Ends
mattered more than chronology: In the process, he inverted their relative
order in time.[49] Containing the same structural elements—a ceremony of
consecration, bishops, a king, and marital as well as motherly themes—
they were made into polar opposites:

> Lothar . . . with the approval of his maternal uncle Liudfrid and of Walther
> . . . and (which is horrible to say) even with the consent of some of his king-
> dom's bishops, crowns and attaches to himself to be, as it were, his wife and
> queen . . . his concubine Waldrada.
>
>   Hincmar bishop of Reims, having gathered his province's bishops, and King
> Charles having come into this same city, venerably dedicates in the Virgin
> Mary's honor . . . that province's mother church.[50]

On the one hand, bishops cooperate with a king's mad consecration of a
whore; on the other, a king participates in an archbishop's collegial conse-

---

[48] *De divortio*, resp. 1, ed. Böhringer, 123:8–27, with (among many possible examples) *AB*
ad an. 833, 11: "*Quod illo* [Hlothario] *renuente, Hludouuicus tristis abcessit, deinceps cum suis*
meditans qualiter patrum suum ab eadem custodia eriperet." Here again the historian would do
well to avoid classifying all emotions within the modern "private"; see the warnings in Gerd
Althoff, "Königsherrschaft und Konfliktsbewaltigung im 10. und 11. Jahrhundert," repr. in
his *Spielregeln der Politik im Mittelalter* (Darmstadt: 1997), at 29–30, and idem, "Empörung,
Tränen, Zerknirschung. Emotionen in der öffentlichen Kommunikation des Mittelalters," in
Spielregeln, 258–81.

[49] This placement puzzled Parisot, *Royaume*, 199 n. 6, given that Nicolas I, *Ep.* 57 (ed.
Ernst Perels, MGH Epp. Kar. 4.2.1 [Berlin: 1912], 361:26–27 with n. 8), seems to indicate
that Waldrada had been consecrated queen on Dec. 25, 862: ". . . *Aganus* [Bergamensis epis-
copus], *quem perhibetis die natalis Domini super adulteros benedictionem, quae maledictio potius*
credenda est, protulisse." See as well the discussion in Staubach, *Herrscherbild*, 145 and n. 212
(447–50).

[50] *AB ad an.* 862, 93–94: "*Hlotharius Vualdradam concubinam, maleficis, ut ferebatur, artibus*
dementatus et ipsius pellicis pro qua uxorem suam Theotbergam abiecerat caeco amore inlectus, faven-
tibus sibi Liutfrido, avunculo suo, et Vualtario, qui vel ob hoc maxime illi erant familiares, et, quod
nefas est dictu, quibusdam etiam regni sui episcopis consentientibus, coronat et quasi in coniugem et
reginam sibi, amicis dolentibus atque contradicentibus, copulat. Hincmarus Remorum episcopus, ve-
niente Karolo rege in eandem civitatem, accitis conprovincialibus suis episcopis, matrem ecclesiam ipsius
provinciae in honore sanctae Mariae sicut et antiqua fuerat sacrata xv kalendas octobris [17 Sept.]
venerabiliter dedicat." Hincmar's constancy in naming his supernatural spouse provides yet
another contrast with Lothar's polygamy.

cration of a church (Hincmar's bride according to the liturgy) in the honor of Christ's Mother.[51]

WHY SHOULD A RITUAL MEAN? WRITING AND RITUAL EVENTS

By juxtaposing Waldrada and Notre-Dame of Reims's consecration, Hincmar sought to ridicule Lothar and to put his union in negative perspective. By describing a liturgical event, the archbishop fought with the pen against the hoped-for effects of another liturgical event. Historians of early medieval culture have taught us that rituals can serve to validate writings.[52] Putting a *libellus* on an altar publicizes as well as confirms the judicial accusation or verdict it contains and lifts it up to the sphere of sacred justice.[53] Louis the Pious's multiple prostrations at Compiègne were both constitutive elements in his deposition and a visual subscription of his written confession. Similarly for Queen Theutberga, according to her enemies, and archbishop John of Ravenna in the *Liber Pontificalis*: Admissions of guilt on vellum and liturgical forms lent one another authoritative force and commemorative power.[54] Given this, it should not be surprising that the obverse relationship obtains as well: Rituals can invalidate writings, and the pen can nullify a public action. Archbishops Theutgaud and Gunthar's attempts to obtain their reinstatement from Nicholas I (r. 858–67) provide a case in point. In analyzing it, we benefit from a plurality of sources.

Two accounts preserved with slight variations in both the *Annals of Fulda* and the *Annals of Saint-Bertin* are critical. They are in effect two rival interpretations of Archbishops Gunthar and Theutgaud's deposition at the October 863 Roman Synod: One is the papal version of the synodal acts, the other the Lotharingian bishops' letter of protest, which also recounts the synod. The historian is fortunate that the death of Rudolf in 865 interrupted his redaction of the *Annals of Fulda* before Lothar II's burial in Piacenza closed the dispute in his enemies' favor. Unlike his work's continuations or Hincmar's *Annals of Saint-Bertin*, then, Rudolf's rendering of events is unlikely to have been contaminated by ulterior knowledge of the

---

[51] For the intimate conceptual relationship between church, Mary, the archiepiscopal office, and the liturgical impression of "forms" of office, see Karl F. Morrison, " 'Unum ex Multis': Hincmar of Rheims' medical and aesthetic rationales for unification," repr. in his *Holiness and politics in early medieval thought* (London: 1985), 592, 596, 609.

[52] See Koziol, *Begging Pardon*, e.g., 68–70, 90, and, for a later period, Michael Clanchy, *From Memory to Written Record: England 1066–1307*, 2d ed. (Oxford: 1993), 254–60. For an earlier period, cf. Mary Beard, "Writing and ritual: A study of diversity and expansion in the Arval Acta," *Papers of the British School at Rome* 53 (1985): 139.

[53] The synod of Troyes (878), Mansi 17 (Venice: 1772), 345–47, provides a good contemporary example of a series of different complaints laid down in individual *libelli*.

[54] Hincmar, *De divortio*, interrogatio-responsio 1, 15, 121:9–121:13; *Vita Nicolai I* 30, *LP*, ed. Duchesne, 2.156:32–157:8.

final outcome. Prudently, Rudolf lay side by side two interpretations of Gunthar and Theutgaud's deposition at the Roman Synod of October 863, the synodal acts themselves and the Lotharingian archbishops' letter of protest after the event. Hincmar, however, establishes a much clearer hierarchy between the two documents; he separates them from one other by placing them under two different years, 863 and 864. Rudolf does hint at a preference for the papal synodal acts over the bishops' version, but he still lets the reader compare and choose.[55] One of Rudolf's continuators, who recast the *Annals of Fulda* a few years later as events moved into the cyclone's eye, resorted to even greater prudence. He chose to cut off the two documents and refer his audience to available copies "in numerous places in Germany."[56] Caution may have been in order in the East Frankish realm where these annals were redacted. If Louis the German did not always back his nephew Lothar, Louis' archchancellor in the 860s was one Grimald, brother of Theutgaud. Owing to his office Grimald possibly supervised the writing of the semi-official *Annals of Fulda*.[57]

Both the papal and episcopal versions polemicized in terms of the received understanding of what was a "good council." As defined in early medieval formularies (*ordines de celebrando concilii*), a good council presupposed the Holy Spirit's presence, made ritually manifest by smooth cere-

---

[55] *AF ad an.* 863, 57–58: ". . . [deposed] *iuste quidem et canonice, ut scriptis suis ipse* [papa] *testatur; iniuste vero, sicut illi rescriptis et assertionibus firmare conantur. Propterea partis utriusque scriptorum seriem his annalibus inserendam esse iudicavi, discernendam rei veritatem lectoris arbitrio dereliquens.*" Rudolf's share of the *AF* ends right after the bishops' letters. On this aspect of the *AF*, see F. Kurze's introduction, esp. vii and n. 1, and the critical survey in Löwe, *Deutschlands Geschichtsquellen*, vol. 6, 678–80. While aware that the annalists' identities are much disputed, for convenience's sake I stick to "Rudolf" to denote the annalist responsible for this stratum of the *AF*.

[56] *AF ad an.* 863, 57–58: ". . . *conantur. Scripturam autem utriusque partis quisquis curiosus scire voluerit, in nonnullis Germaniae locis poterit invenire.*" The bishops' protest seems to have been widely disseminated; see Parisot, *Royaume*, 244, basing himself on Nicholas, *Ep.* 53, ed. Perels, 346:4–7: *per totum pene occidentale clima.* Horst Fuhrmann, "Eine im Original erhaltene Propagandaschrift des Erzbischofs Gunthar von Köln (865)," *Archiv für Diplomatik* 4 (1958): 1–51, esp. 51, gives a sense of the means by which such texts were propagated—"chain letters." For another contemporary multiplication of documents *in multis libellis* sent to almost all bishops in East Francia, see Rimbert, *Vita Anskarii* 41, ed. Georg Waitz, SS rer. Germ. in u.s. 55 (Hannover: 1884), 75. Older historiography in Friedrich Wilhelm Oediger, *Die Regesten der Erzbischöfe von Köln im Mittelalter*, vol. 1 (Bonn: 1954), n° 206, 70. Easy diffusion explains but does not justify the continuator's call to look elsewhere for the two documents. Copies of the papal version were sent personally to Hincmar, who then integrated it in the AB, Ado of Vienne and Wenilo of Rouen, and generically to Louis the German's archbishops, possibly the source for *AF*, see Nicolas I, *Epp.* 18–20 (the intended audience for *Ep.* 21 is unclear), ed. Perels, 284–87.

[57] The exact place where the *Annals of Fulda* were redacted is still unclear, but one hypothesis is that until 863 they were produced near Mainz under the supervision of Grimald; see Löwe, *Deutschlands Geschichtsquellen*, vol. 6, 680–86.

monial and unanimous consensus.[58] No wonder then that the Roman synod's minutes present Nicholas as the mediator or representative of "the
Holy Spirit's judgment and Saint Peter's authority." They assimilate the
Metz synod of 863, which with the approval of corrupt papal legates had
recognized the earlier Lotharingian conciliar decisions, to the model
pseudo-council, the Late Antique "robbery of Ephesus" (449). They condemn any bishops who might join Gunthar and Theutgaud in forming "a
sedition, conjurations, or conspiracies"—perversely inspired groupings.

Nicholas I's biographer would later justify the 863 deposition by accus-
ing the two bishops of forgery.[59] Gunthar and Theutgaud certainly at the
very least propagandized their own version of these specific events. Their
libellus answers the synodal acts within the tropes of the same political culture. Nicholas, not the agentless consent of all (itself invisibly orchestrated
by the Spirit), had stage-managed the council. Could it be called a council
at all? The pope had kept Gunthar and Theutgaud waiting for three weeks
before summoning them without any hint of hostility. Then, in a parody
of conciliar ordines, the doors had been shut and blocked behind the unsuspecting pair, and a mixed crowd of clerics and laymen, as if a gang of rob-
bers, had surrounded them. More latrocinali conspiratione: Inspired by a
"spirit of banditry" rather than by the Holy Spirit, the assembly was not a
council but a mob (turba).[60] The bishops had been forcibly wrenched from
their servants and entourage. They were far away from their ordinary
judges, their Lotharingian colleagues and metropolitans. The proceedings
lacked all the features necessary to law's rites: no canonical examination,
not a single accuser or witness, no judicial debate or use of authoritative
texts, no confession of the accused. This demonstrated the Holy Spirit's

---

[58] See Paul Hinschius, Decretales Pseudo-Isidorianae (Leipzig: 1863), 22–24; see now Die
Konzilsordines des Früh- und Hochmittelalters, ed. Herbert Schneider, MGH Ordines de cele-
brando concilio (Hannover: 1996), 176–86. For "good conciliar ritual," see Roger Reynolds,
"Rites and Signs of Conciliar Decision in the Early Middle Ages," Segni e riti nella chiesa
altomedievale occidentale, 2 vols., Centro Italiano di studi sull'alto medioevo, Settimane 33
(Spoleto: 1987), 1.207–78.

[59] Vita Nicolai I 48, in LP, ed. Duchesne, 2.151–72, here 2.160:21–23, recounting the 863
Roman synod's accusations: Theutgaud and Gunthar had "falsified a letter of the pious pontiff, as is declared in the gestae they evilly composed, which have been kept in the archives
(scrinium) of this see." Nicolas I, in 867, Ep. 53, ed. Perels, 346:15–16, still accused them of
having "woven with some of our suffragants iniquitous tractates and certain fictiones," and of
having erased a bishop's reservations in the Metz synodal acta, 347:21–31. No wonder then
that Levillain, in AB, lxv–lxvi, noting the divergences between AB and AF, believes that the
Lotharingian archbishops' own enemies falsified their capitula!

[60] AF ad an. 863, 61; cf. AB ad an. 863 and 864, 99–103 and 107–108. Compare the Ordo
2, c.12, ed. Schneider, 182:88–89: "Nullus autem tumultus aut inter consedentes aut inter astantes
habebitur," or the original Ordo 1 (Toledo IV), c. 10, 141:41–43: "Tunc enim deus suorum sacerdotum coetui interesse credendus est, si tumultu omni abiecto sollicite atque tranquille ecclesiastica
negotia terminentur."

absence. Nicholas had acted tyrannically, "outside the consent of all." In other words, the unanimity constitutive of early medieval "good ritual" was wholly lacking. The pope had claimed that the Spirit spoke through his mouth; the bishops accused him of having been possessed instead by fury.[61]

Nicholas had assimilated the Lotharingian synods to conspiracies. The bishops' retort played on the very same register. Theutgaud and Gunthar attempted to invalidate their trial by presenting it as canonically improper and by painting it as disorderly and improper in form. Returning now to Hincmar's presentation of the two documents, let us see how he attempted, through the very structuring of his narrative, to invalidate the Lotharingians' protest. The *Annals of Saint-Bertin* taint Gunthar and Theutgaud's letter of protest by sandwiching it between two episodes. Each involves a riotous "bad ritual."

The first of these two episodes will call for detailed commentary further along, where it will be related to other sources. For the time being, a summary will suffice. According to the *Annals of Saint-Bertin*, Gunthar's reaction to his deposition did not limit itself to the redaction of a tendentious protest. In 864, he returned to Rome with Louis II (Lothar's brother). The emperor had transmitted the two bishops to the 863 Roman council under his safekeeping (*fiducia*); Gunthar convinced Louis that, in stripping them of their dignity, Nicolas had insulted him. The emperor flared into anger and resolved to force Nicolas to retract his decision. In 864, Louis entered Rome, the two deposed prelates in tow. But once there, his warriors encountered a penitential procession on Saint-Peter's steps. It was a liturgy of opposition. Nicholas had ordered the litanies to bemoan the emperor's lack of respect for papal authority. The imperial troops dispersed it by force, breaking crosses and killing a man in the process. God's vengeance struck. Louis fell sick and was forced to accept the papal verdict.

The second episode that Hincmar recounted to invalidate the episcopal complaint directly concerned the document itself. Gunthar had entrusted his brother with a mission. Should Nicholas refuse to receive the *libellus*, this Hilduin would place it on Peter's grave. Accordingly,

> Hilduin, in armor and with Gunthar's men, entered without any reverence Saint Peter's church and sought to throw that diabolical writ . . . on Saint Peter's body. The guardians prevented him from doing so, and both he and

---

[61] The pope's words (in *AF ad an.* 863, 59, cf. *AB* 863, 100, 102): ". . . *cum Ephesino latrocinio . . . in perpetuum damnandam nec vocari sinodum . . .*" and ". . . *si cum his coniuncti seditionem, coniurationes vel conspirationes fecerint . . .*" seem to be countered by the bishop's . . . "*facta more latrocinali conspiratione . . .*" (*AF*, 61; cf. *AB* 864, 109). Similarly, the papal *Spiritus Sancti iudicio et beati Petri per nos auctoritate* (cf. *AB* 863, 101) is inverted into (cf. *AB* 864, 109) ". . . *nullaque . . . auctoritatum probatione . . . extra omnium omnino consensum, tuo solius arbitrio et tyrannico furore*" (let us recall that both Holy Spirit and *furor* possess their vessel).

his accomplices began to strike these same guardians with blows, to the point that one of them was killed. Then Hilduin threw that writ on Saint Peter's body, and he and those who had come with him, protecting themselves with drawn swords, exited the church.[62]

The *Annals*'s audience was supposed to understand that Gunthar had sought to appeal liturgically from the pope's judicial court to the Apostle's (or to validate his text with Peter's approval). "On Saint Peter's body" pointed to a sacred spot where one hallowed both pious gifts and righteous protests.[63] In an effort to sanctify Charlemagne's 774 donation to the Roman See, the *Liber pontificalis* depicted an elaborate combination of ritual and writing that culminated in this very heart of Peter's *confessio*. The king placed "with his own hands" a copy of the text "inside over Saint Peter's body, beneath the Gospels which are kissed there."[64] Circa 770/1, Pope Stephen III first "consecrated" a protest letter in Peter's *confessio* before sending it to Charlemagne.[65] Hincmar (or his source) invalidated both

---

[62] *AB* 864, 111. Cf. also Nicolas I, *Ep.* 53, to Louis the German's bishops, dated from much after the fact, i.e., 31 Oct. 867, ed. Ernst Perels, MGH. Epp. Kar. 4.2.1 (Berlin: 1912), 340–51. This letter recounts all of Theutgaud and Gunthar's evil deeds, including "*qualiter nos tyrannice penes sanctum Petrum positos afflixerint, oppresserint et quibus potuerint malis fatigaverint, adeo ut homines eorum adita sancti Petri violaverint et in ecclesia ipsius sanguinem fuderint. Qualiter etiam ibidem nobis matitunales hymnos celebrantibus illi noctu post tribunal ecclesiae ipsius cum complicibus et fautoribus suis contra Calcedonense concilium coniuraverint . . .*" (346:3–13). The *Liber pontificalis* does not document this crisis, which suggests that Nicholas in fact lost.

[63] One did the same at other religious centers. A single example: At the end of the tenth century, Aymo, bishop of Valence deposed a protest on saint Stephen's altar in Arles. Despite Odette Pontal, *Les conciles de la France capétienne jusqu'en 1215* (Paris: 1995), 75, who dates it to 976/78, there is no reason to believe the act took place in King Conrad's presence or during the lifetime of all the witnesses to Aikard's excommunication, for Aymo describes a series of measures—one, a clamor *ante presentiam Gondradi regis senioris nostri*, two, an appeal to *iuditium aeterni regis domini nostri* and to the sword and fire of the *caelestis imperator* since the clamor was in vain, *quoniam nulla ratione ipsum* [Aikardum? regem?] *ad rectitudinem faciendam invitare potui*. He thus asked for the counsel and help of neighboring bishops, who excommunicated Aikard. Then he placed the text (*scriptura*) on the altar, beseeching all the inhabitants of Arles who would read it not to cease announcing its message publicly to all, and not to remove it from the altar until it was known that Aikard and his men had atoned their misdeed ("*. . . ne dimittatis, quin omnibus palam annuntietis, nec sit aliquis qui tollat eam desuper altare beati Stephani, nisi dum lecta fuerit et audita, donec audiatis persecutores dei aecclesiae pro quibus res agitur ad satisfactionem venire*"). Text in Jules Marion, ed., *Cartulaires de l'église cathédrale de Grenoble, dits cartulaires de Saint-Hugues*. Collection de documents inédits sur l'histoire de France 1.43 (Paris: 1869), 59–61.

[64] *Vita Hadriani I* 43, in *LP*, ed. Duchesne 1.498:22–30.

[65] *Codex Carolinus* 45, ed. W. Gundlach, MGH Epp. Merow. et Kar. Aevi 1 (MGH Epistolae 3, Berlin: 1892), 563:33–35: "*Praesentem itaque nostram exhortationem atque adorationem in confessione beati Petri ponentes, et sacrificium super eam atque hostias Deo nostro offerentes, vobis cum lacrimis ex eadem sacra confessione direximus.*" To repulse a Lombard assault, Stephen III's predecessor (r. 752–57) "bound and tied to the venerable cross of our Lord and God the pact

Gunthar's move and the *libellus* by turning the archbishop's paraliturgical protest into a bloody desecration of Peter's *memoria*.

Thus two stories, the one suggesting disrespect for liturgy, the other, an attempt to coerce Saint Peter, function to invalidate (or so Hincmar hoped) the archbishops' written protest. Narratives involving ritual and violence envelope and counter a narrative that spoke as well of forms and procedures violently manipulated.

But it was not so much rituals as *texts* about bad rituals that invalidated the archbishops' written protest. The "bad rituals" themselves may never have occurred. The attack on the procession seems at first sight confirmed by two other sources. But the specifics in this apparent convergence make it impossible to recover what actually transpired in Rome in 864. What can be salvaged through the deep dive into ninth-century waters is why Hincmar and others crafted their stories as they did, and why they chose to configure them as they did. Let us look at the *Annals of Saint-Bertin* again, this time in detail, before moving to the parallel accounts. Rumor had reached Rome that the emperor intended to force, violently if necessary, the Lotharingian archbishops' reinstatement.

> Hearing this, the pope imposed on himself and on the Romans a general fast with litanies,[66] so that God through the apostles' intercession might give the aforesaid emperor good intentions and reverence toward the divine cult and the apostolic see's authority. But as the emperor had reached Rome and was taking lodging[67] near Saint Peter's basilica, the Roman clergy and people, celebrating the fast with crosses and litanies, went to blessed Peter's *memoria*. When they began to ascend the steps before Saint Peter's basilica, the emperor's men threw them flat to the ground and beat them with many blows. Their crosses and banners broken, those who could escape took flight.[68]

. . . that the infamous king of the Lombards had broken" (*alligans connectensque adorandae cruci domini Dei nostri pactum scilicet illum quod nefandus rex Langobardorum disruperat*), *Vita Stephani II* 11, *LP*, ed. Duchesne, 1.443:7–8.

[66] See Hincmar's own *Schedula adversus Hincmarum Laudunensem episcopum* 28, ed. Wilfried Hartmann, *Die Konzilien der karolingischen Teilreiche 860–874*, MGH Concilia 4 (Hannover: 1998), 467, for what the archbishop himself thought such litanies involved: "*Audivimus namque, quia sanctae memoriae Nicolaus papa, sancta romana ecclesia in afflictione posita, auctoritate veteris et novi testamenti*" [Ioel 2.12 and Matth. 11.21] in ieiunio et fletu, *ac* planctu, in cinere et cilicio" *litanias indixerit.*

[67] Carlrichard Brühl, "Die Kaiserpfalz bei St. Peter und die Pfalz Ottos III. auf dem Palatin," reworked in his *Aus Mittelalter und Diplomatik. Gesammelte Aufsätze*, 2 vols. (Berlin: 1989), at 2.7, citing the *Libellus*, ed. Giuseppe Zucchetti, *Il Chronicon di Benedetto monaco di S. Andrea del Soratte e il Libellus de imperatoria potestate in urbe Roma*, Fonti per la storia d'Italia 55 (Rome: 1920), 204:1, identifies the place, an old Carolingian palace.

[68] *AB ad an.* 864, 106. As Herbert Zielinski remarks, the account is highly crafted— Böhmer-Zielinski, *Regesta Imperii*, vol. 1.3.1, *Die Karolinger im Regnum Italiae 840–887(888)* (Cologne: 1991), Louis II n° 215, 91.

In the affray, a man in Louis's service broke the wondrous cross that Empress Helena had given the prince of the apostles, and threw it in the mud. Did the pope know Roman law's provision that those who disturbed litanies should undergo capital punishment?[69] Nicholas locked himself in Saint Peter's church and fasted for two days, triggering God's vengeance: The cross-breaker died and the emperor fell sick with fevers. Louis then sought an understanding with the pope; it was agreed that the two deposed bishops would return to Francia without being restored to their rank.

For Hincmar, the affray takes place near the basilica, on Saint-Peter's steps. In a Beneventine source, Erchempert's *History of the Lombards*, written at some distance from Rome and 864, it is Louis II's reception into Rome (and not a chance encounter with a penitential procession) that provides the setting for this violence: "[A]ccording to the age-old custom, a sacerdotal procession dressed in pure white came to encounter him (*obvium ei*), but he, spurning fear of God, had the clergy be beaten with sticks, and the crosses and all the consecrated vessels (*ministeria*) be trampled underfoot."[70] Can one reconcile these two sources?

Matters reach yet another degree of complexity when one adduces still another text. While using the same structural elements, the late ninth-century *Libellus de imperatoria potestate in urbe Roma* throws the event in a totally different light.[71] Was it actually the same event? The affray occurred somewhere on the road between Saint-Paul and the imperial palace near Saint-Peter. The archbishop who caused trouble is not Gunthar of Cologne, absent from this narrative. Instead, the conflict between the royal and papal offices was triggered by Nicholas's jealousy over the favor and influence John, archbishop of Ravenna, enjoyed with emperor Louis II,

---

[69] Justinian, *Novella* 123.31, ed. Rudolf Schoell and Wilhelm Kroll, *Corpus Iuris Civilis*, vol. 3, 2d ed. (Berlin: 1928), 616–17. It is possible that the law, being present in Justin's Latin *Epitome* (ed. Pierre Pithou and L. Miraeus, *Imperatoris Justiniani constitutiones per Julianum antecessorem* 115.52 = 478 [Basel: 1576], 174–75) was known in Carolingian times. There are hints that some of Justinian's codification was used in the ninth century; the locus classicus is Odilo, *Vita Odonis* 1.5, PL 133, 461.

[70] Erchempert, *Historia Langobardorum Beneventanorum* 37, ed. Georg Waitz, MGH SS rer. Lang., at 248:33–40: ". . . *Cur autem iam dicto augusto supradictum opprobrium Domino permittente Beneventani inferre quiverint, de multis duo inferam: primum quia veniens quodam tempore Romam, ut duos episcopos condempnatos ad pristinam reduceret dignitatem, et dum nollet ei consentiret* [sic] *Nicolaus papa, vir Deo plenus, secundum antiquum morem obvium ei venit candidatum sacerdotalem agmen; at ille, spreto timore Dei, fustibus clerum caedi fecit, cruces vero omniaque sacrata ministeria pedibus calcari, Romamque pene miliari spatio depredatus est vicariumque beati Petri quasi vile mancipium ab officio suo ministerii, nisi dominus restitisset, privare voluit* . . ." Similar (but brief) negative eulogy in *Annals of Xanten ad an.* 869, 27:9–12.

[71] For various hypotheses on the *Libellus*'s date of composition, see *Deutschlands Geschichtsquellen im Mittelalter. Vorzeit und Karolinger*, vol. 4, ed. Heinz Löwe (Weimar: 1963), 425–26 (according to Löwe from the tenth century's first decade).

and by the pope's attempts to unjustly depose John.[72] The Carolingian decided to harden his control over Rome and journeyed to the city with the archbishop. There, the citizens, great and small, organized a successful honorific entry. Upset, the pope reacted:

> As all his [Nicholas's] ambushes against the royal dignity were held for nothing, he ordered monks and virgins consecrated to God belonging to Rome monasteries to celebrate, as if under the pretext of religion, daily litanies which circumambulated the walls (*per circuitum murorum*),[73] and to sing masses against princes who behave evilly.[74]

Needless to say, this striking recuperation of a liturgy of supplication normally used against pagans could hardly please the warriors in Louis's entourage:[75]

> When they heard this, the king's magnates humbly approached the pope and asked him in a friendly manner to forbid such things. But since they were unable to obtain anything from him, they went back, mournful. But one day, as some warriors of the said prince, having gone to Saint-Paul, were coming back, it happened that they encountered these litanies. Impelled by the Ancient Enemy, the warriors lapsed into fury and, because they were faithful to their lord, took vengeance against these people, striking them and beating them with the sticks they carried in their hands. The others fled and threw

---

[72] The *Vita Nicolai* 50, *LP*, ed. Duchesne, 2.160–61, does not make the least allusion to any version of the 864 events but lumps together Gunthar, Theutgaud, and John as plotters against the pope. They were in Benevento at Louis II's court.

[73] One of the first occurrences of circumambulatory processions on a besieged city's walls is Gregory of Tours, *LH* 3.29, 125:10–126:4. The liturgical form harkens back to pagan Rome; see the reaction to Caesar's crossing of the Rubicon as described in Lucan, *Civil Wars* 1.592–606, ed. D. R. Shackleton Bailey (Stuttgart: 1988), 21. Masses and litanies in *supplicatio* might be the prelude to a battle for *sanctam ecclesiam vel populum christianum*, see *Annales regni Francorum ad an.* 791, ed. Kurze, MGH SS Rer. germ. in u.s. 6 (Hannover: 1895), 88–89, *laetanias faciendi per triduo missarumque sollemnia celebrandi*, with Michael McCormick, "Liturgie et guerre des Carolingiens à la première croisade," '*Militia Christi*' *e Crociata nei secoli XI–XIII*, Miscellanea del Centro di studi medioevali 13 (Milan: 1992), 209–40, at 220–33. The letter formed the basis for an item in the formulary "of Saint-Denys," ed. Karl Zeumer, *MGH Formulae*, MGH Leges 5 (Hannover: 1886), 510–11 (from manuscript Paris Bibliothèque Nationale de France Latin 2777, 61r–v). Thus, the 791 event's description became the basis for a new paraliturgical practice. *Laetania* ranged from a full procession or a stational prayer to any supplicatory ritual; see Walahfrid Strabo, *De exordiis et incrementis rerum ecclesiasticarum* 29, ed. Alfred Boretius et al., MGH Capitularia 2.3 (Hannover: 1897), 514:4–6, with Ferdinand Cabrol, article "Litanies," *Dictionnaire d'Archéologie Chrétienne et de Liturgie*, vol. 9.2 (Paris: 1930), 1540–47.

[74] *Libellus*, 204:1–5. The closest parallel in the Roman tradition is the *Vita Stephani II* 10–11, in *LP*, ed. Duchesne, 1.442:17–443:8, where the pope, whom King Aistulf besieged in Rome, organized elaborate processional litanies against his opponent.

[75] *Libellus*, 204:6–15.

away the crosses and the icons they carried (as is the Greek custom), and many were broken.

The aftermath according to the *Libellus* mirrors in negative that in the *Annals of Saint-Bertin*: The emperor was moved to anger and the pope to meekness. Nicolas had to go to Louis and implore pardon for his partisans. The salient structural parallels and oppositions can be summarized with the following diagram:

Hincmar:	————	procession attacked
Erchempert:	*occursus* attacked	————
Libellus:	*occursus*	procession attacked

So what, if anything, had really happened? The texts offer three alternative versions. One might be tempted to search for the actual event behind these texts; this would mean creating yet another alternative narrative.[76] Had Louis been greeted by a respectful and conventional (*secundum antiquum morem*) *occursus* that he had then madly manhandled (Erchempert)? Had the emperor chanced upon a penitential liturgy that bemoaning publicly his hostile intentions, triggered his men's violence (Hincmar)? Or was the aggressive atmosphere at least as much owed to the pope as to the Carolingian, insofar as Nicholas had intended from the beginning to confront the emperor liturgically (the *Libellus*)? Did a largely orderly advent into Rome lead to a few scuffles that the Carolingian's enemies later blew out of proportion (the truth behind Erchempert)? Did Nicholas try to compensate for a smooth *adventus* honoring the emperor by organizing monastic processions (the truth behind the *Libellus*)? Or did he purposefully stage within the imperial lodging's immediate surroundings a quasi clamor that he knew would provoke Louis's faithful men (the truth behind a synthesis of Hincmar and the *Libellus*)? Or did he orchestrate a highly ambiguous *occursus* that served both to honor the imperial office and criticize this particular emperor's policy (one of the truths arrived at through a combination of the three texts)?

One should give up the attempt to reconstruct the events of 864 and rather concentrate on the meanings different authors wanted to convey in recounting them. To do so, one should focus on Roman topography and the ceremonial forms traditionally attached to Roman places. The locus of

---

[76] See e.g., Parisot's collage, *Royaume*, 241–42, 245, which in the main follows the *Libellus* up to the immediate aftermath of the affray, then adopts the *AB*'s narrative line and posits a change of attitude once the imperial side learns that Helena's cross has been broken. Or Duchesne, *LP* 2.170, n. 49, who calls *AB* "the best narrative" but adds that the *Libellus* "also preserved a few interesting details."

the affray, Saint-Peter's steps, happened to be the all-important final station in a monarch's entry into Rome. The "Steps" had played this role in
the seminal year 800 for Charlemagne's *adventus*, providing a precedent
for later Carolingian rulers, before and after 864. In a text we have already
looked at, a victorious Arnulf was honorably received (*susceptus*) at the Milvian Bridge "by the whole Roman senate as well as the Greek *scholae* with
banners and crosses," then received in turn by the pope "in the place called
Saint-Peter's steps" before being crowned and named Augustus (896).[77]
Conversely, if we trust Hincmar's quill, Pope Hadrian II signaled his disapproval of Lothar II by not granting him a ceremonial reception when he
reached Saint-Peter (869).[78] Thus Hincmar and the *Libellus* situated the
confrontation in the expected and highly meaningful space of the arrival
of the imperial *adventus*.

All three texts contain at least one processional ritual (either an *occursus*
or litanies or both) that ninth-century political culture utilized to convey
friendship. All three texts share the knowledge *or the assumption* that such
a ceremonial event took place. Whether it occurred or not, it was expected
to occur. A procession provided medieval political culture with a recognized way to gauge—qualitatively and quantitatively—the relationship between two parties, qualitatively by detailing the nature of the train and its
trappings, quantitatively, by evaluating the length an *occursus* traveled to
meet its recipient. The past—in texts and memory—had supplied various
models that could themselves become the basis of meaningful variation.
The ambient political culture's assumptions and commonplaces concerning what could and should happen can be recovered from the ninth-century
sources. These expectations shaped the horizons of the three authors who
spoke about Louis II and Nicholas I. In this field, Charlemagne's 800 reception loomed large, at least in Frankish memory: an *occursus* twelve miles
from Rome led by the pope in person, a meal on that spot, and on the next
day as Leo waited on Saint-Peter's steps, another *occursus*, which involved
the sending of the city's banners to meet the king and the stationing of
groups of citizens and foreigners on the way.[79] Papal sources document

---

[77] *Annales Fuldenses, Continuatio Ratisponensis, ad an.* 896, 128. See above, at nn. 11–12.
According to the *Vita Leonis III* 18–19, in *LP*, ed. Duchesne, 2.6:17–24, Leo III was also
received at the Milvian Bridge when he returned—triumphantly with Charlemagne's backing—to Rome.

[78] *AB ad an.* 869, 155: "*Ubi nullum clericum obvium habuit, sed tantum ipse usque ad sepulchrum
sancti Petri cum suis pervenit, indeque solarium secus ecclesiam beati Petri mansionem habiturus
intravit, quem nec etiam scopa mundatum invenit.*"

[79] *Annales regni Francorum ad an.* 800, ed. Kurze, MGH SS rer. Germ. in u. s. 6, 110–12.
See also Otto II's reception during Christmas week 967, *Continuatio Reginonis*, ed. Kurze,
Reginonis Chronicon (as n. 36), 179. Richard Trexler, *Public Life in Renaissance Florence* (New
York: 1980), 306–308, underlines the measurability of processions.

other variants.[80] Close to the 864 riot, we find another instance of quantitative and qualitative gauging of a political relationship through a procession. But here the *Liber Pontificalis* managed to recount and locate movements in such a way as to assert papal superiority. Louis demonstrated his friendship for Nicholas, who had just been elected in his presence: From outside Rome, he came forth to meet the papal advent (*obvius in adventum eius occurrit*) and served, on foot, as the mounted pope's groom for an arrowshot's distance.[81]

In text and probably in action, processions were instruments to measure the respective power of two parties in a political relationship. In extreme cases, when the relationship was breaking down, they were expected to break down as well. Thematically speaking, the closest parallel to the 864 textual cluster comes from the *Liber Pontificalis*'s description of Sergius II's 844 reception of Louis II for his coronation. All the magistrates (*universi iudices*) met the king nine miles from Rome with banners (*signa*) and *laudes*; one mile from the city, the procession encountered another train: the *militia*'s various corps (*scholae*), including the Greeks, who sang imperial *laudes* and brought out crosses. Sergius himself waited on Saint-Peter's steps, surrounded by his clergy.[82] This text has its own purpose and logic, which are worth analyzing. There too the writer injected the ritual's description with an element of tension. Tension within a ritual within a narrative has a function and modalities. Where it leads to open conflict, as in the 864 texts, such tension is meant to convey the radical moral superiority of one side over another. Contained, as it is here, it reveals right order, a specific order: The *Liber Pontificalis* sought to enshrine within the proceedings (and therefore make normative) the king's recognition of Sergius II's election, which had taken place without his consent. In recounting the ceremony as it did, it sought as well to legitimize the papal position on two issues. Sergius was refusing to reinstate Ebbo, erstwhile archbishop of Reims; and the pope did not want Rome's greater men to swear an oath of fidelity to Louis himself (as opposed to Emperor Lothar). For the faction whose views the *Vita Sergii* reflects, these were critical signs of liberty from Carolingian power.[83] The narrative argued for this liberty's necessity in symbolic terms,

---

[80] *Vita Stephani II* 25, in *LP*, 1.447:10–15, reception of Stephen II (752–57), to be compared with the *Chronicle of Aniane ad an.* 754 (see below, epilogue, 260). *LP*, 1.429:18–430:5, reception of Zachary (741–52): The exarch of Ravenna travels fifty miles. See also Josef Déer, "Die Vorrechte des Kaisers in Rom (772–800)," *Schweizer Beiträge zur Allgemeinen Geschichte* 15 (1957): 5–63, at 42–45, drawing on the *LP*, 1.378 n.15, 1.343, 1.372, 1.496–97.

[81] *Vita Nicolai I* 8–10, in *LP*, ed. Duchesne, 2.152:14–28.

[82] *Vita Sergii II* 9, in *LP*, ed. Duchesne, 2.88:5–15. The closest ceremonial is Hadrian I's 774 reception of Charlemagne, *Vita Hadriani I* 35, *LP* 1.496:27–497:20, in which the respective distances were thirty miles and one mile.

[83] *Vita Sergii II* 15–16, in *LP*, 2.90:11–21. See ibidem 18, 2.91:1–3, after Louis II's departure for Pavia: "*Tunc vero leti omnes . . . senatus populusque romanus ingenti peste liberati et iugo tiran-*

through the irruption of the miraculous: The ritual almost turned bad. After Louis had taken his host's right hand, and after both had entered Saint-Peter's atrium, a demon seized a Frankish warrior in the royal retinue. The pope reacted, ordering the church's doors to be closed. If later *ordines* can indicate anything about ninth-century understandings of Saint-Peter's liturgical space, these silver gates beyond the atrium led to the locus of imperial consecration and provided a stational point in that ceremony.[84] Louis had to assure Sergius "that he had come there with neither malignity in his spirit nor any wickedness nor evil guile" before the pope opened the doors again and they stepped into Saint-Peter proper to worship.[85] The warrior's possession (or malignity in spirit) suggested symbolically the ever-potential madness of a potentially badly intentioned Frankish king (indeed, his army had plundered and raged in the Roman countryside); the doors' closure signified the Church's sovereign countermeasure against any such hostility: a denial of access to the king-making liturgy. Within the narrative describing Louis's reception, this hint of a devil-inspired crisis overcome ultimately highlighted right order. But in the 864 texts, the demon triumphed, and the rituals turned "bad," dramatizing the bad relationship that obtained between the heads of *regnum* and *sacerdotium*.

Given the precedents provided by this political culture, contemporaries' assessment of the relationship between Nicholas and Louis II in 864 had a strong probability of crystallizing in this space, on the road to Rome's walls or near Saint-Peter, and around a processional ritual. Thus there may have been a real procession; or there may have been merely, without the event, a "first-story" or "Ur-narrative" involving a procession, because a procession provided the best means to quantify and qualify the political relationship between the two men.

Rival interpretations soon surrounded the fact or the fiction: Hincmar's to demonstrate the righteousness of the papal stance against the Lotharin-

---

nice inmanitatis redempti, sanctissimum Sergium praesulem velut salutis auctorem ac restitutorem pacis venerabant." While here (*Vita* 12) Sergius refuses to let the violent Franks come into Rome *hospitalitatis causa* (2.88:32–89:3), in 774, Charlemagne had prayed Hadrian to grant him entry into Rome *sua orationum vota per diversas dei ecclesias persolvenda*, which request the pontiff had granted after they had each sworn an oath to each other, *Vita Hadriani I* 39, in *LP* 1.497:21–25.

[84] See the earliest surviving blueprint, a Roman ordo in the Mainz Pontifical (before 960), ed. Reinhard Elze, *Die Ordines für die Weihe und Krönung des Kaisers und der Kaiserin*, Fontes Iuris Germanici in usum scholarum 9 (Hannover: 1960), 2–3. The ceremony moves from *ante portam argenteam* (2:12) and finishes *ante confessionem beati Petri* (2:20). Interestingly, the best guide to the 844 ceremony is the Ordo of Censius II, ed. Elze, 35–47, from the twelfth-century Roman curia, a text that subordinates the emperor to the pope.

[85] *Vita Sergii II* 10–11, in *LP*, ed. Duchesne, 2.88:16–31. On the *atrium* and its role in processions as a space in which to incorporate the laity, see most recently Kristin Mary Sazama, "The Assertion of Monastic Spiritual and Temporal Authority in the Romanesque

gians; Erchempert's to place within providential history the death of a ruler who had sided against Benevento; the *Libellus* to hint at the evilness of autocratic popes with the aim of justifying a balance of power more in favor of royal *potestas*. Here as in many other cases, the real or imaginary ritual's interpretation weighed more than its actual performance.

Contemporaries were aware that plural interpretations were possible. This awareness led them to imagine (and claim) that their enemies wickedly interpreted ritual events. It also led them to seek to control interpretation as much as, if not more than the ceremonies themselves. Given this, historians need to reevaluate functionalist models of ritual efficacy.

WICKED INTERPRETERS AND TACTICAL INTERPRETATION: WHAT WILL A RITUAL MEAN?

In 869 King Lothar II, embroiled in his divorce, journeyed to Italy. He hoped to strike a compromise with Hadrian II, Theutberga's defender. If we follow Hincmar of Reims, Lothar bribed his brother Emperor Louis II and the empress, and obtained through their mediation a meeting with the pope. In Monte-Cassino, Hadrian sang a mass in the king's presence and received him and his accomplices to communion, but on the following condition: The king had to promise that he had not associated in any way with Waldrada after Nicholas, Hadrian's predecessor, had excommunicated her.[86] Tradition, from Ado of Vienne a few years later to Regino of Prüm and the tenth-century *Translatio sanctae Glodesindis*, would elaborate on Hincmar's crisp but clear message.[87] For the Annals of Saint-Bertin, Hadrian had subjected the king to a judicial ordeal, *iudicium dei*, and Lothar had sought to cheat on it; within two months, the king's transgression resulted in his death. First a pestilence struck the royal entourage; Lothar "watched with his own eyes" his men fall in droves; still, "he refused to understand God's judgment."[88] But in the economy of Hincmar's narrative, the sinful king, blind to the spirit behind the letter of the events, did not die immediately. Lothar had first to incriminate himself further in another

---

Sculpture of Sainte-Madeleine at Vézelay" (Ph.D. diss., Northwestern University, 1995), 32–34, 82–95.

[86] *AB* 869, 154.

[87] Ado (d. 874), *Chronicon*, MGH SS 2.315–24, at 323:7–23; Regino, *ad an.* 869, ed. Kurze, 96–98: ". . . *nequaquam sumere presumas, ne forte ad iudicium et condempnationem tibi eveniat . . .*" John of Saint-Arnulf, *Vita altera Sanctae Glodesindis* 5.59, *AASS* Jul. VI, 220e. See the Annals of Hildesheim and its cognates, MGH SS 3, 48:27–29: "*ab Adriano papa damnatus, domis rediens cum suis pene omnibus periit*" (similar in *Annales Otterburani*, MGH SS 5, 3:46–47).

[88] *AB* 869, 156: ". . . *febre corripitur, et grassante clade in suos quos in oculos suos coacervatim mori conspiciebat, sed iudicium dei intellegere nolens . . .*" Cf. *Annales Xantenses ad an.* 870, 28:17–26 (within the broad eschatological framework of that work's last years).

attempted manipulation of ritual. From Monte-Cassino, he followed in Hadrian's footsteps to Rome. There, contrary to his expectations, no *occursus* greeted him in front of Saint-Peter, he found that not the slightest attempt had been made to clean his lodgings, and he failed to obtain a mass from Hadrian. On the following day, however, Lothar ate with the pope in the Lateran. The two parties read in opposite and irreconcilable ways the papal gestures at the meeting:

> [Lothar] obtained . . . through gifts of gold and silver vases that the Pontiff himself would give him a woolen mantle, a palm-leaf and a *ferula* . . . And he and his men interpreted these [papal] gifts in the following way, that is, that through the woolen mantle he was being re-invested with Waldrada, that the palm-leaf showed him to be the victor in the affairs he had incepted, and that he would distrain with the *ferula* those bishops who resisted him and stood in the way of his will.[89]

For Hadrian, however, these objects clothed Lothar in the costume of a pilgrim or penitent and invited him to bow to the authority of the Church. Mantle, palm, and staff conveyed the political obverse of the Lotharingian understanding (*ut . . . episcopos . . . distringeret*). It is possible (although indifferent for this argument) that at the meeting the two parties had agreed to disagree and to craft with this exchange of gifts an ambiguous message acceptable to both. Indeed for the Annalist there existed two possible readings of the papal presents, but one was true and the other one perverse. In writing about the ceremony of gift exchange, he stamped it with the meaning he preferred—thus marking out the king's own deceitful or blind reading. The meeting became the penultimate act in Lothar's demise and, with the king's doleful communion, provided an explanation of the Carolingian's death as well as of the partition of Lotharingia.

One can document other ninth-century instances where control of a ritual's interpretation was more critical than the performance itself. John VIII's 878 liturgical clamor is a case in point. It is documented in the *Annals of Fulda*'s account of the struggles over the imperial crown opened up by Charles the Bald's death:

> Lambert son of Wido [margrave of Spoleto] and Adalbert son of Boniface [margrave of Tuscany his brother-in-law] entered Rome with a strong band of armed men. They put John, the Roman pontiff, under guard, and forced the leaders of the Romans to swear an oath of fidelity to Karlmann. Once they

---

[89] Hincmar, *AB*, 155, with Percy Ernst Schramm and Florentine Mütherich, *Denkmale der deutschen Könige und Kaiser* (Munich: 1962), 85–86, and Ursula Swinarski, *Herrschen mit den Heiligen: Kirchenbesuche, Pilgerfahrten und Heiligenverehrung früh- und hochmittelalterlicher Herrscher, ca. 500–1200*, Geist und Werk der Zeiten 78 (Bern: 1991), 62–63.

had left Rome, the pontiff entered Saint-Peter's church and transported all the treasures he found there to the Lateran. He covered the altar of Saint Peter with a hair-shirt and shut closed all this same church's doors. And no service pertaining to God's cult was celebrated there for several days, and, dreadful to say, entry was denied to all those who came from everywhere in order to pray there. And all things were in confusion there.[90]

John's own letter collection confirms—up to a point—the Fulda Annalist's report. Early in 878, he had written to "his beloved son count Lambert" to announce that he would in no way receive in Rome his "manifest enemy" Adalbert. In the same letter, the pope had warned Lambert that he would gladly grant him an *occursus* (*honorifice recipere*) as long as the margrave did not come to Rome with the intention of restoring to their positions and possessions enemies of, and traitors to (*infideles*) the pope.[91] By the spring of 878, several papal letters indicate that the "beloved son" had verified his spiritual father's worst fears. John had received with honor (*honorifice*) Lambert in Saint-Peter, but the margrave had treacherously seized Rome's gates and prevented the movement of food and people. He and the pope's *manifestus in omnibus inimicus* Adalbert then "troubled and evilly dispersed by beating them with sticks" monks and clergy who were going to the basilica singing "hymns, spiritual canticles, and the holy litanies." These evil men would not let them sacrifice to God in Saint-Peter. The parallel with the methods Louis II allegedly employed in 864 is striking. The historian should wonder whether one is dealing here with a tradition of political methods when dealing with uppity clergy (which Louis and Lambert shared in) or in oppositional writing (shared at least by Hincmar and papal circles). Faced with such violence, the pope's sole recourse was to demonstrate "sadness" and to weep, "for during these days neither was there any cloth (*vestis*) covering Saint Peter's altar nor was any day or night office solemnly (*ex more*) celebrated there." John leaves unclear whether the stripping of the altar and the cessation of offices directly resulted from the margraves' blockade or (as in the *Annals of Fulda*) were elements in a liturgical protest.[92] One should remark here the importance

---

[90] *AF ad an.* 878, 91.

[91] *Ep.* 83, ed. Erich Caspar, in Paul Kehr, MGH Epp. Kar. 5 (Berlin: 1928), 79:2–4, 7–10, 16–18.

[92] See *Epp.* 73–74, 87–88, 96, 107, esp. *Ep.* 73, ed. Caspar, 67–69, at 68:22–26: ". . . *venerabiles item episcopos, presbyteros atque diaconos et religiosos monachos cum ymnis et canticis spiritalibus sacrisque letaniis ad ecclesiam principis apostolorum venientes, heu pro dolor! more paganorum conturbaverunt et fustibus cedentes nequiter disperserunt, non sinentes illos exire debitumque Deo sacrificium offerre.*" 68:30–69:1: ". . . *ut nequaquam nobis aliud agere nisi flere liceret; nam ipsis diebus nec vestis fuit super altare sancti Petri nec aliquod ibi nocturnum vel diurnum officium ex more celebratum.*" *Ep.* 74, 70:13–17 reports the same misdeeds and complains that Lambert's blockade resulted in

of written propaganda in the struggle against Adalbert and Lambert. The pope himself trusted ritual less than texts' power to initiate communication. Some of the letters he wrote to inform princes and prelates of the margraves' behavior mention "another little work directed to the attention of all Christians," which recounted in full the misdeeds.[93] Further, John informed the 878 synod of Troyes that Lambert's excommunication was written on the walls of Saint-Peter. The text presumably detailed the sanction's causes, including lack of respect for the litanies and the liturgy of protest. The pope hoped that visitors (including pilgrims?) would sympathize.[94]

John VIII may have had good reasons for equivocation. While humiliation of saints involved a purposeful inversion of right order to trigger supernatural wrath and obtain a righting of wrongs, "turning everything upside down" should be read negatively. The Fulda annalist's tone suggests that he considered the pope's actions a manipulation, an impression his negative portrayal of John's later deeds confirms. For John associates with Boso, a man the same *Annals* accuse of poisoning, *raptus*, and conspiracy against Carolingian lordship in Italy:

> The said pontiff then took ship and entered the kingdom of Charles [after having traveled] over the Tyrrhenian sea. He sojourned there for almost the full year. Finally, John returned to Italy with great ostentation. The pontiff was taking along count Boso (who, having snuffed out his own wife's life by poison, had taken by force [to be his wife] from Italy [Ermengard] the daughter of Emperor Louis), and strove with him to plot how he could wrest away the Kingdom of Italy from Karlmann's portion and how he could entrust it [Italy] to Boso's governance.[95]

We can draw our own conclusions. Ritual humiliation did not function automatically to rally support. If it "did act on others and helped to force

---

the pope's loss of *urbis Romae potestatem*. See *Ep*. 107, 99:32–33, presenting the results of Lambert's blockade: "... *ita ut nec ibi aliquam alicui lucernam illuminare nec laudes deo conferre liceret...*" Like the *AF, Ep*. 87, to Louis the Stammerer, 82:39–83:1, mentions forced oaths.

[93] *Ep*. 87 (to Louis the Stammerer), ed. Caspar, 83:4–7; cf. *Ep*. 89, 85:23–29.

[94] Mansi 17.348ab: "*Quodque decretum in praedicta beati Petri ecclesia sciptum, ut ingredientes et exeuntes legant et doleant, eosque* [Lambert, Adalbert, and their followers] *anathematizatos teneant, posuimus.*"

[95] *AF ad an.* 878, 91–92. All these elements are doubtful; see Johannes Fried, "Boso von Vienne oder Ludwig der Stammler? Der Kaiserkandidat Johanns VIII.", *DA* 32,1 (1976): 193–208, at 202–204 and n. 46. But "die rechtgenaue Schilderung und die aufgebrachte Verurteilung der Schliessung der Peterkirche durch Johann VIII." reported "von enttäuschten Rompilgern" (202 n. 46) may not have been objective either. For an earlier, generic condemnation of the stripping of the altars, see below, ch. 3, 90–92, Toledo XIII (683) c. 7, ed. Vives, 423–24.

public opinion on the issue,"[96] its effectiveness depended less on the specifics of its performance than on political agents' control of means of communication and interpretation. Communication: As Geary notes for a late tenth-century case, this was why the canons of Tours blocked entrance to their church to all but pilgrims (*portae ... clausae ... solis peregrinis patuere*).[97] Interpretation: This may be why John VIII's letters equivocate concerning the cessation of offices in Saint-Peter. By the time they were being written, his enemies may have been gaining the upper hand in a war of propaganda and succeeded in presenting whatever had happened as an evil and manipulative clamor. In 878, the competition between orchestrated rumors determined the success of the papal liturgy. Other rituals do not escape this rule.

If we trust some anthropologists and the historians who have used their work, royal funerals are a ritualized crisis. Their ultimate function is the restoration of order; their meaning is to express the continuity of power despite mortality. The most fully analyzed early medieval funeral may be Otto III's, which occurred in 1002. According to Lothar Bornscheuer, pious service to the royal body on its trek to its final resting place allowed the king's distant relative, Duke Henry of Bavaria, to solidify his claims to the throne. Otto had died in Italy; he would be buried in Aachen. Henry took over the corpse when the funeral cortège, having crossed the Alps, reached Bavaria. He honored it, traveled with it, and finally let it go on with others to the Rhineland and Aachen. During this funeral journey through Bavaria, the duke festively and personally translated the royal viscera to a chapel in his main city, Regensburg.[98] We might trust the German historian's thesis, for after all, the Liber Pontificalis argued approximately the same claims with approximately the same words: One of the proofs of Nicolas I's popeworthiness laid in the care with which, before his 858 election, he had carried to the tomb "on his very own shoulders" his predecessor Benedict's body.[99] Yet for a medievalist, funerals survive, as it were, first

---

[96] Patrick J. Geary, "Humiliation of Saints," repr. in Geary, *Living with the Dead in Medieval Europe* (Ithaca [NY]: 1994), 109; see Lester K. Little, "Morphologie des malédictions monastiques," *Annales ESC* 34 (1979): 43–60.

[97] Geary, "Humiliation," 106, quoting a 996/97 document edited in Louis Halphen, *Le comté d'Anjou au onzième siècle* (Paris: 1906), n° 3, 348–49.

[98] Lothar Bornscheuer, *Miseriae regum*, 4–5, 144f., who writes "Heinrich hatte seine intensive Fürsorge um den Verstorbenen geradezu dafür nutzen können, seinen umstrittenen Nachfolgeanspruch demonstrativ zur Geltung zu bringen" (5); cf. most recently Hans Martin Schaller, "Der Kaiser stirbt," in *Tod im Mittelalter*, ed. Arno Borst et al., Konstanzer Bibliothek 20 (Constance: 1993), 59–75.

[99] *Vita Nicolai I* 4, *LP*, ed. Duchesne, 2.151:25–27: "*Suisque eum humeris* [Benedictum], *cum adhuc diaconus esset, usque as apostoli beatissimi Petri basilicam cum aliis diaconibus gestans, propriis manibus tumulo collocavit, dilectionis praemium pandens quod circa eum habebat et amoris integritatem.*" Compare with Adalbold, *Vita Heinrici*, ed. Georg Waitz in Georg Pertz, MGH SS 4

and foremost as texts. We may wonder what an enemy of either Otto III or Duke Henry would have done with the Saxon emperor's last rites. It is significant that the prime source documenting Henry's piety, Adalbold of Utrecht, avoided recounting Archbishop Heribert of Cologne's own funeral piety toward Otto. According to Thietmar of Merseburg, Adalbold's main source, Heribert and Henry vied for control of the dead emperor's last rites in order to acquire greater influence in the election of his successor.[100] At the very least oppositional historiography would have erased Henry's pious performance in the funeral cortège. It might have gone as far as ridiculing the ceremonious transportation.

Black narratives of funerals were as old as their positive counterparts. Since at least Gregory of Nazianzen's wonderfully black-and-white portrait contrasting the funeral cortèges of Constantius II and Julian the Apostate, ecclesiastical authors used depictions of death rites to push for a prince's *consecratio* or *damnatio memoriae*, or rather their equivalents in Christian political culture.[101] What are we to make of the remarkable absence of developed narratives of royal funerals in Gregory of Tours? Had the ceremony lost in importance in the Merovingian world, even though it was both heir to a late antiquity where funerals had been critical for successors' legitimacy, and a cultural satellite of Byzantium where they still were? Unlikely. And had the Merovingian world downplayed it only for royalty and not for the episcopate? Probably not. The first Council of Braga (563) ordered that the corpses of suicides, of catechumens who had died without receiving baptism, and of executed criminals (*qui pro sceleribus suis puniuntur*) were not to be led "with psalms to their burial-place" (a denial of what the council called the *psallendi officium*). It further provided that these people were not to be commemorated during the mass at the offertory (*nulla pro illis in oblatione commemoratio*).[102] Carolingian churchmen adopted these provisions to punish people who died excommu-

---

(Hannover: 1841), 684:36–39: ". . . *ipse* [Heinricus] *suis humeris corpus imperatoris* [Ottonis III] *in civitatem subvexit, pietatis exemplum et humanitatis exhibens debitum.*"

[100] Bornscheuer, *Miseriae regum,* 144f., 208–11; Thietmar, *Chronicon* 4.50–51 and 4.53–54, ed. Holtzmann, 188–194, allowing tensions to show (Henry of Luxemburg begs his brother Henry of Bavaria to let the body go on toward Lotharingia; the majority of the great men present at the funeral orchestrated by Heribert in Aachen promise help to Henry's rival Hermann of Swabia). Like Richildis, Charles's wife, Heribert brings the royal insignia from Italy, and bargains at the head of a faction of magnates; cf. *AB ad an.* 877, 218. See now Warner, "Thietmar," 70–73, for perceptive comments on Thietmar's political interests and on how sophisticatedly he patterns the failed rituals he attributes to Henry's opponents of 1002.

[101] See ch. 3 n. 52, and for the Byzantine "ideal-type" in P. Karlin-Hayter, "L'adieu à l'empereur," *Byzantion* 61,1 (1991): 112–55.

[102] Council of Braga I, cc. 16–17, Mansi 9.779, or José Vives, *Concilios visigóticos e hispano-romanos* (Barcelona: 1963), 74–75; and *AB* 878, 226. See now Ian N. Wood, "Sépultures ecclésiastiques et sénatoriales dans la vallée du Rhône (400–600)," *Médiévales* 31 (1996): 13–28.

nicate for having despoiled ecclesiastical possessions. Church fathers knew the importance of pomp for social identity. In refusing to elaborate on ceremonies that probably still took place on a lavish scale, the bishop of Tours sought to downgrade the centrality of the royal office.[103] It was, as we shall see in the following chapter, a red thread in his *Ten Books of Histories*.

By 875, there was, at least in northern Italy, a liturgy of "conducting" the royal corpse to its final resting place. Andreas of Bergamo, for whom Louis II was a hero, described how the archbishop of Milan, after having forced the bishop of Brescia to hand over the emperor's body, had ordered the clergy of three dioceses to escort it to Saint-Ambrose.[104] Embalmed, it was put on a bier, and led "with every honor and the singing of hymns to God." Andreas himself escorted it through his diocese (at the boundaries of which clergy from another diocese probably took over, as in a relay); he gloried in having carried it for part of that stretch of the road.

The chronicler Andreas clearly respected his deceased emperor. But when one disliked a king, one could underline the discordant elements in his funeral. We see this only two years later, in 877, with Charles the Bald. While the Annals of Saint-Vaast content themselves with a curt "they deposited his body in the same kingdom [of Burgundy] in a small monastic cell until it could be transferred to Francia, and it was later transferred there through various places," Hincmar gleefully parodies his old master's final journey:[105]

He died eleven days after having quaffed the poison, on the second day of the Nones of October [6th of October], in the vilest hovel. Opening him up, those

---

[103] Alain Dierkens, "Autour de la tombe de Charlemagne," *Byzantion* 61,1 (1991): 156–80, believes that the absence of a preexistent Merovingian model accounts in part for the lack of sophistication (until Louis the Pious) of royal funeral rituals. But see below, ch. 3, 108–109.

[104] Andreas of Bergamo, *Historiola* 18, ed. Georg Waitz, MGH SS rer. Lang, at 229:24–36 (poor Latin but eyewitness account): "*Hludowicus imperator defunctus est, pridie Idus Agust., in finibus Bresiana. Antonius vero Bresiane episcopus tulit corpus eius et posuit eum in sepulchro in aecclesia sanctae Mariae, ubi corpus sancti Filastrici requiescit. Anspertus Mediolanensis archiepiscopus mandans ei per archidiaconum suum, ut reddat corpus illud; ille autem noluit. Tunc mandans Garibaldi Bergomensis episcopus et Benedicti Cremonensis episcopus cum suorum sacerdotes et cunctum clero venire, sicut ipse archiepiscopus faciebat. Episcopis vero ita fecerunt et illuc perrexerunt. Trahentes eum a terra et mirifice condientes dies quinto post transitum, in pharetro posuerunt, cum omni honore, hymnis Deo psalentibus, in Mediolanum perduxerunt. Veritatem in Christo loquor: ibi fui et partem aliquam portavi et cum portantibus ambulavi a flumen qui dicatur Oleo usque ad flumen Adua. Adductus igitur in civitate cum magno honore et lacrimabili fletu, in ecclesia beati Ambrosii confessoris sepelierunt die septimane suae. Qui imperavit annos 26.*"

[105] *Annales Vedastini ad an.* 877, ed. B. de Simson, 42:18–20; Hincmar, *AB ad an.* 877, 216–17. There may be a reference to Charles's odorous death in Hincmar's *Visio Bernoldi*, PL 125, 1116c. By 873, Hincmar's earlier love for Charles had cooled off since he had lost favor following the rise of newer royal councillors, Nelson, *Charles the Bald*, 222, 241–42. Cf. Devisse, *Hincmar*, 2.803–24, and Löwe, "Geschichtsschreibung," 185–86.

who were with him removed the innards and poured in wine and the spices they could [find]; having put him in a coffin,[106] they began to transport him towards the monastery of Saint-Denis, where he had requested to be buried.[107] But as they were not able to carry him on account of the stench, they conveyed him in a barrel whose interior and exterior were coated with pitch, and which they wrapped in animal skins. This succeeded in no way in removing the stench. Therefore, having barely made it to a certain monastic cella in the diocese of Lyon, called Nantua, they entrusted to the earth this body with that very barrel.

In all likelihood, the king's body did stink. Most corpses do. Needless to say, stench was not a specifically Carolingian problem, but one acutely posed in the warmer southern climates.[108] Repatriating corpses across the Alps would long prove itself problematic for North European armies active in Italy.[109] Yet nothing forced the archbishop of Reims to dwell on this unpalatable fact. With malice: Hincmar's words, *pro foetore non valentes portare*, echo the death of the godless Antiochus (II Mac. 9.9–10: *et qui paulo ante sidera caeli contingere se arbitrabatur, eum nemo poterat propter intolerantiam foetoris portare*), a biblical model also alluded to in the equally hostile Annals of Fulda's parallel rendering of the event.[110] The *cella*, in its smallness, recalls Hincmar's equally dismissive indications as to Lothar II's burial place, "in some small minster" near Piacenza.[111] Circa 1100, promonarchist historiography would piously rework the account, place the king's first resting place in Vercelli, in the blessed martyr Eusebius's church, and deodorize the stench with a divinely inspired translation to Saint-Denis: "Owing to a vision, his body was transported to France and

---

[106] Regino, *Chronicon ad an.* 877, ed. Kurze, 113, writes *levatum in feretro*.

[107] Nelson, "La mort de Charles le Chauve," 63 speaks rightly of a "separation between the king and his patron-saint" Denis in Hincmar's "cyphered narrative," since Oct. 6 was close to Denis' feast day.

[108] Bodies that did not stink were suspect and some explanation had to be found, see e.g., Ordericus Vitalis, *The Ecclesiastical History*, ed. and trans. Marjorie Chibnall (Oxford: 1969), 2.80–81.

[109] For a near-contemporary Byzantine imperial body's stench, see Karlin-Hayter, "L'adieu," 113 n. 4.

[110] *AF ad an.* 877, 90. The biblical type is mustered as well in Lactantius, *De mortibus persecutorum* 33.7, ed. J. L. Creed (Oxford: 1984), 50, a model text for tyrants' deaths. The parallels go further in Hincmar's case. Antiochus's demise began with his flight (*in fugam versi sunt*) from Persia, like Charles's own in Italy (*fugam iniit . . . terga vertere . . .*). Cf. also *cum magna periit tristitia*, which parallels the synoptic I Mac. 6.9, *renovata est in eo tristitia magna*. But in the *AB* 877, 216, it is Karlmann who *ipse fugam arripuit*. Both the *AF* and the *AB* had access to the same rumors, both painted Charles's death in sinister biblical colors, but both took "patriotic" and necessarily divergent lines in making the other kingdom's ruler run away.

[111] *AB ad an.* 869, 156.

buried with honor in the basilica of the blessed martyr Denis in Paris."[112]
In the feisty archbishop's account, the funeral preparations convey an impression of disorder: The king's familiars stuff Charles with spices as best they can; instead of the corpse, the barrel is wrapped in skins;[113] the Nantua burial *cum ipsa tonna* seems especially ludicrous. Anointed of the Lord, Charles ended up like a pickled herring.

A complicated political chessboard generates and maintains a complicated political culture. While liturgical forms do not constitute the sole objects a political culture manipulates (ninth- and tenth-century authors crafted with special attention the images of women and warfare), they provided a highly efficient way to imagine and gauge—in texts as much as in action— a political situation. We saw this in the case of the 864 narratives. The specific shape ceremonies take under an author's pen depends on culturally received narrative practice and historical capital: Imagination is limited by intelligibility and by considerations of strategic efficiency. Thus, texts do not put forth just any ritual. John VIII's complaints against Adalbert and Lambert highlight violence against Roman processions precisely because this accusation has become traditional and because litanies served to measure power.[114] Hincmar damns Charles the Bald's last years as ruler by inverting the model of a good emperor's funeral that was available in the last quarter of the ninth century. These tactics, as well as the Fulda Annalist's portrayal of Lothar II as perverse interpreter, point to the failings of a functionalist theory of ritual efficacy that would be oblivious to the weight of communication in the shaping of "public opinion."

[112] MS. Paris Bibliothèque Nationale de France Latin 12711, f. 155va, between 1082 and 1103, see Jean-François Lemarignier, "Autour de la royauté française du IXe au XIIIe siècle," *Bibliothèque de l'Ecole des Chartes* 113 (1955): 5–33, at 11–13, 25–36.

[113] See e.g. *Roland* vv. 2964–69, tr. Glyn Burgess (London: 1990): "He had them all cut open before him / And all their hearts wrapped in silken cloth / They are placed in a white marble coffin / They placed the lords in deerskins / And washed them in piment and in wine." Spices were also used to preserve the royal body during its transportation, cf. Otto I's funeral in Thietmar, *Chronicon* 2.43, ed. Holtzmann, 92:11–17, and Louis II's (n. 104 above). Nithard, *Histories* 4.5, ed. Lauer, 138, marveled at his father's body preservation without spices: *corpore absque aromatibus indissoluto*. While it does not involve a body's transportation, the *Vita Droctovei* by Gislemar (d. 889), ed. Bruno Krusch, SS rer. Mer. 3 (Hannover: 1896), 535–43, at 541:20f. and 542:20–24 (chapters 15 and 18) provides a model contemporary "good funeral."

[114] So Koziol, *Begging Pardon*, 306, on rituals being "a currency for measuring power," possibly an adaptation of Mary Douglas, *Purity and Danger*, reed. (London: 1991), 70: "Money provides a standard for measuring worth; ritual standardizes situations, so helps to evaluate them." Yet the effective factor in measuring is not an audience's reaction, which gives a specific meaning to an inherently ambiguous event (*Begging Pardon*, 307–10); rather, as the cases in which we have plural sources show, it is propaganda, which may even determine the audience's reports.

Chapter Three

RITES OF SAINTS AND RITES OF KINGS: CONSENSUS AND TRANSGRESSION IN THE WORKS OF GREGORY OF TOURS

THE LATIN WEST long remained under the receding shadow of the Roman empire. Yet over the course of the sixth century, it seemed increasingly that barbarian kings were there to stay. Some *regna* did disappear, wiped off by rivals or by Justinian's reconquests. But such downfalls were not enough to nip in the bud the mental geography emergent in the West. Its upper classes, content with a distant emperor and a lowered tax burden, possibly never had prayed very fervently for a reversal of the political map the invasions had produced. Now they no longer counted on it. Wisdom lay in providing for the future, with the *reges gentium* cautiously included in the equation. With Gregory the Great, the papacy itself would initiate a new policy that complemented and inflected the traditional orientation toward, and obedience to the emperor: to deal directly with the non-Roman rulers. In Visigothic Spain and in Frankish Gaul, especially, the bishops found themselves compelled to define their authority relative to that of the kings and their officials.

The pen contributed to this definition. Rachel Stocking has recovered in the surviving minutes of Spanish councils the tracks of the uneasy dialogue between Visigothic kings and episcopate. North and south of the Pyrenees, explicit conciliar pronouncements, but also more veiled tensions revealed by twists and turns in writing, afford an analytical point of entry into these interactions. In their specific details and general architecture, the synods' decrees negotiated the boundaries between public power and the Church. The very way in which these meetings were convened and organized, down to the seating arrangements, participated in this process. The Fourth Council of Toledo (633), in laying down the way in which such ecclesiastical assemblies were to convene and proceed, their rituals, and the place in them of lesser clergy and laymen, was as graphically precise as Roman

I presented an earlier version of this chapter at the 1994 International Medieval Congress, Leeds (England), "Gregory of Tours: Rites of Saints and Rites of Kings." For comments on its various drafts, I wholeheartedly thank Martin Heinzelmann; for information on Visigothic canon law, Rachel Stocking.

legislation on seating arrangement at the games.[1] Synods also strove for uniformity in liturgical practice.[2] In Frankish Gaul as well as in the southern kingdom, numerous canons sought to enforce clergy's and magnates' attendance at the mother churches' ceremonies as well as suffragants' respect of metropolitan liturgical models;[3] to lay out ways to inform priests of the precise date of Lent, Easter, and other major feasts; and to prescribe their length.[4] The unanimity that, in a sub-Roman culture, liturgy manifested, called for a scrupulous uniformity over time and space. The Suebic council of Braga (a source later integrated in the Visigothic corpus when that kingdom was absorbed by its greater neighbor) spells out this ideology: "We judge it necessary and very useful that those [practices] which all of us owing to custom kept different and disorderly we should [now] celebrate

---

[1] For Spain, see Rachel Stocking, *Bishops, Councils, and Consensus in the Visigothic Kingdom, 589–633*, (Ann Arbor: forthcoming), ch. 2 for the dialogue between king and episcopate, ch. 5, for the conciliar ordo legislated at Toledo IV (ed. José Vives, *Concilios visigóticos e hispano-romanos* [Barcelona: 1963], 188–90). It passed into Carolingian canon law repertoire, see Paul Hinschius, *Decretales Pseudo-Isidorianae* (Leipzig: 1863), 22–24. For the ordo's influence, Hans Barion, *Das fränkish-deutsche Synodalrecht des Frühmittelalters*, Kanonistische Studien und Texte 5–6, ed. Albert Michael Koeniger (Bonn: 1931; repr. Amsterdam: 1963), 57, and Martin Klöckener, *Die Liturgie der Diözesansynode*, Liturgiewissenschafliche Quellen und Forschungen 68 (Münster: 1986), 40–83. See as well Stocking, "Aventius, Martianus, and Isidore: Provincial Councils in Seventh-Century Spain," *Early Medieval Europe* 6,2 (1997): 169–88.

[2] As Peter Brown, *The Rise of Western Christendom* (Cambridge, Mass.: 1996), 220–21, notices for Visigothic Spain with the Goths' 589 conversion to Catholicism. But the same concerns had existed in Gaul well before. See Orléans IV (541) c. 3, ed. Charles de Clerq, *Concilia Galliae, 511–695*, CCSL 148A (Turnhout: 1963), 132:22–133:25: "*Quisquis de prioribus civibus pascha extra civitatem tenere voluerit, sciat sibi a cuncta synodum esse prohibitum; sed principales festivitates sub praesentia episcopi teneat, ubi sanctum decit esse conventum.*" See as well the following notes.

[3] Agde (506) c. 30, ed. Charles Munier, *Concilia Galliae, 314–506*, CCSL 148 (Turnhout: 1963), 206:256–63: "*. . . convenit ordinem ecclesiae ab omnibus aequaliter custodiri*"; I Braga (561) cc. 2.1–5, Vives, 71–72: "*. . . unus atque idem psallendi ordo in matutinis vel vespertinis officiis . . . ; per sollemnium dierum vigilias vel missas omnes easdem et non diversas lectiones in ecclesia legant . . . episcopi et . . . presbyteri populum . . . uno modo salutent . . . eodem ordine missae* [unum] *. . . babtizandi ordinem*"; Tours II (567) c. 19 (18), CCSL 148A, 182–83, seeks local uniformity in setting the *psallendi ordo* for saint Martin's basilica and "our churches" during the year. Arles (554) c. 1, CCSL 148A, 171:15–19, prescribes that oblations at the altar should be offered by all bishops of the province according to the model of the church of Arles ("*ut oblatae, quae in sancto offeruntur altario, a conprovincialibus episcopis non aliter nisi ad formam Arilatensis offerantur ecclesiae. Quod si aliter aliquis facere praesumpserit, tamdiu sit a communione vel a caritate fratrum seclusus, quamdiu ipsum coetus synodalis reciperit*").

[4] Synchronicity of Easter, *Statuta ecclesiae antiqua* (ca. 475) c. 78 (65), CCSL 148, 178:190–91. Synchronicity for all major feasts, Agde (506) c. 21, CCSL 148, 202:196–203:205. Orléans IV (541) c. 1–2, CCSL 148A, 132:8–21: synchronicity of Easter and equal length for Lent. Auxerre (578–603 or 561–605) c. 2, CCSL 148A, 265:4–6, provides that all priests should send envoys (to their bishop) to learn when Lent will start and announce the date to the people at Epiphany. See the *Collection of Martin of Braga* cc. 63–64, Mansi 9.857.

according to an office united thanks to God's grace."[5] For the Gothic clergy, seventy years later at the Fourth Council of Toledo (633), territorial unity mysteriously relates to liturgical unity: One *ordo* will regulate all sacraments—psalmody and prayer, mass, vespers, and matins—for one liturgy (*ecclesiastica consuetudo*) should be held by those who are "contained in one faith and kingdom."[6] Consequently, the fathers will extend a Spanish observance to the (recently conquered) province of Galicia's churches "for the sake of the unity of peace."[7] The canons' high concern for the meticulous and seamless performance of ecclesiastical liturgy places them on a cultural continuum with late Roman conceptions of *religio*. The third-century A.D. grammarian Servius reports how, in the middle of the Apollinian games, a messenger had informed the Roman people of the sudden arrival of Hannibal's Carthaginian troops; to fend off the Punic threat, everyone had left the theater hurriedly. Yet even though he was no longer in the presence of any human audience, a lone mime had played his part all the way to the end, preventing a full break in the solemnity.[8] Liturgy was to be performed regardless of interruptions; should a priest or bishop, owing to sickness, suddenly falter during the consecration of the host, another cleric will immediately take up the eucharistic ceremony where the celebrant left off.[9] If the councils sought uniformity, it was perhaps to forestall manipulation, or, to call a spade a spade, individual clerics' use of the liturgy to serve ends different from those of the episcopal collective. The Thirteenth Council of Toledo documents the existence in Visigothic Spain of a liturgical protest we have already discussed, the clamor. But it is not with approval. The council's fathers condemned to deposition and enslavement

> those men who . . . when they consider themselves injured by some quarrel with their brethren, are immediately seized by an insane temerity, strip the altars, take off the sacred vestments, take away the luminaries, and impelled

---

[5] Braga I (563) second allocution, ed. Vives, *Concilios*, 70.

[6] Toledo IV (633) c. 2, ed. Vives, 188.

[7] Toledo IV (633) c. 9, ed. Vives, 194 (blessing lamps and tapers during vigils).

[8] See Florence Dupont, *L'acteur-roi* (Paris: 1985), 51. Servius, *In Vergilii carmina commentarii*, vols. 1–2: *Aeneidos librorum VI–XII commentarii* 8.110, ed. Georg Thilo (Leipzig: 1884), 2.214:29–215:6.

[9] Toledo VII (646) c. 2, ed. Vives, 253: "*Censemus igitur convenire, ut quum a sacerdotibus missarum tempore sancta mysteria consecrantur, si aegritudinis accidat cuiuslibet eventus quo coeptum nequeat consecrationis expleri misterium, sit liberum episcopo vel presbyteri alteri consecratione exequi officium coepti; non enim aliud ad supplementum sui initiatis mysteriis conpetit quam aut incipientis aut subsequentis completa benedictio sacerdotis, qua nec perfecta videri possunt nisi perfectionis ordine compleatur. Quum enim sumus omnes unum in Christo, nicil contrarium diversitas format, ubi efficaciam prosperitatis unitas fidei repraesentat: quod etiam consultum cuncti ordinis clerici indultum esse sibi non ambigant, sed ut praemissum est praecedentibus libenter alii pro complemento succedant.*" Toledo XI (675) c. 14, 366, asks officiants to provide for replacements in case of emergency.

by their evil-mindedness withdraw the cult of divine sacrifices. Thus, unable to avenge themselves on human beings, they [instead] impinge against God's rights, which is worse.[10]

The council's avowed logic exalted God above selfish ends, public worship over private vengeances. The same discourse, as we saw, would serve John VIII's East Frankish enemies in their condemnation of the 878 stripping of the altars.[11]

Synodal decrees have sometimes fossilized for our paleontological benefit a dialogue between the two powers. Works of historiography and hagiography were by nature monologues.[12] Yet they too could be meant to convey an image of the right relationship between *regnum* and *sacerdotium*. In one case at least, the image's crafter employed "rituals" (the liturgy, but other ceremonial forms as well) to give rhythm and power to his argument.[13] Gregory of Tours' *Ten Books of Histories* and hagiographical works will allow us to explore the narrative mustering of that harmony and consensus that consiliar canons considered necessary for the Christian community—the *ecclesia*.[14]

Gregory's ecclesiology owed much to an intellectual tradition associated with Ambrose of Milan.[15] Like Ambrose's successor Augustine, he thought in terms of the Two Cities. But their articulation is none too obvious. The *Libri Historiarum*'s preface opposing the holy deeds of the saints and martyrs to the kings' madness is famous; this dichotomy encompassed contem-

---

[10] Toledo XIII (683) c. 7, ed. Vives, 423–24. The council also condemns those clerics who would "cover the sacred altar with any other vestment of lugubrious nature."

[11] Above, ch. 2, 80–81.

[12] Marc Reydellet, *La royauté dans la littérature latine* (Rome: 1981), remains the best guide to this literary accommodation.

[13] Despite discussions with B. Jussen over his now published "Liturgie und Legitimation, oder: Wie die Gallo-Romanen das römische Reich beendeten," *Institutionen und Ereignis*, Veröffentlichungen des Max-Planck-Instituts für Geschichte 138, ed. Reinhard Blanker and Bernhard Jussen (Göttingen: 1998), 75–136, I remain convinced that Gregory testifies more to the situation at the end of the sixth century than to a process that took Gaul from 400 to 600.

[14] Most recent biography and bibliography in Ian Wood, *Gregory of Tours* (Bangor: 1994), and Martin Heinzelmann, *Gregor von Tours (538–94). "Zehn Bücher Geschichte". Historiographie und Gesellschaftskonzept im 6. Jahrhundert* (Darmstadt: 1994). See the table of abbreviations for the full references to Gregory's works. Henceforth, *LH* shall stand for the *Libri Historiarum Decem*; *VP* for *Vita Patrum*; *GM* for *Liber in Gloria Martyrum*; and *GC* for *Liber in Gloria Confessorum*. Adriaan H. B. Breukelaar, *Historiography and Episcopal Authority in Sixth-Century Gaul: The Histories of Gregory of Tours interpreted in their historical context*, Forschungen zur Kirchen- und Dogmengeschichte 57 (Göttingen: 1994), 54–55, repertories references in the *LH* to the other works; they prove that Gregory thought they were complementary.

[15] Jean-Rémi Palanque, *Saint Ambroise et l'Empire Romain. Contribution à l'histoire des rapports de l'Eglise et de l'Etat à la fin du quatrième siècle* (Paris: 1933).

porary bishops and rulers.[16] Like Ambrose, however, Gregory could look at kings as members of the *ecclesia*. No contradiction here, or at least none peculiar to him: With a logical consistency now lost to us, since at least Origen of Alexandria, Christian exegetes saw in kingship simultaneously an instrument of God and an instrument of the devil. But each wrote with different emphases depending on his political ideals and the individual rulers whom he faced.[17]

Gregory recognized that practically speaking bishops could not coerce kings. We learn much about his ideals as well as his sense of (unfortunate) effective limits in the *Histories'* chapter 5.18, which we shall return to, devoted to Bishop Praetextatus's trial at a council presided over by the evil Chilperic. De facto, only God, justice itself, could condemn the king.[18] Conversely, while the secular ruler could try bishops, such an action took place before an episcopal assembly and proceeded, in form as well as for penalties, according to the canons.[19] In a case in which he was personally concerned, Gregory cleared himself of the accusation by celebrating mass at three altars and then swearing an oath, but insisted that this form of purgation, while not as constricting as those required of laymen, still impinged on his canonical rights.[20] But if only God could condemn the king, it was because Chilperic, not rulers in general, refused to be corrected. Episcopal inability to judicially judge the secular ruler did not mean, however, that he should escape rebukes. For the bishop of Tours, Christendom

---

[16] As noticed by Walter Goffart, *The Narrators of Barbarian History* (A.D. 550–800): Jordanes, Gregory of Tours, Bede, and Paul the Deacon (Princeton: 1988), 233. See Chilperic's characterization as a new Diocletian, *LH* 4.47, 184:11–12.

[17] See Gerard Caspary, *Politics and Exegesis: Origen and the Two Swords* (Berkeley: 1979), and the application to Pope Gregory I, Carol Straw, *Gregory the Great: Perfection in Imperfection* (Berkeley: 1988).

[18] *LH* 5.18, 219:9–12: "*Si quid de nobis, o rex, iustitiae tramitem transcendere voluerit, a te corrigi potest; si vero tu excesseris, quis te corripiet? Loquimur enim tibi; sed si volueris, audis; si autem nolueris, quis te condemnavit, nisi is qui se pronuntiavit esse iustitiam?*" (Gregory speaking at Praetextatus's trial). But the author's exhortations to his episcopal colleagues in the same chapter (218:1–8) make clear that this inability to correct Chilperic is not normative; it owes everything to this *specific* king's evil character. I disagree here with Marc Reydellet, "Pensée et pratique politiques chez Grégoire de Tours," *Gregorio di Tours*, Centro di studi sulla spiritualità medievale, Convegno 12 (Todi: 1977), 181, 184–85 (opposing in a rather unmedieval way "une conception moralisante plutôt que politique," but cf. 195–96).

[19] See Praetextatus's trial, below at nn. 52f., as well as Guntram's judicial dealings with treacherous bishops. Late antique judicial practice put bishops accused of crimes under secular power's jurisdiction, yet they had to be judged in a synod; before the middle of the sixth century, the clergy sought to limit the reach of lay judges and tribunals and maintained that bishops could only be tried by their colleagues. See Paul Hinschius, *System der katholischen Kirchenrecht*, 6 vols. (Berlin: 1869–97), 4.794–97, 849–57. But much of Hinschius's data stems from the *LH*!

[20] *LH* 5.49, 260:27–261:9.

was divided in three orders, and the two leading groups, lay rulers and upper clergy, had mutual responsibilities. It pertained to saints (in Gregory's works not exclusively but overwhelmingly bishops) to educate, rebuke, and resist kings. Thus, the holy man Leobardus exercised "solicitous care vis-à-vis the people, judicial inquisition (*inquisitio*) vis-à-vis the kings, assiduous prayer for all ecclesiastics who feared God."[21] Of Nicetius bishop of Trier, Gregory writes that he "was very respected and honored by King Theuderic, because Nicetius had often revealed to Theuderic his sins in order to improve him through his reprimands."[22] Gregory himself harangued his peers during the council King Chilperic had convoked to judge one of their colleagues and exhorted them to vocal action. Being responsible ex officio for all souls, it was their episcopal duty to speak out, preach, and "put before the king's eyes his sins."[23] That cowardice led the council to another course of action should change nothing as to our appraisal of Gregory's ideology.

Gregory expressed this understanding not through explicit theorizing but rather through narrative patterns. Since Walter Goffart's *Narrators of Barbarian History* and especially Martin Heinzelmann's *Gregor von Tours*, it has become impossible to see in the *Histories* a mere series of confused episodes chaotically juxtaposed.[24] In his fundamental study, the German historian in particular has aptly revealed how carefully constructed Gregory's narrative is. While it may be that Heinzelmann overemphasizes the theme of harmonious cooperation between kings and bishops, he has made limpidly clear how the bishop of Tours has both a *Geschichtstheologie* and an ecclesiology concerned with the relationship of *regnum* to *sacerdotium*, and how this relationship is constructed through anecdotes.

The anecdotes's stage is often some ritual. Rituals are so present in Gregory of Tours's works that one might almost fail to see them. In the bleak worldly city that the *Histories* present, they often provide a setting for violence and bloodshed. Thus, Bishops Salonius and Sagittarius attack their episcopal neighbor of Saint-Paul-Trois-Châteaux during the banquet

---

[21] *VP* 20.3, 292:31–293:1; cf. James, 133: "*Tantum sensum acumine erudivit, ut miraretur facundia elocutionis eius. Erat enim dulcis alloquio, blandus hortatu, eratque ei sollicitudo pro populis, inquesitio pro regibus, oratio assidua pro omnibus ecclesiasticis deum timentibus.*"

[22] *VP* 17.1, 278:24–25; tr. James, 114.

[23] Gregory first tells them to give Chilperic a "*consilium sanctum atque sacerdotalem* [sic]," *LH* 5.18, 218:1–3, 5–8: "*Mementote, domini mi sacerdotes, verbi prophetici, quod ait, Si viderit speculator iniquitatem hominis et non dixerit, reus erit animae pereuntis* [Ez. 33.6]. *Ergo nolite silere, sed praedicate et ponite ante oculos regis peccata eius, ne forte ei aliquid mali contingat et vos rei sitis pro anima eius.*" Cf. also *VP* 5.2, 228–29, James, 49–50; and *LH* 7.22, 342:1–15. As Breukelaar, *Historiography*, 252–58, remarks, Gregory expresses here his conception of the balance of judicial power between *regnum* and *sacerdotium*.

[24] E.g., *Gregor*, 131, on a meaning that "bei isolierten Betrachtung der einzelnen Texte nicht sichtbar wird." See as well Breukelaar, *Historiography*, passim.

commemorating Victor's accession.²⁵ Thus, Kings Lothar and Childebert draw their dead brother Chlodomer's children to their death by pretending they want to make them kings.²⁶ Thus, Queen Fredegunda's agents murder Sigebert as he is ceremonially raised on a shield.²⁷

These anecdotes obey a general pattern. Rituals involving royalty or royal officials range across a spectrum encompassing the wholly negative but almost never reaching the wholly positive. At the one end, we find Chilperic's self-serving manipulation of ceremonial forms in Praetextatus of Rouen's trial, at the other, Guntram's adoption of episcopal liturgy to lead the Rogations against an epidemic. The greater majority of developed descriptions of rituals involving secular power cluster in the black negative; Guntram's rituals, which range from light gray to pure white, proportionally to his reliance on episcopal guidance, constitute a notable and meaningful exception. But neither is the clergy a simple ensemble with respect to salvation. There is not any neat fit between, on the one hand, the Augustinian two cities, and, on the other, kings and bishops. For Gregory as well as for his namesake Pope Gregory the Great, there is as well such a thing as a wicked, worldly ecclesiastical ruler. This explains that narratives implicating bishops in liturgy can be negative—thus Salonius and Sagittarius's expedition during their episcopal enemy's accession anniversary. A bad bishop's liturgy will fail—thus (implicitly, as ever so often) Cautinus of Clermont's Rogations.²⁸ Yet Gregory knows which is the better order within the *ecclesia*. The greater majority of episcopal rituals is placed in the positive, at or beyond the point defined by Guntram's Rogations. When set on the hagiographic marches between this world and Heaven, a borderland in the main controlled by saintly bishops, rituals tend to be harmonious occasions of civic consensus—both within the earthly community and between the saints and their terrestrial clients.

Partisanship moves Liudprand of Cremona to construct rituals in specific ways. He utilizes his political culture's values to attack or exalt individual rulers—the hated Berengar or the beloved Otto. Gregory is viscerally hostile to Chilperic, a grandson of Clovis, and to his wife Fredegunda. But unlike the hatreds expressed in the *Antapodosis*, those in the *Histories* aim well beyond individual persons. Reydellet errs in stating that Gregory criticizes only individuals, not institutions.²⁹ The bishop of Tours' bile did not

²⁵ *LH* 5.20, 227:11–14; Thorpe, 285.
²⁶ *LH* 3.18, 118:6–7; Thorpe, 180.
²⁷ *LH* 4.51, 188:10–15; Thorpe, 248.
²⁸ Contrast *LH* 4.5, 138:8–20 (instituted by Cautinus's predecessor Gallus *itinere pedestri* from Clermont to Brioude) and *LH* 4.13, 145:8–13 (Cautinus runs away *equo ascenso* out of fear during the ceremony *reliquo psallentio*). See Breukelaar, *Historiography*, 48.
²⁹ Reydellet, *La royauté*, 351. One should agree with Reydellet's well-proven thesis that Gregory is reconciled with the idea of a non-Roman monarchy.

originate in an inability to stomach Chilperic and Fredegunda's moral failings, but from an ecclesiology inseparable from conflict over political issues.[30] These, such as the royal taxation of episcopally run civitates, are unsurprising apples of discord given the power constellation obtaining in sub Roman Gaul. The sum total of Gregory's attacks against specific individuals and specific misdeeds constructs an argument against a specific form of monarchical rule. Avoidance of statements of principle in favor of suggestive mosaics characterizes the bishop's style: Edward James has shown how Gregory seeks to uphold ecclesiastical asylum not by proclaiming the general rule of its sanctity but by recounting a set of stories in which sanctuary violation is supernaturally punished. There, Gregory does not lay out explicitly his agenda, but he is clearly and specifically arguing against the *Theodosian Code*'s restrictive provisions. In this, as we shall see in the next chapter, he belonged to a longer Latin tradition.[31] Walter Goffart has also demonstrated a similar tactic vis-à-vis legal provisions protecting the Jews and especially their synagogues. Heirs of Roman legitimacy in the West, the so-called barbarian kings warranted the *Code*.[32]

Arguments about such problems were inextricably tied with contending models of the right relationship between *regnum* and *sacerdotium*. One camp's success on a specific issue validated its vision of the broader equilibrium; the vision conversely served to back positions on specifics. No wonder then that Gregory defended his general model of the *ecclesia* with the same narrative tactics he employed for asylum or Jewish status.

Both Gregory's position and the one he associated with Chilperic had been made possible by Gaul's destinies in Late Antiquity. Clovis's baptism had sealed an alliance between the Frankish kings and the Gallo-Roman aristocracy. The latter had, since roughly 400, reinvested its fortunes in church offices, especially the episcopacy. The alliance entailed a balance of power between kings and bishops south of the Loire, where the latter retained the greatest authority.[33] Like all equilibria constantly threatened and

---

[30] Reydellet, *La royauté*, 419. *Contra*: Heinzelmann, *Gregor*, 42–45.

[31] See below, ch. 4, 152–53.

[32] Edward James, "*Beati pacifici*: bishops and the law in sixth-century Gaul," in *Dispute and settlements: Law and human relations in the West*, ed. John Bossy (Cambridge: 1983), 25–46. See Walter Goffart, "The conversions of Avitus of Clermont, and similar passages in Gregory of Tours," repr. in his *Rome's Fall and After* (London: 1989), 298–99, and also Jacques Fontaine, "Hagiographie et politique, de Sulpice Sévère à Venance Fortunat," *Revue d'Histoire de l'Eglise de France* 62 (1976), 121 (on Sulpicius): "*L'ensemble de ces épisodes est loin de définir une idéologie politique en forme. Du moins ont-elles laissé une série d'exemples qui donnent une certaine 'image d'Epinal' du pouvoir temporel.*"

[33] For this divide, see most recently Raymond Van Dam, *Saints and Their Miracles in Late Antique Gaul* (Princeton: 1993), 1–50. The insights provided by Martin Heinzelmann, "Neue Aspekte der biographischen und hagiographischen Literatur in der lateinischen Welt (1.-6. Jahrhundert)," *Francia* 1 (1973): 27–44, allow one to see the issue in terms of local power

renegotiated, this balance of power spoke through a specific vocabulary. In the late fourth century, Ambrose of Milan had understood and expressed the relationship between emperor and Church in the language of Late Roman politics. The autocratic *dominus* governed without respect for the senatorial *mos maiorum* and the senatorial order's liberties. Analogically, a bad Christian ruler placed himself above the Church. In the Ambrosian model, religion (as interpreted by the bishops) provided the emperor with a bulwark against the temptations of autocracy. Such was the meaning of Ambrose's funeral oration on Theodosius. The imperial embrace of Christianity had granted the emperor supernatural protection (symbolized by the nail of the Holy Cross embedded in the imperial helmet) but also put a bridle into his mouth (symbolized by his horse bit, which also contained a nail). The role that had once pertained to senatorial liberties had devolved upon the collegial authority of the bishops, endowed with "free speech," *parrhésia*.[34] Gregory, following Ambrose, wished to guard against the real or imaginary dangers of what one may call a "Christian Dominate." This may explain a notable trait of his literary production, namely, that it by no means centers on the imperial idea and pays scant attention to the East.[35]

Although one cannot rule out that Gregory invented whole cloth his evidence for the sake of an audience that already disliked strong royal authority in Church matters, it is not improbable that the real Chilperic had sought to ape the Eastern rulers. Understandably—legitimacy still lay

---

versus royal power, in a fight for commemoration. On the authority of Clovis and his successors in Church matters, see Eugen Ewig, "Christliche Expansion im Merovingerreich," in *Kirchengeschichte als Missionsgeschichte*, ed. Heizgünter Frohnes et al., 2 vols. (Munich: 1973–78), vol. 2:1, *Die Kirche des früheren Mittelalters*, ed. Knut Schläferdiek, 126–27 (with bibliographical references n. 38): "Synodalhoheit mit Recht auf Einberufung und Vorgabe von Verhändlungsgegenständen ... Verfügungsgewalt über die Bistümer und ... Bindung des Zugangs zum geistlichen Amt an königliche Anordnung oder Genehmigung."

[34] *De obitu Theodosii* 40–51, ed. Otto Faller, CSEL 73 (Vienna: 1955), 392–98. On episcopal *parrhésia*, see now Peter Brown, *Power and Persuasion in Late Antiquity* (Madison: 1992), passim. For Ambrose, see Francis Dvornik, *Early Christian and Byzantine Political Philosophy: Origins and Background*, 2 vols., Dumbarton Oak Studies 9 (Washington DC: 1966), 2.672–83, esp. 2.674–75. The fiction of Christian moderation in governance was reactualized, albeit directed not against the ruler but against his rivals, with Charlemagne's *Libri Carolini*: The acts of the episcopal synod of Frankfurt posturingly and polemically denounced Byzantine government as absolutism, thus serving the hegemonic Frankish king's interests. See Eugen Ewig, "Zum christlichen Königsgedanken im Frühmittelalter," repr. in Ewig, *Spätantikes und fränkisches Gallien*, 2 vols. (Munich: 1976), 1.3–71, at 54–59, and I Deug-Su, *Cultura e ideologia nella prima età carolingia*, Istituto storico italiano per il medioevo, studi storici 146–47 (Rome: 1984).

[35] Goffart, *Narrators*, 223–24, notes that Gregory avoids all mention of Justinian, 160. (But see the hostile story in *GM* 102, 105–107, tr. Van Dam, 124–26.)

heavily with the Roman world. Ernst Stein detected long ago an echo of Tiberius's legislation in Chilperic's edicts.[36] Regardless of actual bonds and actual Byzantine exemplarity on Chilperic, the Chilperic of the *Histories* exemplifies and embodies this rejected Byzantine style of governance. Perhaps Gregory means to signify exactly this when he shows the king taking pride in a Byzantine gift.[37] His Chilperic is infested with vices traditionally associated in the West with the bad late Roman emperor.[38] Like Justinian, Chilperic intervenes in theological disputes: He seeks to redefine Trinitarian formulas.[39] He oversteps royal power's limits by seeking to convert the Jews. As Goffart has shown, this episode ends in unmitigated disaster and bloodshed, unlike the story that Gregory pairs with it, an episcopally-led conversion of the Jews. We shall return to these twinned narratives' liturgical components.[40] The king is shown involved in circus games—that is, with the wrong rituals. Indeed, Chilperic builds amphitheaters, *eosque populis spectaculum praebens*, a pursuit criticized indirectly through the apposed and opposite example of Tiberius II (d. 582). At his accession, prior to his coronation, the Byzantine emperor broke with custom: He did not proceed into the hippodrome to open circus games, but visited the shrines of the saints (God rewarded him, since a dangerous conspirator submitted to him after this).[41] The message of this diptych could not be clearer. First, as we

[36] Ernst Stein, *Studien zur Geschichte des byzantinischen Reiches* (Stuttgart: 1919), 108, 115 n.6; idem, "Des Tiberius Constantinus Novelle *Perì èpibolés* und der *Edictus domni Chilperici regis*," *Klio* 16 (1920), 72–74. See also Eugen Ewig, *Die Merowinger und das Imperium*, Rheinisch-Westfälische Akademie der Wissenschaften, Vorträge G.261 (Opladen: 1983), 33–40. Michel Rouche also argues for a tight *imitatio imperii* in his "Les baptêmes forcés des Juifs en Gaule mérovingienne et dans l'Empire d'Orient," *De l'antijudaïsme antique à l'antisémitisme contemporain*, ed. Valentin Nikiprowitzy (Lille: 1979), 105–24.

[37] *LH* 6.2, 266:17–267:3.

[38] See Goffart, *Narrators*, 223–24 and n. 484, idem, "Conversions," 297–300. Goffart also notes that Gregory systematically abases the mighty (*Narrators*, 209–11), and contrasts the instability implicit in the last scene involving royalty, *LH* 10.27–28, with the sempiternity suggested by the list of bishops in the final chapter, *LH* 10.31, 519–22, 526–36.

[39] In *LH* 5.43 Gregory discusses with an Arian, and in 5.44, Chilperic tries to impose an *indicolum* on the Trinity. Implicitly, Chilperic apes Gregory in invoking the authority of the patriarchs, the prophets, and the Law. Compare Gregory: "... *quam omnes patriarchae, prophetae, sive lex ipsa vel oraculis cecinit* ..." (ed. Krusch, 252:8–9) and Chilperic: "*sic* ... *prophetis ac patriarchis apparuit, sic enim ipsa lex nuntiavit*" (ed. Krusch, 253:3–4). See Goffart, "Conversions," 300. It was part and parcel of Merovingian kings' legitimacy to manifest interest in theology; Childebert I asked Pope Pelagius I to profess his orthodoxy (as the West understood it since Leo I) over the dispute of the Three Chapters. See Ewig, *Merowinger*, 15–17, with *Epp. Arelatenses* 48 and 53–54, MGH Epp. Merow. et Kar. Aevi 1 (Berlin: 1892), 70–72 and 76–80.

[40] See Goffart, "Conversions," 300–306, and below at n. 122.

[41] Gregory of Tours, *LH* 5.17, 5.30, 216:13–14, 235:5–12, with Heinzelmann, *Gregor*, 52, 126. Heinzelmann, 48, points out that the opposition between Tiberius and Chilperic is set

shall see in the following chapter, hagiographers had long opposed sanctity
(and especially martyrdom) to the rituals of the arena. Second, R. A. Markus has shown how the Church fathers, between 400 and 600, increasingly
made rejection of the *pompa diaboli* and *spectacula* a test of Catholicity.[42]
Tiberius thus falls on one side of the divide, Chilperic on the other. Finally,
Gregory highlights the king's disregard for the law of the Church—this
will be evident when we return to Praetextatus' trial.

AUTOCRATIC KINGSHIP AND MANIPULATED RITUALS: CHILPERIC

In the *Histories*, Chilperic stands for an autocracy that would extend itself
over religious matters rather than seek episcopal guidance. Gregory
stamps with a negative seal this kind of governance by, among other
means, underlining the ruler's readiness to manipulate ritual. Three episodes deserve detailed analysis; they deal respectively with *adventus*, divination, and law.

Chilperic's advent into Paris stands at the very midpoint of the *Sixth
Book of the Histories*, a location that signals that this chapter constitutes the
keystone of that book.[43] After Charibert's death (567), his three surviving
brothers, including Chilperic, had divided his kingdom and neutralized
his capital. They had sworn an agreement not to enter Paris without the
others' assent. *LH* 6.27 recounts and indicts Chilperic's transgression.
Right before Easter, the king makes his advent into Paris, "preceded by
the relics of many saints in order to avoid . . . the malediction written in
the pact." Among these saints may have been those who had warranted
the *pactiones*, Polyeuctes, Hilary, and Martin. If Chilperic involved Polyeuctes in this sham, it was a terribly bad idea, at least in Gregory's hagiographic universe: The saint was known to severely punish those who broke

---

up from the very beginning of the section devoted to this worst of Frankish kings, *LH* 5.2.
For Tiberius as a figure exemplifying the qualities Chilperic lacks, see as well Breukelaar,
Historiography, 234–35. On the amphitheater and Byzantine accession ceremonies, see Sabine
MacCormack, *Art and Ceremony in Late Antiquity* (Berkeley: 1981), 249–54 (for Corippus,
In laudem Iustini). In *LH* 5.17, Gregory may also be opposing Chilperic's circus games to the
rites of friendship binding Guntram and Childebert (kisses, enthronement, banquet, gifts),
their proposal to resolve territorial dispute if necessary by God's judgment on the battlefield.

[42] Robert A. Markus, *The End of Ancient Christianity* (Cambridge: 1990), and the same's
programatic "The sacred and the secular: from Augustine to Gregory the Great," *Journal of
Theological Studies*, n.s. 36:1 (1985), 84–96. See below, ch. 4. But the games had several ideological valences. Procopius, reporting that Frankish rulers watched horse races in Arles, took
it not as a sign of impiety but as a signal of their usurpation of the *imperium*, along with the
minting of coins in their own effigy. See Procopius, *Gothic Wars*, in *History of the Wars* 7.33,
tr. H. B. Dewing, 7 vols. (London: 1914–40), 4.438:6.

[43] Heinzelmann, *Gregor*, 132.

oaths sworn in his name. Furthermore, as bishop of Tours, Gregory could not take lightly the slight on his own Martin, and on Hilary, whose devotee he was. Gregory specified the date of Chilperic's *adventus*: before Easter. He may have meant to accuse the king of parodying Christ's advent into Jerusalem on Palm Sunday. But Chilperic himself was probably only following the canons of royal ceremonial.[44] The *Libri historiarum* placed the final words concerning this event in a royal mouth: According to Chilperic's brother Guntram, this manipulation led directly to the perpetrator's death.[45]

A second episode is devoted to, and structured by, rituals of divination. The king's rebellious son Merovech has sought asylum in Saint Martin's basilica in Tours. Merovech and his faithless accomplice Guntram Boso pace about and search for ways out of the dead end in which they have put themselves. Both turn to divination—Guntram Boso to a rustic witch, who predicts him unhoped-for successes. Merovech consults twice his host, Bishop Gregory, or rather the Bible through episcopal mediation. The two rebels are not the only ones in this single chapter to get guidance from above or attempt to communicate with the supernatural. So as to capture Merovech, Chilperic hopes to be allowed to violate the asylum the saint guarantees. He sends an envoy to Tours with a letter to Martin, to be deposited on the altar of the basilica with a blank piece of parchment. The king expects Tours's saintly patron to give his position in writing on a (to Gregory evident) point of canon law: whether he, Chilperic, might be allowed to forcibly expel his son from sanctuary. Martin does not deign to give an answer.[46]

Besides indicting Chilperic, chapter 5.14 serves a didactic purpose—to convey a lesson concerning access to truth. Supernatural messages are sought or obtained five times; the central and third benefits Gregory, gracing him with a personal vision; the narrative arranges the other four in an onionlike structure around it:

---

[44] Chilperic may have been following normal royal practice. See, for a later era, Hans-Martin Schaller, "Der heilige Tag als Termin mittelalterlicher Staatsakte," *DA* 30, 1 (1974), 1–24.

[45] *LH* 6.27, 295; cf. 7.6, 329:10–19. For Polyeuctes, see *GM* 102, 105:20–24, Van Dam, 124.

[46] *LH* 5.14, 207–13, at 211:15–212:2, Thorpe, 269. On asylum as an apple of discord between bishops and kings, see above, n. 30. Gregory seems to be hinting as well that Chilperic expected him to collaborate [in the French sense of the term] and forge a favorable Martinian answer. No lesser an authority figure than Clovis prescribed the death penalty for people of any order who trusted in *divinatio, auguria, sortes qua mentiuntur esse sanctorum* at the council of Orléans I (511), c. 30, CCSL 148A, 12:173–76, whose agenda he had defined; cf. closer to Gregory's time, Auxerre (573/603 or 561/605), c. 4, CCSL 148A, 265:13–16. On this text, see Jussen, "Liturgie und Legitimation," 126–29. But *LH* 5.14 seems to me more aimed at princes than at female prophetesses. Gender is instrumentalized.

1. Gregory reads a biblical passage for Merovech but the latter cannot see patent truth.[47]
2. Guntram consults a prophetess; her false speech deceives him.[48]
3. Gregory has a vision (true sight).[49]
4. Chilperic consults Martin; the saint remains tellingly silent.[50]
5. Merovech opens three biblical books and sees his true fate.[51]

In the first and fifth attempts, Merovech, whom Gregory assists, employs the ritual of the *sortes biblicae*, that is, opens the Bible to find out his fate. On the initial one, he remains obdurately blind to God's message. On the last, his woeful future jumps to his eyes. Guntram Boso and Chilperic are the actors of the second and fourth attempts. Guntram Boso gets a long and false prophecy from the pythonissa; Martin spurns Chilperic. The woman's patently false predictions stand opposed to the truthful Christian rites of divination. In all cases but the third, central one, information is, or would be mediated. Only Gregory can directly access truth. Structurally at least, the bishop's vision makes Merovech pass from blindness to sight. The two episodes placed immediately before and after the vision frame it and are meant to be read in conjunction. Guntram Boso and Chilperic's failures mean that without episcopal mediation, *potentes* will hear only the lying speech of pagan superstition or the saints' reproachful silence. Left to themselves, secular officials, like the pagans of yore, treat the saints' relics like magical objects that can be handled to give automatic results. The saints naturally resist such attempts.[52] Chilperic's attempt is thus both manipulative and misguided, being opposed to the God-given order that regulates access to truth in a Christian society.

Praetextatus' trial provides a third case of Chilperic's misguided handling of rituals. Recounted by the longest chapter in the *Histories*, 5.18, it calls for a detailed analysis. Praetextatus has incurred Queen Fredegunda's hatred. Her husband Chilperic summons a council to convict him of treason: The bishop will be accused of conspiring with the queen of a rival

---

[47] *LH* 5.14, 210:2–3: "*Illo quoque non intelligente, consideravi hunc versiculum ad Dominum praeparatum.*"

[48] *LH* 5.14, 210:4–17.

[49] *LH* 5.14, 210:17–211:4: "*Denique . . . Cum autem haec in posterum impleta fuissent, tunc a liquidum cognovi, falsa esse quae promiserant arioli.*"

[50] *LH* 5.14, 211:15–212:2.

[51] *LH* 5.14, 211:5–17: "*Merovechus vero non credens phitonissae . . . In his responsibus ille confusus, flens diutissime ad sepulchrum beati antestetis. . . .*" See Breukelaar, *Historiography*, 246–47, for a similar analysis.

[52] Gregory's hagiography is filled with examples of frightened secular magnates who would buy off holy anger yet meet a deserved death: *GC* 66, 67, 337–38, tr. Van Dam, 72–73; *GC* 70, 338–39, tr. Van Dam, 74–75; *GC* 78, 345:3–21, tr. Van Dam, 81–82; *GM* 78, 90–91, tr. Van Dam, 101–103.

kingdom, Brunechildis, and another rebellious son of Chilperic, Chramm. The greater majority of the bishops are ready to abandon their colleague and willing to let the king have his way. Only Gregory resists—in Ambrosian fashion—Chilperic's will. His speeches, ironic to the king, exhortative to his colleagues, define the mutual powers in judicial matters of the *ecclesia*'s two leading orders.[53]

To impose this interpretation, Gregory the author presents Chilperic as an evil manipulator of two political rituals, the popular denunciation of a bad official and prostration in the hope for pardon. Karl Hauck has well analyzed the subepisode devoted to the first manipulation. Furious at the bishop's resistance, the irate king threatens to organize a popular demonstration in Tours against Gregory; a claque will enter into a dialogue with the king and shout hostile slogans (*vociferare*) according to a set script. Chilperic refers here to an established practice. In Late Antiquity, public officials had to take popular *voces*, orchestrated or not, seriously; reported to their superiors, they could make the difference between rewards or punishments. In 331 Constantine had decreed that popular acclamations praising or blaming governors were to be recorded and transmitted to him "if they are truthful *voces* and not spread by client-groups."[54] Chilperic, then, is threatening to have his agents pretend to represent the people of Tours's consensus and complain that their bishop is not fulfilling equitably his judicial duties. As he tells Gregory, this should ensure

> ". . . that you may be marked out to be infamous (*noteris*) among the people, and that it may be fully obvious that you are unjust to all. For I shall convoke the people of Tours and tell them: 'Shout slogans (*voceferamini*) against Gregory, and say that he is unjust and grants justice to no man.' And, after they have shouted this, I shall answer them: 'How can you, who are smaller men, [expect justice from Gregory when] I, who am king, cannot find justice from him?' "[55]

Gregory counters that it will be evident to all that the demonstration is a sham organized by the king. Thus, Chilperic, not Gregory, will be publicly made infamous (*notaberis*).[56] Cowed by this retort, the king backs down and

[53] Sycophantic bishops also belong to the hagiographic—even Martinian—tradition: Fontaine, "Hagiographie et politique," 118. On this episode, Ian N. Wood, "The secret histories of Gregory of Tours," *Revue Belge de Philologie et d'Histoire* 71:2 (1993): 253–70, at 268–69.

[54] *Codex Theodosianus* I.xvi.6 (see CTh VIII.v.32), analyzed by Cameron, *Circus Factions*, 238–41, and Charlotte Roueché, "Acclamations in the Later Roman Empire," *Journal of Roman Studies* 74 (1984): 186–87. Constantine's words parallel *Severus Alexander* 22.6, in *Scriptores Historiae Augustae*, 2 vols., ed. Ernst Hohl, et al. (Leipzig: 1965), 1.267:16–21, where Severus honors and rewards "*praesides provinciarum, quos vere, non factionibus laudari comperit.*"

[55] *LH* 5.18, 219:13–18; with Karl Hauck, "Von einer spätantiken Randkultur zum karolingischen Europa," *FMSt* 1 (1967): 42–43.

[56] *LH* 5.18, 219:19–220:1: "*Quod vero falso clamore populo, te insultante, vociferat, nihil est, quia sciunt omnes a te haec emissa. Ideoque non ego, sed potius tu in adclamatione notaberis.*"

gives up the idea. But he fails to avoid infamy, at least in the *Histories*. The text, as it were, "marked him out" as a ruler willing to use a claque to propagate untruths.

In the *Histories*, the king is not the only character to try to benefit from popular demonstrations (nor, as we shall see shortly, was Chilperic's figure isolated in the Late Roman and Byzantine political imaginary). Public pressure could profit a bishop who faced a king. When Gregory stood accused of slandering Queen Fredegunda, the people began to growl, wondering aloud, "Why are these things impuned to the bishop of God? Why is the king prosecuting these charges? [etc.]."[57] Just as much as the encroaching *potestas extera*, rebellious and ambitious priests threatened any bishop from inside his church. Dissatisfied with an appointment, the priest Cato ordered a group of poor (*pauperum caterva*) to shout out (*clamorem dari praecepit*): "Why are you abandoning us, your sons, good father? [etc.]." In and of itself, the text of such slogans does not provide the clue that they are manipulated. Almost the same words mourned the agony of a holy bishop: "Why are you abandoning us, good shepherd? [etc.]."[58] The only means of differentiating between honesty and stage management lay in suggesting spontaneity or imputing agency.[59] Devilish imitation readily and effectively fakes the ritual symptoms of good consensus. Understandably, then, it takes the eye of an expert (Bishop Gregory) to distinguish between true and counterfeit ritual.

Manipulated crowds shouting prearranged slogans belonged to the inheritance shared by the Latin West and the Byzantine East. The *Life of Stephen the Younger*, written in 808 by the saint's namesake Stephen the Deacon, culminates in the martyrdom of the iconodule Stephen (Nov. 20, 764), abbot of the Auxentian monastery near Nicomedia, at the hands of the courtiers loyal to the iconoclast emperor Constantine V (741–75). What interests us here is Constantine's earlier attempt, in 762, to engineer Abbot Stephen's downfall. The emperor first commands his courtier George Syncletos to associate with the holy man, become one of his monks, and receive the tonsure from him. Constantine then convokes the people in the hippodrome for an assembly (*selention*). There, staging a dialogue with his subjects, he complains that his enemies have kidnapped George. The people roar that the guilty party should be bitterly punished. A few days later, at another assembly—a motley crowd encompassing (ridicu-

---

[57] *LH* 5.49, 260:32–261:2.

[58] *LH* 4.11, 2.23, 142:3–9, 68:22–27. For parallel passages, see Felix Thürlemann, *Der historische Diskurs bei Gregor von Tours: Topos und Wirklichkeit*. Geist und Werk der Zeiten 39 (Frankfurt am Main: 1974), 102–104. For ambitious priests miraculously controlled, see also infra, at n. 125.

[59] See Rouché, "Acclamations," 184, 187. See chapter 4, at nn. 21, 32.

lously) all age groups from the elderly to the newborns, and (not a good thing) mixing men and women—the emperor announces that thanks to a revelation, he has been able to recover his courtier. The emperor produces George, dressed as a monk. As the people clamor the Jews' slogan (*phōnēn*) "Crucify him," George is stripped of the habit and his monastic baptism is erased by a sort of second baptism. The courtier is then dressed back in the garb of the military aristocracy, with helm (*perikephalaian*) and soldier's vestment (*stratiōtikon*). Constantine himself attaches George's sword [through a belt] to his shoulders.[60] Aroused by this ceremony, the mob rushes out to burn Stephen's monastery. The reference to Christ's martyrdom, the monstrous rebaptism, the inversion of right order, which transforms into a soldier with the *cingulum militare* a man who had belonged to the higher calling of monasticism: All of this points to the shamelessness of a ruler who does not shy from manipulating rituals.

Gregory of Tours's portrait places Chilperic squarely in this gallery of impious kings. Further down in chapter 5.18, the wicked ruler manipulates the ritual of humiliation and pardon. Chilperic, in a first round, has been defeated by Pratextatus' refusal to admit his guilt. He tries to trap him through the use of another, well-established ritual, whose stage he sets with the help of two bishops. Their Turonian colleague has no lost love for them; we are given all the elements to deduce that they are Bertramm of Bordeaux and Ragnemod of Paris (future godfather to one of the king's sons, Theoderic).[61] Chilperic orders these two men to go to Praetextatus, and to tell him, "as if you were giving him your own advice,"

'You know that King Chilperic is pious, touched by compunction, and quickly swayed to mercy; humble yourself at his feet (*sub eo*) and say that you perpetrated these things he alleges. Then all of us, prostrate at his feet, will beseech him to give you his pardon'[62]

---

[60] *Vita sancti Stephani iunioris*, PG 100, 1070–1186, here 1131–37, with Cameron, *Circus Factions*, 302–303. I have been unable to consult the ed. and French translation by M.-F. Auzépy, *La Vie d'Etienne le Jeune* (Aldershot: 1997). See Charles Diehl, "Une vie de saint de l'époque des empereurs iconoclastes," Académie des Inscriptions et Belles-Lettres, *Comptes rendus des séances de l'année 1915* (Paris: 1915), 134–50. See Ihor Sevcenko, "Hagiography of the Iconoclast Period," repr. in *his Ideology, Letters and Culture in the Byzantine World* (London: 1982), at 4–5, 21 and nn, as well as Gilbert Dagron, *Empereur et prêtre. Etude sur le "césaropapisme" byzantin* (Paris: 1996), 195–96.

[61] Compare *LH* 5.18, 219:1–2: "*duo tamen adulatores ex ipsis—quod de episcopis dici dolendum est . . .*" with ibidem, 219:4–5: "*ad dexteram eius Berthramnus episcopus, ad levam vero Ragnemodus . . .*" They are probably also to be identified with some of the *quosdam de adolatoribus suis* (*LH* 5.18, 222:6–7) who deceive Praetextatus by promising him ritual help at the council (they have to be partakers in the council if they can promise that they will fall at the king's feet). Cf. *LH* 6.27, 295:5–6: Ragnemod was *compater* to Chilperic.

[62] *LH* 5.18, 222:8–13.

"Deluded by these words," Praetextatus accepts. What exactly is he deluded into? Chilperic's sycophants effectively convey to their episcopal colleague Praetextatus a proposal to agree in advance of the council's next session on a ritual. Episcopal self-humiliation will trigger royal pardon. Bertramm and Ragnemod promise that the bishops will unite and force the king's hand by joining in the bishop of Rouen's prostration. The offer can only seem reasonable; given the strength of Praetextatus' position, the ritual will allow Chilperic to save face; simultaneously, the bishop will regain favor. His victory would not be politically expedient. Were he cleared by his colleagues at the expense of the royal dignity, Praetextatus could only expect the king's hatred.

As in Ottonian and Salian Germany,[63] self-abasements mediated in avance were common in the world of Gregory of Tours. Later in the *Histories*, the reader will meet count Leudast and the Visigothic prince Hermenegild. Leudast, a former count of Tours, having slandered Queen Fredegunda's virtue, had lost royal grace. He obtained, thanks to the magnates' plea and mediation (*depraecante omni populo*), an audience with King Chilperic, at whose feet he prostrated himself in a call for mercy. But it was utter foolishness on his part to try a few days later to regain Fredegunda's grace by prostrating himself at her feet in church without a prearranged understanding. As we shall see, it led to his death.[64] We learn elsewhere in the *Histories* that the specific degree of self-abasement could be negotiated, even, it seems, fixed by oath. Hermenegild, having unsuccessfully rebelled against his father Leovigild, the ruling king, opened negotiations with him through his brother Reccared. Comforted by the mediator's oath, Hermenegild expected that Leovigild would not humiliate him to the point of despoiling him of the trappings of his rank. He was deceived. Stripped of his royal vestments, he was sent into exile with only one servant—not a fitting retinue for a king's son.[65] Other sources confirm that there was, in sixth-century Merovingian Gaul, an economy of mutual public prostrations, often in holy places, that served political actors to save face. It well antedates the phenomenon identified for eleventh-century Loire valley

---

[63] See, among other works by the same, Gerd Althoff, "Demonstration und Inszenierung. Spielregeln der Kommunikation in mittelalterlicher Öffentlichkeit," reed. in his *Spielregeln der Politik*, 229–57.

[64] *LH* 6.32, 302–304.

[65] *LH* 5.38, 245:9–15: "*Leuvichildus misit ad eum* [Hermanagildem] *fratrem eius* [Reccaredem], *qui, data sacramenta ne humiliaretur, ait, 'Tu accede et prosternere pedibus patris nostri, et omnia indulget tibi'. At ille poposcit vocare patrem suum, quo ingrediente* [aecclesiam], *prostravit se ad pedes illius. Ille vero adpraehensum osculavit eum et blandis sermonibus delinitum duxit ad castra; oblitusque sacramenti, innuit suis et adpraehensum expoliavit eum ab indumentis suis induitque illum veste villo; regressusque ad urbem Tolidus, ablatis pueris eius, misit eum in exilio cum uno tantum puerolo.*"

France.[66] In her *Vita Radegundis*, the nun Baudovina recounts how saint Radegund and the husband from whom she had fled, King Lothar, negotiated her new status. A mediator was involved. Bishop Germanus of Auxerre prostrated himself, "weeping, before Saint Martin's tomb," at the feet of Lothar, and beseeched him on Radegund's part not to snatch her from her monastery. This plea and these gestures were reciprocated with Lothar's own display of sorrow, counterprostration at Germanus's feet "on the threshold of [the church of] Saint-Martin," and admission of guilt. Finally, the king sent the bishop to Poitiers to prostrate himself at Radegund's feet and ask her to forgive him.[67] And so it was done, reinstating some equilibrium and the honor of all parties.

In *Histories* 5.18, then, the episcopal envoys are proposing to stage a ritual whose potential meanings were well established in contemporary political culture. Negotiation bore on the specific interpretations to be attached to the parties' gestures. On this basis, the council resumes on the following morning. The controversy between bishop and king rises to new heights—an escalation that prepares the dramatic atmosphere that makes meaningful a ritual of pardon.[68] Unexpectedly—for the innocent observer—"Bishop Praetextatus prostrated himself to the ground and said, 'I sinned in Heaven and against you, O most merciful (*o rex misericordissime*) king; I am a horrible murderer; I sought to kill you and to elevate your son to your throne.'" Pratextatus is playing his role with appropriate gestures (the agreed-upon prostration) and speech (hyperbolic self-accusation and call on the ruler's *misericordia*). The *o rex misericordissime* answers the sycophants' promise, *rex . . . cito flectatur ad misericordiam*; it signals to the bishop's colleagues and stage partners that it is their turn to enter the play. But the bishop (and possibly the others as well) is a dupe; Chilperic, unexpectedly—for Praetextatus—intervenes in the script and forestalls any further appeal to his mercy:

> As [Praetextatus] said this, the king prostrated himself at the bishops' feet, and said: "Hear, o most pious bishops! This execrable man confesses himself guilty of this crime!"[69]

---

[66] See Koziol, *Begging Pardon*, 233ff. The works of Treitinger (as n. 86) and Alföldi (as n. 112), document widespread historical and literary antecedents to "begging pardon and favor."

[67] Baudovinia, *Vita sanctae Radegundis* 2.7, ed. Bruno Krusch, SS rer. Merov. 2 (Hannover: 1888), 382:12–25: "[Germanus episcopus] *vir deo plenus, lacrimans prosternit se pedibus regais ante sepulchrum beati Martini cum contestatione divina . . . Sic rex . . . poenitentia ductus . . . prosternit se et illi ante limina sancti Martini pedibus apostolici viri Germani, rogat ut sic pro ipso veniam peteret beatae Radegundis, ut . . . Sic vir apostolicus dominus Germanus Pictavis veniens, ingressus in monasterium, in oratorium dominae Mariae nomini dedicatum prosternit se ad sanctae reginae pedes, pro rege veniam poscens . . .*"

[68] As elegantly suggested by Koziol, *Begging Pardon*, 311–16.

[69] *LH* 5.18, 222:21–23.

John Lackland would later be accused of a similar tactic with a similar objective: To avoid granting pardon to a bishop, the king negated an episcopal prostration with his own.[70] But we do not need the twelfth century for parallels. Leudast's demise provides us with a contemporary example that involves Chilperic's very family: After the ex-count had thrown himself at Fredegunda's feet in the church, the hostile queen burst into tears and riposted with a similar counterprostration.[71] In *Histories* 5.18, the royal abasement triggers a collective episcopal reaction. The bishops follow Chilperic's hidden ritual agenda and let loose a flow of tears, not for their colleague but for the wounded majesty: "[W]eeping, they raised up the king from the ground."[72] Praetextatus is condemned on the strength of his confession and of a collection of canons forged overnight.[73]

Gregory's Praetextatus, soon roughed up and sent into exile, is a worthy companion to the Byzantine hagiographer's Stephen the Younger. For the Merovingian reader of the *Histories*, Chilperic would have stood indicted as willing to pervert one of the most useful ritual forms of reconciliation available to sixth-century political society. Manipulated rituals, like counterfeit miracles, signaled that the manipulator was dominated by *libido dominandi* and, as such, a tyrant unfit to rule. Chilperic was punished—as Gregory subtly indicates in the chapter heading summarizing the incident, "Concerning Bishop Praetextatus and the death of Merovech."[74] God's hand struck the wicked king in his own son.

GOOD KINGSHIP'S UPPER LIMIT: GUNTRAM'S RITUALS

Bad King Chilperic means bad rituality. How does "good King" Guntram handle rituals? For Gregory, royal power necessarily falls short of the ideal,[75] especially when it rejects the cooperation and guidance of good

---

[70] See J. E. A. Joliffe, *Angevin Kingship*, 2d ed. (London: 1955), 102, n.1, citing the *Canterbury Chronicle*, ed. W. Stubbs, II, 59: "*Rex vicissim procidit ad pedes eius* [archiepiscopi] *et ridendo et irridendo dixit, 'Ecce, tantum tibi feci quantum tu mihi.'* "

[71] *LH* 6.32, 303:4–11.

[72] *LH* 5.18, 222:23.

[73] *LH* 5.18, 222:23–223:9.

[74] As pointed out by Heinzelmann, *Gregor*, 105.

[75] See Heinzelmann, *Gregor*, 128–29: "Die geringere Durchschlagskraft [compared to Die Abgeschlossenheit und Kohärenz der Darstellung einer schlechten Königsherrschaft am Beispiel von Leben und Tod Chilperics] bezüglich des Themas 'der gute König' liegt . . . auch an der theologisch-typologischen Deutung, die einer solchen Königsherrschaft im Rahmen der ecclesia-Ideologie unseres Autors tatsächlich zukommen konnte. So stellte für den Theologen Gregor die Beschreibung der christlichen Gesellschaft ('ecclesia') unter einem "wahrhaft christlichen" König zwar ein anstrebbares Ziel dar, gleichzeitig war ihm jedoch voll bewusst, dass die endgültige Realisierung eines solchen idealen Projektes nicht in der Gegenwartsgesellschaft, sondern erst zum Zeitpunkt des Jüngsten Gerichts möglich sein

bishops. Hence, even in "good King" Guntram's case, a feeling of danger and incomplete consensus overshadows royal rituals. It is only when the king conforms to the episcopal model because he adopts episcopal values that his rituals near (and in one case reach) seamlessness.

Historiography and Merovingian Rituals

There exists a gap between Gregory's constructions and sixth-century practices. The bishop downplays the participation of kings as a group in rituals (especially the liturgy). Gregory's aims are twofold: to exalt the chosen few in that group (Guntram) and to highlight purely ecclesiastical rites. Historians often place the beginnings of a "Christian kingship" (whatever this may mean) with the Carolingians. Henri Pirenne thus contrasted the *état profane mérovingien* and the *état religieux carolingien*. This is partly the product of the convergence of two points of view, or rather of two refusals to see: Both Merovingian churchmen and Carolingian historiography desired to downplay the piety of Merovingian royalty. The Carolingians' ability to obfuscate the qualities of both predecessors and contemporary rivals could still deceive the like of Eugen Ewig. The great early medievalist drew on *The Fourth Book of the Chronicle of Fredegar* and on the *Liber historiae Francorum*, two pro-Carolingian sources, to argue that the monarchy's "christianization" had proceeded very slowly since Clovis's baptism. There was a telling acceleration: The process had picked up during the first half of the seventh century, but then dropped back *ins Stocken*. This short-lived jump in royal use of Christian forms corresponded to an era of Pippinid influence: The Carolingians' ancestors stood behind the throne of the Merovingian Dagobert, subking in Austrasia.[76] But this seeming surge may be more a product of Carolingian historiography, eager to highlight ancestral piety to the detriment of rivals, than the reflection of an actual evolution over time or of the actual "advance" in religio-political matters of a lone aristocratic kindred, the Pippinids/Carolingians.

In recent years, increasingly, the veil with which Carolingian-era writers covered Merovingian kingship has been rent. Not only did it hide, it also distorted. Worst of all, perhaps, it made the deposed Merovingians look like half-pagans, and Merovingian Francia half-christianized. Carolingian historiography retroactively invalidated as well the Merovingians' right to

---

'würde.' I would insist that this very incompleteness is a critical part of Gregory's ideology of kingship, well suited to his real and ideal interests. Let us note here that if, for Gregory, Guntram is the "good king," Venantius Fortunatus does not shy from calling, in the context of a synod, Chilperic *rex bone*; see *Carmen* 9.1, v. 55, ed. Friedrich Leo, MGH Auctores Antiquissimi 4 (Berlin: 1881), 202.

[76] Henri Pirenne, *Mahomet et Charlemagne*, 4th ed. (Paris and Bruxelles: 1937). See Ewig's comments in "Zum christlichen Königsgedanken," 17, 20–21.

rule by depicting a perverse relationship between *nomen* and *mos*, between power and ceremony. Such was the opening argument of Einhardt's *Vita Karoli*. If one follows Karl Hauck, this well-known description of a lazy ruler transported in a peasant oxcart to the Franks' yearly assembly caricatured almost beyond recognition a royal ceremonial, the circuit (*Umritt*) of the land. According to Einhardt, when festively receiving ambassadors in the royal hall or presiding assemblies of the realm, the Merovingian kings were only puppets. Behind the throne, the Carolingian mayors of the palace orchestrated everything. Otherwise put, Merovingian kings almost never participated in public rituals, and when they appeared to do so they had little actual control over them. By the first quarter of the ninth century, when Einhardt redacted the *Vita*, this had long been the official Carolingian version.[77] Thus the *Annals of Lorsch*:

> They didn't have any *potestas* in the kingdom but for the fact that charters and privileges were written under their name; they had hardly any royal *potestas* but did what the Franks' mayor of the palace wanted. On the day of the Marchfield, according to the age-old custom (*secundum antiquam consuetudinem*), the people offered gifts to the kings; on that day, the king sat on the royal throne, the army stood around him in a circle, and the mayor of the palace stood before him. [The king] ordered whatever the Franks had decreed. But on the next as on the following days, he sat at home.[78]

As for Merovingian historiography, what survives Carolingian rewritings was characteristically reluctant to exalt kingship, because the churchmen who produced it—chief of them Gregory—saw in the *regnum* a necessary but rival order. Yet fragmentary evidence suggests that the Merovingian reality differed from what competitors, contemporary or posterior, depicted. Frankish kings employed the then-current liturgical language to present their authority; and conversely, some local churchmen sought to exalt their saints by an association with royalty. A prime example of this can be found in royal burials *ad sanctos* (downplayed in the *Histories*) and the liturgy commemorating the royal family. According to hagiography,

---

[77] Einhardt, *Vita Karoli* c. 1, ed. Louis Halphen (Paris: 1923), 8–10, "*ut speciem dominantis effingeret*" (to fake the appearance of a ruler). See Hauck, "Von einer spätantiken Randkultur," 37. For a redatation of the *Vita*, and otherwise considerations very germane to this essay, see Matthew Innes and Rosamond McKitterick, "The writing of history," in Rosamond McKitterick, ed., *Carolingian culture: emulation and innovation* (Cambridge: 1994), 193–220, at 204–207. For Carolingian obfuscations, see Patrick J. Geary's concluding remarks to his *Before France and Germany* (New York: 1988), and Ian N. Wood, *The Merovingian Kingdoms: 450–751* (London: 1993), as well as Patrick Geary, Stephane Lebecq, and John J. Contreni in *French Historical Studies* 19, 3 (1996): 755–84; Felice Lifshitz, *The Norman Conquest of Pious Neustria. Historiographic Discourse and Sanity Relics 684–1090* (Toronto: 1995), 11–12; Yitzak Hen, *Culture and Religion in Merovingian Gaul, A.D. 481–751* (Leiden: 1995), 197–205.

[78] *Annales Laurissenses minores ad an.* 753 [750], MGH SS 1, 116:7–21.

several of Clovis's sons each favored his chosen saintly bishop, sought his conversation, erected a church over his tomb, and had themselves buried near him. The *vitae* attest to local interest in royal piety, and the liturgy for the dead, to royal interest in saintly intercession. It has even been asserted that the highest ranking churches in the Frankish kingdom, the *basilicae maiores*, obtained their preeminence thanks to the tombs of kings they contained.[79] The *Life* of a former queen converted to the monastic life, Radegund, documents royal participation in the liturgy. When she became a nun, Radegund "divested herself of the noble costume which she was wont to wear as queen when she walked in procession on the day of a festival with her train of attendants."[80] Radegund's hagiographer, Venantius Fortunatus, has left in his panegyristic poems a trove of information on Merovingian liturgical practices, involving kings, queens, and their aristocracy.[81] They were so much part of the routine of royalty that a king, when minor, might be represented by one of his followers in their performance. Fortunatus praised one Count Sigoald "who fed the poor for the king's sake," in the hope that God would grant this youngster, Childebert, long life and that he may stand at the summit of rulership; Sigoald, further, represented Childebert at "sacred festivals" to provide for thousands of infirms.[82]

Finally, Frankish kings could not but emulate those to whom they were tied by marriage or rivalry, and a glance at neighboring realms reveals the liveliness of liturgical idioms. Even nations such as the Lombards, whose historiography labors under handicaps similar to the Merovingians (for why should popes or Byzantines have cared to highlight the kings of Pavia's

---

[79] See Karl Heinrich Krüger, *Königsgrabkirchen der Franken, Angelsachsen und Langobarden bis zur Mitte des 8. Jahrhunderts*, Münstersche Mittelalter-Schriften 4 (Munich: 1971).

[80] Venantius Fortunatus, *Vita sanctae Radegundis* 1.13, MGH SS rer. Merov. 2 (Hannover: 1888), 369:1–3.

[81] *Carmen* 6.6, "De horto Ultrogothonis," v. 19, ed. Friedrich Leo, MGH Auctores Antiquissimi 4 (Berlin: 1881), 147, tells of Childebert's visits to the saints' shrines: "*hinc iter eius erat, cum limina sancta petebat.*" Queen Theudechild behaves like Radegund in providing for orphans and widows and, like her, "hides her gifts to her fellows out of fear they would forbid them" (*Carmen* 4.25, vv. 11–16, ed. Leo, 94). But this is not simply female piety, for Gogo, perhaps as *nutricius* of Childebert II, not only hunts ostentatiously but helps the needy, the wardless young, and widows (*Carmen* 7.4, vv. 27–30, ed. Leo, 156). And one should remember, praising Childebert as builder of churches in Paris, the famous "*Melchisedech noster merito rex atque sacerdos / complevit laicus religionis opus / publica iura regens ac celsa palatia servans / unica pontificum gloria, norma fuit*" (*Carmen* 2.10, vv. 21–24, ed. Leo, 40). Brian Brennan, "The image of the Frankish kings in the poetry of Venantius Fortunatus," *Journal of Medieval History* 10, 1 (1984): 1–11, rightly underlines the Byzantine monarchic ideals in Venantius's works (and in this case the connection to Melchisedech in Ravenna), but strangely makes Gregory an objective touchstone of royal practice: "One only has to read the narrative of Gregory's History to learn that the Frankish kings were not as Venantius pictures them."

[82] *Carmen* 10.17, vv. 19–26 and 31–32, ed. Leo, 249–51 at 250. See as well idem, *Vita sancti Germani* 13, MGH SS rer. Merov. 5 (Hannover: 1920), 381–82.

piety?), have left telling tracks. At the very end of the seventh century, a scribe penned a verse history of Lombard rulers' pious dealings with the Church. They culminated on a liturgically perfect council led by the author's king, Cunipert. In one of the two manuscripts that preserve it, the poem was placed with the acts of the council of Chalcedon—the maintenance of orthodoxy being a hallmark of Catholic kingship. It begins with the Lombards' conversion from Arianism to Catholicism under Aribert, and moves on to his son Berthar's forced conversion of the Jews. Berthar, we learn, was also a "lover of the Church" (*amator ecclesiae*) and a founder of monasteries (*a fundamentis constrictor coenubii*). The poet ends on the Synod of Pavia, presided by Cunipert, *ecclesiarum ditator et opifex*. Pavia spoke of unity, for it proclaimed the acceptance (against the dissent of the Patriarchate of Aquileia) of the fifth ecumenical council of Constantinople. A mass celebrated the recovery of consensus:

> *Namque ovantes ingressi ecclesia, iureiurandum adfirmant concordiam / atque uniti karitatis vincolum, ostias simul offerentes Dominum, eucharistiam concord(e)s participant* Rejoicing, they enter the church, confirm through the swearing of oaths that their heart is one, and united by the bond of charity, they offer together a sacrifice to the Lord by participating with one heart in the Eucharist].[83]

But the most vibrant (or rather, the, to us, most visible) early medieval political culture straddled the Pyrenees. The Visigothic kingdom, long considered an anomaly, helps to fathom the extent to which its Merovingian neighbors brought together rituals and power.[84]

Gregory himself provides indirect evidence that Merovingian kings—good or bad—used the language of the Catholic liturgy. They must have attended Mass fairly frequently. In one case, Guntram takes advantage of the prescribed silence before the reading of the Epistle to ask his people not to kill him, and they answer with a prayer for the king (Jean Mabillon deduced from this passage that there was already an *oratio pro rege* at a fixed place during the mass under the Merovingians).[85] Eager to indict Fredegunda for impiety, Gregory shows her hired assassins in wait for enemy kings in churches—a space within which canon law, both Roman and Mer-

---

[83] *Carmen de synodo Ticinensi* (ca 698), ed. Ludwig Bethmann, MGH SS rer. Lang., 189–91. See as well Hans Belting, "Studien zum beneventanischen Hof im 8. Jahrhundert," *Dumbarton Oaks Papers* 16 (Washington, D.C.: 1962), 141–93, notably 160.

[84] See above, at nn. 1–2. What Michael McCormick, *Eternal Victory*, could reconstruct of the Visigothic liturgy of war is in itself suggestive of a high degree of ceremonial activity using the language of religion.

[85] Jean Mabillon, *De liturgia gallicana libri tres*, 1.3.11 (Paris: 1729), 21, with *LH* 7.8, 331:1–10. See as well *LH* 8.4, 373:15–23.

ovingian, strictly forbade the bearing of arms.[86] From this we learn that Guntram regularly went to matins, and attended saints' festivals, at which he might take communion. Churches are the best place, explains a would-be murderer caught near the altar during Saint Marcel's feast at Châlons: "[W]e could not find another way to approach him with swords, except in church, where he is known to be safe and may stand without fearing anything."[87] From yet another assassination attempt, we gain confirmation of what Venantius's poem to Sigoald documents, that there existed a royal ritual of almsgiving. It was notoriously hard to come into the ruler's presence. Still, Fredegunda assumed that two of her clerics, disguised as beggars, could approach Childebert, prostrate themselves at his feet, ask for alms, and then stab him with poisoned daggers.[88]

We owe this information only to Gregory's animosities, not to his desire to exalt Merovingian piety, for the bishop was reluctant to show Frankish kings too involved in Christian liturgy. Witness the deaths of rulers in the *Histories*: Unlike the saint (and unlike the emperor in Late Roman historiography) the dying or dead king does not provide an occasion for developed expressions of consensus. To the contrary, Chilperic's body, deserted by his followers in the aftermath of his assassination, was taken care of only by a lone bishop.[89] So barren was Gregory's text of honors for Chilperic that a

---

[86] If Theodosius II's edict of 431 on asylum, Mansi 5.442de, had exemplary value in the West, even kings were not supposed to carry arms into a church: "*et nos . . . dei templum ingressuri, foris armas relinquimus et ipsum etiam diadema deponimus; et quo submissius imperii speciem praeferimus, eo magis imperii nobis maiestas promittitur.*" See Otto Treitinger, *Die oströmische Kaiser- und Reichsidee nach ihrer Gestaltung im höfischen Zeremoniell. Vom oströmischen Staats- und Reichsgedanken* (Jena: 1938; reed. Darmstadt: 1956), 9, 150. How early Roman emperors began giving up their sword is unclear. In a recently rediscovered sermon of Augustine that Honorius I "took off his diadem" when he came to pray to Peter's *memoria* in Rome in 403/4, but there is not any mention of a sword. See Sermo Mainz 12.26 = Dolbeau 5.26, in François Dolbeau, *26 sermons au peuple d'Afrique* (Paris: 1996), 55–56, 76, ll. 521–34. Closer to Gregory, see Orleans III (538), c. 32 (29), CCSL 148A, 125–26, 295–97: "*. . . sacrificia vero matutina missarum sive vespertina ne quis cum armis pertenentibus ad bellorum usum expectit*"; and Châlons (639–54) c. 17, CCSL 148A, 306:97–307:100: "*. . . ut nullus secularium nec in ecclesia nec infra atrium ipsius ecclesiae qualecumque scandalum aut semultatis penitus excitare non praesumat nec arma trahere aut quecumque ad vulnerandum vel interficiendum penitus appetere* [under pain of excommunication]."

[87] *LH* 8.44, 410:14: "*procedente rege(m) ad matutinus ac praeunte cereo*"; *LH* 9.3, 416:3–4. This is another example of the evil Fredegunda's willingness to take advantage of ritual forms (see as well *LH* 10.18, 509:9, *in oraturium*).

[88] *LH* 8.29, 391:16–392:3, 393:3–5; tr. Thorpe, 457–58, recounting Fredegunda's instructions and the clerics' confession: "*adsimilantes vos esse mendicos. Cumque pedibus eius fueritis strati, quasi stipem postulantes . . . ut nos egenos adsimularemus. Cumque pedibus tuis provoluti aliquid stipendii quaereremus . . .*"

[89] For another method of *damnatio memoriae* through description of funerals, see Gregory Nazianzen's *Oratio* 5.16–18, a comparison between Constantius II and Julian's, ed. Jean Ber-

later author felt the need to amplify it in pomp and attendance.[90] Understandably, precisely those royal figures most marginal and furthest from Gregory's circle of enmities receive relatively more developed funerals in the *Histories*: the Christianizer of the Franks, Clovis's Queen Clotild, and two sets of young princes murdered by their relatives (Theudoald and Gunthar, and Clovis and Merovech, whose exequies are orchestrated by, respectively, Clotild and Guntram).[91] Massive attendance and pomp were reserved for the saints; they expressed community. Thus the dying Pelagia asked her son Aredius to expose her body "for four days so that all the servants and maids might come and see my body, and so that none of those whom I have supported with the highest care might be excluded from my funeral."[92]

Finally, we should give a second look to Chilperic himself. Redacting the king's epitaph, Gregory scornfully recounts that the bad king produced bad verses and hymns.[93] But Venantius Fortunatus did not share his friend Gregory's verdict on Chilperic's intellectual achievements. In a poem dedicated to the king, he praised the Merovingian's superiority. Vis-à-vis other *reges*, Chilperic was endowed with higher literacy, better verses, and peerless religious wisdom.[94] We can leave to literary historians the issue of the king's actual talents. Gregory and Fortunatus's pronouncements were equally biased, for they were uttered in the context of divergent political

---

nardi, SC 309 (Paris: 1983), 322–29, commented upon by McCormack, *Art and Ceremony*, 132–33.

[90] *Liber Historiae Francorum* 35, ed. Bruno Krusch, MGH SS rer. Merov. 2 (Hannover: 1888), 304:1–10, adding that the bishop dressed Chilperic in "royal vestments" and that Fredegund and the whole army accompanied the body. In the original, Malulf "spends the night in hymns" alone by the body; in the *LHF*, hymns and psalmody accompany the whole cortège.

[91] See above, ch. 2 at n. 81. Materials conveniently gathered by Krüger, *Königsgrabkirchen*, 48–49 (Clovis, *LH* 2.43, 93:14–15), 114–15 (Childebert I, *LH* 4.20, 152:8–10), 131 (Lothar, *LH* 4.21, 154:12–14), 131 (Chilperic, *LH* 6.46, 321:5–10). For Clotild, see *LH* 4.1, 135:16–20. For Theudoald and Gunthar, see *LH* 3.18, 119:13–15. For Clovis and Merovech, see *LH* 8.10, 376:13–19.

[92] *GC* 102, 363:1–5; tr. Van Dam, 103. On consensus at and through saints' funeral, see further below, 119, the discussion of *VP* 13.3.

[93] *LH* 5.44, 254:1–3, and *LH* 6.46, 320:6–9: "*Conficitque . . . et alia opuscula vel ymnus sive missas, quae nulla ratione suscipi possunt.*" Perhaps Gregory refers to some canonical prohibition; cf. the Collection of Martin of Braga, c. 67, Mansi 9.857: "*Non oportet psalmos compositos et vulgares in ecclesia dicere.*"

[94] *Carmen* 9.1, vv. 104–10, ed. Leo, 204: "*doctrinae studio vincis et omne genus. / regibus aequalis de carmine maior haberis, / dogmate vel qualis non fuit ante parens. / te arma ferunt generi similem, sed littera praefert: / sic veterum regum par simul atque prior. / admirande mihi nimium rex, cuius opime / proelia robor agit, carmina lima polit.*" Cf. v. 144, 205: *sis quoque catholicis religionis apex.* This praise was dedicated to the king *quando synodus Brinnaco* [Berny, 580] *habita est*—where Gregory himself was on trial (see Brennan, "Image," 6), which no doubt irked the bishop of Tours all the more!

agendas. No matter what, they testify that religious learning and culture provided a field for competition among kings. One of Chilperic's own poems, a hymn to Saint Médard, survived to fuel modern-day evaluations of late antique culture. It shows that in this competition a king might take the quill himself (or use the services of a third party to write in his name). Médard stood patron to the kingdom centered on Soissons. Soissons had been the capital of the last among Clovis's four sons to survive, Lothar (d. 561), who had founded a church in the saint's name. After Lothar's death, it had been allotted to Chilperic's share. Chilperic had had to flee his city before his brother Sigebert—who then had proceeded to rebuild Médard's church. But the victor was assassinated in 574. The Swedish philologist Dag Norberg proposes that the king composed the hymn shortly after Sigebert's death and his return to the city. Taking this hypothesis further, Chilperic's poetry may have been an element in a royal liturgy of thanksgiving.[95] Whether or not one can contextualize the composition this precisely, Chilperic's hymn testifies to a language of public royal devotion to a saint associated with the king's capital—not unlike the evidence we have for Saint Denis under Charles the Bald and the Capetians. Gregory, who disliked kings who did not listen to bishops, could not be too keen to relay such information.

Guntram: Apex of Royal Rituals

But King Guntram did, in the main, listen to bishops. His A.D. 585 *adventus* and sojourn in Orléans allows Gregory to delineate the upper limit of a king-centered rituality.[96] A positive counterpart to Chilperic's oath-breaking entry into Paris, the Orléans *adventus* is met, appropriately, with a show of consensus. The king accepts citizens' invitations to dine in their houses, and he trades presents with them, manifesting the horizontal, egalitarian dimension of politics. Gregory's Latin, in its symmetries, conveys the tit-for-tat of reciprocity: *multum ab his muneratus muneraque ipsis proflua benignitate largitus est.* All the ethnic groups present in the city participate in the *occursus*, singing hymns. But the Jews do so with an ulterior motive: to

---

[95] Dag Norberg, *La poésie latine rythmique du Haut Moyen Age,* Studia latina Stockholmiensia 2 (Stockholm: 1954), ch. 2: "La poésie du roi Chilpéric," 31–40, text in Karl Strecker, MGH Poetae Latini 4:2 (Berlin: 1923), 457–59. Venantius Fortunatus associated Medard to Sigibert in 565/7: *Carmen* 2.16, vv. 161–64 (almost the finale), ed. Leo, 48: *"en tua templa colit nimio Sigeberethus amore, / insistens operi promptus amore tui. / culmina custodi qui templum in culmine duxit, / protege pro meritis qui tibi tecta dedit."* Sigibert was ultimately buried in Saint-Médard of Soissons, his refoundation, *LH* 4.51, 189:9–11. In the ninth century at least, a Byzantine ruler, Leo VI (886–912) composed and preached homilies, as well as hymns that were then sung, see Gilbert Dagron, *Empereur et prêtre,* 136, 204, 218, 242.

[96] I would nuance here the position taken by Heinzelmann, *Gregor,* 57–59.

gain the king's favor and to obtain the reconstruction with public funds of a synagogue the Christians had destroyed. The good Guntram sees through their ploy and, anticipating their request, preemptively denounces them at the banquet that follows his entry. Right handling of ceremonial forms includes the ability to prevent their manipulation by others. Now an *adventus* often involved petitions by the citizenry; Gregory highlights how Guntram nips the Jewish demand in the bud (indeed, before it can even be made), in order to make him into an exemplar of royal obedience to ecclesiastical norms.

For ritual and political theory—Ambrosian political theory—merge in this episode. It refers unmistakably to the famous incident of Callinicum (388), which Ambrose (as later generations saw it) had made a test case of the place of the emperor within the Church.[97] As the 388 crisis had come to be recounted, a monkish mob had leveled a synagogue, provoking Theodosius I's anger. The emperor (r. 379–95) had instructed the bishop of the city to pay for the building's reconstruction. Preaching during the Mass, Ambrose had rebuked Theodosius, stopped the Mass, and refused the emperor access to the eucharist as long as he did not rescind the order. In his sermon, the bishop had recalled how the tyrant Maximus (later Gallo-Roman hagiography's favorite imperial whipping boy) had been overthrown because he had ordered Christians to rebuild the synagogues they had burned in Rome.[98] The Ambrosian tradition, mediated by Sulpicius Severus and other Gallo-Roman hagiographers, was alive and well in Gregory's writings.[99] We shall return to the *Vita patrum*, where Nicetius of Trier interrupts the Mass to force a king to chase out his excommunicate followers. The bishop of Tours himself adopted Ambrose's persona. In a dream, he "resists" Guntram at the altar when the king, having suddenly entered

---

[97] I am following here Goffart, "Conversions," 298–99.

[98] The original (but less influential) dossier is Ambrose, *Epp.* (*extra collectionem*) 1a-1, ed. Michaela Zelzer, CSEL 82:3 (Vienna: 1982), 145–77. The reference to Maximus is *Ep.* 40.23, 173; Ambrose lauches into the theme of *parrhésia* in 40.2, 162–63: "*Sed neque imperiale est libertatem dicendi negare neque sacerdotale quod sentias non dicere.*" For the incident as it came to be remembered, see Paulinus of Milan, *Vita sancti Ambrosii* 22–23, ed. Michele Pellegrino, *Vita di S. Ambrogio* (Rome: 1961), 80–84. For the specific Jewish issue, see Gavin I. Langmuir, "From Ambrose of Milan to Emicho of Leiningen," Centro italiano di studi sull'alto medioevo, Settimane di studio 26 (1978), *Gli Ebrei nell'alto medioevo*, 2 vols. (Spoleto: 1980), 1.313–68, esp. 327–35. On the Jews in Gaul, see Bernard S. Bachrach, *Early Medieval Jewish Policy in Western Europe* (Minneapolis: 1977), ch. 3; Michel Rouche, "Les baptêmes forcés," 105–24; and Brian Brennan, "The conversion of the Jews of Clermont in A.D 576," *Journal of Theological Studies* n.s. 36 (1985): 321–37.

[99] See Fontaine's important article, "Hagiographie et politique," which stops short of Gregory's era.

Martin's basilica during Mass as the oblations have already been placed on the cloth, tries to snatch away the wicked Eberulf from sanctuary.[100] Guntram does not repeat his imperial predecessors' mistakes.[101] But if the king avoids Jewish manipulation, expressing willingness to be a more perfect Theodosius in Gregory's book, the sum total of the rituals centered on his person in Orléans hint at the frailty of royal rule: They are incompletely consensual. While Guntram shows himself ready to amend and correct his breaches of etiquette, especially at Bishop Gregory's behest,[102] the fact remains that the ceremonies that he organizes are not seamless. The king flares into anger both during a festive banquet he gives to the bishops and during Mass. In the first episode, Guntram breaches decorum, verbally berating treacherous bishops, then tries to reinstate ceremonial order: "He washed his hands, received a benediction from the bishops, and sat again at the table, [showing] a joyful and hilarious face, as if he had expressed nothing concerning the offenses committed against him."[103] Midway through the banquet, Guntram asks each bishop to contribute a cleric to sing the anthem. He then displays confiscated gold, which he intends to give to the poor and the churches, and finally asks for episcopal prayers on his and his nephew's behalf. In so doing, he attempts to place himself literally in the role of orchestrator of harmony and make himself the center of a network of gifts and countergifts. But decorum breaks down again when the king proclaims his hostility to Bishop Theodore of Marseilles. Furthermore, the king almost interrupts the Mass when he learns that one of the bishops whom he suspects of treason is to be the celebrant.

---

[100] *Vita Patrum* 17.2, 729; tr. James, 115–16. See the discussion below, at nn. 128–130. Gregory's dream: *LH* 7.22, 342:1–15, esp. 8–10: "*Ego vero, expansis manibus, contra pectus regis meum pectus aptabam,*" and 14: "*Dum . . . ego regem viliter resisterem . . .*" (below, n. 131). The normative show of strength was possible before Ambrose, at least in the imaginary: See Eusebius of Caesarea, *Historia Ecclesiastica* 6.34, ed. Gustave Bardy, SC 41 (Paris: 1955), 137; tr. Select library of Nicene and post-Nicene fathers, ser. 2, I (repr. Grand Rapids: 1986), 278, where a bishop of Antioch refuses full admission to the church to emperor Philip the Arabian (244–49) until he confesses and cleanses himself from his "many crimes." John Chrysostomos reworked this story in his sermon on Babylas, *PG* 50, 533f., and used it against the defunct emperor Julian.

[101] For the opposite legislative practice in Theodoric's Ostrogothic Italy, see Bachrach, *Jewish Policy*, 30–31. For Roman Law's provisions, see CTh XVI.viii.9, 20, 21, 25, 27, with Brennan, "Conversion," 334–35. CTh XVI.viii.35 provides for the replacement of forcibly alienated Jewish buildings and donations, and for compensations should the land on which they stood have been consecrated to the Christian cult. For Orléans, see Bernard Blumenkranz, *Juifs et Chrétiens dans le monde occidental, 430–1096* (Paris: 1960), 310–11.

[102] When rightly admonished, the king will stick to ecclesiastical norms: In *LH* 8.6, 374–75, he finally gives in to Gregory's mediation when the bishop presents to him, for a return in the royal grace, Garachar and Bladast, hosts of Saint Martin's sanctuary.

[103] *LH* 8.2, 312:12–15.

Unlike Governor Albinus of Marseilles in an earlier chapter of the *Histories*, Guntram ultimately allows the liturgy to take place.[104] The incident thus places the king in a light shade of gray between the black disrespect evidenced by the evil secular official and the white of ideal liturgical seamlessness. Yet ultimately the author leaves his reader on a hopeful note. Gregory and Guntram trade visions recounting—in liturgified form—Chilperic's spiritual deposition and death. The two godsent glimpses into the otherworld compliment their recipients, bishop and king, here put on a level of parity, and complement one another. The evil king is shorn of his hair and "enthroned" into Hell, and author Gregory has Bishop Gregory tell the good king that "it was his evilness that, through your prayer (*oratio*), led to his death."[105] The vision, noteworthily, presents a liturgy of deposition, which calls on the Merovingian custom of shearing the hair of royals to exclude them from *potestas*, and on the rite of episcopal *incathedratio*, the elevation to the bishop's throne.

As Martin Heinzelmann has shown, cooperation between *regnum* and *sacerdotium* peaks in *Histories* 9.21. Guntram effectively performs the duties that Bishop Gregory thought incumbed upon a Christian king. He strikes peace with his nephew, organizes a council, offers the bishops a banquet and jokes with them, discussing God, churches, as well as the defense of the poor.[106] Like a saintly bishop, King Guntram performs a miracle, and Gregory tells us that he himself heard demoniacs invoking the king's name and confessing their crimes. *Virtutes*—both moral and miraculous—go with an ability to embrace episcopal rituality. In Gregory's hagiography, wonders can accompany important liturgical occasions, such as episcopal accessions.[107] But normally good rituals go with good bishops. No wonder then that Guntram's miracle comes after the king's adoption of episcopal forms. The king is first presented acting *acsi bonus sacerdos providens remedia* to fend off an epidemic moving north from Marseilles—the religious remedies of rogations, fasting, vigils, and alms. He follows to the letter the

---

[104] Contrast *LH* 8.7, 375:10–22 with *LH* 4.43, 178:3–14.

[105] *LH* 8.5, 374:6–21: "*Et quis Chilpericum interemit, nisi malitia sua tuaque oratione?*" reinforced if one reads *a te tonsato capite* for *ante tonsato capite* (6; 9) in Gregory's vision. Understand, owing to his evil nature, Chilperic deserved death; it came about because Guntram prayed for it. See Breukelaar, *Historiography*, 128, 237, and Heinzelmann, *Gregor*, 58–59, who notes that Tetricus of Langres and Nicetius of Lyons (two of the three bishops who, in Guntram's vision, end up breaking Chilperic's bones and throwing him into an infernal cauldron) were Gregory's maternal grand-uncles. I thank Martin Heinzelmann for converting me to this meaning despite my stubborn reluctance.

[106] Heinzelmann, *Gregor*, 63–65. See *LH* 9.20–21, 434–442.

[107] E.g., Gregory of Langres (a relative of Gregory), *VP* 7.2, 238:5–7; tr. James, 61–62: "*Nam cum inergumini eum in primo die episcopatus sui confiterentur, rogabant eum presbiteri, ut eos benedicere dignaretur.*"

model of the liturgy Bishop Mamertus of Vienne had instituted: *indixit populis ieiunium, instituit orandi modum, edendi seriem, erogandi hilarem dispensationem.*[108] By following these forms, he was thought to be no longer simply a *rex*, but also a *sacerdos domini.*[109]

Should we follow Reydellet in arguing that Gregory can tolerate the king's reported powers only by assimilating him to a bishop?[110] Over the course of the *Histories* Guntram oscillates between traits associated with *regnum* and *sacerdotium*, in being both prone to anger and of recognized virtue.[111] But Gregory also wants to show the true royal road. The ruler will be able to journey on it if he adopts episcopal values. The symptom, test, and reward of this assimilation, which Gregory hopes for but believes is hard to attain, is to be found in the domain of rituality. Good ritual being par excellence episcopal, the king's one moment of perfect rituality and hence of sanctity comes about through an exact imitation of the sacerdotal model.

The picture Gregory wove was far from innocent. Legitimacy hinges on regularity in performance as well as on regularity in the language through which political actors communicate. In sub-Roman Gaul this idiom comprised gestures and rituals, and contemporaries were well aware of this. By these standards, Chilperic's rule is illegitimate, and Guntram's, imperfect. The one cannot be expected to act according to the established *mos* (indeed,

---

[108] *LH* 2.34, 83:17–84:4. It was indeed the right season, between Easter and Ascension (cf. 83:5). In Gregory's hagiography, rogations are the characteristic episcopal response to disasters, especially epidemics, see *VP* 6.6, 234:15–27; also in *LH* 4.5, 138:8–25 (mid-Lent), *LH* 10.30, 525:15–18. But here again what Gregory presents as extraordinary royal behavior may well have been ordinary. The council of Orléans I (511) c. 27, CCSL 148A, esp. 12:164–65, over which Clovis presided and whose agenda he determined, provided for pre-Ascension rogations with fasts and litanies. The king meant them to involve the full community; consequently, slaves of both sexes should be freed from work on those three days *quo magis plebs universa conveniat*. While nothing indicates that Clovis personally led the rogations, he certainly legislated Church liturgy.

[109] *LH* 9.21, 441–42. See Heinzelmann, *Gregor*, 63–65, 182–83.

[110] *La royauté*, 421–25.

[111] Anger: *GC* 86, 354:1–10; tr. Van Dam, 92; *LH* 8.7, 375:13; *LH* 10.10, 494:17–19. Virtues: *GM* 75, 88:26–27: "King Guntramn so dedicated himself to spiritual behavior that he abandoned the trappings of the world (*saeculi pompis*) and spent his wealth on churches and the poor" (tr. Van Dam, 98). Various sins: *LH* 5.35, 242:2–3 (sins in obeying his queen's murderous deathbed *praeceptum iniquitatis*). More important, and pace Breukelaar, *Historiography*, 238, Gregory recounts *after* Guntram's miracle an unjust deed that the king regrets, *LH* 10.10, 494:4–19, see esp. 17–19: "*Multum se ex hoc deinceps rex paenitens, ut sic eum ira praecipitem reddidisset, ut pro parvolae causae noxia fidilem sibique virum necessarium tam celeriter interemisset.*" Still after Orléans, God makes Guntram sick because, believes Gregory, "*cogitabat . . . multus episcoporum exsilio detrudere*" (including Theodore), *LH* 8.20, 387:10–12.

he perverts ritual *mores* for his own ends).[112] The other proves himself often unable to follow proper ceremonial. Or, to turn from this modern Weberian reading to a very Durkheimian Augustine: No *religio*, be it true or false, can do without visible signs and sacraments which bind together the community; thus those who spurn them are sacrilegious. Chilperic is akin to the pagan rulers of the *City of God*, who manipulated religion for politics' sake.[113] Alone, without episcopal guidance, Guntram cannot succeed in weaving coherently enough the texture of ritual. These kings cannot be fully the center of a community. That role devolves upon the saints.[114]

CHURCH RITUALS: CONSENSUS AND TRANSGRESSION

Indeed, Catholic rituals are, par excellence, unmanipulated (despite opponents' perverse doubts) and resistant to manipulation. Unmanipulated: One would almost believe that no agent stands to orchestrate the liturgy. Style reenforces the message, for as those strands of modern French scholarship that have evacuated agency, Gregory loves the passive mode. Miraculous honors are paid to the saints until human beings recognize the presence of their relics in a site.[115] The holy dead sometimes participate in the liturgy, dividing their voices to strengthen opposite priestly choirs. Demoniacs indicate the exact date of a holy anniversary and lead the congregation to celebrate the feast all over again. A holy man can tell the exact moment when the Mass is taking place in a distant church, thus allowing for perfect synchronization between two churches (the miracle, through its extreme character, reflects the concern of conciliar legislation for the synchronicity of ecclesiastical festivals).[116] Such agentless occasions are arenas of peace, characterized by plenty and lack of decay, like the yearly festival of Edessa. There, "no quarrels arose among the people, no flies landed on carcasses, no thirsty person was without water." There, after the celebration, the precincts were cleansed by rain, leaving the church courtyard as pristine as if no one had ever walked it.[117] When there is agency, the ideal is group

[112] On the near equivalency of *ritus* and *mos*, see Andreas Alföldi, *Die monarchische Repräsentation im römischen Kaiserreiche*, reed. (Darmstadt: 1970), 7 and 10 n. 6.

[113] See below, ch. 4, at n. 96, Augustine, *Contra Faustum* 19.11.

[114] This corresponds to other structural characteristics of the *LH*: Breukelaar, *Historiography*, 258, 270–71, notes that the "active dead" are overwhelmingly bishops, and that there are, proportionally to the numbers in each order, many more good clergy than good secular officials.

[115] *GC* 29, 316, Van Dam, 43; *GC* 72, 340–41, Van Dam, 76–77; perhaps *GC* 21, 310:17–311:10, Van Dam, 3

[116] *GC* 46, 326, Van Dam 57; *GM* 89, 97:27–98:5, Van Dam, 89.

[117] *GM* 32, 57–58; tr. Van Dam, 52. Contrast the pagan festival at Javols, which is yearly threatened by violent storms, *GC* 2, 299:16–26; tr. Van Dam, 19.

action.[118] Unmanipulated despite perverse doubts: In the *Gloria Martyrum*, the Arian king Theudigisel attempts to expose a Catholic miracle as fraudulent, and fails. A Catholic church contained a pool, whose waters would rise to a constant level for Easter baptism and then dry out totally until the following Easter. The miracle warranted the superiority of Catholic baptism over that of the heretics. The king sealed the building, posted guards, and even had trenches dug all around it to intercept putative underground pipes—but this neither stopped the miracle nor revealed any trick.[119] Resistant to manipulation—witness Gregory's extraordinary boast that poison poured in the Eucharistic cup would not harm one taking communion in the orthodox Trinity's name.[120]

Gregory's church rites thus conform to the ideals of Gallic and Visigothic conciliar legislation: uniformity, smoothness, synchronicity, and independence from agency for its effects. The invisible psalmody at the unknown saints' grave verifies (supernaturally) a 517 conciliar decree, that relics may be placed in rural oratories only if there happen to be priests in the area who will recite "frequently" there the Psalms.[121]

But the model as I just outlined it is incomplete. Saintly and episcopal rituals are not simple seamlessness. First, because (as in Rome in 844) tensions accompany or preface the good rituals. Second, because some of Gregory's narratives actually show a good bishop doing what is, to us, and what would have been, to his enemies, manipulation of ritual. The first issue is easily dealt with. Everything depends on how one defines the narrative unit, and on whether the narrative ends on a ritual of consensus. In the case of Guntram at Orléans, the narration closed on a feeling of conflict. But let us consider the following example. Two communities, fighting over the body of a saint, miraculously unite through funeral ritual. One of the two groups of villagers begs to be incorporated in the obsequies as soon as they see the pomp (*quod illi cernentes, paenitentiam moti*) the other side has prepared—"the placing of choirs singing psalms along the road with crosses, candles, and the sweet smell of censers." The two "people" join and celebrate the liturgy as peers (*pariter*).[122] In another episode, the civic

---

[118] *GC* 20, 310:6–9, contrasting two similar miracles witnessed by respectively only a few people and all the people and correlating this difference in audiences to "evidence of power . . . [and] a reinforcement of grace" [tr. Van Dam, 34–35]. On clean power, consensus, and absence of manipulation, see Peter Brown, *The Cult of the Saints* (Chicago: 1981).

[119] *GM* 23–24, 51–53, tr. Van Dam, 42–44.

[120] *LH* 3.31, 127:2–9: Amalasuntha poisoned the chalice from which her mother was to partake in the Arian eucharist—a clear proof of the presence of the devil at the heretics' altar.

[121] Epaon (517), c. 25, CCSL 148A, 30:175–79.

[122] *VP* 13.3, 267:8–19; James, 97–98: "*Cumque haec et huiuscemodi inter se verba proferrent, et Lipidiacenses, effosam humum, deposito sarcofago, eum* [Lupicinium] *sepelire niterentur, convocatis matrona solatiis, fugatis paginsibus, rapuit sanctum corpus ac ferre coepit in feretro ad vicum Transaliacensim, dispositis in itenere psallentium turmis cum crucibus cereisque atque odore flagrantis thimia-*

unity of Clermont is restored and reinforced, after initial violence, through the baptism of the Jews.[123] Gallo-Roman hagiographers had read their Max Gluckman and Victor Turner. Or perhaps they had consulted the theologians who, from Augustine to the early modern missionaries, underlined that it was necessary to destroy bad pagan consensus in order to establish true Christian unity.[124]

Correspondingly, bishops will rupture the liturgy. We have the case of Bishop Gallus, who miraculously makes his deacon sing off tune when the man wants to sing out of place, usurping another clerk's role during a conciliar Mass. Chided, Deacon Valentinianus will perform wonderfully on a later, authorized occasion.[125] We have a case of liturgical clamor (one of

---

mitis. *Quod illi cernentes, paenitentiam moti, miserunt post matronam, dicentes, 'Peccavimus resistendo tibi. Profecto enim cognoscimus, in hoc esse Domini voluntatem. Nunc autem petimus, ut non abiciamur ab huius funeris obsequiis, sed admittamur officiis eius.' Illa quoque permittente, ut sequerentur, coniunctus est uterque populus. Et sic pariter usque ad Transaliacensim vicum venientes, celebratis missis, beatum corpus cum summo honore gaudioque sepelierunt. . . . Uterque tamen locus unius sancti praesidiis commonitur."*

[123] See Brennan, "Conversion," 311, 324, 330–31, who underlines the ideal of *consensus omnium* and the importance of a prior show of disruption. Notice the contrast between the conversion led by Avitus in Clermont, *LH* 5.11, 205–206, esp. *"ut fiat unus grex et unus pastor . . . coniuncti in unum,"* and the one led by Chilperic. The latter episode's first act, *LH* 6.5, shows the king silenced in theological debate by the Jew Priscus just as Priscus is then silenced by Gregory: *"ad haec rege tacente, in medio me ingerens* (269:11–12) . . . *silenti eo"* (271:18–19). The second act, *LH* 6.17, 286–87, begins with a royal order that the Jews should convert, follows with the faked conversion of most Jews, conflict within that community, violence within the context of a ritual occasion, and ends on the massacre of almost all the Jewish parties involved as well as on the desecration of a church through the bloodshed. See Goffart, "Conversions," 300–306, and Heinzelmann, *Gregor*, 48.

[124] See, e.g., Las Casas, *Apologética historia*, paraphrased by Anthony Pagden, *The Fall of Natural Man* (Cambridge [UK]: 1982), 134, as well as Augustine, *Letter* 93, esp. 5.16–18, PL 33, 329–30: with the help of coercion, the heretic can overcome the heavy fetter of custom (*consuetudinis vinculum grave*) and peer pressure, and so enter the bond of peace (*ad pacis vinculum*).

[125] *VP* 6.5, 233:19–234:2, tr. James, 56–57. Gallus owed his ascent in the church to his cantorial abilities, *VP* 6.2, 231:1–14, James, 53. Another bishop related to Gregory, Nicetius of Lyons, silences a deacon who would intone a response, by revealing that the man is possessed. The demon speaks the truth concerning the deacon through man's very own mouth: "Let him be quiet! let him be quiet! May the enemy of justice not be so bold as to sing!" (*VP* 8.4, 244:17–27; James, 69). The concern with cantors is evident also in Orléans, where Guntram selects for singing one deacon from the entourage of each member of the council, to demonstrate conciliar harmony, *LH* 8.3, 372:20–373:2. See also a miracle of harmony, *GC* 46, 316, tr. Van Dam 57. Voice was an important element in determining a clerical pecking order, first, because like Rome, Late Antique Gaul placed a premium on oratorial abilities, second, because voice expressed spirit—both vital and supernatural (a link Gregory makes, dwelling on Gallus's power over both voices and souls). On the former aspect, see, e.g., Florence Dupont, *L'acteur-roi, ou le théâtre dans la Rome antique* (Paris: 1985), 31–32; on the latter, see Aline Rousselle, *Porneia. De la maîtrise du corps à la privation sensorielle* (Paris: 1983), 20–27, as well as her "Parole et inspiration: le travail de la voix dans le monde romain," *History and Philosophy of the Life Sciences* (1983), 5.129–57.

the first attested in the West).[126] We have especially the Ambrosian-style confrontation between Nicetius of Trier and King Childeric, alluded to above. Independent information suggests that Nicetius was not beyond publicly standing up to a ruler, at least through a letter, and long distance. The target was Emperor Justinian, whom Nicetius berated for backing the heresies of Nestorius and Eutychius, calling on him to renounce publicly his error or go down to Hell in the heresiarchs' company.[127] In the *Libri Historiarum*, Nicetius refuses to consecrate the Eucharist unless the king expels his excommunicate followers from the church. When the king balks, immediately, a man is seized by a demon and begins to shout hostile comparisons between Nicetius and Childeric. He proclaims

> in a loud voice . . . both the virtues of the saint and the crimes of the king. He said that the bishop was chaste and the king was an adulterer, that the former was humble in his fear of Christ, and the latter was proud in his royal glory, that the priest would be discovered by God without blemish and the other would soon be destroyed by the [devil] author of his crimes.[128]

The rhythmic declamation is a supernatural transposition of secular lauds, in which a choir alternately praises a contender and curses his opponent.[129] Frightened, the ruler asks the saint to expel the demoniac, and yields—tit for tat—to his earlier demand. Nicetius exorcizes the man, the Mass resumes, and the incident yields a meeker king. As for the possessed, he is—like the supernatural agents of riots in Cassius Dio—nowhere to be found after the dispute's supernatural resolution.[130]

Here the argument rebounds. Bad rituals are manipulated. Good rituals are (in the main) ultimately seamlessly consensual. But some rituals demonstrate openly the saint's power: A higher purpose seizes the ritual occa-

---

[126] *GC* 70, 339:15–34; tr. Van Dam, 74–75. See now Lester K. Little, *Benedictine Maledictions: Liturgical Cursing in Romanesque France* (Cornell: 1993), esp. 83–84.

[127] *Epp. Austrasicae* 7, ed. Wilhelm Gundlach, MGH Epistolae 3 = Epp. Merowingici et Karolini Aevi 1 (Berlin: 1892), 118–19. This letter was equally paradigmatic as, if differently paradigmatic than the *LH*, insofar as it belonged to a collection gathered for the *ars dictandi*, see W. Gundlach in *Neues Archiv* 13 (1888): 365–87, at 378. On Nicetius, see Nancy Gauthier, *L'évangélisation des pays de la Moselle* (Paris: 1980), 172–89.

[128] *VP* 17.2, 279:25–28, James, 115–16: "*Coepitque voce valida inter supplicia torturae suae et sancti virtutes et regis crimina confiteri. Dicebatque episcopum castum, regem adulterum; hunc timore Christi humilem, illum gloria regni superbum; istum sacerdotio inpollutum a deo in posterum praeferendum, hunc ab auctore sceleris sui velociter elidendum.*"

[129] See, e.g., Pacatus, *Panegyric* 37.3 to Theodosius I, ed. Edouard Galletier (Paris: 1955), 103–104, with Alföldi, *Repräsentation*, 83: "*Cuncta cantu et crotalis personabant. Hic tibi triumphum chorus, ille contra tyranno funebres naenias et carmen exequiale dicebat. Hic perpetuum victis abitum, ille victoribus crebrum optabat adventum.*" With Gregory, triumphal hymns and funeral dirges have become predictions of eternal life and eternal death, contrasting advents, as it were, into Heaven and Hell.

[130] For Cassius Dio, see ch. 4, 133–34.

sion and coordinates it to its ends. A secular official, even King Guntram, cannot interrupt Mass in order to seize a person secular power defines as criminal—recall Gregory's paradigmatic dream of Ambrosian resistance.[131] But the bishop can interrupt Mass and let the demons seize a man in order to perform another ritual, exorcism, all at once purifying the church from those the clean power of the church defines as criminals.

We are thus dealing with a double structure. It combines two axes. In the one superiority is a factor of the degree of consensus manifested in the ritual. In the other superiority manifests itself in the shocking ability to transgress the consensus expressed in ritual in order to fashion a higher-level consensus. The one axis allows the ranking of political foci, revealing, for instance, the inferiority of the group centered around the king vis-à-vis the saint-centered community; the other axis permits the expression of superiority within a social ensemble (revealing, for instance, the ultimate power of a bishop over the whole cultic community). We can assume that outside the hagiographer's folia secular magnates would have been tempted to play the transgressive axis. But the hagiographer imaginarily and pre-emptively transfers such attempts into the realm of self-serving manipulation of ritual, which can only result in severely damaged consensus.

The reader may accuse me of having projected these thoughts into Gregory of Tours's brain. But I hope to have suggested how carefully constructed his narratives involving rituals are, and how we can almost think, next to Gregory the hagiographer, of Gregory the reader of social anthropology—an anthropology he used in the service of politics.

---

[131] Above, at n. 100: *"Putabam me quasi in hac basilica sacrosancta missarum solemnia celebrare. Cumque iam altarium cum oblationibus palleo syrico coopertum essit, subito ingredientem Gunthchramnum regem conspicio. . . ."* The same Justinianic Novel 123.31, which punished with death the interruption of litanies, also provided for the death penalty for those who interrupted the Mass; see above n. 69, ch. 2.

Chapter Four

THE LATE ANTIQUE MATRIX:
MARTYRDOM AND RITUAL

> When the people saw itself so assembled [in the Arena],
> it had to marvel at itself, for it had been thus far accus-
> tomed only to see itself run pell-mell, to find itself in a
> milling crowd, without order, and lacking in discipline.
> But the beast with multiple heads and minds, which had
> floated and wandered to and fro, now saw itself united
> into a noble body (*Körper*), defined as a unit (*Einheit*),
> bound together (*verbinden*) and fastened in a single
> mass, a single form animated by a single spirit (*Geist*)
> —Johann Wolfgang von Goethe, *Travels to Italy*

IN GREGORY OF TOURS'S WRITINGS, liturgy-centered consensus, but also transgression within ceremonial, served to measure cohesion and superiority. The sub-Roman world to which he belonged, and in which these indexes had currency, would have seemed all at once familiar and alien to the persecuted Christians of the first centuries. For if the Merovingian understandings of liturgy and ceremonial descended from the matrix of late antique political culture, including, as we shall see, their oppositional facet,[1] this engendering owed little to nature and everything to human agency. Aware of the value the wider society in which they dwelled attached to a number of "rituals," early Christians employed them for their own ends and, in the doing, transformed these cultural practices in shape, logic, and meaning. Given their opposition to the Roman order, they could not but diverge in their interpretation of the very forms they borrowed from late antique political culture. Then as, for example, later in the world of the Carolingian elites, the actual performance of rituals mattered less than

---

I presented portions of this chapter at King's College, London, in March 1995; its substance follows closely my article, "Martyre et ritualité," dans l'Antiquité Tardive. Horizons de l'écriture médiévale des rituels," *Annales* 48, 1 (1997): 63–92. My thanks to members of the U.C. quarterly seminar (September 1997), and especially to Bill North, for suggestions toward improving it.

[1] Walter Goffart, "Conversions," 299, rightly sees in the *passiones* what "tutored [the Merovingian world] in these precedents" of hostility to secular power. Cf. as well Fontaine, "Hagiographie et politique."

the reading authors offered of them. Even more, their actual existence may not have mattered much. Victory on the field of meaning would determine power and identity. This chapter is devoted to the Christian sects' hijacking of a civic ritual, the execution of criminals. When they could claim the condemned as their own, they called it martyrdom.

In analyzing martyrdom in these terms, one is faced with a dynamic of continuity and change that one is tempted to gloss with the social scientific notions of cultural reproduction and production, communication and distinction. The gloss would run as follows: To the imperatives of intelligibility for the sake of propaganda (*fidei*) and communication was conjoined the need to assert distinctiveness, without which the Christian groups could not create and maintain their identity. On the one hand, the nascent *ecclesia* could not but employ the preexistent forms available in the late antique world. For martyrdom, Glenn Bowersock has even argued that given the need to communicate with the majority, Christian discourse drew more from the repertoire of the dominant pagan group than from those of another dominated culture, Judaism. The Christian death for God looked more like a Roman *devotio* than like the Old Testament self-sacrifice (even though the earliest Christians had not rejected the Jewish model as belonging to a bygone age in Providential History but, rather, taken it up in the New Testament).[2] Rome, then, seems like one of those hierarchical societies in which the dominant group's values and practices overdetermine those of subjugated groups.[3] But on the other hand, while mechanisms of acculturation, communication, and cultural reproduction may have been at play in the competitive market for religious wares that existed in the late antique Mediterranean, processes of distinction were necessary: The Christians, noteworthily through martyrdom, argued their difference and generated group identity.[4]

But to remain at this level of analysis is to stop at "Religion As a Cultural System."[5] While the historian can approach late antique Christianities as

[2] See Glen W. Bowersock, *Martyrdom and Rome* (Cambridge [UK]: 1995), 44, 54–55.
[3] Compare Marshall Sahlins, *Islands of History* (Chicago: 1985), ch. 2.
[4] See Peter Stockmeier, "Christlicher Glaube und antike Religiosität," *Aufstieg und Niedergang der römischen Welt*, ed. Wolfgang Haase, vol. 2.23.2 (Berlin: 1980), 899–900, on the dialectical interplay of distinction and communication. Pierre Bourdieu, *La Distinction: critique sociale du jugement* (Paris: 1979), remains a stimulating point of entry into the issue. Yet as shall be argued here, distinction must work differently when a culture has a harder-to-negotiate, Book-centered religious core. Compare, for the ethnic paradigm, *Strategies of distinction: the construction of ethnic communities, 300–800*, ed. Walter Pohl and Helmut Reimitz (Leiden: 1998) to, for a Book-centered religion, Kathryn A. Miller, "Guardians of Islam: Muslim Communities in Medieval Aragon" (Ph.D. diss., Yale, 1998).
[5] Cf. Clifford Geertz, "Religion As a Cultural System," repr. in Geertz, *Interpretation of Cultures* (n.p.: 1973), 87–125.

"cultures," and even conceptualize Christianity's self-understanding of its difference as "cultural," the specificities of this self-understanding force one to modify substantially the analysis. The general dynamic of cultural reproduction and production was guided intimately by specific Christian attitudes. A good share of the Christian groups' foundational texts conveyed a message of radical rupture from the surrounding *saeculum*. Recent scholarship has reemphasized the malleability and fungibility of most religious movements, cults, and associations active within Rome's empire. Syncretism ruled the age. So with their vociferous desire not to assimilate (no matter how much they borrowed from the host cultures), late antique Christianities still seem exceptional.[6] Cast backward, the shadow of the social sciences' fundamental categories obscures these categories' very origins. Historically seen, it is precisely the radical and rare desire of Christians to be different, which Early Modernity remembered with special intensity owing to the confessional wars, that led to the emergence of the notion of social group, understood as a unit all at once *religio* and *societas*. This genesis still conditions modern analysts' use of the notion, especially in allowing some scholars to draw linear equations whose related variables are "religious identity" and "group identity."[7]

In other words, that Christianity, to an unprecedented degree if one excepts Judaism, self-consciously underlined difference over accommodation made it and makes it the archetypal group, defining its boundaries through distinction.[8] The tautological ease with which one can retroactively fit the world of the martyrs into a modern sociological framework, however, must not obfuscate, first, the exceptionality in late antiquity of early Christianity, and, second, the specificities of the practices with which Christians asserted uniqueness. Otherwise, we shall merely verify the eternal laws of theory, and in so doing lose the historicity both of past cultural practices and of present social scientific models.

In exploring the topic of early Christian martyrdom, it becomes necessary to assume, heuristically, a high degree of coherence in late antique

---

[6] See most recently Mary Beard, John North, and Simon Price, *Religions of Rome*, vol. 1 (Cambridge, [UK]: 1998).

[7] See below, chapters 5 and 6.

[8] For the importance of groups in Western history since early Christianity, see Otto Gerhard Oexle, "Soziale Gruppen in der Ständegesellschaft," in *Die Repräsentation der Gruppen*, ed. Otto Gerhard Oexle and Andrea von Hülsen-Esch (Göttingen: 1998), esp. 34–39. The firmness of the contours of Western "religions," after having been exported *conceptually* by scholars from modern monotheism into non-Western cultures, has been adopted *culturally* by some of these ensembles. As a result, they now operate more like Christianity. For an Indian example, conceptualizing these influences, see Harjot Oberoi, *The construction of religious boundaries: culture, identity and diversity in the Sikh tradition* (Oxford: 1994).

Mediterranean culture. Its texture and inner tensions, as well as the processes of production and reproduction of this matrix, evidently, would deserve an analysis in their own right. Still, since any historical exposition
calls for arbitrary beginnings, it stands here simplified and somewhat static.
It will serve as the context for two explorations. The first is the Christian
appropriation, through writing at the very least, of death in the arena. It
aimed at demonstrating the superiority of the Christian dispensation over
the pagan *saeculum*, and highlighted in particular its believers' access to
higher prescience and truth. Since any tactic's efficiency is a factor of the
signifying power and seductiveness of the tropes it mobilizes, one must
explore martyrdom's field of meaning in contemporary non-Christian culture. Conversely, martyrdom appears sometimes in texts not so much to
underline some group's superiority but rather to give meaningfulness to a
phenomenon that does not necessarily belong to the narrowly defined political field. Still, the aura of power late antique culture attached to civic
ceremonies greatly contributed to this function. Strategy and meaningfulness interacted dialectically. Accordingly, in the chapter's second part,
we shall explore a less polemical use of martyrdom: how it served to explain
the transformations of urban space and time in the age opened by Constantine's conversion. This will in turn lead us back to a key specificity of
the Christian groups that has provided a red thread for the past chapters,
scriptural interpretation.

Two examples will serve as points of entry into these processes. Both
deal with martyrdom. Both come from Carthage circa 200. The one is
the anonymous *Passio Perpetuae et Felicitatis*, the other Tertullian's attacks
against gentile rituals. But since, as has just been argued, these texts' intelligibility to contemporary audiences depended on their inscription in the
dominant gentile culture, we must first turn to the Roman understanding
of the arena.

ROMAN EXECUTIONS AND CHRISTIAN MARTYRDOM

We may trust that we know what martyrdom was. Yet even the deeds of
saints take part of their meaning from the dominant culture of the persecutors. We should remember, then, that the late antique audiences that saw
a Christian die thought they were watching an execution. An execution
according to set forms, death by the sword or by the ax, on the cross, by
drowning, by fire, by fighting the beasts.[9] These onlookers would not have
found totally alien the Foucauldian concept of "theater of punishment,"
given that public power meted out many such penalties as *spectacula* (Greek
theama), and this, often, literally, in a theater, amphitheater, or hippo-

---

[9] See Theodor Mommsen, *Le droit pénal romain*, (Fr. tr. Paris: 1907), vol. 3, 229–66.

drome. Like the martyrs, gentile audiences would have attributed a religious value to the event. With the criminals' annihilation, the games restored the political order.[10]

Criminals not only went to their death during public festivals but were often forced to play some role, unpalatable to them when they were Christians but vastly meaningful to the onlookers. I will not delve into this point, which K. M. Coleman has masterfully treated.[11] Martial's *De spectaculis* describes and comments on numerous minidramas staged with live criminals but often leading to their death. Some served to verify mythology: "[L]et the fable be endowed with faith." They were meant to have a religious valence. Thus Martial called the elaborate machinery that allowed Hercules to ascend toward the celestial spheres "not a work of artifice but a work of piety."[12] According to Tertullian, "often criminals (*noxii*) play the part of (*induunt*) these gods of yours; we saw at one time Attis being castrated . . . and that man who was burning alive was dressed as Hercules (*Herculem induerat*)."[13] Urged on by the pain of Nessus's poison, Hercules had freely opted for self-immolation. The *noxii*, however, had no choice. They did not keep their *libertas*. Owing to their condemnation, they had become *servi poenae*, slaves to their penalty.[14] Now slaves of the State, they could no longer freely dispose of their own body. Their death

---

[10] Keith Hopkins, "Murderous Games," in his *Death and Renewal: Sociological Studies in Roman History* (Cambridge [UK]: 1983), 9–10. Carlin R. Barton, *The Sorrows of the Ancient Romans: The Gladiator and the Monster* (Princeton: 1993), 11–46, suggests instead that senators or knights chose to become gladiators in an attempt to recover an aristocratic freedom the principate had destroyed.

[11] K. M. Coleman, "Fatal charades: Roman executions staged as mythological enactments," *Journal of Roman Studies* 80 (1990), 44–73. See as well the reading, inspired by Michel Foucault, *Surveiller et punir* (Paris: 1975), by David Potter, "Martyrdom and Spectacle," in *Theater and Society in the Classical World*, ed. Ruth Scodel (Ann Arbor: 1993), 53–88; and more recently Kate Cooper, "The Voice of the Victim: Gender, Representation and Early Christian Martyrdom," *Bulletin of the John Rylands Library* 80,3 (1998): 147–57.

[12] Martial, *De spectaculis* 5 (citation), 7, 8, 12–13, 16 (citation), 21b, in Martial, *Epigrams*, ed. Walter C. A. Ker, 2 vols. (Cambridge, Mass., and London: 1919), 1.6, 6–8, 8, 10, 12, 16. Cf. Strabo, *Geography* 6.2.6, ed. Horace Leonard Jones, vol. 3. (Cambridge, Mass.: 1983), 84–85. Coleman, "Fatal charades," 60–66, analyzes all these texts with great nuance. On Martial, see Magnus Wistrand, *Entertainment and violence in Ancient Rome: The attitudes of Roman writers of the first century* A.D. (Göteborg: 1992), esp. 22, 69.

[13] *Apologeticum* 15.4–5, ed. Jean-Pierre Waltzing (Paris: 1929), 36.

[14] This seems to be the meaning of *Digest* 48.19.8.11 (Ulpian), ed. Theodor Mommsen, Paul Krueger, and Alan Watson, (Philadelphia: 1985), vol. 4, 847:31–848:1: "*Quicunque in ludum venatorium fuerint damnati, videndum est an servi poenae efficiantur; solent enim iuniores hac poena adfici. Utrum ergo servi poenae isti efficiantur, an retineant libertatem, videndum est. Et magis est ut hi quoque servi efficiantur: hoc enim distant a caeteris, quod instituuntur venatores, aut pyrrichiani, aut in aliam quam voluptatem gesticulandi, vel aliter se movendi gratia.*" Cf. 48.19.12, 849: *confestim poenae servi fiunt,* and 48.14.29, 852, with Mommsen, *Droit pénal,* 3.289–92. I agree here with Potter, "Martyrdom As Spectacle," 65.

script did not belong to them; to live their last moment, they got cloaked in an alien identity that made the event all the more a thing of the gentile community.[15]

The Games, Staging Ground for Consensus and Opposition[16]

It was indeed desirable that everything should take place according to a set scenario—hence patterns, forms, some would say, ritual. Spectacles, either of the stage or of the circus, provided the universally acknowledged litmus test of civic unity and order. True, ancient authors knew well that *spectacula*, *munera*, and *ludi* generated emulation and competition, humors that at times overspilled into conflict and bloodshed. Some viewed the phenomenon with untrammeled cynicism. Juvenal's famous saying on "bread and circuses" need not be elaborated upon.[17] Long after the Empire's Christianization, and perhaps echoing a Christian critique of gentile forms of communication, the Byzantine chronicler John Malalas would attribute the origins of chariot races and circus factions to Romulus's wiles. With Remus's murder, Rome's cofounder had depleted an already scant legitimacy. So Romulus "built the hippodrome . . . wishing to divert the mass of the people of Rome because they were rioting and attacking him owing to his brother . . . Then the inhabitants of Rome were divided into the factions and no longer agreed among themselves, because thereafter they desired their own side's victory and supported their own faction as if it were a religion." Malalas assumes that each color tended to align itself with politi-

---

[15] And indeed the mythological reenactments necessitated the lack of freedom of their actors. Thus in Apuleius's *Golden Ass*, the ass Lucius's partner for public fornication in the amphitheater, a woman of high birth, had to have committed an especially degrading crime to be so exposed. She became *vilis . . . bestiis addicta*. Lucius himself feared the *infamia publici spectaculi*. See *Der goldene Esel*, ed. Edward Brandt and Wilhelm Ehlers (Munich: 1989), 432–34 and 444.

[16] Cf. Monique Clavel-Lévêque, "L'espace des jeux à Rome: champs de lutte et lieux d'obtention du consentement," *Mélanges . . . Roland Fietier* (Annales littéraires de l'Université de Besançon 287, Paris: 1984), 197–226, reworked in eadem, *L'empire en jeux. Espace symbolique et pratique sociale dans le monde romain* (Paris: 1984)—inspired by Marxist anthropology. See as well the analyses, building on Bourdieu's logic of practice, of Egon Flaig, "Repenser le politique dans la République romaine," *Actes de la recherche en sciences sociales* 105 (1994): 18–25; cf. the expanded version, "Entscheidung und Konsens. Zu den Feldern der politischen Kommunikation zwischen Aristokratie und Plebs," in *Demokratie in Rom?* ed. Martin Jehne, et al. (Stuttgart: 1995), 100ff; Flaig, *Den Kaiser herausfordern. Die Usurpation im Römischen Reich*, Historische Studien 7 (Frankfurt: 1992), 38–93. See as well Thomas Wiedemann, *Emperors and Gladiators* (London: 1992).

[17] Juvenal, *Satire* 10, vv. 78–81, ed. P. de Labriolle and J. Gérard (Paris: 1921), 127; cf. Paul Veyne, *Le pain et le cirque* (Paris: 1976), 84ff.

cal groups and options. The king consequently favored the factions rival to those that supported his enemies.[18]

Perhaps because it was known to be only too frail, rulers valued expressions of popular consensus. They prized its obtainment, especially at events staged in the circus or the theater. Claudian's panegyric for Honorius described the interaction between the emperor and the people in the circus in terms of a mutual increase in sacrality accruing from a give-and-take between the imperial majesty's presence and the assent, marked by applauses, of the *plebs*.[19] Creating sacrality, the dialogue also sacralized order, insofar as (in the circus at least) people sat according to their status. According to Suetonius, Augustus capped his Roman reforms by "correcting and putting back in order the excessively confused and dissolute customary way in which one watched spectacles." The prince cared for some dialogue with the people, but only if the latter was organized according to its orders; he separated the senators from the commons, soldiers from civilians, married men from bachelors, mature from underage, and fenced off noncitizens, including women, in the area the farthest from the stage.[20] Harmony was thus implicitly hierarchical. Yet just as there are dangers in taking medieval texts for simple reflections of reality, it is fallacious to make late antique men and women (whether authors or actors in the political field) the unconscious or passive objects of some mental structure standing outside them. That sacrality that in the games' dialogue balances hierarchy and community is for Suetonius a conceptual tool and perhaps even an ideological touchstone; it provides the author with a norm that his main characters, the emperors, virtuously verify or shamefully transgress. Harmony or disharmony were often in the beholder's self-interested eye. In Apuleius's *Apology*, one Pontianus expresses that "one considers a divine omen the harmony (*consensus*) of an acclamation [shouted in] common (*publicae vocis*)."[21] In the economy of the story, though, the man, a dubious character, is trying to convince with this argument that the local town's

---

[18] *Ioannis Malalae Chronographia* 7.4–5, ed. L. Dindorf, B. G. Nieburh, et al., Corpus scripturarum historiae byzantinae 26 (Bonn: 1831), 176–77; Australian tr. by Elisabeth Jeffreys et al., *The Chronicle of John Malalas* (Melbourne: 1986), 92–94.

[19] Claudian, *Panegyricus dictus Honorio Augusto sextum Consuli* 611–17, ed. John Barrie Hall (Leipzig: 1985), 287–88: "*O quantum populo secreti numinis addit imperii praesens genius, quantamque rependit maiestas alterna vicem, cum regia circi conexum gradibus veneratur purpura vulgus assensuque cavae sublatus in aethera vallis plebis adoratae reboat fragor unaque totis intonat Augustum septenis arcibus echo!*" See Alan Cameron, *Claudian. Poetry and Propaganda at the Court of Honorius* (Oxford: 1970), 382–83.

[20] Suetonius, *Augustus* 44.1–5, ed. Henri Ailloud, 3 vols. (Paris: 1931–32), 1.101–102.

[21] Apuleius, *Apologia* 73.3, ed. Paul Valette (Paris: 1924), 87; earlier, 72.4, 86, Pontianus is said to act *callide*. Cf. Charlotte Roueché, "Acclamations in the later Roman Empire: New evidence from Aphrodisias," *JRS* 74 (1984): 188.

approval dictates that Apuleius should marry Pontianus's mother. The literary depiction of a manipulation of one of Roman political culture's formulas suggests that the presence in texts of ritual consensus (or disharmony) can equally be owed to polemical or strategical intentions.

Regardless of the awareness that consensus was not always spontaneous, in Rome as well as in the provinces, the people prized their ability to be in dialogue with its rulers and their representatives. In the *Life of the Twelve Caesars*'s implicit normative system, the *civilis princeps* holds the middle ground between aloofness at the games and excessive participation in them. Or, as the anthropologists would say, he practices judicious role distancing. In this, the good emperor is the direct ancestor of Gregory the Great's prelate, who should strike a balance between familiarity and superiority.[22] Excessive familiarity carried a negative valence, and ancient historians painted bad emperors as demagogues. Commodus's descent in the arena fueled oppositional critique.[23] He died an evil death. When still praetorian prefect, Titus had manipulated the dialogue's rules *incivilius et violentius*: He planted agents in the theaters and in the camps, who requested there *quasi consensu* the punishment of people suspect to him. But in Suetonius's biographies, improvement characterizes good men after their accession to emperorship. Titus *princeps* verifies this: He promised to give gladiatorial games in which the spectators' will, not his, would run the show. He even condescended to favor a side, that of the Thraecian fighters, a partisanship that allowed him to debate with the people "with voice and gesture." Suetonius reassures his potential aristocratic reader: In so doing, Titus preserved equity and his majesty.[24] A bond with the people can also be demonstrated spatially. Pliny praises in his panegyric Trajan's chosen position in

[22] Andrew Wallace-Hadrill, "Civilis princeps: Between citizen and king," *JRS* 72 (1982): 32–48, delineates the Roman ideal. Gregory the Great, *Moralia in Iob* 21.13.20, ed. Marcus Adriaen, CCSL 143A (Turnhout: 1979), 1081:14–19. See as well the horizontal rituals of the Carolingians (Nelson, "Carolingian royal ritual," 156, 169–71), and late antique parallels (or models) in Cassius Dio, *Roman History*, *Epitoma* 65.10.4–65.11.1 and 68.7.2–3, trans. Ernest Cary, reed., 9 vols. (Cambridge, Mass.: 1955–69), 8.278–81 and 8.370–71 (Vespasian and Trajan). Cf. the modern anthropological notion of "role distancing," Erving Goffman, *Encounters* (New York: 1961), 107–108, 135, 141–42, and for an application, George E. Marcus, "Three Perspectives on Role Distance in Conversation between Tongan Nobles and their 'People,' " in *Dangerous Words*, ed. Donald L. Brenneis and Fred R. Meyers (New York: 1984), 243–65.

[23] Cassius Dio, *Epitoma* 73.10.2–3, 14.1, 17.1–22.3, ed. Cary, 9.90–93, 98–99, 104–17.

[24] Suetonius, *Divus Titus*, 6.2 and 8.3–5, ed. Ailloud, 3.71 and 3.74 (citation): "*Quin et studium armaturae Thraecum prae se ferens saepe cum populo et voce et gestu ut fautor cavillatus est, verum maiestate salva nec minus aequitate.*" The following paragraph, 8.6, shows that the dialogue belongs to the field of *popularitas* ("*Ne quid popularitatis praetermitteret, nonnumquam in thermis suis admissa plebe lavit*"). As Nelson, "Carolingian Royal Ritual," 156 n. 50, remarks, the passage served as a model for the baths that Charlemagne, according to Einhard's biography, shared with his aristocracy (in Carolingian parlance, the *populus*) to mark *familiaritas*.

the circus: He placed himself in such a way that he could be seen by all citizens just as much as he could see them. The equality in visual access and the dialogue of popular and imperial gazes signal a limited power.[25] Yet equilibrium means limits in two directions. The ruler had to accede to some of the demands that the *plebs* conveyed with rhythmic slogans, but could not yield constantly. Nor, for that matter, always refuse. An emperor gambled away popularity when, like Domitian, he enjoined silence through a herald to the collective petitioneers.[26] But one gambles for desirable stakes. An emperor refused to interact with his subjects in an attempt to establish a greater degree of distance and therefore of authority. In certain cases, ad hoc aloofness could meet with the ancient historians' approval,[27] and perhaps as well (but here one enters squarely the realm of speculation) with that of part of the audience. The balancing game entailed dangers, for any component signal could be misinterpreted, honestly or purposefully, but it seems to have been unescapable. Thus, through combinations of signals of proximity and distance, *plebs* and *princeps* constantly renegotiated their status. The crowd knew it was a sign of its collective honor when the *princeps*, his representatives, or (in the semiautonomous cities) the civic magistrates, acquiesced in its demands.[28] At the games, it could clamor for more beasts and more human victims. Some of these were Christian.

Crowd honor was that of a collective, which had authority. Classical political culture considered that the expression of popular wishes at the games had quasi-constitutional value.[29] Cicero could argue that the Roman people indicated its verdict (*iudicium*) or will especially in three places: public assemblies, elections, as well as at the gatherings held for (circus and theatrical) games and for gladiatorial shows (*contione, comitiis, ludorum gladiatorumque consessu*). In that latter context, the people came in greatest number (hence more representatively) and enjoyed the greatest *libertas*. One might suspect a bias in Cicero's presentation of the loci of popular author-

---

[25] Pliny the Younger, *Panegyricus Traiani* 51.3, ed. Marcel Durry, *Lettres de Pline* (Paris: 1947), 140.

[26] Suetonius, *Domitian* 13.2–3, ed. Ailloud, 3.92. Tiberius steered an extreme course: The people having forced him (*coactus*) to manumission an actor, he rarely attended spectacles, *ne quid exposceretur*, Suetonius, *Tiberius* 47.1, ed. Ailloud, 2, 37. Cassius Dio, *Historiae* 59.13.3–7, ed. Cary, 7.298–301, paints a situation in which communication between Gaius Caligula and his people no longer functions in the least.

[27] Cassius Dio, *Epitoma* 69.6.1–2, ed. Cary, 8.434–35: Hadrian imitates Domitian, because he wanted to lead according to his dignity rather than by flattering the people. Cf. ibidem 69.16.3, 8.454–55: The emperor refuses to accede to the people's clamors as it would mean to transgress the law. On these episodes, see Traugott Bollinger, *Theatralis licentia. Die Publikumsdemonstrationen an den öffentlichen Spielen* (Ph.D. diss. Basel, Winterthur: 1969), 66, 43.

[28] On honor, see Barton, *Sorrows*, 34–36.

[29] The sources to A.D. 238 have been conveniently catalogued and analysed in Bollinger, *Theatralis licentia*.

ity. At this moment of Roman political life, this Roman orator had more friends in the theater than in more straightforwardly "political" popular assemblies.[30] But Cicero could not put forward an idea that contemporary political culture would have automatically rejected as absurd. One forges values less easily than events. Dio Cassius and Herodian's histories, and closer to Republican times Tacitus's writings, testify to the force, sometimes yielded to, sometimes resisted, of popular *voces* (Greek *boai*). To account for the exact dialectic of might and right that empowered slogans is beyond the scope of this study, but whatever its logic, the phenomenon did not limit itself to Rome. In the semiautonomous cities, similar occasions afforded commoners a rare opportunity to exercise judicial power; as a group, they could vote by acclamation a person to death.[31] Depending on authorial partisanship, the sources present acclamations as either divinely inspired—an origin marked by spontaneity and simultaneity—or manipulated.[32] Staged or innocent, the *voces*, not unlike their descendants, the medieval litanies of the saints and *laudes regiae*, consisted in rhythmic shouts or chants that allowed variations and relative innovation.[33] Consequently, praiseful slogans could be turned on their head in conflictual circumstances. After the death of Commodus, if we trust Dio Cassius, the people "now chanted, with certain changes that made them utterly ridiculous, all the slogans that they had been accustomed to utter with a kind of rhythmic swing in the amphitheatres."[34] Cadence alone conveyed meaning; thus

---

[30] Cicero, *Pro Sestio* 50.106, 54.115–59.127, ed. Jean Cousin (Paris: 1965), 105, 199–226; Bollinger, *Theatralis licentia*, 25–27; Hopkins, "Murderous Games," 14; Claude Nicolet, *Le métier de citoyen dans la Rome républicaine* (Paris: 1988), 480–87.

[31] Jean Colin, *Les villes libres de l'Orient gréco-romain et l'envoi aux supplices par acclamations populaires*, Collection Latomus 82 (Bruxelles: 1965), here 117–30, redundant with the same's "Les jours de supplice des martyrs chrétiens et les fêtes impériales," *Mélanges André Piganiol*, 3 vols. (Paris: 1965–66), 3.1565–80. For examples in Christian sources, Cyprian of Carthage, *Ep.* 59.6.1, ed. G. F. Diercks, CCSL 3C:2 (Turnhout: 1996), 2.346:163–347:167: "... *totiens ad leonem petitus, in circo, in amphitheatro dominicae dignationis testimonio honoratus ... clamore popularium ad leonem denuo postulatus in circo ...*", or the *Acts of the Martyrs of Lyon*", 38, ed. Antoon A. R. Bastiaensen, *Atti e passioni dei martiri* (Rome: 1987), 75:5–6, where the *dēmos* clamors for, and obtains the punishments it wants to be inflicted upon the condemned.

[32] Rouché, "Acclamations," 183–84.

[33] Record has been kept of senatorial acclamations calling for the demise of an enemy; those of the commons were probably not very different; see the *Scriptores Historiae Augustae* (Iulus Capitolinus), *Maximinus* 16.3–7, ed. Ernst Hohl et al., 2 vols. (Leipzig: 1965), 2.15:26–16:11. For medieval *laudes*, see Ernst Kantorowicz, *Laudes regiae: A Study in Liturgical Acclamations and Medieval Ruler Worship* (Berkeley: 1946). See, however, Reinhardt Elze, "Die Herrscherlaudes im Mittelalter," repr. in his *Päpste-Kaiser-Könige und die mittelalterliche Herrschaftssymbolik* (London: 1982), 207, who doubts *laudes* had any constitutive authority. On innovation, see Rouché, "Acclamations," 189–90.

[34] Cassius Dio, 74.2.3, tr. Cary, 9.124–27; cf. Alan Cameron, *Circus Factions: Blues and Greens at Rome and Byzantium* (Oxford: 1976), 236.

Dio's Vespasian thought of punishing the Alexandrians not only for insulting words but as well because "there was something in their broken anapaestic rhythm that roused his ire"—the accent fell on the second half-foot instead of on the first. This mode may have been especially well suited for acts of parrhesia; tragedians employed it for the parabasis, that is, the moment when the chorus surged forward and spoke out the playwright's political grievances.[35] This culture, and one suspects, all cultures, knew how to inflect its customary language to convey new messages.

Tragedy provided oppositional behavior with more than a model for chanted oppositional slogans. In his *On the Death of Peregrinus*, the satirist Lucian underlined the love of his semifictional antihero, the Sophist Proteus Peregrinus, for tragic things—tragedian's clothes and tricks borrowed from tragedy. Peregrinus used them as props in self-aggrandizing shows of parrhesia before an emperor, Antoninus Pius, whom he knew had too much clemency to put him to death.[36] Interestingly for our purposes, in the course of his histrionic career, the Sophist had at one time converted and captured the loyalty of a Christian sect. After his excesses led to his expulsion, he planned to cremate himself at the height of the Olympic Festival, "all but in the theater" in a "spectacle" (*theama*).[37]

Lucian's satire and Dio's historical works suggest how, being an occasion for consensus, the *spectacula* afforded opponents an occasion to sway that consensus. When disruptors failed, they could console themselves that they had at least broken the illusion of unanimity. Demonstrative opposition in the tragic mode belonged to the stock-in-trade of the philosophic enemies of the empire. Opposed to Titus and Berenice's marriage, a Cynic philosopher "entered the theater when it was full and denounced the pair in a long, abusive speech." The provocator was flogged. Another sophist who sought to imitate him did not get away so lightly: He was beheaded. Dio had no lost love for the "yelping" Cynic dogs, but in this case their antics expressed and mobilized a strong enough popular opinion. The young Flavian got the message; he sent away his oriental lover.[38] When opposers succeeded, they created a new consensus. Dio's disingenuously crafted description of the fall of the praetorian prefect Cleander in 190 is justly famous:

> As the horses were about to contend for the seventh race, a crowd of children ran into the circus, led by a tall maiden of grim aspect, who because of what afterwards happened, was thought to have been a *daimona*. The children

---

[35] Cassius Dio, 65.8.5, tr. Cary, 8.272–73.

[36] Lucian, *On the Death of Peregrinus* 14 and 21, ed. and tr. A. M. Harmas, *Lucian*, vol. 5 (Cambridge, Mass.: 1955), 16–17 and 24–25.

[37] Lucian, *Peregrinus* 21, 24–25.

[38] Cassius Dio, 65.15.5, tr. Cary, 8.290–91.

shouted in unison (*suneboēsan*) many bitter words, which the people took up, to then shout every conceivable insult. And finally the throng leapt down from the seats and set out to find Commodus . . . calling out many blessings on him and many curses upon Cleander.[39]

In turn emperors might seek to erase parrhesia's effects by making a public spectacle of the offenders. Roman law attests to this practice.[40] But such a propagandistic move's success could never be counted on. Success did not result automatically from such a gambit. It depended partially on the struggle between the rival interpretations of the contending groups. Peregrinus's fiery death was dismissed as a fraud by Lucian, but the author still allows his modern readers to see that for other contemporary observers the self-immolating Sophist had been a holy man. Reporting with some critical distance the fate of one opposer, Dio provides us with a case in which neither emperor nor critique seems to have imposed his reading:

> An Egyptian, Serapio, had told the emperor to his face . . . that he would be shortlived and that Macrinus would succeed him . . . Serapio had at first been thrown to a lion for this. But when, as the result of merely holding out his hand (as is reported) the animal did not touch him, he was slain. And he might even have escaped this fate (or so he declared) by invoking certain *daimones* if he had lived one day longer.[41]

Serapio's death in the arena, bathed as it is in rumors of the miraculous (all the more as Macrinus's accession verified his prophecy), takes us closer to the martyrs.

Martyrdom: Imaginary Hijacking of the Dominant Political Culture

If we trust Christian authors, martyrdom was crucial for their community. The stakes did not merely consist in the conversion of those outside. Neither were they merely the creation of heroes for the new faith through an appropriation of the ambiguous prestige enjoyed by the gladiator—who (according to a recent book) vowed himself freely to death in a constitu-

---

[39] Cassius Dio, 73.13.3–4, ed. Cary, 9.96–99. For the events, see C. R. Whittacker, "The revolt of Papyrius Dionysius, A.D. 190," *Historia* 13 (1964): 348–69, Bollinger, *Theatralis licentia*, 34–35, 38, and Cameron, *Circus Factions*, 185–86.

[40] *Digest* 48.19.38.2 (Paulus), ed. Mommsen et al., 4.853: "*Actores seditionis et tumultus populo concitato pro qualitate dignitatis aut in furcam tolluntur aut in bestiis obiiciuntur aut in insulam deportantur.*"

[41] Cassius Dio, 79.4.4–5, tr. Cary, 9.346–49. For this episode, see Igor Gorevich, *O Kritike Antropologii Zhivotnikh* (Towards a critique of animal anthropology), vol. 2: *Zvyeri i Anektoti*, (Kaboul-Kishinev: 1987), 303–305, whom I thank for the reference.

tional order where even the upper classes had lost their *libertas*.[42] The blood of the martyrs may have been the seed of the Church, as Tertullian had it, but martyrdom was equally about order within the community. In a letter preserved in Eusebius's *Ecclesiastical History*, Dionysius, bishop of Alexandria, arguing for the reintegration within the *ecclesia* of the lapsed, exalted "martyrdom for the sake of preventing division [within the Church]" over and above death "for refusing to worship idols."[43] The *Passion of Montanus and Lucius* reports a martyr's last speech. To pagan eyes, Montanus may have seemed yet another Proteus Peregrinus, "a sophist enamored of death who was pronouncing his own funeral oration before his demise."[44] But the hagiographer, unlike Lucian, sympathized with his hero's ideals. Montanus called on the Christians to be steadfast in the face of persecution, on apostates and heretics to return to the fold, on women to preserve their purity, on the common people to follow the clergy, and last but not least on the clergy not to squabble.[45] Death, Montanus or his hagiographer hoped, would sanctify this model order. In this belief Christians agreed with their gentile persecutors—*tuo sanguine sancietur disciplina*, to quote the concluding sentence of the official presiding at Cyprian of Carthage's trial.[46] But for them, like Cyprian himself, what was sanctified by blood was a *tradita divinitus disciplina* triumphant over the *disciplina Romana*.[47]

Thus, given its importance for both the civic group and the Christian group, the spectacle of death in a public space could only be contentious.[48] In dealing with gentile society, the Christian adopted a strategy involving

[42] Cf. Barton, *Sorrows*, ch. 1.

[43] Dionysius to Novatus, in Eusebius, *Ecclesiastical History* 6.45, ed. Gustave Bardy, SC 41 (Paris: 1984), 161.

[44] Lucian, *Peregrinus* 32, tr. Harmas, 36–37.

[45] *Passio Montani et Lucii* 14, ed. Herbert Musurillo, 226–29: "*Generaliter autem docebat ut praepositos venerarentur. Praepositis quoque ipsis concordiam pacis insinuans, nihil esse melius aiebat quam praepositorum unanimem voluntatem. Tunc et plebem posse ad sacerdotum obsequia provocari et ad vinculum dilectionis animari, si rectores plebis pacem tenerent.*" Cf. also the *Acts of Pionus* 12–14, ed. Bastiaensen, 172–81.

[46] *Passio Cypriani* (both recensions) 3.5, ed. Bastiaensen 216:22, 225:20.

[47] Cyprian, *De lapsis* 5, ed. Maurice Bévenot, CCSL 3 (Turnhout: 1972), 223:89–90; cf. Andr[e]as Alföldi, "Zu den Christenverfolgungen in der Mitte des 3. Jahrhunderts," repr. in his *Studien zur Geschichte der Weltkrise des 3. Jahrhunderts nach Christus* (Darmstadt: 1967), 285–311, here 305–306.

[48] See David Nicholls, "The theatre of martyrdom in the French Reformation," *Past and Present* 121 (1988): 68 (who employs Protestant martyrologies as descriptions of what actually happened). Potter, "Martyrdom As Spectacle," 70–71 and n. 3, remarks upon the oppositional potential of executions (but for practice, not texts). For the Reformation, my colleague Brad S. Gregory leans toward the substantial conformity of martyrdom narratives to real events as far as executions are concerned—see his *Salvation at Stake: Christian Martyrdom in Early Modern Europe* (Cambridge, Mass.: 1999), 16–21.

the appropriation and subversion of established meanings. First, at the most basic level, that of language.[49] Second, that of documentary forms. The acts of a trial (*acta*) served to legitimize the judge's decision; martyrs' *Acts* such as the *Acta Scillitanorum*, carefully patterned after the Roman judicial model, justify instead the Christian position.[50] Under Constantine, the great historian Eusebius of Caesarea would implicitly admit that *Acta* served a propagandistic function. The bishop attributed to the pagan opponent his own group's strategy; he reported (or imagined) that Maximinus Daia had ordered the forgery of *Acts of Pilatus and the Savior* besmirching Jesus' character and ordered schoolchildren to learn them by heart.[51] Ritual forms were also to be appropriated.[52] The two groups viewed the rites associated with execution/martyrdom through opposite lenses. The best example may be that wonderfully crafted document, the *Martyrdom of Perpetua and Felicitas*. Like many *Passiones*, this narrative served modern historians' reconstructions of the circus games, yet the hagiographer intended primarily to utilize the game's framework and pervert (or rather, convert) its meanings and meaningfulness for his or her own community's ends. In the *Martyrdom of Perpetua* as in many other instances of the genre, it is remarkable how much the martyrs control their fate.[53] They also control the interpretation of the civic ritual, in part through their actions, gestures, and words, in part through their visions, in part through the hagiographer's comments.

Later *passiones* emphasize that the pagans and Christians who watched a martyr's death in the arena accessed different and hierarchized levels of

---

[49] As programmatically stated by Averil Cameron, *Christianity and the Rhetoric of Empire: The Development of Christian Discourse* (Berkeley: 1991), 122–23.

[50] Hans Armin Gärtner, "Die Acta Scillitanorum in literarischer Interpretation," *Wiener Studien* 102 (1989): 156–57. Bowersock, *Martyrdom*, 36–38, believes in the fundamental authenticity of sections in *Acta* depicting judicial processes. Cf. as well Giuliana Lanata, *Gli atti dei martiri come documenti processuali*, (Milan: 1973), 15f, 38–40. Wiedemann, *Emperors and Gladiators*, 80, puts the matter well: "The martyr-acts reverse the Roman world's assumptions about justice and law: the executions of Christians show that the executions carried out by the pagan world are the opposite of public guarantees of social order".

[51] *Ecclesiastical History* 9.5.1–2, 9.7.1, ed. Gustave Bardy (Paris: 1984), 3.50–52.

[52] See Carl Andresen, "Altchristliche Kritik am Tanz—ein Ausschnitt aus dem Kampf der Alten Kirche gegen heidnische Sitte," in Heinzgünter Frohnes and Uwe W. Knorr, *Kirchengeschichte als Missionsgeschichte*, vol. 1, *Die Alte Kirche* (Munich: 1974), 356–57, assuming that to worship the Divinity with both body and soul was a concept alien to "Great Church" Christians (but not to heretical groups, see *Acta Ioannis* 94–96: "I represented the whole learning through a mime").

[53] See Coleman, "Fatal charades," 59, on Saturus's martyrdom, whose numerous twists and turns are there to show that he suffers the death he had predicted for himself. The best reading of the Passio is a book by Joyce Salisbury, *Perpetua's Passion: The Death and Memory of a Young Roman Woman* (New York and London: 1997), published the same year as my

reality. As prophesied in Proverbs 2.5, "You shall find a divine sense," the elects acquired "spiritual senses" that allowed them to reach a spiritual understanding of the material happening.[54] The pagans, in this Christian logic, did not perceive a reality at all, but a shadow. In Prudentius's *Peri stephanon*, only the baptized can see Lawrence's transfiguration on the grill; his burnt flesh smells delicious to the Christians but reeks in the pagans' nostrils—symbolizing the former's election to eternal life and the latter's damnation.[55] But the earliest *Acta* had already employed dual-level reading. In the *Martyrdom of Polycarp*, the magistrate calls on the bishop to clamor "Death to the godless (*atheous*)." Polycarp conforms to the order, but reorients the slogan's meaning. He turns to "the lawless (*anomōn*) pagan crowd" and transfixes it with his gaze, then turns this gaze toward Heaven. The martyr's suicide recycles Roman *devotio*, which vows to death (here, spiritual) the enemy. Polycarp's eyes draw a path between those who are condemned to (real, spiritual) death, and their divine executioner; his clamor's double entendre, which the echo between *atheos* and *anomos* underlines, reveals the blindness of the true victims in this game, the pagans.[56]

In the economy of the *Martyrdom of Polycarp*, the moment of death opens fleetingly a window onto the relationship between appearances and reality. But the interplay between carnal and spiritual vision and sense structures entirely the *Passio Perpetuae*. Perpetua's fourth vision precedes the narrative of the following day in the arena and provides its authoritative interpretation—according to *mysterium*.[57] The martyrs' death in the arena is actually

---

"Martyre et ritualité." On a number of topics our analyses parallel one another. Cf. especially *Perpetua's Passion*, 128–44.

[54] Cf. Karl Rahner, "Le début d'une doctrine des cinq sens spirituels chez Origène," *Revue d'ascétique et de mystique* 13 (1932): 113–45. See Sabine MacCormack, *The Shadows of Poetry: Vergil in the Mind of Augustine* (Berkeley: 1998), 73–88, on pagan interpretation and the Christian interpretation of pagan texts as if they had only a literal sense. Dio Chrysostom, *Oratio* 12.33, ed. J. W. Cowhoon, 5 vols. (London-Cambridge: 1950) 2.34–37, provides a good example of the way in which pagan ceremonies meant to activate inner understanding.

[55] Prudentius, *Peri Stephanon Liber*, 2, vv. 373–96, ed. Maurice Lavarenne (Paris: 1963), 43. See Igor Gorevich, *O Kritike Antropologii Zhivotnikh*, vol. 1, *Prichasheniye i Shashlik*, 5–8, whom I thank for the reference. That the different perceptions signal different fates is grounded in 2 Cor. 2–14:16: "*Deo autem gratias qui semper triumphat nos in Christo Iesu et odorem notitiae suae manifestat per nos in omni loco, quia Christi bonus odor sumus Deo in his qui salvi sunt et in his qui pereunt, aliis quidem odor mortis in mortem, aliis autem odor vitae in vitam.*" Cf. Origen, *Contra Celsum*, ed. Marcel Borret, *Origène. Contre Celse* 1.48, 2 vols. (Paris: 1967), 1.202:27–204:39.

[56] *Passio Polycarpi* 9.2, ed. Bastiaensen, 16:10–13. In 15.2, 24:7–8 when Polycarp is set on fire, his hagiographer smells as well a delicious odor, that of freshly baked bread, not burnt flesh. Cp. Daniel Boyarin, *Dying for God: Martydom and the Making of Christianity and Judaism* (Stanford: 1999), 51, on a Jewish rabbinical parallel to this Christian double entendre.

[57] *Passio Perpetuae et Felicitatis* 10.1–15, ed. Bastiaensen, 128–30. Cf. recently Louis Robert, "Une vision de Perpétue martyre à Carthage en 203," *Comptes-rendus de l'Académie des Inscrip-*

an agonistic victory over the devil. The true game master is not just any civic magistrate, but God himself.[58] Such a guiding spirit converts the *damnatio ad bestias* to the highest level of significance.

Numerous other details in the *Passio* speak of this conversion from letter to spirit. Traditionally, at least in Carthage, citizens shared with the people earmarked to fight the beasts (*bestarii*) a final meal consecrated to the God Liber, the *coena Libera*.[59] Perpetua and her companions attended such a banquet on the eve of the games. Yet, "as far as they were concerned (*quantum in ipsis erat*)" what they partook of was not a *coena Libera* but a Christian communal meal, *agapes*, perhaps a "Last Supper."[60] To impose this understanding, and to break the sham impression of community, the martyrs confronted the pagans: "[W]ith the same steadfastness they threw words at the face of the people, threatening them with God's Judgement, professing that their passion would be a blessing, and mocking the curiosity of those who flocked [to see them]." One of the condemned, Saturus, underlined the true rift hidden behind the meal: "Today friends and tomorrow enemies? But note carefully our faces, so that you may recognize us *in die illo*"—a double entendre, for it meant both the morrow and the day that pagans were blind to, the Last Judgement. According to the *Passio*, stunned by these words, many gentiles converted.[61]

Legally, these criminals could have been forced to die in the modes the crowd and presiding magistrate had chosen. But when the soldiers attempted "to force the men to don (*induere*) the garb of victims vowed to Saturn, the women those of victims consecrated to Ceres," Perpetua masterfully rejected the travesty.[62] To refuse idolatrous garb was simultaneously to invalidate part of the civic ritual's meaning and power for a pagan audience. A miracle confirmed this first assertion of freedom; each martyr ob-

---

tions et Belles-Lettres (Paris: 1982), 228–76; Brent D. Shaw, "The Passion of Perpetua," *Past and Present* 139 (1993), 3–45; Salisbury, *Perpetua's Passion.*

[58] See Barton, *Sorrows*, 20 n. 32. Cf. Bowersock, *Martyrdom*, 52–54: "a performance orchestrated by God."

[59] Cf. Tertullian, *Apologeticum* 42.5, ed. Waltzing, 91: "*Non in publico Liberalibus discumbo, quod bestiariis supremam cenantibus mos est.*" Werner Weismann, "Gladiator," *Reallexikon für Antike und Christentum*, ed. Theodor Klauser et al. (Stuttgart: 1981), 32.

[60] *Passio*, 17.1, ed. Bastiaensen, 138:1–3: "*Pridie quoque cum illam cenam ultimam, quam liberam vocant—quantum in ipsis erat, non cenam liberam sed agapem—cenarent . . .*" My 1997 reading here paralleled that of Salisbury, *Perpetua's Passion*, 137. But Salisbury suggested further (138–39) that the martyrs, in marching into the arena, reconsecrated to their purposes the *pompa*, and that in singing psalms they took over as well the arena's musical message.

[61] *Passio*, 17.2–3, ed. Bastiaensen, 138:7–10.

[62] *Passio*, 18.4–5, ed. Bastiaensen, 140. Cf. Rudolf Freudenberg, "Probleme römische Religionspolitik in Nordafrika nach der *Passio SS. Perpetuae et Felicitatis*," *Helikon* 13–14 (1973–74): 174–75: In gladiatorial fights, *addicere* signals the contractual abandon of one's life.

tained the death he or she had hoped for. For the hagiographer, these men and women were by no means *servi poenae.*

At the opening of the games, the martyrs further tilted the understanding of the event. They threatened the spectators as well as Hilarianus, the presiding officer, with godsent torments in the other world. Here the martyrs use an oppositional idiom we have already met with the 190 supernatural circus demonstration against Cleander.[63] The people reacted and clamored for the offenders to be beaten with whips (the punishment inflicted to the Cynic detractor of Titus's marriage), unwittingly displacing the ritual one step further toward a Christian meaning, for the victims "rejoiced that they had obtained some of the Lord's torments."[64] When Saturus was doused with his own blood, the crowd itself gave witness through its clamors to this second baptism (*tanto perfusus est sanguine ut populus revertenti illi secundi baptismatis testimonium reclamaverit*). In other words, insofar as martyr means witness, the people (still blindly) testified to a witnessing. Historians have interpreted diversely the crowd's shouts, "*Salvum lotum, salvum lotum.*" Did these words mean "well washed" (irony and cruelty on the part of onlookers belonging to a culture addicted to the baths)? Or were they a reference to baptism?[65] But the scholarly disagreement reflects a purposeful ambiguity. In the text, like Saturus's taunt at the *coena Libera,* the shouts belong simultaneously to the realms of letter and spirit; unwittingly, the people's slogans participate in the Christian *mysterium.* The pagans had sought to make Perpetua and her companions gruesome and passive figures in their civic rites; they have been transformed themselves into actors in the rite of baptism by the Holy Spirit.[66]

The Christians wrote and publicized *passiones* and *acta* in an attempt to impose their partisan interpretation on a public event whose factual mise-en-scène they did not control. They insinuated that there existed a transcendental meaning, of which God denied understanding to their oppo-

---

[63] Above, 133–34. Cf. also Cassius Dio, *Epitoma* 74.13.4–5, tr. Cary, 9.148–49: "invoking the Gods and cursing the soldiers"—the invocations being possibly sloganlike (*tous theous epiboomenos*) and alternating with the curses (*oute . . . oute*).

[64] *Passio,* 18.9, ed. Bastiaensen, 140.

[65] Franz Dölger, "Gladiatorenblut und Martyrerblut. Eine Szene der *Passio Perpetuae* in kultur- und religionsgeschichtlicher Bedeutung," *Vorträge der Bibliothek Warburg* 3 (1926), 196–203.

[66] The Spanish friars' tactic in Mexico—to make the natives "act" in political ceremonies or religious plays "parts" with a hidden or unobvious meaning to which the *padres* alone were privy—thus belonged to an age-old repertoire. See Richard Trexler, "We Think, They Act: Clerical Readings of Missionary Theatre in Sixteenth-Century New Spain," in *Understanding Popular Culture: Europe from the Middle Ages to the Nineteenth Century,* ed. Steven Kaplan (Berlin and New York: 1984), 189–227, at 191.

nents, which secretly informed the event. For the hagiographers, and perhaps for the martyrs as well,[67] death in the arena did not restore the *romana disciplina* and did not sacralize the civic community. Rather, God had established it as an instrument for the making of their own community.

A general Christian hostility vis-à-vis the *spectacula* may indicate nothing more than a rejection of their through-and-through idolatrous nature. With their references to mythology along with the procession of divine images and statues that opened them (the *pompa*), they were fully cultic. But one must go further. Is it coincidental that we owe to Tertullian—a fellow countryman and contemporary of Perpetua and Felicitas—both the sharpest attacks against festivals and the first testimony to the baptismal formula, the abjuration of the devil, his works, and his *pompa*?[68] During late antiquity, the Christian imaginary would progressively construct games and Church rites into polar opposites.[69] Tertullian's own rhetorical comparisons are telling. Public authority has banned factions, he says in his *Apology*, "lest the polity (*civitas*) be rent into parts, which would easily disturb elections (*comitia*), comices (*concilia*), reunions of the *curia*, public assemblies (*contiones*), even *spectacula*." Yet the Christians are not a *factio* but "a [legal] body (*corpus*), owing to (*de*) a shared understanding (*conscientia*) of *religio*, the unity in *disciplina* and an alliance in hope; we come together to form an association and make a congregation, in order to solicit God by our prayers." Then Tertullian details the organization and virtues of the grouping (*coitio*, *coetus*, or *congregatio*), and ends on the shared rites practiced by this body: prayers, charity, and especially well-lit banquets, which the Christians open by washing their hands, at which one sings canticles, and which are concluded with an oration.[70] By contrast, festivals in the honor of the emperors consist in nothing else but unbridled disorder: One takes out beds and braziers (for meals and sacrifices), one gives mutual banquets so numerous that the city transmutes itself into a huge tavern, and people

---

[67] Cf. Potter, "Martyrdom and Spectacle," 70–71, and Salisbury, *Perpetua's Passion*, for whom the Passion is Perpetua's diary. Yet it is almost impossible to reconstruct each event and even to prove that it actually happened owing to the importance for both sides of executions/martyrdoms, the paucity of sources, and the absence of pairs of narratives that might give us the pagan and the Christian version of the same deaths.

[68] Cf. Jan H. Waszink, "Pompa Diaboli," *Vigiliae Christianae* 1 (1947): 13–41.

[69] Robert A. Markus, *The end of Ancient Christianity* (Cambridge: 1990), 107–10, believes that after a first spurt circa 200, for the *spectacula* this construction happened late and progressively, between 400 and 600. Between 400 and 600, they were neither Christian nor pagan, but "secular." Ramsay MacMullen, *Christianity and Paganism between the Fourth and the Eighth Century* (New Haven: 1997), has taken issue with this.

[70] Tertullian, *Apologeticum* 38.2, 39.1–2, 39.14–19, ed. Waltzing, 80, 81. Cf. Stockmeier, "Christlicher Glaube," 896–97.

run herdlike to violent, immodest and libidinous games.[71] The same opposition implicitly informs the martyr Saturus's vision in *Perpetua*, where the
saints condemn strife within the Carthaginian *ecclesia* and compare it to the
agitation of circus factions.[72] The North African rhetor had written the
Apologeticum to plead aggressively with the gentiles. In his even less moderate *On the Spectacles*, written to shame his congregation, Tertullian paints
the games into the ultimate disorder destructive of communal peace. As
soon as the magistrate throws down his hand flag (*mappa*) to signal the
games' opening, madness seizes the onlookers; they are possessed with fury,
anger, and discord. This unreason manifests itself in the groundlessness of
their acclamations, be they hostile or favorable. Tertullian concludes: "Is
there anything more biting than the circus, where one spares neither the
princes nor one's fellow citizens?"[73] Desirous to force a radical separation
between the groups, he feared nothing more than an easy come-and-go
allowing movement from God's assembly to the devil's assembly (*ecclesia*).
Rendered ambiguous, words and gestures would loose their identity-de-
fining specificity: Hands raised to God would also move to praise mimes;
the same lips would render witness to the liturgy and to the gladiator. The
latter might even be praised into undying glory with the slogan "from eternity into eternity."[74]

The comparison between Tertullian's writings and the *Passio Perpetuae*
allows one to perceive two paradoxically complementary tactics. Circa 200
in North Africa, Christians condemned their coreligionists' attendance at
the civic spectacles because (among other things) it blurred the distinctiveness of the elements of the *ecclesia*'s ritual system and consequently obfuscated Christian identity. But when confronted with Christian deaths in
the context of these spectacles, they sought to take advantage of the ambiguity inherent in signs by reading into these civic rituals a Christian signification, and they tried to commemorate martyrdom by transmuting the
games into a setting for providential history.

Beyond Constantine: Instrument of Polemics and Sign of Meaningfulness

A riot occurred in the city during which one shouted against the leader as if
he had deserted the common safety. Furthermore, as Maxentius was giving
circus-games for the anniversary of his accession, suddenly the people shouted

---

[71] Tertullian, *Apologeticum* 35.2, ed. Waltzing, 75.

[72] *Passio Perpetuae* 13.6, ed. Bastiaensen 134:12–14: "*Dixerunt* [martyres episcopo] *Optato:*
'*Corrige plebem tuam, quia sic ad te conveniunt quasi de circo redeuntes et de factionibus certantes.*'"

[73] *De Spectaculis*, 16.4:12–15, 16.7:25–26, ed. Marie Turcan, SC 332 (Paris: 1986), 234–36.

[74] *De Spectaculis*, 25.5:17–22, ed. Turcan, 290.

with one voice that Constantine could not be conquered. Troubled by this acclamation, Maxentius withdrew, and calling to himself some senators, ordered a consultation of the Sibylline Books. There it was found that on this very day the enemy of the Romans would perish.

In Lactantius's account of the demise of Constantine's first opponent, Maxentius, a miraculous consensus leads the usurper, besieged in Rome, to turn to an oracular text. The *Sibylline Books* give an apparently unambiguous answer. Emboldened by his own blindness to the prophecy's literal meaning, Maxentius leads his troops to battle over the Milvian Bridge, there to die.[75]

Less than a generation after Lactantius's *On the Death of the Persecutors*, the Christian propagandist Eusebius also wanted posterity to believe that the most prestigious pagan prophetic texts, the *Sibylline Books*, had predicted Christ's victory. Texts were available. Since the first century, Jews and Christians had produced forged Sibylline Books that carefully imitated all aspects of the pagan original to tap its authoritative value. According to Eusebius's *Life of Constantine*, the oracles announced the Empire's conversion and the accession to power of the Christian basileus Constantine, enemy of paganism: When the emperor opened in 325 the Council of Nicea, he interpreted in these (self-serving) terms the Sibyl's prophecy to the bishops.[76] In this strategy, the text of the opponent contains the irreducible proof of its own supersession by a new dispensation. This technique was at the very core of Christian identity: The relationship Church Fathers established between Old and New Testament provides its most obvious analogue and probable model.[77] The *Sibylline Books'* fate in the writings of Eusebius—who was also a hagiographer—sheds light on the hijacking of ritual, or rather of textual depictions of rituals, in the *Acta* of the first Christian centuries. Forced by a fact, persecution, but aware as well of the centrality that theater and circus enjoyed in the civic and cultic life of the empire, the Christians worked on the ritual space of the *ludi circenses*. The martyrs (or their hagiographers) stage their own death rites within the ritual context of the games and explode the latter. In other words, martyrdom

---

[75] Lactantius, *De mortibus persecutorum* 44.7–8, ed. J. L. Creed (Oxford: 1984), 64: "*Fit in urbe seditio et dux increpitatur velut desertor salus publicae. Tuncque repente populus—circenses enim natali suo [Maxentius] edebat—una voce subclamat Constantinum vinci non posse. Qua voce consternatus proripit se ac vocatis quibusdam senatoribus libros Sybillinos inspici iubet, in quibus repertum est illo die hostem romanorum esse periturum.*"

[76] Ramsay MacMullen, *Enemies of the Roman Order* (Cambridge, Mass.: 1966), 145–52, 154f. The *Oratio Constantini* is an insert in Eusebius of Caesarea, *Vita Constantini*, ed. I. A. Heikel, *Eusebius Werke* (Leipzig: 1902), 1.7.179f.; PL 8, cols. 449f., Alfons Kurfess, *Sibyllinische Weissagungen* (Berlin: 1951), 208f.

[77] See Gerard Caspary, *Politics and Exegesis: Origen and the Two Swords* (Berkeley: 1979).

reveals the meaning enclosed in its pagan shell, a significance hidden to the pagans, blind puppets of God, the Supreme *Editor*.[78]

Beyond Constantine: Theorizing Religio *and the Political Sphere*

With Constantine's victory, the opposition constructed in early Christian times between the *spectacula* and Church rites was enlisted for new tasks and therefore transformed.[79] This reutilization of the *spectacula*—now no longer the real target of polemics—accounts in part for the stigma that remained attached to them in the *très longue durée*. Rival Christian groups assimilated their adversaries' rites to the games and argued that they labored under the same vices as pagan shows. In the East, Catholics accused Arians of having borrowed for their liturgy the theatrical techniques of the mime. In North Africa, Augustine sought to discipline his congregation by assimilating the practices with which it honored the saints to the disorderliness of pagan rituals. He employed the same tactic in trying to besmirch the memory of those martyrs whom his rivals the Donatists claimed as their own. Given that he recycled the images of fury and gregarious behavior his North African countryman Tertullian had painted circa A.D. 200, one justly suspects that we hardly have here an objective portrait of Donatist death.[80]

The struggles among Church factions did not alone raise the issue of ritual. The emperor's conversion made all the more acute the problem

---

[78] This strategy is similar, but in the field of texts and imagination, to the actual incorporation of another group's rituals into one's own. See for example how Madagascar's Merina kings captured and subordinated to royal ceremonial the descent groups' circumcision ritual—Maurice Bloch, *From blessing to violence: History and ideology in the circumcision ritual of the Merina in Madagascar* (Cambridge [UK]: 1986), 117.

[79] Hermann Reich, *Der Mimus. Ein litterar-entwicklungsgeschichtlicher Versuch*, 2 vols. (Berlin: 1903), 762–65. Like Cicero four hundred years before (see Florence Dupont, *L'Acteur-Roi*, 31–34), authors such as Jerome betrayed a profound ambivalence: They were willing to study actors' skills and learn from them as counseled in manuals of rhetoric; at the same time, they had to posture repulsion.

[80] He transforms into frenzied suicides the deaths of men and women his sectarian opponents considered martyrs. Augustine, *Contra Gaudentium* 1.28.32, ed. Michael Petschenig, CSEL 53 (Vienna: 1910), 230:30–231:5: "... *cum idololatriae licentia usquequaque ferveret ... isti paganorum armis festa sua frequentantium irruebant. Vovebant autem pagani iuvenes idolis suis quis quot occideret. At isti gregatim hinc atque inde confluentes tamquam in amphitheatro a venatoribus more immanium bestiarum venabulis se oppositis ingerebant, furentes moriebantur, putrescentes sepeliebantur, decipientes colebantur*" (... when the licence of idolatry still burned strong everywhere ... these men rushed on the weapons of the pagans who were celebrating their festivals ... Herdlike, they flowed together hither and tither, and akin to ferocious beasts in the amphitheater they impaled themselves on the hunting spears that were put before them. Possessed by fury, they died; rotting, they were buried; deluding [others into believing this had been martyrdom], they were worshipped). See Claude Lepelley, "Iuvenes et circoncellions: les derniers sacrifices humains de l'Afrique antique," *Antiquités Africaines* 15 (1980), 264.

Tertullian had raised. For some Church fathers, given the accelerated rate of exchange between civic and Christian forms, it became quite critical to underline more sharply the difference between them. In this context, Vigilantius's attacks on the cult of relics must have been unsettling. "You have brought [into the Church] the rites of the gentiles under the mantle of religion," wrote the Spanish priest, criticizing in particular the practice of lighting candles before them even in daylight. Jerome's feeble reply, that one had to execrate this cultic act when it honored idols but accept it when it honored the saints,[81] would hardly have received a passing grade in the conceptual world of Tertullian.

Jerome's correspondent Augustine of Hippo addressed the issue as well. In several of his works, he gave some thought to the function and effect of rituals, both to plead for their importance and to inveigh against their self-serving use. Between 413 and 415, Augustine constructed in the *De civitate Dei* an opposition that ostensibly contrasted the gentile political dispensation and the Christian order, yet could be turned against any emperor desirous of manipulating the Faith to the benefit of his power.[82] In worldly polities, leaders allied to the demons manipulated religion (both beliefs and rites) in order to consolidate their selfish power over the commons:

> The demons can only get control of men when they have deluded and deceived them; in the same way the leaders (*principes*) of men (who were not men of integrity but the human counterparts of the demons) taught men as true under the name of religion things they knew to be false. By this means they bound them tighter as it were (*velut aptius alligantes*) to the citizen community (*civilis societas*) so that they might bring them under control (*subditos possiderent*) and keep them there by the same technique. What chance had a weak and ignorant individual of escaping from the combined deceits of the statesmen and the demons?[83]

Augustine was Roman. "Religion" (in the modern sense of the term) comprised both beliefs (*opinio*) and ceremonies (*religio, ritus*).[84] Consequently,

---

[81] *Contra Vigilantium* 4, 7, PL 23, 342c–43a, & 346a, with MacMullen, *Christianity*, 115–16. Cf. Lactantius's derisive comments about pagan gods needing luminaries, *Divine Institutes* 6.2.1–8, ed. Samuel Brandt, CSEL 19 (Prague: 1890), 481:14–483:8.

[82] Peter Brown, *Augustine of Hippo: A Biography* (Berkeley: 1967), 313–14: After the sack of Rome, worried citizens had turned to the games for reassurance.

[83] *De civitate dei* 4.32, 126:8–14; tr. Henry Bettenson, *City of God* (Harmondsworth: 1972), 176. Compare Lactantius (following an Euhemerist model popular as well in the early modern era): Gods were often human political leaders whom their heirs (or themselves) had divinized for crass political purposes. See his *Divine Institutes* 1.22.21–26:88–109, ed. Pierre Monat, SC 326 (Paris: 1986), 236–38: Jupiter bound (*copulabat*) to himself in political alliances and friendships other rulers, an *amicitia* sealed by the construction of joint temples, rites, and feasts.

[84] Cf. below, 146.

the ruling class's position, "that it was expedient for communities (*civitates*) to be deceived in matters of *religio*,"[85] had a corollary in the ceremonial sphere:

> Varro . . . openly declared . . . on the subject of religious rites (*in religionibus*)[86] that there are many truths which it is not expedient for the general public (*vulgus*) to know, and, further, many falsehoods which are good for the general public (*populus*) to believe true . . . Varro here at least reveals the whole policy of the so-called sages, by whose influence cities and peoples are governed.[87]

But in God's polity, politics are justly subordinated to religion as means to ends, in a hierarchical relationship akin to that ideally obtaining between the peace of the body and the peace of the soul. As we shall see, this oppositional construction entailed an appropriation of the idea of common good to the benefit of the City of God. Conversely, Augustine classifies any political power that would not serve God as segmentary, sectarian, private. For Livy, Numa Pompilius, Rome's second king, had pretended to receive the nightly guidance of the nymph Egeria in legislating religious ceremonies that would domesticate the fierce spirits of the first Romans. In the ancient world, to invent rituals for the common good was perfectly acceptable; a practice's origins did not have the same validating or invalidating valence as in a Judeo-Christian universe that knew absolute beginnings and ends.[88] Creationist monotheism injected into the European tradition a correlation between *Genesis* and *Geltung* that lasted well into the nineteenth century.[89] Numa's "invention" fueled Prudentius's criticism of pagan cults in *Peri Stephanon*.[90] The poet's contemporary Augustine uses this episode to nail in, *ab urbe condita*, paganism's original sin: the self-serving deceit with which the Roman upperclass manipulates religion.[91]

---

[85] *De civitate dei* 4.27, 121:15–16, tr. Bettenson, 169.

[86] Augustine, *De diuersis quaestionibus octoginta tribus*, ed. A. Mutzenbecher, CCSL 44 (Turnhout: 1970), 42:25–26 (adopting Cicero's definition in the *De inventione*): "*Religio est quae superioris cuiusdam naturae, quam diuinam uocant, curam cerimoniamque affert.*"

[87] *De civitate dei* 4.31, 125:15–20, tr. Bettenson, 174–75.

[88] *De civitate dei* 6.4, 169:16–18 (cf. Bettenson, 232): Chronologically speaking, human communities first come into being and institute their religions, but the true religion came first and instituted the celestial *civitas* ("*Vera autem religio non a terrena aliqua civitate instituta est, sed plane caelestem ipsa instituit civitatem*"). See Livy, *Ab urbe condita* 1.19, ed. B. O. Foster (Cambridge, Mass.: 1919), 1.66–68.

[89] On this, see below, ch. 5, 182–84.

[90] Prudence, *Peri Stephanon* 10, vv. 402–403, ed. Lavarenne, 133: "*Inventa regum pro salute publica Pompiliorum nostra carpunt secula.*" For Tertullian, *De prescriptione hereticorum* 40.6, ed. R. F. Refoulé and P. de Labriolle, SC 46 (Paris: 1957), 146, the devil had inspired Numa's rituals; they were to be deceitful copy of Jewish law's customs (*morositas*).

[91] *De civitate dei* 7.34–35, esp. 34 *in fine*, 214:29–215:37.

Augustine develops the opposition between public and sectarian in his discussion of systems of signs in the *De doctrina christiana* (396–427). He contrasts those *signa* that are "divinely instituted as if for the common good (*tanquam publice*) for the love of God and of one's neighbor" with those "that waste the hearts of wretched human beings by [inducing] private desires (*privatas appetitiones*) for temporal things." These bad signs are produced "by some pestilential community (*societas*) of humans and demons" and are akin to "the instituted pacts of some faithless and fraudulent alliance (*infidelis et dolosae amicitiae*)."[92] The bishop of Hippo stands on its head the once-dominant understanding: that the cult of the Gods and of the emperors warranted the common good and that Christians were an exclusive sect.

Some of Augustine's more precise formulations stem from the Manichees' attack against Christian cultic forms. Faustus had inveighed against Christianity that it differed neither in belief nor in rites from paganism. Augustine counters this accusation in the *Adversus Faustum Manichaeum* (397), a text alluded to in the *City of God*'s discussion of rites.[93] The bishop of Hippo's ultimate line of defense is not our main concern. It parallels his criterion for evaluating whether a war is just or unjust: intention.[94] In the case of the saints, cult aims at inciting humans to imitate their example as well as at obtaining a participation in their merits and prayers. On the way to this solution, Augustine delivers important thoughts on ritual. He agrees with Faustus that two elements define a religious group and distinguish it from another: its beliefs (*opinio*) and rites (*cultus, ritus*).[95] The latter are absolutely necessary: A *religio*, regardless of its ultimate relationship to truth, can only bind human beings together if it draws them together with visible signs and sacraments; the power of such *signa et sacramenta* is beyond words, which explains that one considers attacks against them sacrilegious.[96]

---

[92] *De doctrina Christiana* 2.23.36, ed. G. M. Green, CSEL 80 (Vienna: 1963), 59:30–60:16. The same opposition between public and selfish private informs Augustine's discussion of miracles and sorcery, see above, introduction, 10.

[93] *De civitate dei* 6.11, 83, refers to *Adversus Faustum*'s defense of Jewish ceremonies.

[94] *De civitate dei* 1.21, 23:4–9.

[95] Augustine, *Contra Faustum* 20.3, ed. Joseph Zycha, CSEL 25:1 (Vienna: 1891), 537:4–8 (Faustus speaking, but Augustine accepts these categories): "*Schisma, nisi fallor, est eadem opinantem atque eodem ritu colentem quo ceteri, solo congregationis delectari discidio. Secta vero est longe alia opinantem quam caeteri, alio etiam sibi ac longe dissimili ritu divinitatis intuisse culturam.*" Cf. Markus, *End*, 102.

[96] Augustine, *Contra Faustum* 19.11, on circumcision and Jewish alimentary prohibitions, ed. Zycha, 510:1–7: "*In nullum autem nomen religionis, seu verum seu falsum, coagulari homines possunt, nisi aliquo signaculorum vel sacramentorum visibilium consortio conligentur, quorum sacramentorum vis inenarabiliter valet plurimum, et ideo contempta sacrilegos facit. Inpie quippe contemnitur, sine qua non potest perfici pietas.*" The beautiful insistence on the prefix *con* linguistically reinforces Augustine's thesis on community.

When one pastes independent works together, one risks getting glued up in a pseudosynthesis. Yet there are enough intertextual links between *Against Faustus*, the *City of God*, and *On Christian Doctrine* to suggest the following. Despite his criticism of Numa's guile and of Varro's cowardly lack of sincerity, Augustine was Livy's heir. He should be seen as an intermediary between Livy and Durkheim, between Roman conceptions of order and early social anthropology.[97] Like the pagans, Augustine considered that *religiones* were essential. As any human association, the *ecclesia* depended for its cohesion on public (understand: common) signs and sacraments. Yet one had to distinguish between good and bad communities. One criterion among others consisted in the contrasting ways in which they used *religiones*. A tangle of deceitful signs held together unjust (understand: unsubordinated to God's justice) associations; their rulers readily manipulated these *signa* for their private ends. This dual "belief," in the importance of rites and in their devilish manipulation in communities that did not give God his due, would be bequeathed to medieval political culture. It is, as part 2 of this essay argues, critically absent in many anthropologically inspired analyses of medieval "ritual" owed to twentieth-century historians.

Remembering Martyrdom to Convey Meaningfulness: Space and Time

Patristic constructs (or historians' reconstruction of patristic constructs) do not in themselves demonstrate their own cultural importance. To get a hint of their hold, we have to turn to the role of martyrdom and rituals in other genres produced by the post-Constantinian Church with other agendas. Robert A. Markus has recently reexamined post-Constantinian critiques of the *pompa diaboli*. In his opinion, they were critical in the work of reclassification that progressively fashioned a dichotomous opposition between paganism and Christianity intolerant of the erstwhile religiously neutral no-man's-land of civic space.[98] One may disagree with him over the cultic colorlessness of the games. After all, the *saeculum* was never a fully neutral zone; the term itself carried too much negativity, as in the devil's epithet, *princeps saeculi*, the Prince of this World.[99] But it remains that the great

---

[97] Cf. John Bossy, "Some elementary forms of Durkheim," *Past and Present* 95 (1982): 3–18, for Durkheim's early modern ancestors.

[98] Markus, *End of Ancient Christianity*. In this book, Markus seems to have extended the notion of "the secular," which he revealed to be present in the thought (but not in the vocabulary) of Augustine (see Markus, *Saeculum*), to make it a general, if threatened, feature of late antique mentalities between 400 and 600.

[99] The semantic field of "*saeculum*" hardly suggests neutrality; see, e.g., the penances provided by a council, perhaps in Cordoba (ca. A.D. 354) 5, ed. Jesus Suberbiola Martínez, *Nuevos concilios hispano-romanos de los siglos III y IV. La colección de Elvira* (Malaga: 1987), 119 (long version): "*Matronae vel eorum mariti ut vestimenta sua ad ornandam seculariter pompam non dent; et si fecerint, triennio temporis abstineantur*"; 131 (shorter version): "*Nullus fidelis ad pompam seculi vestimentum suum det.*"

English historian has opened up a key dossier: late antique Christianity's construction of its identity through its conceptualization of ritual forms.[100]

The remembrance of the age of the martyrs served to formulate and make meaningful the transformations that the Christian victors felt had occurred with the onset of what Augustine called "these Christian times."[101] It served, in fact, to *effect* this transition. It would be inscribed in the calendar. Bede (d. 725) begins his martyrology with the *natalis* of one Almachius, who had interrupted (and as a result found death during) games given for the first day of the year with the words: "Today is the octave of the Lord's Birthday! Desist from idolatrous superstitions and polluted sacrifices."[102] By the sixth century, and probably already in the fourth, the hagiographic type of the "Mime-martyr" had appeared.[103] It conveyed a similar but more complex argument. In these romanced passions, a pagan mime stages at the games a Christian ritual—more often one of the most important, baptism. But perverse imitation engenders unexpected effects: Mimesis functions *ex opere*, regardless of the actor's earlier faith and indignity. At the very moment where he parodies the sacred gestures, the mime believes and proclaims to the crowd his newborn faith. The onlookers at first see in this profession only the second act of the play. They laugh; the presiding official even pitches in the plot and sends soldiers in the arena to arrest the true-false convert. All believe that one has reached a third act well suited to the general parody: The exhibitionist sectarian will suffer martyrdom. Progressively, faced with the mime's repeated proclamations and increased antipagan provocations, the audience comes to realize that the mime has truly converted, truth merges with assumed make-believe, and he dies a saint's death. The hagiographic novel conveys a message: The mime-martyr's passion demonstrates the irresistible superiority of Church rituals, in

---

[100] This is a verbal shortcut, since evidently "late antique Christianity" is not an agent.

[101] Cf., for Byzantium, the wonderful article owed to Sabine MacCormack, "Christ and Empire, Time and Ceremonial in Sixth-Century Byzantium," *Byzantion* 52 (1982), 287–309.

[102] AASS Ian. I (Anvers-Bruxelles: 1643), 31; *Premier martyrologe de Bède*, ed. J. Dubois and G. Renaud, I.R.H.T. Bibliographies, Colloques, Travaux Pratiques 12 (Paris: 1976), 5; cf. PL 123, 205d–207a. Cf. Hippolyte Delahaye, "Saint Almachius ou Télémaque," *Analecta Bollandiana* 33 (1914): 421–28, who identifies too readily the Almachius of the Latin martyrologies with the Greek Telemachus in Theodoret, *Historia Ecclesiastica* 5.26, given that "un chrétien zélé qui vient déranger la foule dans ses plaisirs et trouve la mort au milieu des gladiateurs, cela ne s'est pas vu deux fois à Rome vers le commencement du Ve siècle" (423–24).

[103] Werner Weismann, "Gelasinos von Heliopolis, ein Schauspieler-Märtyrer," *Analecta Bollandiana* 93 (1975): 39–66; numerous versions of Genesius's legend exist, see Weismann, "Die 'Passio Genesii mimi' (BHL 3320)," *Mittellateinisches Jahrbuch* 12 (1977): 22–43, and Joseph van der Straten, *Les manuscrits hagiographiques d'Orléans, Tours et Angers*, Subsidia Hagiographica 64 (Bruxelles: 1982), 288–92. Weismann lists similar narratives in his *Kirche und Schauspiele. Die Schauspiele im Urteil der lateinischen Kirchenväter* (Würzburg: 1972), thus Ardalio, AASS Apr. II (Anvers: 1675), 215, or Philemon, AASS Apr. I (Paris: 1865), 751–53.

the more frequent version represented by baptism (in which one renounces the *pompa diaboli* including theater), over gentile "communication" rites, represented by what may have been its most beloved forms, the mime.

The function that one of these mime-martyrdoms plays in John Malalas's *Chronicle* illustrates how such narratives could help think time. The last story to be told in book 13, Gelasinos's death at games presided over by the last pagan emperor, occurs at the central hinge of the work, right before Constantine's conversion, the first episode in book 14.[104] The emperor's baptism represents the takeover from the inside of the heretofore pagan political structure; Gelasinos's martyrdom symbolizes the equally epochal triumph of Christian rituals from within the arena. On the part of a chronicler interested in the amphitheater to the point of attributing the invention of chariot races to Romulus, *ab urbe condita*, this was an elegant idea. But not an isolated idea. Another author, Prudentius, utilized Lawrence's martyrdom, located in Rome, "venerable mother of temples," to retroactively announce the metamorphosis of the Empire. Lawrence's glorious death was both a triumph over paganism and a prophecy of the final victory, Constantine's.[105] Like the *Aeneid*, the *Peri stephanon* places back into the past an oracle announcing a new order; ritual gives meaning, drama, and density to the providential event.

With the mime-martyrs we have an example of the use of martyrdom to make sense of chronological watersheds. The remembrance of the saints could also be used to give meaningfulness to topography or transformations in space.[106] In his *Oration on the Martyr Gordios*, Basil, bishop of Caesarea, tells his congregation the story of the first martyrdom in that city.[107] Like the author of the *Passio Perpetuae*, the bishop hijacks a gentile event for a Christian purpose, but for a purpose visible only from the perspective of the post-Constantinian present. A renowned Christian centurion, Gordios

---

[104] Malalas, *Chronographia* 12.49–50, ed. Dindorf and Nieburh, 314–15, tr. Jeffreys et al., *The Chronicle*, 170–71.

[105] Prudence, *Peri Stephanon* 2, vv. 1–16, 429–520, ed. Lavarenne, 32, 44–47. On the christianization of time, see Markus, *End*, 97–106.

[106] See Sabine MacCormack, "Loca sancta: The Organization of Sacred Topography in Late Antiquity," Robert Ousterhout, ed., *The Blessings of Pilgrimage* (Urbana: 1990), 7–40; Markus, *End*, 139–55; for a later era Amy G. Remensnyder, *Remembering Kings Past: Monastic Foundation Legends in Medieval Southern France* (Ithaca: 1995), 69–74, 197–98. Richard Krautheimer, *Three Christian Capitals: Topography and Politics* (Berkeley: 1983), Peter Brown, *The Cult of the Saints* (Chicago: 1981), 8, 42–43, and Gilbert Dagron, *Constantinople imaginaire* (Paris: 1984), have addressed the contemporary models of a new civic topography. Evelyne Patlagean, "Ancient Byzantine hagiography and social history," in *Saints and their Cults*, ed. Stephen Wilson (Cambridge [UK]: 1983), 101–21 at 109–11, deals with Byzantine hagiography's use of space.

[107] On the relationship between monument, *memoria*, and writing in Roman culture, see Mary Jaeger, *Livy's Written Rome* (Ann Arbor: 1997).

abandons the military life when the rulers decree persecution—leading to chaos and division in Caesarea—and withdraws to the neighboring mountains. There, he prepares himself with fasts, vigils, prayers, and meditations on the Scriptures, like an athlete for the upcoming fight. For exile is only temporary; asceticism prefaces a martyrdom that will change the face of the city. Gordios does not select just any moment in the civic calendar: At a festival celebrated for "a demon who loves war," the entire city fills the theater to watch chariot races. In late antique political culture, such manifestations of unity signify the established order's legitimacy. But the bishop paints this "*consensus omnium*" in highly pejorative colors. How positive can a unity be that takes in schoolboys, slaves, and women of the lowest origins? Worse, the festival brings together Greeks, Jews, and "a great multitude of Christians" who, unguardedly, sat together "in the council of vanity" [cf. Psalm 1] and did not refuse to pervert themselves (*ecclinontes*) with evildoers." It is to disrupt this impious consensus that Gordios descends from his mountain and enters the theater, there to put himself in the center, *eis to meson*.

The martyr's arrival immediately reorients the crowd's attention ("the theater turned to the unexpected spectacle [*theas*]") and polarizes it with equal swiftness. Civic unity is shattered, for the people now shout conflicting slogans (*boe summiges*): The Christians applaud the interloper and the pagans call on the presiding magistrate to do away with him. Here Basil the hagiographer draws on conventional tropes of hagiography: In this genre, the martyr's challenge often results in the conversion of the audience, sometimes in whole, more often in part;[108] split, the audience is also divided in its chants, some praising the martyrs' God, some demanding that the presiding officials do away with the "magicians," who resist tortures so wonderfully.[109] The representatives of public power, to forestall the mar-

---

[108] Collective conversion in the amphitheater, *Vita secunda Faustini et Iovitae martyrum*, AASS Feb. II, 813–17, at 816; in the stadium, with destruction of the idols, *Passio Bonifatii* 2.8 (BHL 1413), AASS Mai. III, 280–83, at 282 (*"factus est ploratio a turba et vociferatio magna dicentium, 'Magnus est deus Christianorum; magnus est deus sanctorum martyrum; Christe fili Dei, salva nos; universi enim in te credimus et ad te confugimus; pereant universa simulacre gentium.' Et impetum fecit omnis plebs et destruxit aram, et iudicem lapidaverunt"*); collective recognition in the amphitheater of the Christian God, *Acta Martinae* 5.42, AASS Ian. I, 15–16, at 16. Partial conversion of the audience in the amphitheater, *Acta sancti Primi et Feliciani* 6, AASS Jun. II, 152–54, at 154 (1,500 men with their whole families out of 12,000 total *exceptis pueris et mulieribus*), *Passio Potiti* 4.16–20, Ian. I, 754–57, at 757 (2,000 out of 30,000), *Passio Viti* 2.14–16, AASS Jun. II, 1021–26, here 1025 (1,000 men out of 5,000 *virorum absque mulieribus et infantibus, quorum erat multitudo inaestimabilis*).

[109] Schism in an audience convoked *ad spectaculum* (meaning, prophetically, of both martyrdom and the arena), see *Passio Firmini et Rustici* 1.8, AASS Aug. II, 419–22, at 421 (BHL 3023): "*Haec videntes populi qui aderant versi in stuporem dixerunt, 'Magnus est deus christianorum; alii autem a diabolo caecati qui ex parte Anulini stabant coeperunt clamare dicentes,' Tolle magos*

tyrs' predictable impact on the crowd, can even decide to interrogate them secretly and execute them swiftly.[110]

With such topoi at hand, Basil depicts with magnificent rhetorical art the destruction of civic consensus and its re-creation around a new center. The crowd finds unity only in an enthrallment of the senses. All forget the horses and the charioteers, and the noise produced by the chariots' presentation is in vain. Eyes and ears have found their definitive focus: "[N]o eye strove to see anything but Gordios, no ear wanted to hear anything but his words." Here the bishop recycles the tropes panegyrists mustered in descriptions of the emperor's *adventus*.[111] Once the magistrate imposes silence through a herald, "Gordios is listened to, Gordios is watched." A stereotypical confrontation between archon and martyr follows, and finally the former condemns the latter to be executed. Now comes the spatial (as opposed to topical) reorientation. The whole city, mobilized again (but for the real, incomparably more valuable show), leaves town and recreates around the place of execution as if a kind of new arena. When Gordios is beheaded, the people's acclamation (*boē*) marks his victory and the birth of a new consensus. Simultaneously, it signals the victory of the spectacle of martyrdom over that provided by the pagan chariot race. Even more (for such was Basil's avowed purpose), in depicting the crowd's itinerary, it explains the recent reorientation of civic space. Caesarea's urban geometry underwent a sort of symmetrical inversion, as sacral places and foci of communitarian togetherness were projected from the center to the periphery, from within the city's walls and the theater to the suburbs and *tōn marturōn stadion*, the martyrs' stadium.[112]

Basil's wishes are clear. He hopes that the new topography will be as eternal as martyrdom is eternal. It may not be fortuitous that he explains perhaps more convincingly than any other Church Father how the recitation of *Acta* provides a spectacle powerful enough to replace the civic

---

atque maleficos, ne filii nostri seducantur ab eis . . . Populi vero cum vidissent mirabilia quae facta sunt dixerunt ad Anulinum, 'Quid hoc fecisti ut adduceres huc magos istos? Civitas Veronensis in perditione est; tolle eos a nobis.' "

[110] Passio Maximi Cumae 10, AASS Oct. XIII, 319–25, at 322 : "Haec audiens praeses tremefactus est et ne seditio fieret in populo iussit infantem caedi"; see as well the Acta sancti Justi et Pastoris 2, AASS Aug. II, 154.

[111] Cf. (both on Julian) Ammianus Marcellinus, Res gestae libri, ed. Wolfgang Seyfarth et al. (Leipzig: 1978), 1.252:8–10, and Mamertinus, Gratiarum actio Iuliano 6.3–5, ed. Edouard Galletier, Panégyriques latins, vol. 3 (Paris: 1955), 21: "Voces gaudentium oppresserat miraculi magnitudo."

[112] Homily 18, On Gordios the Martyr, PG 31, 489–508. See Jaeger, Livy's Written Rome, ch. 2, who explicates how the Livian narrative of the Sabines' rape, a story of political conflict resolved into political union, becomes a story about the shaping of the urban landscape.

games.[113] As Basil tells us in another of his sermons, preaching about the martyrs provokes an anamnesis that brings back their deeds *eis meson*, and allows the audience to visualize them. The rhetor's speech functions like an artist's tablet painting.[114] Only from the standpoint of a silent reading culture can we forget the impact of a text read aloud and presented in public like a live image. In Caesarea, year after year, the performance repeated itself, explaining all at once the waning of the games and civic topography.

Martyrdom's role in texts that rendered meaningful chronology and topography fostered its preservation as a narrative element. But this marker of significance transmitted simultaneously a model of oppositional behavior, within or through ritual. The first martyrdoms had aimed at imposing the superiority of one dispensation over another; now one demonstrated a political order's illegitimacy (or lesser legitimacy) by attacking its rituals. The offensive could be "real," through deeds, but imaginary as well, through texts. Since the first *Acta martyrum*, hagiographers (a category from which one would be hard put to distinguish historians) knew how critical it was to impose one's interpretation on a ritual, be it one's own or one's opponents'.

Two examples shall illustrate the transformation in Christian idioms. Both are associated with an important figure, Ambrose of Milan. In the first, a hagiographer underlines the superiority he is pleading for through rituals. In 422, Paulinus, a cleric belonging to the Milanese church, wrote the first *Vita Ambrosii*. One of its aims was to define and delimit vis-à-vis one another two spheres, those of episcopal and of imperial power. Paulinus drew on his hero's letters, especially those Ambrose had written Theodosius I concerning the incidents of Callinicum and Thessaloniki. He turned what had been probably mostly a written (and confidential) debate between emperor and bishop into a confrontational drama set on the stage of the Christian liturgy, out of which Ambrose emerged victorious.[115] A miracle served the same agenda. According to the *Vita*, Honorius gave games (*Lybicarum ferarum munus*) in Milan. The people came en masse.

---

[113] See Weismann, *Kirche und Schauspiele*, 108ff, Suzanne Poque, "Spectacles et festins offerts par Augustin d'Hippone pour les fêtes des martyrs," *Pallas* 5 (1968): 103–25, esp. 110–11.

[114] Homily 19, PG 31, 507–26, here 508c–509a. Quintillian, *Institutio Oratoria* 6.2.29–32, ed. Ludwig Radermacher (Leipzig: 1907), 1.327:18–328:10, explains how rhetorical art allows an audience to visualize an event (such as a violent crime). Cf. A. J. Woodman, *Rhetoric in Classical Historiography* (London: 1988), and Roos Meijering, *Literary and Rhetorical Theories in Greek Scholia* (Groningen: 1987), 20–30.

[115] See Rudolf Schieffer, "Von Mailand nach Canossa", *DA* 28 (1972): 333–70. Ambrose himself had not included the letters on Callicicum and Thessaloniki in his official collection.

The presiding official, prefect Eugenius, ordered Stilicho to send soldiers to Milan's main church, entrusting them with a mission: to seize one Cresconius from the basilica where he had found asylum. Seeing Stilicho's men, Cresconius took refuge at the altar; Ambrose and his clergy formed a protective circle around him. But their smaller numbers failed to restrain the soldiers; Stilicho's henchmen grabbed Cresconius and, "rejoicing, returned to the amphitheater." In the meantime, prostrate before the altar, the bishop cried and implored God—a precocious example, perhaps, of a liturgical clamor.[116] His action triggered supernatural retaliation, for in the arena the leopards unleashed against Cresconius attacked the soldiers who had "staged a triumph over the Church." Stilicho, terrified, underwent penance; Cresconius escaped the death penalty; he was sent into exile instead, and soon afterward obtained his pardon.[117]

Like Gregory of Tours more than half a century later, Paulinus aimed at supporting with the pen the Church's customary right of asylum and judicial intercession, which imperial legislation sought to roll back.[118] The hagiographer did not limit himself to the narrative stick; he offered to representatives of public power a positive example. Right after Theodosius's victory over the usurper Eugenius, the emperor had granted Ambrose the pardon of two rebels who had sought sanctuary in a church. The victor had even "groveled at the bishop's feet, professing that he owed his safety to his [Ambrose's] merits and prayers."[119]

For his ends, Paulinus mustered recycled topoi of martyrdom. The arena still provided a charged space for the confrontation between public power and holiness. But this monument now stood conjoined to a topographical counterpart signifying episcopal authority, the basilica. The beasts that favored the saint's cause also sprang out of the *Acta*'s repertory.[120] But they turned against the soldiers more to signify the immunity of the building in which the saint resides than to show that God and not the magistrate determined the martyr's death. As in earlier hagiography, Paulinus subordinated the civic ritual to a demonstration of the superiority of the order

---

[116] Cf. Lester K. Little, *Benedictine Maledictions: Liturgical Cursing in Romanesque France* (Ithaca: 1993).

[117] Paulinus, *Vita sancti Ambrosii* 34, ed. Michele Pellegrino, *Vita di S. Ambrogio* (Rome: 1961), 100.

[118] James, "*Beati pacifici*"; L. Wenger, "Asylrecht," *Reallexikon für Antike und Christentum*, vol. 1 (Leipzig: 1950), col. 841.

[119] Paulinus, *Vita Ambrosii* 31, ed. Pellegrino, 96:20–22.

[120] Beasts submit to the martyrs: *Acta sancti Primi et Feliciani* 6, AASS Jun. II, 152–54, here 154 ("*Et dixerunt beati martyres: 'Praeses iniquitatis, ecce ferae cognoscunt creatorem suum'* "); *Passio Viti* 2.14–16, AASS Jun. II, 1021–26, at 1025; *Passio Potiti* 4.16–20, Ian. I, 754–57, at 757. Beasts devour some of the persecutors: *Acta Martinae* 5.42, AASS Ian. I, 15–16, at 16; *Vita prima sancti Faustini et Iovita*, AASS Feb. II, 810 (*ministri* and priests of Saturn devoured when they bring their idols into the arena to convert the saints).

he wanted to argue for. The opposition between two spaces, church and amphitheater, and the associated rituals, the supplication liturgy and the games, allowed the author to rank vis-à-vis one another two authorities, that of the bishop and that of secular power. We saw how Gregory of Tours would employ it, in turn, to contrast two types of government, King Chilperic's and Emperor Tiberius's. The one built amphitheaters, the other opened his reign with a visit of Constantinople's churches rather than with a procession into the circus.[121]

A more radical formula belonged as well to the repertory the first Christian centuries bestowed upon their medieval heirs: a provocation in the context of a ritual event in which the whole community officially participated and that it considered an expression of its consensus. Geoffrey Koziol has recently analyzed a number of "cases" of ritualized protests disrupting political liturgies.[122] As in his earlier work, he assumes that ritual in general is a direct index of an authority's legitimacy or illegitimacy—a radical shortcut that avoids the strategies that led to the writing down of each of these "cases." But authors, not events, measure power.

Traditions associated with Ambrose also provide an illustration of a second legacy of late antique political culture: the demonstration of superiority through the interpretation of rituals. The bishop of Milan, relayed by his hagiographer, recounts the invention in Bologna of two saints' relics. Vital and Agricola had been buried in that city's Jewish cemetery. Ambrose organized a solemn ceremony, which the two communities, Christian and Jewish, witnessed. The narrative positions the two groups' relationship on a model structurally akin to that of the martyrs and pagans in the *Passio Perpetuae*. Spatially, the Jews make up the ritual's outer circle—like the Carthaginian crowd. The Christians, within that circle, make history. Ambrose was a masterful exegete; he probably meant to suggest through this concentric setup the hierarchical inequation between *textus* and *mysterium*, between shell and true contents. The organization of the dialogue between Jews and Christians confirms this; the two groups recite alternately biblical quotations (like circus slogans called *voces*) that answer one another. The former supply the letter (surface sense) and the latter the spirit (the inner meaning). In all instances, the Christian quotation reveals the truth hidden in the immediately preceding set of verses uttered blindly by the Jews. The Old Testament people, like the Carthaginian pagans, act in a ritual they do not control, proving by this very lack of autonomy Christian superiority. Ambrose and his staff may depend on the Jewish remembrance of Vital and

[121] Gregory of Tours, *LH* 5.17, 5.30; cf. above, ch. 3, 97–98.

[122] Geoffrey G. Koziol, "England, France, and the Problem of Sacrality in Twelfth-Century Ritual," in *Cultures of Power*, ed. Thomas N. Bisson (Philadelphia: 1995), 124–48, drawing principally on Eadmer.

Agricola's martyrdom, especially to discover the place where the saints lay buried. Yet in the last analysis, "the Jews showed that they had knowledge of the martyrs, but not the Word's knowledge, in other words, [they had knowledge of the martyrs], but not according to the knowledge of the Sole Good and of the Sole Truth."[123] Ambrose called on doubting Thomas's example to nail in, as it were, his point: "One would have said that the martyr was crying out to the Jews: *Put your hand in* [the wound at] *my side, and desist from incredulity, and have faith instead*" (John 20.27).[124] To have access to the mystery hidden in the ritual event proves authority. Ambrose claims it at this very point with his quill. Participation in a ritual is not an index of status, let alone superiority. Superiority, rather, is conveyed through the control of interpretation and through a demonstrated ability to reveal the event's hidden meaning.

Late antiquity provides the medievalist with a world in which Christian discourse had not yet reached a monopolistic position. There, he or she can observe narrative strategies anticipating those present in the early Middle Ages. What are evidently phantasmatic plots on the part of the Passiones and Acta's authors, meant to hijack the dominant culture's rituals, point to the less immediately obvious medieval practices, and especially to the clerical ability to fully reinterpret or even invent whole cloth a ritual event.

In late antique political culture, ritual was supposed to signify and create consensus. For polemicists, then, to demonstrate the illegitimacy of the enemy's order entailed destroying its rituals, in reality (through action) or imagination (through writing). When antagonism was less radical, and authors and stage masters sought to express superiority without excluding, they tried to make the other's ritual a satellite of their own (that is, to

---

[123] *Exhortatio virginitatis liber unus* 1.8, PL 16, 353c–354a: "*Circumfundebamur a Iudaeis cum sacrae reliquiae eveherentur; aderat populus ecclesiae cum plausu et laetitia. Dicebant Iudaei:* 'Flores visi sunt in terra [Cant. 2.12]' *cum viderent martyres. Dicebant Christiani:* 'Tempus incisionis adest [Cant. 2.12], iam et qui metit mercedem accipit [Ioan. 4.36]. Alii seminaverunt et nos metimus martyrum fructus.' Iterum audientes Iudaei voces plaudentis ecclesiae, dicebant inter se:* 'Vox turturis audita est in terra nostra [Cant. 2.12].' *Unde bene lectum,* Dies diei eructat verbum et nox nocti indicat scientiam [Ps. 18.3]: *Dies diei Christianus Christiano, nox nocti Iudaeus Iudaeo. Indicabant ergo Iudaei quod habebant scientiam martyrum, sed non scientiam verbi, id est non secundum illam solius boni et solius veri scientiam,* Ignorantes enim dei iustitiam et volentes se iustificare iustitiam dei non receperunt [Rom. 10.3]." The pseudo-Ambrosian *Ep.* 3, PL 17, 747–49, here 747c–748a, intensifies the confrontation, for there the Jews do not participate in Christian rejoicing but rather mourn déplorent (*lugentes*) the Christian triumph. The *Exhortatio* is a telling text in the light of Boyarin's thesis (*Dying for God*, 93–126) that Judaism and Christianity had elaborated martyrdom more or less synchronically and in relation to one another's traditions, and that both had fought to claim that martyrdom was exclusively theirs.

[124] *Exhortatio virginitatis liber unus* 1.9, PL 16, 354a–b.

force it into a subordinate position in their own ceremonies), or to claim that it took its true meaning only in a framework defined through their own interpretation. No wonder then that for Tertullian, the devil was an evil interpreter.[125]

This chapter faced two quandaries. It shares the first with all of this essay's first part. How does one cross the bridge to historical reality from the river bank of highly crafted texts produced by a culture of interpretation? The second problem is how to avoid circular reasoning in an analysis whose objects are the early Christian *coetus, congregationes,* or *coitiones* (to use Tertullian's Latin terminology), that is, the very entities that provided early modern social thought with its archetypal social group (a key way station on the road to Max Weber being medieval religious communities, *religiones*).[126] The first issue is better left to the general conclusion. But one can already suggest that cultural characteristics (such as the purpose of martyrdom) are as much facts as events are. And in some cases the presence of a plurality of texts, especially when they belong to different genres, allows one to stand on firmer ground. Marcus Aurelius is more likely to have been acquainted with Christian practice than with the sects' hagiography. When the emperor exhorts himself in his notebooks to die philosophically, and not "tragically, as Christians do," he gives indirect evidence of the highly crafted nature of martyrdom and of the cultural subrepertoire the Christians had adopted, that of tragedy.[127] As for the second quandary, it is overcome by a tighter, historicized reconstruction of the relationship between Christian *coetus* and Christian *religiones*.

The Christian grouping was not defined by the enactment in common of a set of arbitrary signs. Augustine had underlined that most *signa* owed their significating force to an arbitrary (and usually, but not always collective) human or demonic decision. This was the case for pagan *religiones*, such as augury.[128] Despite their often consensual origin, these signs and the

---

[125] See *De testimonio animae* 3.2, ed. R. Willems, CCSL 1 (Turnhout: 1954), 178:7–10: "*Satanam . . . quem nos dicimus malitiae angelum, totius erroris artificem, totius saeculi interpolatorem*"; or *De spectaculis* 2.7, ed. Turcan, 90:31–33: "*Multum interest inter corruptelam et integritatem, quia multum est inter institutorem et interpolatorem.*"

[126] Medieval monastic institutions and religious sociations (called *religiones*) were defined by rules (of which the most famous is the *Rule of Saint Benedict*). Rules are written authorities prescribing, among other things, a precise, hence patterned, behavior. Cf. Asad, "Discipline and Humility in Christian Monasticism," in Asad, *Genealogies of Religion* (Baltimore: 1993), 125–67, and Oexle, "Soziale Gruppen."

[127] Marcus Aurelius, *Meditations* 11.3, ed. A. I. Trannoy (Paris: 1925), 124, opposing a preparedness for death arrived at "rationally and with dignity and if you wish to be seen as sincere, atragōdōs, without theatrical pose" to the Christian death "by irrational obstination."

[128] *De doctrina christiana* 2.24.37, 61:17–21: "*Quod manifestissime ostendit ritus augurum, qui et antequam observent et postquam observata signa tenuerint, id agunt ne videant volatus aut audiant*

pacts they corresponded to were categorized (in Augustine's model) private. Other *signa*, much rarer, signified something because they originated in the divine will. The signs related to the Christian *coetus*, then, could not be the product of human agency, collective or individual. God was their author. This was the true public realm. Yet both honest and mendacious signs tie together communities, and consensus can be found equally in good, neutral, and bad communities.[129] How did a community, then, demonstrate its divine institution? It did so by linking itself to key moments of providential history, and by tying the letter of its existence to a higher *mysterium*. The *coetus* around Perpetua did not define itself through her death as performance alone; it was critical to commemorate a martyrdom that itself pedagogically explained the relationship between letter and spirit. It constituted itself through a claim that it had the right understanding of the spirit behind the letter. As a corollary, it could identify clearly the truth behind a performance, and, if necessary, act accordingly. The demonstrative nature of approval and opposition in early medieval political culture, then, is not to be explained primarily by some general rule of ethology or of symbolic action.[130] It was the meaningful and fully intelligible corollary of a specific religious world vision.

---

voces avium, quia nulla ista signa sunt, nisi consensus observantis accedat." In this particular case the decision is individual, not collective.

[129] See above, 144–47.

[130] Cf. Ruth Schmidt-Wiegand, "Gebärdensprache im mittelalterlichen Recht," *FMSt* 16 (1982): 363–79, drawing on Konrad Lorenz.

PART II

From Theology to the Social Sciences, ca. 1500–ca. 1970

Alle prägnanten Begriffe der modernen
Staatslehre sind säkularisierte theologische
Begriffe. Nicht nur ihrer historischen
Entwicklung nach, weil sie aus der Theologie
auf die Staatslehre übertragen wurden . . .
sondern auch in ihrer systematischen
Struktur, deren Erkenntnis notwendig
ist für eine soziologische Betrachtung
dieser Begriffe.
—Carl Schmitt, *Politische Theologie*

From Theology to the Social Sciences, ca. 1500–ca. 1970

Rituals have become a fixture in titles of history books, articles, and professional conference sessions. Jack Goody's annoyed warning, that the concept of ritual has become so broad as to be useless, has been met at best as an annoyance that has to be acknowledged—but little more.[1] Like resistance, which some voices now argue should be resisted,[2] the term is just too fashionable to be given up.

This omnipresence and breadth are not, however, beyond explanation. In an age in which, in academic circles at least, religious belief is not quite understood any longer, the concept of "ritual" has inherited the mantle of another concept, "religion," and plays the same structural role in many explanatory models. To give a first approximation, "rite"—what the Christian tradition considered the more material half of religion as against *opiniones*—has come to occupy most of the field that religion once covered. To understand the modern concepts of ritual as well as whether and how they help in analyzing medieval documents, one must therefore follow the postmedieval destiny of the notion of religion as much as that of liturgical rites. But—and this is where the approximation is only that—one should be aware of the distance between the rite of medieval religion and anthro-

Thanks for help on this second part to Tim Brook, Dan Gordon, Brad Gregory, Hal Kahn, Luc Ferrier, Kathryn Miller, Paul Robinson, Aron Rodrigue, Marcel Sebök, Martial Staub and Zeev Sternhell.

[1] Jack Goody, "Against ritual: loosely structured thoughts on a loosely defined topic," in Sally F. Moore and Barbara G. Meyerhoff, *Secular Ritual* (Assen: 1977), 25–35; compare Koziol, *Begging*, 289. Barbara Boudewijnse, "The conceptualization of ritual: A history of its problematic aspects," *Jaarboek voor Liturgie-onderzoek* 11 (1995): 31–56, at 42–43, has noted rightly the lack of response to Goody's challenge.

[2] Sherry Ortner, "Resistance and the Problem of Ethnographic Refusal," *Comparative Studies in Society and History* 37,1 (1995): 173–93; Michael F. Brown, "On Resisting Resistance," *American Anthropologist* 98,4 (1996): 729–35.

pological "ritual." The latter category was built on the former, but with major accretions and distortions. The category was broadened to encompass practices that medieval Catholic thinkers would never have accepted as rites—at least not as rites in a true religion. One cannot, then, satisfy oneself with a simple lexicographic study and follow the fate of one term, such as "rite" or "ritual."[3] Nor is it enough to concentrate on Reformation-era changes in sacramental theory to the detriment of other transformations.[4] Finally, the category's elements were attributed roles and effects, some of which the Middle Ages might have recognized, some of which they would not.

The Protestant Reformations and the Catholic reactions to them, the encounters with non-European groups on the frontiers of the colonial empires, the Enlightenment and the French Revolution's aftermath, all contributed to these transformations. Before turning to them, however, a note of warning must be sounded. This second part of the essay belongs to the genre of *longue durée* intellectual history, and no longer focuses on cultural history. It is about the formation of a concept with one eye to the 1900 horizon and the other to the Middle Ages, not about the actual workings of "rites," "ceremonies," and other solemnities in the centuries separating these two moments. And since it ultimately aims at a confrontation of medieval and twentieth-century notions, it looks at the process of formation not for the sake of the process, but with the end product in mind. Because of the essay's double horizon, medieval and contemporary, it is legitimate to take a bird's-eye-view and compare ideas whose holders would have violently disagreed with one another. In the vein of German *Begriffs-geschichte*, this second part is not interested so much in the chronological evolution of ideas but in the systemic structural baggage that the concept, as it is now in usage among medievalists, has accumulated over time, over the course of a plurality of specific historical instantiations.[5] This is not "genealogy" in the Foucauldian sense. The approach here employed may share with Michel Foucault an interest in discontinuities and the belief that the historicization of an intellectual object, here atemporal "ritual," serves

---

[3] One flaw in the otherwise inspiring piece by Talal Asad, "Towards a Genealogy of the Concept of Ritual," reed. in his *Genealogies of Religion* (Baltimore: 1993), 55–79. See also Barbara Boudewijnse, "Conceptualization," and eadem, "British Roots of the Concept of Ritual," in *Religion in the Making*, ed. Arie L. Molendijk and Peter Pels (Leiden: 1998), 277–95.

[4] The focus of the most satisfying chapter in Edward Muir, *Ritual in Early Modern Europe* (Cambridge [UK]: 1997), 155f.

[5] Cf. Reinhart Koselleck, "Introduction" to Otto Brunner et al., *Geschichtliche Grundbegriffe*, 6 vols. (Stuttgart: 1972), 1.xxi: Since at any moment in time a concept is made up of different strata of meaning accrued from different historical time, its "geschichtliche Tiefe, die nicht identisch ist mit ihrer Chronologie, gewinnt einen systematischen oder einen strukturellen Charakter."

to reveal and critique its essentialist use.[6] But it trusts with *Begriffsgeschichte* that the twisted intellectual continuities that do exist between past and present have had an essential and hardly reducible impact on the concept as it is currently employed by medievalists. This *longue-durée* continuum, with its distortions, has both endowed "ritual" with an almost automatic legitimacy and saddled it with complicated connotations. Like the term "feudalism," "ritual" evokes a set of semantic fields regardless of the intentions and definitionary caution of the scholar employing it. In a sense, then, whereas the earlier four chapters have vociferously emphasized authorial intent, this second part disregards many of the coherences and dissonances within and among works. The essay, in the last intention, is about early medieval political culture and the twentieth century's theorizing of it, not about the waters that flowed between them. Finally, it may be objected that I perform on twentieth-century historiography the same kind of reductionist reading that I feel historians fall prey to when using social scientific models. I feel comfortable with the accusation, a stock-in-trade of the profession. For generalizing about a body of contemporary scholarship in an attempt to delineate shared straits (at the evident cost of neglecting individual nuances) and point out its common problems vastly differs from imposing on the primary sources a misleading thought-world.

[6] Michel Foucault, "Nietszche, Genealogy, History," trans. in Paul Rabinow, ed., *The Foucault Reader*, New York: 1989, 76–99, esp. 77–78, 81, 99. My thanks to Lou Roberts and Martial Staub who have helped me define my position relative to, respectively, Foucauldian genealogy and *Begriffsgeschichte*.

Chapter Five

RITES, RITUALS, AND ORDER, CA. 1500–CA. 1800

THE REFORMATION, CEREMONIES, AND ORDER

The Reformation's success in sixteenth-century Europe can be explained partly by the skill with which its propagandists mustered against the Roman Church notions basic to the medieval definition of Christendom. They positioned themselves on the side of the spiritual against a putative carnal, and attributed to the enemy a mindless ritualism, recycling for their polemical descriptions of Catholic rites late antique depictions of pagan cults, but perhaps more pointedly the opposition between the New Law and the Old Law. Catholic rites were all "ceremonies," just as Jewish rites had all been "ceremonies." Unlike the few sacraments now acceptable to the Reformers, they were at best dispensable dross, at worst a cause of perdition. It will be remembered that according to patristic understanding the Jewish "ceremonies" had been emptied of all meaning when Christ had fulfilled the promises of the Old Dispensation that these *caerimoniae* symbolized. Thomas Aquinas thus carefully distinguished between purely ceremonial commands, now prohibited in Christendom, and *praecepta iudicialia*, secular provisions that might be adopted in a Christian State.[1] Since the relationship between *regnum* and *sacerdotium* could be conceived in terms of the contrast between the Old Law and the New Law, the distinction between ceremonies and sacraments could also be correlated to the hierarchized complementarity of Polity and Church.[2]

With the sixteenth century, this correlation became quasi axiomatic. Conceptually speaking, the moderate Protestant Reformers relocated the religious practices that they did not reject, and yet that they did not consider sacraments, in the domain of the political.[3] Religious practices—as

---

[1] See Thomas Aquinas, ST I II 103 a. 3–4 and 104, *Opera Omnia*, vol. 7 (Rome: 1892), 254–61.

[2] See Thomas Aquinas, ST I II 98–103, *Opera*, 7.200ff., especially 102 a. 2 and 103 a. 3, 7.229 and 7.254–55.

[3] Peter Burke, "The repudiation of ritual in early modern Europe," repr. in his *The historical anthropology of early modern Italy* (Cambridge [UK]: 1987), 227–28, rightly dates to the Reformation the distinction between "ritual" and "ceremony," the former having a mystical dimension, the latter being pragmatic and political. But more precisely, as discussed in the introduction and in the conclusion, the era articulated and theorized a preexistent binary opposition. For formulations of this dichotomy, see Max Gluckman, *Politics, Law and Ritual in Tribal Society* (Oxford: 1965), 251, or (critically) Luc de Heusch, "Introduction à une ritologie

opposed to Faith and the preaching of the Word—were less necessary for, and therefore less numerous in, a New Dispensation Church that, compared with Ancient Israel, was more spiritual. But, for the Protestants, a visible church, insofar as it did not only comprise the elect and could not be reduced to this invisible core, needed as any society to maintain order. The *Augsburg Confession* (1530), and the *Apology* (1531) that its main author, Phillip Melanchthon (1497–1560), penned for it, neatly poised the *ecclesia* between the twin extremes of pure materiality and pure spirituality. The true Church could not be equated to a political society. "It is not only a society in external things and rites like other polities," a mere "external polity," wrote Melanchthon. He further distinguished it from that most carnal of religious associations, Ancient Israel, which had been made "distinct from the pagans by civil rites" (what a German version of the *Apology* translated as "*Polizei und bürgerliches Wesen*," police and civility). But for all its spirituality, the true Church wasn't immaterial. Even though it had to be considered as "principally a society, in the hearts, of the Faith and the Holy Spirit," it too had an external component. First, external marks—the pure doctrine of the Gospel and the right administration of the sacraments—allowed it to be recognized outwardly. Here Melanchthon represented a wider Protestant consensus. Most other Reformers would have recognized that the Lord's Supper and Baptism served (to quote Calvin) as a *marque et enseigne* that testified that an individual belonged to the church ("like a man-at-arm who bears the livery of his prince to profess he belongs to him"). But this was far from being the sacraments' primary role; it paled next to the principal reasons for their institution: to signal the remission of sins, to make humans participate in Christ's death, and to unite them to Him and His "benefits."[4] A second set of practices, however,

---

générale," in Edgar Morin et al., *L'Unité de l'homme. Invariants biologiques et universaux culturels* (Paris: 1974), 679–713 at 680–83. Jonathan Z. Smith, *To Take Place: Toward Theory in Ritual* (Chicago: 1987), 96–102, esp. 100, argues that the Reformation induced a shift toward a notion of ritual as merely figurative. But the link he posits between the Eucharistic position of extreme Reformers such as Zwingli and Calvin and the notion that *all* rituals are "outward representation rather than inward transformation" isn't obvious and cannot be direct. Why should a minority Protestant understanding of the Eucharist have determined the evolution of wider European thought on all solemnities? For this reason, the following pages have privileged instead the view of ceremonies (as opposed to sacraments) that Lutherans and Anglicans held, since it is more likely to have have had an impact on the notion of "ritual."

[4] Calvin, *Institutes* 4.15.1, trans. John T. McNeill and Ford Lewis Battles, *Institutes of the Christian Religion*, 2 vols., Library of Christian Classics 20–21 (Philadelphia: 1960), 2.1303–04. For a limpid discussion of the Genevan reformer, see François Wendel, *Calvin. Sources et évolution de sa pensée religieuse*, 2d ed. (Geneva: 1985), on this point 242–43. Melanchthon, *Repetitio confessionis augustanae* (1551), in *Opera Omnia*, ed. Carl G. Breitschneider et al., CR 28 (Brunswick: 1860), 416–17 (where Melanchthon speaks of the Lord's Supper as *nervum publicae congregationis*, as *congregationis vinculum*, and as *vinculum . . . mutuae benevolentiae*).

had a principally external role. According to Melanchthon, the Church should hold to the rites or *Kirchenordnungen* that "could be kept without sin" because they "fostered quiet and good order" in it.[5] In this discourse, implicitly, four sets of dyads were put in correspondence: (1) polity— Church; (2) Old Testament—New Testament; (3) ceremonies—Spirit; (4) order—salvation.

This was how the Lutherans explained nonsacramental practices. In so doing, they assimilated them to "political ceremonies," fostering the crystallization of this category, the forerunner of our "secular rituals."[6] For in attacking the Catholic Mass (in the Middle Ages associated with much of what we would now consider "ritual") Luther and others forced a strict conceptual disjunction between religious rites and civic or political solemnities. Of course, in the *practice* of Protestant societies the modern observer (and perhaps contemporaries as well) can notice a mixture of "religion" and "politics" in solemnities.[7] And, of course, medieval authors were not unable to distinguish between the two; they just rarely did, and when they did, they thought more in terms of a continuum. One rare such medieval case is Thomas Aquinas's incidental discussion of the principal audience of religious vows (God or humans), which he contrasted to the solemnities of knighthood and marriage.[8] More often, when an author associated politics to rites, it was for polemical, not analytical, reasons, to brand practices as

---

[5] Phillip Melanchthon, *Apologia Confessionis* 7.5, ed. in *Bekenntnisschriften der evangelisch-lutherischen Kirche*, 6th ed. (Göttingen: 1967), 234; *Augsburg Confession* 15.1, in *Bekenntnisschriften*, 69; *Apologia* 7.13–15, 236–37. Cf. as well the *Solida declaratio* 10.7 in the Formula of Concord of 1577/80, in ibidem, 1056 (equation of acceptable ceremonies with means of order and discipline).

[6] In sixteenth-century usage, the field covered by the adjective "politicus" can be extremely wide and often corresponds to the secular. See, e.g., the *Confession of Erlauthal* (1562), in *Bekenntnisschriften* 299:28–30 and 45–46: In the Eucharist, one can use any bread that "the Church uses generally for secular usages (*in usu politico*)" and any alcohol a given people uses "in its kingdom." See Volker Sellin, art. "Politik," in Brunner et al., *Geschichtliche Grundbegriffe*, 4.808.

[7] As when reading of the punishments for infanticide that hapless women underwent in Protestant cities, see Lünig, *Theatrum* 34:2.11–12 (as n. 28 below) 3.1405–10. See as well the comments in Burke, "Repudiation," 230, and Muir, *Ritual*, 180 and passim (on rites of antiritualism).

[8] Thomas ST 2.2 q. 88, a.7, *Opera Omnia*, vol. 9 (Rome: 1897), 253–54, discussing whether the actions done outwardly in a *solemnitas* are directed to God or to humans, and concluding that it depends on the nature of the "reality" that the solemnity bears on, with the examples of knighting, marriage, and (Thomas's topic) the vow: "*Respondeo dicendum quod unicuique rei solemnitas adhibetur secundum illius rei conditionem, sicut alia est solemnitas novae militiae, scilicet in quodam apparatu equorum et armorum et concursu militum, et alia solemnitas nuptiarum, quae constitit in apparatu sponsi et sponsae et conventu propinquorum. Votum autem est promissio Deo facta. Unde solemnitas voti attenditur secundum aliquid spirituale, quod ad Deum pertineat; id est secundum aliquam spiritualem benedictionem, quae ex institutione apostolorum adhibetur in professione certae regulae.*"

secular or profane in spirit.[9] By contrast, the post-Reformation world readily conceptualized solemnities by arranging them dichotomously between religion and politics. This angle of vision allowed the sixteenth century to look at every religious solemnity that was not sacramental as essentially social and political in function, and therefore to analyze both the nonsacramental component in a religion's practice and the solemnities of secular polities fundamentally in terms of order.

We may turn to polemics and misrepresentations to further underline this general drift. It will be recalled that many Protestants agreed that participation in the sacraments marked out membership in the Church, but that this function was at best secondary.[10] It is on the background of this understanding that one should consider Melanchthon's misrepresentation of his Protestant brethren and rival, Huldrich Zwingli (1484–1531). He accused him of having stated that the two authentic sacraments (and not only accepted ceremonies) were political in function and only that. Melanchthon excoriated Zwingli for having allegedly stated

> that the Lord's Supper was instituted for two reasons. First, that it be a mark (*nota*) and testimony of our profession [of Faith], just as a specific shape of cowl is a sign of a specific [monastic] profession. Then they believe that it pleased Christ [to institute] this mark, that is a banquet, mostly to signify a mutual conjunction and friendship between Christians, because symposia are signs of pact and friendship. But this is a civil [German: *menschlich*] opinion; it does not make manifest the main usage of the things that God transmitted to us, [but] speaks only about the exercise of charity, which profane and civil [German: *weltliche*] human beings understand in some manner, [and] does not speak of the Faith, which few human beings understand as what it is.[11]

If Zwingli understands Baptism and the Lord's Supper in such a manner, Melanchthon argued, his church will differ in no way from a mere *politia*

---

[9] The late medieval tendency was actually to place what the modern social scientist might judge "secular" in a religious framework. For an example, exceptional in the genre of administrative ordinances, of this phenomenon, see Olivier de la Marche, "L'estat de la maison du Duc Charles de Bourgoingne" (1474), in *Mémoires*, ed. Henri Beaune, vol. 4 (Paris: 1888), 1–94, esp. 2, 3, 8, 9, 20, 31, 67–68.

[10] Above, at nn. 4–5.

[11] Phillip Melanchthon, *Apologia Confessionis* 14.68, ed. in *Bekenntnisschriften*, 369 (I indicate telling German renditions of the Latin). This is not quite the true Zwingli; the closest statements to the position mispresented here may be Zwingli, *De peccato originali declaratio* (1526), ed. Emil Egli et al., CR 92 = Zwingli V (Leipzig: 1934), 358–96, at 392 ("*baptismus ecclesiae Christi signum est, non aliter, quam exercitus aliquis signatur; non quod signum hoc coniungat ecclesiae, sed qui ei iam coniunctus est, publicam tesseram accipit*"); and the *Gutachten im Ittinger Handel* (1524/5), CR 90 = Zwingli III (Leipzig: 1914), 511–38 at 535 (mutual pledge of brotherhood through sacrament on the analogy of *Eidgenossenschaft*). See as well the other texts referred to in J. V. Pollet, *Huldrych Zwingli et le Zwinglianisme* (Paris: 1988), 80–83, 95ff. W. P. Stephens,

externa. Melanchthon misrepresented Zwingli's position. But in his polemic, he revealed an understanding of the polity that had to be widespread if his argument was to be effective: rites define a *secular* polity vis-à-vis similar groups and keep it together. Just like ceremonies annexed by the Protestant churches, secular rites fostered order—what the sixteenth century called "police."

In an age of polemics, no Christian church wanted to be reduced to the "political" and assimilated to the Jewish synagogue or to a mere *politeia*. Understandably, therefore, Catholic authors ferociously criticized the idea that the rites attached to the Roman Church's sacraments were civic in function and did not form an essential part of God's worship. Luther's dogged antagonist Johannes Cochlaeus (1479–1552) denounced the Protestant claim that "they were done only for some reason of police (*politicum . . . finem*), so that the less educated might learn to hear the Word, take the sacraments, and preserve the public peace."[12] Francisco Suarez (1548–1617) followed the same line of argument. He denied that the ceremonies annexed to the sacraments (and the outward worship of God) could have only a social and political role—the maintenance of order. The influential Jesuit theologian rejected indignantly the idea that they might be tools—à la Numa Pompilius—to control the commons.[13] Was it that Counter-

---

Zwingli: An Introduction to his Thought (Oxford: 1992), 80, 83, 94–110, traces the evolution of the Swiss Reformer's views on the Eucharist (my thanks to Brad Gregory for this reference).

[12] "*Defensio ceremoniarum Ecclesiae adversus errores et calumnias trium librorum D. Ambrosii Moibani Vratislaviae Concionantis . . .*" Per D. Io. Cochalaeum Canonicum Vratislaviensem (Alexander Weissenhorn, Ingolstadt, 1644, original 1543 and 1544), D3(v)–D4(r): "*Quas autem Adiaphoras dicis (Quales sunt inquis, ferie, quedam et dies pro verbo audiendo a patribus instituti, item ieiunia, vestitus ecclesiastici, state hore in quibus fiunt coetus piorum) pessime describis, dum doces, ut solummodo propter politicum aliquem finem fiant, unde rudiores discant audire verbum, sacramentis uti, et publicam tranquillitatem servare, sed non obligent conscientiam, neque sint cultus Dei. Haec autem tua sententia maxime repugnat proprio et principali fini Ceremoniarum, quia omnes in honorem et cultum Dei venerationemque sanctorum instituuntur. Si autem propter alium finem instituuntur utpote vel propter crapulam, vel propter vanam gloriam et nominis proprii memoriam, ut inde institutor videri aut laudari ab hominibus velit, iam perversus est finis, perversa item ratio Ceremoniarum, et potius pompae mundanae quam Ceremoniae Ecclesiasticae dici merentur, eo quod non propter Deum, sed propter homines videantur institutae.*" The Lutheran Ambrose Moibanus (d. 1554) was a preacher in Bresslau and pastor of St. Elizabeth Church, where he sought to reform the rites. My thanks to Ralph Keen for this information.

[13] *Disputatio* 15.2.3 (on Aquinas, ST III, q. lxv, a. 4), *Opera Omnia*, 28 vols. (Paris: 1856–78), 20.286: The heretics "say . . . that what we share with them—that is, [those ceremonies] we do for the sake of worship (*cultus*) and as pertaining to the virtue of religion—is superstition. For even though in giving the sacraments one must observe measure and a fitting setting, so that all may be done with honor and according to order (as is said in I Cor. 14), nevertheless they want this to be only for the sake of some human police (*politia*), and not with the aim of worship and religion—for this they say is superstitious"; cf. *Opus de virtute et statu religionis* 2.1.1.1, *Opera Omnia*, 13.77: "Some thought that one can allow these external signs with

Reformation thinkers would hardly have wanted to think that many of their Church's practices were primarily concerned with order rather than salvation? Or rather that the late medieval theology they drew on did not see the liturgy in a primarily political light? One suspects that Cochlaeus, having edited in 1540 Pope Innocent III's *De sacramento altaris*, was in tune with late medieval understandings.

Like a secular polity, a church was a society. All "external polities" had to provide for order through laws and ceremonies. But for the Reformers, uniformity in rites, despite its role in secular polities, was not essential for the unity of a religion. Belief in the same core of doctrine was.[14] Melanchthon assimilated enforced "ritual" uniformity to the active essence or "form" of the ultimate opposite to the Church, the most secular and tyrannical of all societies, Antichrist's kingdom. Pushed to its logical extreme, then, the ends-and-means relationship between "police" and ritual would yield tyranny.[15] The true sacraments had an enormously intense impact on the senses; idolatrous rites shared in this intensity, which explained their potential as instruments for excesses in authority. Moderate Reformers ascribed to the sacraments a propaedeutic efficiency—like images, they struck the human heart and eased in the hearing of the Word. Thus, for

---

regard to God's worship (*cultus*) on account of the commoners (*vulgus*) but that in fact they serve in nothing with respect to God's worship." See as well Luther's opponent Cajetan, *Commentary on Aquinas*, T I II q. 99 a. 3, in Aquinas, *Opera Omnia*, 7.202, who brands as a perverse practice (characteristic of pagan legislators) the invention of any "human law that would organize divine cult . . . and make it serve peace among human beings, as if God was worshipped principally for this reason."

[14] E.g., *Confessio Helvetica posterior* 17, 27 (1562), in *Bekenntnisschriften*, 199:38–40, 218:19–37. Cf Calvin, *Institutes* 4.1.12. We are interested here in sixteenth-century *notions* insofar as they could influence the early social sciences; the sixteenth-century *practice* could be quite different insofar as Protestant princes and polities often enforced uniformity in ceremonies in the territories they controlled. See Susan Karant-Nunn, *The Reformation of ritual* (London: 1997), 119–22.

[15] *Apologia* 15.18, 300: "They condemn us for saying that it is not necessary for the true unity of the church that rites instituted by human beings be everywhere the same. Daniel 11 signifies that new human cults (*cultos*) are the very form (*forma*) and *politeia* of Antichrist's kingdom." See as well Melanchthon, *Repetitio confessionis augustanae*, 437: "Granted that there must be some honorable rites for the sake of order, nevertheless, human beings, prone to superstition, easily corrupt these rites, and invent that such observations merit remission of sins and justify before God. They transform signs into divinities, just as many attributed divinity to statues. And many, either out of superstition or for tyranny, accumulate rites, so, as a result, superstition increases the rites of satisfaction in the church, and Nabuchadnezzar and Antiochus create gods (*ut nominant, Nabogdonosor, Antiochus*) and institute a cult that they also want their subjects to observe, because they consider that a consensus in religion fosters the kingdom's concord and quiet. Here new laws and new divinities are not put forth out of superstition, but for tyranny."

Melanchthon, a rite was "as if a picture of the Word."[16] Catholics understood the power of ecclesiastical rites in comparable ways. The influential seventeenth-century liturgist Edmond Martène justified his massive compilation, *On the Ancient Rites of the Church*, by drawing on Gregory the Great's famous assimilation of images to scriptures for the illiterate: "[E]cclesiastical rites . . . lead in no small manner to illustrate dogma; indeed, they are as if books to the uneducated faithful, in which in some way the Church's faith is adumbrated."[17] This dovetailed perversely with the more extreme Protestant critique. Forbidden rites functioned like the superstitious images that iconoclasts destroyed, rightly fearing their impact. An idol referred to something all at once illusory and very real—a distortion of perception endowed with efficient force. Like idols, the superstitious papist liturgy made human vices into tangible objects of worship.[18] Historians of ideology have noticed the connection between the theological discourse on idolatry and the Marxist notion of religious (and economic) "fetishism."[19] As we see, the notional ancestors of eighteenth-century fetishism were elaborated within a discourse that related them to issues of group cohesion and of the sensual nature of rites. The early modern explanation of ritual potency in terms of iconicity is still with us. They

---

[16] See Melanchthon, *Apologia confessionis* 24.69, *Bekenntnisschriften der evangelisch-lutherischen Kirche*, 369: "*Ceremonia est quasi pictura verbi seu sigillum. Et sicut verbum ad hanc fidem excitandam traditum est, ita sacramentum institutum est, ut illa species incurrens in oculos moveat corda ad credendum*"; ibidem, 13.5, 292–93: "*Sicut autem verbum incurrit in aures, ut feriat corda; ita ritus ipse incurrit in oculos, ut moveat corda. Idem effectus est verbi et ritus, sicut praeclare dictum est ab Augustino, sacramentum est verbum visibile, quia ritus oculis accipitur et est quasi pictura verbi, idem significans, quod verbum*"; Hungarian Confession (1562) 35, in *Bekenntnisschriften der reformierten Kirche*, ed. Ernst Friedrich Karl Müller (Leipzig: 1903; repr. Zürich: 1987), 416:37–42; Consensus Tigurinus (1549) 7, 160. Good exposition of the power of images in Muir, *Ritual*, 192–95, with further bibliography.

[17] Edmond Martène, *De antiquis ecclesiae ritibus*, 4 vols. (Paris: 1699; reed. Anvers: 1736), dedicatory epistle; same themes in Giuseppe Catalani, *Caeremoniale episcoporum in duos libros distributum* (Rome, 1744), praeloquium ad lectorem 19, xii, and in Angelo Rocca Camerle, *Thesaurus pontificiarum sacrarumque antiquitatum necnon rituum, praxium ac ceremoniarum* . . . 2 t. (Rome, 1745), 1.144–45: "All cultic acts (*actiones*) bearing on idols were sins; however, the sacred ceremonies of the Christian religion . . . are not lacking in most august mysteries, as blessed Denys the Aeropagite says [in his *Ecclesiastical Hierarchy*] when he teaches for which reason the holy apostles instituted ceremonies: 'Our lords . . . wove (*texerunt*) celestial sacraments with visible signs, and transmitted divine realities under human images, and made present the spiritual majesty in material figures, so that we might be transported, corresponding to our way and ability to comprehend, to a more august understanding of the mysteries by visible figures as if through some auxiliaries.' "

[18] See Carlos M. N. Eire, *War against the Idols: The Reformation of worship from Erasmus to Calvin* (Cambridge [UK]: 1986), 203f.

[19] See Kurt Lenk, introduction to *Ideologie. Ideologiekritik und Wissenssoziologie* (Frankfurt: 1984), 14–16.

tempt some to decipher rituals as the illiterates were supposed to.[20] They tempt others to insist on rituals' coercive impact on the senses—on how through ritual "religion [is] an extreme form of traditional authority."[21]

In downplaying the importance of rites for the *spiritual* unity of the religious group, the Reformers returned to a theme Augustine had advanced in polemics against the Donatists, but that was neither the sole one to occupy the late antique field nor the only position put forward by the Bishop of Hippo.[22] It is important for us to inventory the Augustinian alternatives—(1) force, (2) dogma, (3) *"religiones"*—and realize how much they correspond to those advanced, next to institutions, by sociology: (1) coercion, (2) intellectual, cultural, or emotional consensus, (3) ceremonial practices. Over the course of the immediately subsequent centuries, Anglicans and even Gallicans would come to accept versions of the Reformers' position—common rites did not fashion *ecclesiastical* unity—but in the even longer *durée*, between 1500 and 1900, a shared *religious* ritual would be increasingly considered constitutive of another unity—the unity of the *social* group.

The transformation of categories occurred outside ecclesiology as well.[23] On the eve of Maximilian of Hapsburg's 1562 coronation in Frankfurt, Protestant electors and princes debated whether they could take part in the solemnities. Consulted, the Lutheran theologian Balthasar Bidenbach devised a justification. What they would participate in was not a religious service (*non Deo cultum*), part of the hated Catholic Mass or "other papal ceremonies," but a *politicum officium*, a State duty incumbent upon them

[20] See Talal Asad, "Discipline and Humility in Christian Monasticism," in his *Genealogies of Religion: Discipline and Reasons of Power in Christianity and Islam* (Baltimore, 1993), 126–30 for what he sees as a dominant idea in modern anthropology: Rituals are symbols and therefore to be interpreted.

[21] As perceptively remarked by Asad, "Towards a Genealogy," 60, commenting on Clifford Geertz. I add here that there is as well a parallel between the Protestant discussion of impact on the senses and Bloch's Marxist understanding of the coercive power of ritual; see Maurice Bloch, "Symbols, song, dance and features of articulation: Is Religion an extreme form of traditional authority?" repr. in his *Ritual, History and Power* (London: 1989), 19–45.

[22] Compare Augustine, *Epp.* 93.11.46 and 185.6.24, ed. A. Goldbacher, CSEL 23 and 67 (Prague-Vienna-Leipzig: 1895 and 1911), 23:21–25 and 488:24–489:1 (where the disciplinary bond of peace is on a par with the sacraments in constituting (?) the *unitas ecclesiae*), with *Contra Faustum* 19.11, ed. Joseph Zycha, CSEL 25:1, (Vienna: 1891), 510:1–7, cited above ch. 4 n. 96 (where sacraments are a sine qua non of social groups) and Hilary of Poitiers, *De Trinitate* 8.7–9, ed. P. Smulders, CCSL 62A (Turnhout: 1980), 320–21 (on the source of the unity of the community of Acts 4—not a common will but its source, baptism).

[23] See Hubert C. Ehalt, "Ritus und Rationalität im Herrschaftsstil des 17. und 18. Jahrhunderts," *Beiträge zur historischen Sozialkunde* 7:1 (1977): 8–12.

by virtue of their rank.[24] It was religiously safe to involve oneself in the coronation as long as this distinction was clear to the world. The complex of actions around the royal coronation, in 1562 and later, was transformed to accommodate Protestant princes' objections to what smacked of the Catholic liturgy.[25] Similar practical accommodations (often at first highly ambiguous) were found for Elizabeth of England's coronation as well as for the insular healing touch.[26] But what should arrest us in Bidenbach's manifesto is the theoretical solution: the dichotomy between rite and political ceremony.

The Protestant position could lead to an understanding of ritual as a form of communication underpinning order. We find it in Johann Christian Lünig's massive *Theatrum ceremoniale historico-politicum* (Leipzig, 1719–20).[27] Lünig's three-volume treatise contains more than an impres-

---

[24] Edited in B. Carptzov, *Commentarius in legem regiam Germanorum* (Leipzig: 1640), 763–68, and cited in Rudolf Hoke, "Ein theologisches Gutachten von staatsrechtlichen Tragweite," in Peter Leischning, Franz Pototschnig and Richard Potz, *Ex aequo et bono. Willibald M. Plöchl zum 70. Geburtstag*, Forschungen zur Rechts- und Kulturgeschichte 10 (Innsbruck: 1977), 106–15.

[25] Hoke, "Gutachten", 114–15. See as well Hans Joachim Berbig, "Zur rechtlichen Relevanz von Ritus und Zeremoniell im römisch-deutschen Imperium," *Zeitschrift für Kirchengeschichte* 92 (1981): 204–49, at 238f. for entries, funerals, victory celebrations, birthdays. According to Berbig, the Reformation brought about a reconfiguration of political rites, but it was actually Enlightenment rationality (the desire to base authority on reason) that caused their demise.

[26] Marc Bloch, *Les rois thaumaturges*, reed. (Paris: 1983), 327f., 333f. For Thomas Cranmer (1489–1556), *Questions and answers on the sacraments* (1540), ed. J. I. Packer and G. E. Duffield, *The works of Thomas Cranmer* (Appleford: 1965), at 27–28, the "divers comely ceremonies and solemnities used" in the inauguration of the king's ministers, religious as well as civil, are there "not of necessity, but only for a good order and seemly fashion" and are not constitutive. See as well his famous *Speech at the Coronation of Edward VI* (1547), in ibidem, 20–23, at 21, denying the constitutive power of coronation and anointing. Richard C. McCoy, "The Civic Progress of Elizabeth and the Troublesome Coronation," in Janos M. Bák, *Coronations. Medieval and Early Modern Monarchic Ritual* (Berkeley: 1990), 217–27, argues that the queen redirected the emphasis of the accession solemnities onto her procession to Westminster. Both McCoy and David Sturdy, "Continuity versus Change: Historians and English Coronations of the Medieval and Early Modern Periods," in Bák, *Coronations*, 228–45, at 240, take the plurality of narratives concerning Elizabeth's coronation to be symptomatic of the problem. Wolfgang Sellert, "Zur rechtshistorischen Bedeutung der Krönung und des Streites um das Krönungsrecht zwischen Mainz und Köln," in Heinz Duchhardt, *Herrscherweihe und Königskrönung im frühneuzeitlichen Europa* (Wiesbaden: 1983), 21–32, at 27–29, cites German thinkers who argued along Cranmer's line: The coronation was a product of royal status, not its cause.

[27] Which is not to say that insistence on the relationship between ceremonial and rank order is particularly Protestant, see e.g., the epistle to the reader in Théodore Godefroy, *Cérémonial de France*, rev. ed. Denys Godefroy (Paris: 1649), iii. See most recently Milos Vec, *Zeremonialwissenschaft im Fürstenstaat: Studien zur juristischen und politischen Theorie absolutistischer Herrschaftsrepräsentation*, Studien zur europäischen Rechtsgeschichte 106 (Frankfurt: 1998).

sively wide array of solemnities, illustrated with a multitude of lengthy examples. In a series of introductions, the author develops as well a theory of ceremonials. According to Lünig, they are the product of the human being's fallen nature. The sin of pride leads rulers to want their subjects to demonstrate their obedience and reverence through "outward signs"; other sins, such as a lust for entertainment, fuel the multiplication of ceremonies. But, says Lünig, while, bluntly speaking, ceremonies and solemnities owe their original being to sin, "one should not throw out the baby with the bath-water." Wise men, such as Moses, have always perceived that "for the conservation of a certain order, without which human society cannot survive, certain rites and ceremonies are necessary." Once purified of superstitious elements and excesses, they become a tool for human well-being.[28] They provide a kind of code of comportment regulating public interaction among rulers and with their inferiors and subjects, which both makes behavior predictable—a factor for peace—and manifests the political pecking order. They serve as the vectors of messages—from the simple and necessary "distinction" setting apart ruler from ruled, to the esteem one wants to convey to one's diplomatic partner.[29] The commons (*Pöbel*), devoid of reason, will find there the sensible signs to awe them into subservience. Indeed, they expect that the prince, being the image and representative of a God of order, will exhibit an orderly governance.[30] Lünig can be cynical; the sincerity of the actors is not his concern; he underlines how one honors not only out of friendship but out of political need, and how one must dissimulate occasionally; and he notices that ceremonial can be used in an aggressive way as a kind of continuation of war—as when the French and Swedish ambassadors during the negotiations of the Peace of Nimwegen

[28] Johann Christian Lünig, *Theatrum ceremoniale historico-politicum, oder historisch—und politischer Schauplatz Aller Ceremonien*, 3 vols. (Leipzig: M. G. Weidmann, 1719–20). Here I summarize 1.1 ("*Von Ceremoniel insgemein*"), 1.1–2.

[29] In attributing these roles to ceremonies, Lünig's theory dovetails with that of Gerd Althoff, *Spielregeln* (see my review, forthcoming in *Annales* 52 (2001), and my commentary in *Les tendances récentes de la médiévistique allemande*, ed. by Otto Gerhard Oexle and Jean-Claude Schmitt (Göttingen and Paris, 2001).

[30] *Theatrum* 1.1, 1.4, and ibidem 4.1 ("*Von grosser Herren Cammer- und Hausz-Ceremoniel insgemein*"), 1.292, with Hubert C. Ehalt, *Ausdrucksformen absolutischer Herrschaft* (Munich: 1980), 65–67, who cites along the same lines one of Lünig's contemporaries, Julius Bernhard von Rohr, and others. See as well Wolfgang Weber, "J. B. von Rohrs Ceremoniel-Wissenschafft (1728/9) im Kontext der frühneuzeitlichen Sozialdisziplinierung," in *Zeremoniell als höfische Aesthetik in Spätmittelalter und Früher Neuzeit*, ed. Jörg Jochen Berns and Thomas Rahn (Tübingen: 1995), 1–20, and Andreas Gestrich, "Höfisches Zeremoniell und sinnliches Volk. Die Rechtfertigung des Hofzeremoniells im 17. und frühen 18. Jahrhundert," in ibidem, 57–73. Compare yet another jurist, Johannes Limnäeus (1592–1663): The coronation makes publicly known who is the ruler and stabilizes his authority insofar as "it renders him more sacred and venerable to the people" (cited in Sellert, "Bedeutung der Krönung," 28–29).

denied protocolary honors to their Brandenburg-Prussia enemies, or when
the French managed to drive a wedge between the Holy Roman Emperor
and the German princes over whether the latters' envoys could be called
ambassadors and receive ambassadorial treatment.[31] The political rites of
opponents—whether the French king's healing touch or the practices tied
to the papal court—excite his irony. For these, he returns to the polemical
accents of the sixteenth century and to a less positive vision of ceremonial.
The healing touch is a "tradition" doubted by many scholars and probably
invented by clerics to keep the laity superstitious;[32] "Rome is the source of
all ceremonies through which the majority of European courts are today
in thrall."[33] Here Lünig is joined by Lutheran ceremonialists: Christian
Hoffmann argues that the papacy promulgated so many Rituals and Books
of Ceremonies, and gave them the force of law, because "rites and ceremonies can insinuate a certain authority (*imperium*)"; it aimed at fencing in
the greatest princes "in the worship (*cultus*) and observance" of the See of
Rome.[34] Lünig is also pessimistic: Given that until the end of the world
emulation (*Jalousie*) among princes and states will not disappear, there will
always be ceremonials.[35] But for all his cynicism and pessimism, Lünig does
consider ceremonies effective. Through their peace-making effect, they
compensate for one of the effects of the Fall—constant war.[36] In two places

[31] *Theatrum* 1.1, 1.7: "*Mit einem Worte das* Ceremoniel *ist ist* [sic] *heute zu Tage bey intricaten Hofleuten nichts anders, als wie ein Scherwentzel, der nach Bewandnisz der Sache alle Farben anneh-men, und so wohl denen Feinden dadurch Tort zu thun, als auch denen Freunden ein* Douçeur *zu erweisen, dienen musz; ob man gleich auch zugestehet, dasz selbiges gewisser massen eine Ordnung sey, wodurch man, wenn derselben* accurat *nachgegangen wird,* effectuiren *kan, dasz niemanden weder zu viel noch zu wenig geschehe.*" For ceremonial and politics within the domestic arena, see Barbara Stollberg-Rilinger, "Zeremoniell als politisches Verfahren. Rangordnung und Rangstreit als Strukturmerkmale des frühneuzeitlichen Reichtages," in *Neue Studien zur früh-neuzeitlichen Reichsgeschichte,* ed. by J. Kunisch, Zeitschrift für Historische Forschung Beiheft 19 (Berlin: 1997), 91–132.

[32] *Theatrum* 11.1, 1.1318: "*Was aber auf diese* Tradition *zu halten, das werden diejenigen gar leichtlich begreiffen, welchen aus der Historie bekannt ist, wie die Clerisey in den ehemaligen Zeiten der mehr als Egyptischen Finsternisz den Aberglauben der einfältigen Läyen durch allerhand* Glauco-mata *gar künstlich zu unterhalten gewust*"; cf. 11.2, 1.1318–19, on origins of the Reims oil.

[33] *Theatrum* 13.1, 2.199–200. See as well 15.1, 2.289 (reminding his reader, in criticism of clerical ordinations and other Catholic rites, of the abolition of Old Law's ceremonial and levitical prescriptions with Christ's incarnation), as well as the critical description of a Spanish auto-da-fé of the 1580's, 15.4, 2.292–93.

[34] Christian Godfried Hoffmann, *Nova scriptorum ac monumentorum . . . collectio. opus ad illustarandam historiam civilem, ecclesiasticam, litterariam, necnon jurisprudentiam publicam et pri-vatam . . .* Vol. II: *Praeter varia ad caeremoniarum disciplinam pertinentia Librum Diurnum Ro-manorum Pontificum et . . . librum sacrarum caeremoniarum, quibus Romani Pontifices uti consue-verunt, exhibens* (Leipzig: 1733), here at 9 n. g and 35.

[35] Publisher's preface to volume 2, a4v—a neat, quasi-secular version of the scholastic be-lief that there will be religious rites and sacraments until the Parousia, see below, at n. 134.

[36] *Theatrum* 8.1, 1.984. War is a product of the inequality introduced by the Fall.

at least, the *Theatrum* seems to anticipate Norbert Elias. Lünig reproduces a late sixteenth-century theory of the origins of knightly tournaments and their solemnities—"through which the aristocracy was forced to lead an honorable, godfearing, and virtuous life."[37] And barely five years after the death of the founder of Versailles, Lünig can comment that "the otherwise hot-headed and proud French have been so bewitched by the precision in Ceremonial their great Louis has shown, and by the imposing state he has established with so much orderliness, that it is still debatable whether they respect him with an almost slavish fear more owing to his great [military] deeds than owing to his extraordinary magnificence."[38] We shall return to the notion that "rituals" can replace the wielding of force. Shared with, and in some cases mediated by a plurality of thinkers from Blaise Pascal to Auguste Comte, it still haunts modern discussions of early medieval society.[39]

We have met in medieval documents an implicit opposition between rites with vertical referents and rites devoid of them. It might seem at first glance the exact equivalent of the modern dichotomy ritual-ceremonial, heir to the Protestant distinction between sacraments and good ceremonies. It is not, for as we saw in the first part of this book, the early medieval opposition is a tool for polemics.[40] A solemnity that should refer to a *mysterium* lacks in this vertical referent because the individual or group involved

---

[37] *Theatrum* 27.2, 3.1165, drawing on the extraordinary fantasy of Franciscus Modius (1556–97), *Pandectae triumphales, sive pomparum et festorum ac solennium apparatuum, conviviorum, spectaculorum, simulacrorum bellicorum equestrium et pedestrium . . . quot hactenus ubique gentium concelebrata sunt; posterior hastiludiorum per Germaniam traditorum initia . . .* 2 t. in 1 vol. (Frankfurt am M.: 1586), who placed the origins of tournaments under the reign of Henry I of Saxony (r. 919–36).

[38] *Theatrum* 1.1, 1.5: "*Die sonst hitzigen und hochmüthigen Frantzosen, sind durch ihres grossen Ludwigs bezeigte* accuratesse *im* CEREMONIEL, *und seinen so ordentlich eingerichteten prächtigen Staat dermassen bezaubert worden, dasz es noch zweifelhafftig ist, ob sie ihn mehr wegen seiner grossen Thaten, als wegen seiner ungemeinen* Magnificenz *mit einer fast sklavischen Furcht* respectiret."

[39] See below, ch. 6 at n. 44. Cf. Karl Leyser, *Rule and Conflict in an Early Medieval Society: Ottonian Saxony* (Oxford: 1979); idem, "Ritual, Zeremonie und Gestik: das ottonische Reich," *FMSt* 27 (1993): 1–26; Koziol, *Begging*, 59; Althoff, *Spielregeln*. For the later Middle Ages, Mervyn James, "Ritual, Drama and Social Body in the Late Medieval English Town," *Past and Present* 98 (1983): 3–29, at 13–14, 23, 26, assumes that the Corpus Christi rites were prominent in towns because these entities lacked "alternative symbols and ties of lordship, lineage and faithfulness, available in countrysides," and were more present where town government was less autocratic (13–14, 23, 26). Compare Max Gluckman, *Politics, law and ritual in tribal society* (Oxford: 1965), 110. Auguste Comte, *Considérations sur le pouvoir spirituel,* in *Oeuvres*, vol. 4, 4th ed. (Paris: 1912), 176–215 at 188: "When the voluntary and moral consent of each, granted to a shared social doctrine can no longer determine the necessary contribution of individual to public order, there remains no other solution to maintain some kind of harmony than the sad alternatives of force or corruption."

[40] A role it retained—understandably—in the early Reformation era: Witness Melanchthon's method of attacking uniformity in rites (above, 169).

in it is wicked or inferior. But in the Protestant understanding, the dichotomy, while a product of confessional controversies, has become analytical. A given solemnity will lack in *mysterium* simply because it belongs to a genre, ceremonials, inferior in essence to the sacraments in proportion to the inferiority of politics to salvation, but positive as an instrument of order.

THE BROADENING OF THE FUTURE FIELD OF "RITUAL"

We owe the fuzziness of our modern concept of ritual in part to the sixteenth century. Confessional struggles, antiquarianism, and encounters in the context of European imperialism all contributed to this swollen grab bag. Catholics and Protestants of all stripes polemicized about the exact position of the boundaries between sacraments, permissible ceremonies, and superstitious ceremonies, as well as about the nature of these subdivisions. In the doing they publicized a catalogue of a whole range of practices. To demonstrate how, over the course of time, a sea of unnecessary ceremonial inventions, the mark of Antichrist, had submerged "true doctrine,"[41] the Lutheran "Magdeburg Centuriators" working under the leadership of Matthias Flaccus [or Flacius] Illyricus (1520–75) combed through patristic and medieval documents. Hounding every addition to, and distortion of, the hard sacramental core of the Lord's Supper and Baptism, they effectively ensured the collection of information not only on funerary rites, masses for the living and the dead, but also, for example, on the cult of relics (and princely participation in it), and practices such as the handshake (*porrextio dextrae*) or the washing of the poor's feet, *adventus*, penance and pardon, and installations of rulers.[42] The Catholics reacted by publishing quantities of medieval liturgical materials but also by compiling their own information on incriminated practices with the intention of showing their great antiquity.[43]

The Humanist interest in the classical world was a second contributor to the widening catalogue of solemnities. Antiquarians fascinated by the glories of Rome or hoping for the favors of patrons who saw themselves its heirs combed the archives no less diligently than the Centuriators. Some might have a confessional intent in mind, as when publishing books with titles tellingly alluding to the "Conformities" (understand, a participation

---

[41] [Matthias Flaccius Illyricus et al.], *Ecclesiastica historia* [or: *Centuriae*], 13 vols. (Basel: 1560–74), *Sexta Centuria*, Preface to European princes (Basel: 1562), 11.

[42] See, e.g., *Ecclesiastica historia*, 4.461, 7.150, 9.242, 7.186–87.

[43] Prosper Guéranger, *Institutions liturgiques*, 4 vols. (Paris: 1878–85), 1.408ff., documents this reaction. The Jesuit Johann Gretzer's works (ibidem, 1.522) are exemplary in their breadth.

in the same essential form) between Ancient Paganism and Catholicism.[44] But other authors were not so aligned. In a work published in the century's last decade, Casellius documented pell-mell the following *ritus*: grant of legal protection (*tuitio*), execution of monsters, treatment of executed persons, solemn migration of nations, military oath, gladiatorial oath, omens (*impetrare*), selling slaves, *gesticulatio* (in arena, in theater, for gods), *supplicia* in Constantinople (parading on donkey, tonsure), crowning, ordeals, punishment of vestal virgins, and *parentalia*. He closed his work on various and sundry Roman gestures: those of cutting one's hair or nails in times of tempest, those made to avoid lightning, those for magic to ward off hail, those for breaking an association (*societas*), announcing enmity or amity, breaking chains, dealing with statues of good rulers and tyrants, the dedication of virgins, and marriage.[45]

Finally, European expansion brought in another harvest of information, gathered from fields as far as Africa, America, and even China or Japan. Ultimately, as Anthony Pagden has shown, it led to a shift in explanations of human nature and culture. The mendicant missionaries who followed in the train of Spanish conquistadores noticed among the Mexica "an elective kingship, the punishment of crimes and excesses, [the custom] of going out to received distinguished persons when they arrive in their villages, feelings of sadness, the ability to weep . . . and to express gratitude when good manners require it." Next to political order, penal law, and common humanity, the Franciscan author of this report highlighted that the Indians shared in the European practice of the *occursus*.[46] Observers of the 1585 Japanese embassy to Venice noticed differences concerning ceremonial; one commented that "in these rites and conversation [the Japanese] have customs so different from all the other nations as if they had contrived to

---

[44] Cf. Bernard Dompnier, "L'Eglise romaine, conservatoire des religions antiques. La critique protestante du culte des saints et des images au XVIIe siècle," in *Les religions du paganisme antique dans l'Europe chrétienne, XVI–XVIIIe siècle* (Paris: 1988), 51–68, using among others F. du Croy, *Les trois conformitez: Assavoir, l'harmonie et convenance de l'Eglise romaine avec le paganisme, judaïsme et heresies anciennes* (n.p.: 1605), and Pierre Mussard, *Les conformitez des ceremonies modernes avec les anciennes* (Leiden: 1667).

[45] Jacques Durant Casellius, *Variarum libri duo in quibus praeter veterum ritus, varii Auctores, vel emendantur, vel illustrantur* (Paris: 1582). In France, one of the prime monuments of antiquarianism was Bernard de Montfaucon, *L'Antiquité expliquée et illustrée en figures*, 15 vols. (Paris: 1719–24); see e.g., 4.152–61 on triumphs. Cf. Philip Jacks, *Antiquarians and the Myth of Antiquity: The Origins of Rome in Renaissance Thought* (Cambridge: 1995).

[46] Jacobo de Testera O.F.M. (1533), *Cartas de Indias* (Madrid: 1877), 64–65, cited and translated in Anthony Pagden, *The Fall of Natural Man: The American Indian and the origins of comparative ethnology* (Cambridge [UK]: 1982), 75. The most sensitive exposition of the mind of the sixteenth-century missionaries may be Sabine MacCormack, *Religion in the Andes* (Princeton: 1991).

do everything in reverse from the others."[47] As we shall see, the missionaries writing about China in the seventeenth century sang the same tune of cultural difference. By the early eighteenth century, Lünig's *Theatrum* reported ceremonies not only from European courts, but also from the West's margins, Carinthia, Muscovy, and especially Turkey, as well as from the more distant world, Persia, Morocco, Abyssinia, Mughal India, the Kingdom of Pegu (in modern Birma), Siam, Tonkin, Congo, Brazil, Japan, and China.[48] Since his express purpose was to provide a practical manual for European courts, he refrained from multiplying useless evidence.[49] Still, it is clear that he was fascinated. He devoted the greatest number of pages to the Ottoman Empire, which in early modern reality and imagination belonged both inside and outside Europe, insisting both on pomp and on a cruel side expressed in executions as well as the bloody rite of circumcision.[50] We saw how Reformation thinkers connected ceremonies, the secular, and the political. Turkey, like China for other authors, provided a monstrously excessive avatar of this relationship, an extreme where the severest despotism and the greatest ceremonialism met.[51]

With Jean-Frédéric Bernard (1690–1752), we meet another significant aspect of the widening.[52] The author's Protestant leanings are evident; God had created rites in the true religion; humans had made them up in all others, including the corrupt versions of Christianity.[53] For being unsur-

---

[47] Cited by Patricia Fortini Brown, "Measured Friendship, Calculated Pomp: The Ceremonial Welcomes of the Venetian Republic," in Barbara Wisch and Susan Scott Munshower, eds., *"All the world's a stage." Art and Pageantry in the Renaissance and Baroque*, vol. 2, *Triumphal Celebration and the Rituals of Statecraft* (University Park [PA]: 1990), 137—186 at 149 (Brown's translation).

[48] Lünig, *Theatrum* 11.74–83 (coronations), 2.157–66; 36.1–10 (various), 3.1461–72.

[49] Cf. Lünig, *Theatrum* 36.1, 3.1461.

[50] Lünig, *Theatrum* 35.1f., 3.1441–61.

[51] Lünig, *Theatrum* 35.1, 3.1441–42: The Koran makes for a tyrannical polity and the blind obedience of the people; the rulers are treated almost like gods even though the subjects curse them in their heart. As a result, there are many court ceremonies and ceremonies of daily life, partly unknown in Europe, partly different, "*und also bewandt sind, dasz man sowohl der Unterthanen Knechtische Ehr-Furcht vor ihre Herren, als auch diese ungezämten und Tyrannischen Hochmut daraus erkennen kan*" (they are observed in such a way that one can tell from them both the servile respect [German] of the subjects for their lords as well as the latter's undomesticated and tyrannical pride). "*Doch musz man ihnen zugestehen, dasz sie in ihrem Ceremoniel so scrupuleux und eigensinnig sind, dasz sie, ohne die grösten Schwürigkeiten, [sic] nicht im geringsten davon abweichen wollen.*"

[52] Jean-Frédéric Bernard, *Histoire des religions et des moeurs*, 7 vols. (Amsterdam: 1723–37; reed. Paris: 1819).

[53] Bernard, *Histoire*, 1.13: "God instituted Himself those [rites] that had to serve Him in the true religion. Humans established others for the false religions. In both religions, human motives multiplied them ad infinitum. . . . True religion became less and less spiritual, but wider in ceremonies; false religion became more mysterious and more opinionated."

prisingly biased, the work is not lacking in conceptual value: Announcing
the ethological models that place ritual on a continuum with basic animal
gestures, Bernard asserted that a number of these invented ceremonies
were simply a systematization of instinctively natural motions of the human
body.[54] But we call on it here for a different purpose than foreshadowing.
Like Lünig's *Theatrum*, this massive, seven-volume *Histoire des religions et
des moeurs* incorporated non-European materials. These encompassed
birth ceremonies, marriage, funerals, naming, oaths to rulers, initiations,
monasticism and asceticism, rulers' coronations and deaths, as well as peace
making. Bernard's last volume, tellingly entitled *The Form Shared by the
Ceremonies Practiced in the Greater Part of Christendom and Those of the Ancient Greeks and Romans*, covered a spectrum of Catholic rites, but placed
them on a continuum with Greco-Roman rites and what modern scholarship calls "popular rituals": Funerals, ordeals, the feast of fools, charivaris
and *danses des chevaux de bois*, Corpus Christi processions all belonged
together. The invitation was open for twentieth-century historians and
folklorists to analyze pell-mell, with a single set of conceptual tools, a congeries of medieval practices the natives themselves would have vehemently
kept separate.[55]

THE CHINESE RITES CONTROVERSY

One should however dispel any impression that early modern thinkers were
mired in some inability to establish distinctions within this widening category. The dichotomy between religious rites and political ceremonies was
not vulgarized and made into a common notion through interconfessional
polemics alone. It permeates the so-called Chinese Rites Controversy (ca.
1635–ca. 1742).[56] This highly publicized and bitter dispute pitted two

---

[54] Bernard, *Histoire*, 1.31–32: "Nature gave to the human being some movements through
which it expresses, almost without wanting to think about it, its heart's afflictions and its
mind's worries . . . Such is also the use the human being makes of its hands when in a pressing
need it asks God for His grace, or when wanting to stir an oppressive enemy's compassion.
It would be most absurd to want to rank these motions with ceremonies: they can enter this
category only after having been made methodical, and this is what all religions' rituals have
done in mixing ceremony to these very simple movements nature gave us at birth."

[55] Bernard, *Conformité des cérémonies pratiquées dans la plus grande partie du Christianisme avec
celles des anciens Grecs et Romains = Histoire*, vol. 6, reed. (Paris: 1819). Cf. Jacques Le Goff and
Jean-Claude Schmitt, eds., *Le Charivari* (Paris: 1981).

[56] On the rites controversy, see David E. Mungello, *Curious Land: Jesuit Accommodation and
the Origins of Sinology*, Studia Leibnitiana Supplementa 25 (Wiesbaden-Stuttgart: 1985); idem,
The Chinese Rite Controversy: Its History and Meaning, Monumenta serica 33 (Nettertal: 1994).
I benefited the most from Paul Rule, *K'ung-tzu or Confucius? The Jesuit Interpretation of Confucianism* (Sydney: 1986). The Chinese side of the encounter has been told—in French—by

Catholic camps against one another, the first comprising mostly Jesuits, the second made up mostly of mendicant friars and their supporters. Two topics were under debate. First, whether the Chinese terms that the Jesuits in China used to denote the Christian God were ambiguous and misleading; second, whether the missionaries and their converts could participate in certain Confucian solemnities. Only the latter will concern us here. Fortunately for the specialist of Europe, the controversy progressively lost touch with Chinese realities,[57] so we need not delve into them, although it would be very interesting to examine how far the image of a Chinese polity maintained by rites corresponded to indigenous seventeenth-century conceptions and how much this image came to influence later anthropology of China to the detriment of facts.[58]

The debate was an open one from at least 1676 on. In that year, the Dominican friar Domingo Fernandez Navarrete published the first volume of his *Tratados de la monarchia de China*.[59] In the following decades, the work would be translated into French and excerpted (even its nonpublished parts).[60] The controversy vulgarized information and models that found their way into the books of Jansenist thinkers and, in the following century, Enlightenment philosophers. By 1719, Lünig felt that his audience had read so much on the cult of Confucius that he could allow himself to summarize.[61] Mendicants and Jesuits all agreed that many Chinese solemnities were superstitious enough that Christians should not partake in them; the

---

Jacques Gernet, *Chine et christianisme* (Paris: 1982), trans. *China and the Christian Impact: A Conflict of Cultures* (Cambridge [UK]: 1985), with good pages on the conflicts that arose over (the non-Chinese categories of) "religion and politics"; for the intersection of the two outlooks on this question, see as well Erik Zürcher, "Jesuit accommodation and the Chinese cultural imperative," in Mungello, *Chinese Rite Controversy*, 31–64.

[57] Cf. Rule, *K'ung-tzu*, 92–94.

[58] Reading J. G. A. Pocock, "Ritual, Language, Power: An Essay in the Apparent Political Meaning of Ancient Chinese Philosophy," in *Politics, Language and Time* (New York: 1971), 42–79, and Patricia Buckley Ebrey, *Confucianism and Family Rituals in Imperial China: A Social History of Writing about Rites* (Princeton: 1991), one has the definite impression that Confucian and Catholic understandings of rites shared much. Are we facing here a real convergence, to be contrasted with other cases in which missionaries imported alien, Christian notions of rituals into the picture they drew of the cultures they sought to evangelize, as argued for Latin America, Africa, and the Pacific by Laura Nader, *Harmony Ideology* (Stanford: 1990)?

[59] Domingo Fernandez Navarrete, *Tratados historicos, politicos, ethicos y religiosos de la monarchia de China. Descripcion breve . . . Añadense los decretos pontificios, y proposiciones calificadas en Roma . . .* (Madrid, 1676).

[60] Copious excerpts in the *Lettre d'une personne de piété Sur un Ecrit des Jesuites contre la Censure de quelques propositions de leurs PP. Le Comte, Le Gobien, etc touchant la Religion des Chinois, faite par la Faculté de Théologie de Paris* (Cologne, 1701)—possibly by Noël Alexandre, O.P., since published by the same Köln printer (the "heirs of Corneille d'Egmont") as Alexandre's *Conformité* (1700).

[61] Lünig, *Theatrum* 36.7, 3.1465–67.

missionaries' polemical documents mention the (to Christian eyes) more outrageous ones either to taint by association other practices the Jesuits allowed or to demonstrate Jesuit honesty and integrity in forbidding sinful rites and allowing indifferent ones. Specifically, the debate focused on policy vis-à-vis two solemnities. First, could converts and missionaries partake in Chinese funeral rites that (depending on the reports) involved fasting, torches, and images? Second, could converts aspiring to be officials render solemn honors to Confucius, including offerings of food and flowers, candles, incense burning, and genuflections? The Jesuits built their Maginot Line on the notion that Confucianism was essentially and in its origins not a religion, but an ethic aiming at stabilizing society and fostering good governance; accordingly, these solemnities were not "religious but civil or political," a formula they repeated ad nauseam.[62]

The controversy drew on discussions of the public behavior of Catholic minorities attending solemnities in heretical countries. It dovetailed with another issue, made famous by Thomas Hobbes and Benedict/Baruch de Spinoza: whether the State could impose on the individual the performance of public acts of religious obeisance (as opposed to private, inner faith).[63] Like these debates, the Rites Controversy generated an awareness of the cultural arbitrariness of ceremonial signs. The French Jesuit Louis Le Comte argued that:

[62] So much ad nauseam that the full evidence, like a great saints' full miracles, cannot be mustered in a footnote. The *Encyclopédie*, s.v. "Chinois, Philosophie des," 3.342f., certainly saw in this distinction the key to the controversy.

[63] Cf. Francisco Suarez, S.J., *Defensio fidei Catholicae adversus Anglicanae Sectae errores* 6.9.13 and 6.9.21 (Cologne: 1614), reed. by Luciano Pereña et al., *De iuramento fidelitatis regis Angliae* (Madrid: 1978), 169, 179. Compare, e.g., Francisco Furtado, S.J., *Informatio antiquissima de praxi missionariorum* 10 (s.d., s.l.), 8: "It does not help to say that the soul of the deceased [pagan] is in Hell, and that therefore one shouldn't display any reverence to him, since in Europe Catholic subjects are not in the least forbidden to display some political honors to the body of a deceased heretical king," as well as the same's *Scriptum . . . ad P. Antonium Rubinum* 30 (bound with the preceding text), 16: "I don't believe theologians will make it an obligation to one or several subjects of an heretical king, who are Catholics (but for good reasons secretly so), to betray themselves at the death of their king, by offering themselves to suffer martyrdom only so that they do not confer upon their king funerary honors, by carrying a torch in their hand, or by putting on a vestment of mourning, or by observing other political ceremonies in the honor of the deceased king that other courtiers customarily perform." This was pointed out by Carl Schmitt, *Der Leviathan in der Staatslehre des Thomas Hobbes. Sinn und Fehlschlag eines politischen Symbols* (Hamburg: 1938), 86f.; trans. George Schwab and Erna Hilfstein, 56–57. Cf. Hobbes, *Leviathan* 3.42, ed. Tuck, 343–44, 389; Benedict de Spinoza, *Tractatus Theologico-Politicus* 18, ed. R. H. M. Elwes, *A Theologico-Political Treatise* (New York: 1951), 245: "[T]he rites of religion and the outward observances of piety should be in accordance with the public peace and well-being, and should therefore be determined by the sovereign power alone"; cf. as well ch. 5 (ceremonies "ordained for the preservation of a society"), 76, and ch. 17 (how the Jews' daily rites nurtured their love of fatherland to the point that it became second nature), 229.

Most human actions are in themselves indifferent and signify essentially only what [meaning] people attached to them when they were first instituted. In France we doff our hat to salute those we honor; in Siam, one must take off one's shoes to appear with respect in the prince's presence; and in China civility requires that one be with hat and boots on, even in the presence of the Emperor.... Nations, to act as well as to speak, have a language specific to them; and foreigners' manners, like their speech (*paroles*), are always shocking and ridiculous for those who ignore their true meaning (*sens*).[64]

Such cultural sensitivity was not the exclusive property of enlightened Jesuits. Their vilified opponent, Navarrete, remarked on the regional differences within China. To illustrate them, Navarrete gave the example of the opposite valences of right and left in North and South China, and even compared them to the shift these directions had undergone between Roman and medieval times. For the Dominican too it was "not only useful but necessary" to learn Chinese *cortesias* "in order to deal with so policed (*politica*) and civilized (*urbana*) a nation."[65] It is doubtful that this general awareness of the cultural arbitrariness of signs should be connected primarily to changed understandings of the Eucharist. Le Comte drew rather on the basic exegetical notion of letter and spirit (*sens*), exterior and interior meaning, bark and marrow, when explaining that buildings and practices associated with Confucian solemnities belonged to the realm of the nonreligious:

Those who stop at the bark of things and never care to penetrate the true meaning (*sens*) of China's characters often wax indignant concerning these two words [*miao* and *tçi*], which according to them signify *temple and sacrifice*, but which I translate into our language by these other two words, *hall and banquet*, or *palace and gift*.[66]

Like other Jesuits, Le Comte pleaded that the *sens* one had to consider was that attached to the ceremony at the original moment of its institution. From the standpoint of twentieth-century cultural anthropology, one may find more germane Navarrete's rejoinder that one should rather focus on contemporary Chinese practice and the general population's understand-

---

[64] Louis le Comte, *Lettre à monseigneur le Duc du Maine Sur les Ceremonies de la Chine, in Des Ceremonies de la Chine* (Liège: 1700), 10–11.

[65] Navarrete, *Tratados* 2 ("Del govierno Chinico") 6 ("De las costesias Chinicas") 1–3, 69–70.

[66] Le Comte, *Lettre*, 93–94. Cf. Antonio de Santa Maria, O.F.M., Fr. tr., Antoine de Sainte-Marie, *Traité sur quelques points importans de la mission de la Chine ... Traduit de l'Espagnol* in *Anciens Traitez de divers auteurs sur les Ceremonies de la Chine* (Paris: Louis Guerin, 1701), 4–7 and 10–11.

ing of the solemnities under dispute.[67] But just as for exegetes—and their heirs, the first social scientists—the true meaning of Abel's sacrifice was to be found *ab origine* and *sub specie eternitatis*, so for the Jesuits it was in the age of Confucius that one was to seek the keys to an evaluation of Confucian rites' true (political, not religious) function. Tellingly, their opponents, and the boards that judged in Rome the controversy, did not much challenge this principle. The influence of exegesis is clear from Leibniz's opinion on the question. He praised his Jesuit informants for having followed in searching for the original situation the attitude of the Apostle Paul, who had respected the Athenian altar to the Unknown God for what it was when originally instituted as opposed to how it was used in the idolatrous present (cf. Acts 17.23). And Leibniz went on to relate the superiority of the Jesuit scholar over contemporary Chinese understandings to that of the outside observer over natives and to that of the Christian exegete of the Old Testament over Jewish interpreters:

> Who does not know in our own day that Christian scholars are much better interpreters of the most ancient books of the Hebrews than the Jews themselves? How often strangers have better insight into the histories and monuments of a nation than their own citizens! This is even more likely concerning doctrines more than twenty centuries removed from the Chinese, who are quite possibly not as equipped with the interpretive aids as we, informed about Chinese literature, and especially aided by European methods.[68]

Leibniz brings together two themes, the superiority of the scientist and the truth of origins. Theology and early sociology both used beginnings as a heuristic fiction that allowed one to map out and hierarchize the relation-

---

[67] *Tratados* 7 (Navarrete's annotations to Roman answers to Martin Martinez's queries of 1656), 472–73: "*Ni viene a proposito el dezir, que labarse las manos, usar de vestido limpio, ayunar, abstenerse de actos venereos etc, son actos indifferentes; porque aunque es verdad que secundum se lo son, como hincar las rodillas, quitar el sombrero, etc, pero determinanse a ser politicas, ò religiosas, hic, et nunc por la intencion, objeto, y otras cosas.*" Cf., in a similar vein, the Answers of Jean François Aleonissa O.F.M. to Cardinal Casanate's questions of 1 June 1699, in Noël Alexandre, O.P., *Conformité des cérémonies chinoises avec l'idolatrie grecque et romaine pour servir de confirmation aux Dominicains missionaires de la Chine* (Cologne: 1700), 140 (Italian original) and 189 (Latin). Should one rely only on the ancient classics (which seem to support the Jesuit position that the incriminated rites are political in nature) or on their more recent interpretations (which according to the mendicants demonstrate that the rites are religious)? Aleonissa argues that these "Ritual Books" (the term for Catholic manuals on the liturgy) are not private compilations but are based at the very least on the common understanding (*sensus*) and practice (*praxis, usus*) of the Chinese nation.

[68] Leibniz, *On the Civil Cult of Confucius* (1700–01) 9–11, trans. Daniel J. Cook and Henry Rosemont, *Writings on China* (Chicago: 1994), 64. My thanks to Luc Ferrier, who prodded me ceaselessly to read Leibniz.

ships between entities that were in fact coeval. The narrative made some entities come into being earlier (or at a more privileged moment in sacred time) than others in order to indicate their logical and essential, not temporal, priority. Like the Jesuits, Durkheim would turn to origins to prove that the function of rites was social;[69] like them he would dismiss posterior accretions of native interpretation as inessential and even misleading.[70] The concentration on beginnings, a characteristic of early social scientific theories of religion that much surprised E. E. Evans-Pritchard, owed everything to anthropology's theological ancestry.[71]

Jesuits and mendicants agreed that China was a country where all social classes practiced ceremonies bearing on every aspect of life,[72] and understood their role to be the maintenance of order.[73] Louis Le Comte phrased

[69] Compare Augustine, De genesi ad litteram opus imperfectum 7.28, PL 34, 231: "Commodissime in illo libro, quasi morarum per intervalla factarum a Deo rerum digesta narratio est, ut ipsa dispositio, quae ab infirmioribus animis contemplatione stabili videri non poterat, per hujusmodi ordinem sermonis exposita quasi istis oculis cerneretur," taken up with more explanations in the De Genesi ad litteram libri duodecim 4.33.51–52, ed. Joseph Zycha, CSEL 28 (Prague: 1894), 131–33 ("omnia mens simul angelica potest, quae singillatim per ordinem conexarum causarum sermo distinguit"), with Durkheim, FE, 10–11 and n. 1, trans. Fields, 6–8 and n. 3 ("It will be seen that I give the word origins, like the word primitive, an entirely relative sense. I do not mean by it an absolute beginning but the simplest social state known at present—the state beyond which it is impossible for us to go"). The "Social Contract" is another such instance of the heuristic use of pseudotemporality.

[70] Durkheim, FE, 3; trans. Fields, 2: "The reasons the faithful settle for in justifying these rites and myths may be mistaken, and most often are; but the true reasons exist nonetheless, and it is the business of science to uncover them." The elision of native exegesis was axiomatic for many functionalists, see, e.g., Radcliffe-Brown and Bronislaw Malinowski, cited by George Stocking, After Tylor: British Social Anthropology, 1888–1951 (London: 1995), 328–29, 272, 286. Tellingly, Malinowski allowed native exegesis of magical, hence individual, practices, but not of religious, hence social, rites). Stocking, 131, traces this attitude to at least Frazer.

[71] See E. E. Evans-Pritchard, Theories of primitive religions (Oxford: 1965), 73, 101f. For the Fathers, origins could validate as well as invalidate, cf. Augustine (above, ch. 4 at nn. 88–91) and Lactantius, Divine Institutes 1.23.5:22–23, ed. Pierre Monat, SC 326 (Paris: 1986), 242: "Non ergo isti glorientur sacrorum vetustate quorum et origo et ratio et tempora deprehensa sunt."

[72] Charles Le Gobien, Eclaircissement donné à Monseigneur le Duc du Maine in his Histoire de l'Edit de l'Empereur de la Chine en faveur de la Religion Chrestienne (Paris: 1698), 217–18: "Among them, ceremonial does not simply regulate as among us the manner and circumstance of religious worship's [public] actions, the public duties rendered to princes, ambassadors, and first magistrates, and certain magnificent offices that custom or the laws prescribe, but it touches every status and the most common duties of civil life."

[73] Cf. nn. 79–84 below, and Le Comte, Lettre, 32–33: "Even though one finds everywhere in these books [the Chinese Classics] the traces of a good Religion, one sees, nevertheless, evidently, that the authors sought almost no other end than the good order of the State; their laws concern only the police, civil ceremonies, the means for preserving the peace and quiet of the empire."

it in the Augustinian vocabulary of the *vinculum*: "the whole nation considers them to be the tightest bond (*lien*) of civil society."[74] Indeed, the primacy of the political explained the omnipresence of rites in China, and Le Comte's cohort Charles Le Gobien went as far as to say that the Chinese in effect worshiped "la politique."[75] This was also the eighteenth-century verdict of Montesquieu on the Romans and of Bishop Warburton on Ancient paganism in general.[76] Using the somewhat pejorative term that in the sixteenth century had denoted persons who put the salvation of the State above their religious beliefs, Le Comte stated that the Chinese "were much more *politiques*" than other nations.[77] Here Jesuits and mendicants still agreed; but they disagreed on the ultimate moral value of such a relationship between religion and order.

Both used the Augustinian grid, assuming that pagan *religio* fulfilled a combination of entertainment (fable or myth), noetic (natural theology), and political roles.[78] Both subscribed to a model, also derived from Augustine, widespread in the seventeenth century, that of the double religion: The esoteric beliefs of the pagan elites differ from the doctrines they teach the masses.[79] For Le Comte, the original lawmakers of China had used

---

[74] Louis Le Comte, *Lettre*, 29. Cf. the Augustinian definition, "*Civitas, quae nihil aliud est quam hominum multitudo aliquo societatis vinculo conligata*" (a civic community is nothing else than a multitude of human beings bound together by some bond of association)—*De civitate Dei* 15.8, 464:66–67.

[75] Le Gobien, *Histoire de l'Edit de l'Empereur de la Chine* 1 (Paris: 1698), 9: "La politique est la divinité qui règne souverainement à la Chine, et à laquelle on se fait un devoir de tout sacrifier."

[76] Montesquieu, *Dissertation sur la politique des Romains dans la religion* (read 18 June 1716), in *Oeuvres complètes*, 2 vols. (Paris: 1880), 116–24, at 124: "*Les Romains, qui n'avoient proprement d'autre divinité que le génie de la République*"; William Warburton, *The Divine Legation of Moses* 2.5.1, 3.2, 2d ed., 2 vols. (London: 1738), 1.274, 1.321: "They believed in a local tutelary deity, by whose direction they were formed into Society; and that, Society, as such, was the subject of Religion." See as well below, at n. 96.

[77] Le Comte, *Lettre*, 43. Cf. Rule, *K'ung-tsu*, xiii: "China was both a source and a test-case for the new ideas about religion and its social role."

[78] Cf. João Rodriguez's memorandum to the Jesuit General Claudio Acquaviva of 22 Jan. 1616, calling Confucianism a *doutrina civil e fabulosa popular* (cited in Rule, *K'ung-tzu*, 75–76 from the original in the Rome Jesuit Archives). The categories come from *De civitate dei* 6.5.

[79] Nicolò Longobardo, cited fairly faithfully by Navarrete in *Tratados* 5, praeludio 3.5, 257: "The three sects of China follow completely this way of philosophizing [described by Plutarch and Augustine], and hold two manners of doctrine. One is secret, and they hold it to be true. Only the Literati understand it, and they teach it covered with symbols and enigmatic figures. The other is public (*vulgar*), and is a metaphor of the first. The Literati hold it for false as to the meaning (*sentindo*) given to the words, and they use it for external police (*politica exterior*) and for the divine, civil, and poetic (*fabuloso*) cult, with which they lead the people to the good and rein it away from evil." For Le Comte, cf. Rule, *K'ung-tzu*, 134. Navarrete rediscovered in the Roman archives of the Office of the Propagation of the Faith a treatise by Longobardo, an early seventeenth-century Jesuit who opposed accommodation; it was

"natural feelings for the common good" in instilling through ceremonies
a reverence for paternal power, which would reinforce social order. This
first "spirit of piety and *politique*" had been over time corrupted by the
influence of Buddhism.[80] But Navarrete saw something more nefarious in
the relationship between religion and politics in China. Here the Dominican harkened back to a position developed by sixteenth-century missionaries to America: A highly structured social order went hand in hand with a
luxuriating and idolatrous religiosity, for rulers absolutely needed to manipulate religion to remain in power. In the words of a Jesuit father, the
Chinese elites had to keep the people "occupied with idolatry."[81] For
Navarrete, even Chinese toleration of alien faiths betrayed the absolute
primacy of politics. The literati's studied willingness to allow a plurality
of doctrines could only be detrimental to salvation; it smacked of the attitude of the "politiques" during the European wars of religion—which a
Spaniard, perhaps, could not view with as much indulgence as a French
Jesuit. Order, not Truth, was the ultimate Good. And for the sake of civic
peace, the Chinese did not stop at this wicked indifference toward existing
cults: "[T]he political (*la politica*) and human wisdom have enlarged their
ambit to such a point" that they made idols to control the people.[82] Like
Buddhist and Taoist priests, Confucian literati believed in a form of atheis-
tic pantheism, but taught otherwise in public to control the commons.[83]
For Navarette, in defending Confucian ceremonies and arguing that they
were purely political and served order, the Jesuits thus came dangerously
close to giving a stamp of approval to the Machiavellian model of "political
religion."[84]

---

translated into French as *Traité sur quelques points de la religion des Chinois. Par le R. Pere Longobardi*, in *Anciens Traitez* (as n. 66 above), here 11, 26. Cf. Rule, *K'ung-tzu*, 77f.

[80] Le Comte, *Lettre*, 44.

[81] Pagden, *Fall*, 172–79, drawing on José de Acosta S.J., *Historia natural y moral de las Indias*
(1590) 5.16, ed. Edmundo O'Gorman (Mexico: 1962), 242. See as well Sabine MacCormack,
"The Limits of Understanding: Perceptions of Greco-Roman and Amerindian Paganism in
Early Modern Europe," in Karen Ordahl Kupperman, ed., *America in European Consciousness,
1493–1750* (Chapel Hill: 1995), 79–129 at 88–96, with further bibliography.

[82] Navarrete, annotations to Longobardo, *Tratados* 5.17.2.5, 288: "*Demanera, que en estos
puntos entran respetos justos, y razon de estado. Tanto como esto se ha dilatado la politica, y prudencia
humana, que se estiende a hazer Dios verdadero al que no lo es, a lo que aun carece de vida vegetativa.*"

[83] Longobardo, apud Navarrete, *Tratados* 5.3, 256–58; Fr. trans. in *Traité* (cf. nn. 66 and 79
above), 24–26. Cf. the citation above, n. 79.

[84] Navarette's position is paraphrased in *Lettre d'une personne de piété*, 63 (translated here)
25–26: "Let this [Jesuit] father not speak of a human faith and of purely moral and natural
virtues (as he feigns to interpret [Confucianism] in his first clarification and in a preface to
the *Exposition of Chinese Worship*), and even less of a political Religion (*Religion politique*) as his
Brethren have dared to put forward in this same preface, unaware that they were thus falling
into the fantasy of *political Religion*, which exists only in *Machiavelli's* ideas." For the image of

For our purposes, we should highlight the two most noteworthy effects of the Chinese Rites Controversy. First, the starting point of this discussion: the vulgarization of the distinction between civil or political solemnities and religious rites. Second, that for minds as influential as Montesquieu and Hegel, the Chinese Empire came to provide an example, even more radical in its lack of spirituality than carnal Israel, of a polity essentially held together by solemnities. For Hegel, external worship is omnipresent, constitutes the whole of Chinese religion, and instills morality—the fulfillment of one's duties. It is such that every sphere of life falls under the governance of the external authority of government (as opposed to "immanent interior life").[85] In Montesquieu's *Spirit of the Laws*, China comes out as a country governed not so much by force as by rites.[86] Their political centrality dooms to failure the efforts of the missionaries, for their apostolate strikes at the heart of the Chinese "general spirit." Montesquieu holds that each nation is endowed with a "general spirit," a notion that approximates some modern understandings of "culture" insofar as it is a fairly inflexible characteristic of a human group and a constraint on its horizons. It is composed of a plurality of factors, "climate, religion, laws, precepts of government, past examples, mores, manners," but in any given nation one of them becomes predominant.[87] In the Chinese case, it is manners, and this for political reasons that also factor in the Empire's cultural essence. Seeking order before all, the lawmakers of China have instituted a multitude of "rites and ceremonies" to honor fathers, and instilled patriarchal values. They benefit the emperor and his magistrates, whom the population regards as "fathers," and foster love between generations. This, reciprocally, reinforces the honorific code of respect: "All of this shaped the rites and these rites the nation's general spirit." Montesquieu draws a very Catholic-sounding conclusion to predict the ultimate failure of Catholic missions:

Machiavelli during the wars of religion, see Donald R. Kelley, "Murd'rous Machiavelli in France," *Political Science Quarterly* 85 (1970): 545–59; for the new meaning of *political*, see Sellin, art. "Politik," *Geschichtliche Grundbegriffe*, 4.811–13.

[85] See Georg W. F. Hegel, *Lectures on the Philosophy of Religion* (1827), E. trans. Peter C. Hodgson et al., 3 vols. (Berkeley: 1984–87), 2.561. The first nineteenth-century French translation, owed to Antoine Véra, *Philosophie de la Religion de Hégel*, 2 vols. (Paris: 1878), 2.140f., insists further on this identity in China of "culte," "religion," and "politique" by annotating the text with Hegel's Jesuit documentation.

[86] In one of his wonderful articles, François Héran remarks how "in Montesquieu the Chinese ... embodies the ideal-type of complete ritualism"—"L'institution démotivée. De Fustel de Coulanges à Durkheim et au-delà," *Revue française de sociologie* 28:1 (1987): 67–97, at 79.

[87] *Esprit des Lois* 19.4, ed. Robert Derathé, 2 vols. (Paris: 1973), 1.329.

Excise one of these practices and the State will totter . . . If one notices that
these external practices constantly refer to a feeling that must be impressed in
all hearts, and which will, from all these hearts, shape the spirit that governs
the Empire, one will understand that it is necessary that this or that particular
[ritual] action be done.[88]

The modern reader is nevertheless left with a fine analysis of the relationship between rites and (dare we say?) *conscience collective*.[89]

THE DOUBLE-DOCTRINE MODEL, FUNCTIONALISM, AND IDEOLOGY

The double-doctrine model that the missionaries used deserves further
attention on at least two grounds. First, the model puts the accent on the
mysteries that obfuscated the true beliefs of the elite, and so led to a heightened reflection on the role of symbols, emblems, and ceremonies for pagan
societies. Second, the model allows the historian to explore the relationship
between early versions of, respectively, the ideological and functionalist
understandings of "ritual."

The double-doctrine model ultimately derived from Augustine. Or
rather, early modern thought used the Church Father's authority to sys-
tematize a congeries of ideas, which had freely floated in late antique paganism and Christianity.[90] According to the model, pagan (and even heretical Christian) religious elites held a different creed from the one they
peddled to the masses. In some variants of the model, the elites held a more
or less pure version of the original natural religion of humankind; in some
others, while false, these beliefs did not run counter to Christianity; in yet
others, they consisted in rank atheism or Epicurean materialism. The hidden doctrine could contain teachings bearing on natural philosophy or cos-
mology; it could as well simply initiate into the actual nonexistence of the
gods and simultaneously into the necessity to maintain their cult for the
masses. Next to this dogma, which they kept secret, the leaders devised for

[88] *Esprit des Lois* 19.19, ed. Derathé, 1.341. For Montesquieu, "manners" are the opposite
of laws insofar as the former are "inspired" and depend more on the general spirit, but the
latter are laid down and depend rather on a specific institution (19.12, 334).

[89] Cf. Durkheim, FE, 536, 605–606; trans. Fields, 379, 426.

[90] See Manuel, *The Eighteenth Century Confronts the Gods* (Cambridge, Mass.: 1959), 65–
69, 121–22; Jan Assmann, *Moses the Egyptian: The Memory of Egypt in Western Monotheism*
(Cambridge, Mass.: 1997), 83, 102, with reference to Celsus, mediated by Origen, *Contra
Celsum* 1.12, ed. Marcel Borret, SC 132 (Paris: 1967), 1.108; Plutarch, *Isis and Osiris*, esp.
5, 352b–c, ed. Christian Froidefond, *Oeuvres Complètes* 5:2 (Paris: 1988), 179–80; Clement,
Stromata 5, 7.41.1, ed. Alain Le Boulluec, SC 278 (Paris: 1981), 90–92. See in general Jean
Pépin, *Mythe et allégorie. Les origines grecques et les contestations judéo-chrétiennes*, 2d ed. (Paris:
1976). Ramsay MacMullen, *Paganism in the Roman Empire* (New Haven: 1981), 77–78 nn.
16–19 and 144–45 n. 38, inventories the ancient proof-texts on allegory and esoteric beliefs.

the people a utilitarian religion that insisted on rewards and punishments in the other life, but also appealed to the baser instincts. The priests hid their core belief either out of prideful desire for distinction, or because it happened to be antithetical to the public doctrine preached to the commons, often for the sake of the maintenance of order. Divulging what they felt was the truth would have ensued in the destruction of their leadership and of political harmony.

In the opinion of Augustine as well as of many Thomists, pagan religions concentrated single-mindedly on social utility and so employed solemnities and mysteries for instrumental purposes.[91] The link between the ceremonial and the social was axiomatic for one of the most widely read authors of the eighteenth century, William Warburton (1698–1779). In 1738–41, the future Bishop of Gloucester published his *Divine Legation of Moses*.[92] The book's thesis is simple. All religions invented by human beings maintain the social order; to do so, they all teach the immortality of the soul as well as rewards and punishments after death. Moses' Law, which does not, therefore must have been divinely inspired rather than made by men. To establish his premise, Warburton dwelled at length on the political role of religion outside the Judeo-Christian revelation.

The Anglican prized order. He might—like Etienne de La Boétie earlier or Marx later—call a man-made religion a "drug"; he still appreciated its efficiency.[93] Thus, even when looking at paganism, he could not quite accept that religions had been fully invented and that they were fully false. The founding legislators had not quite created them out of nothing; each had found a preexisting religion and, unable to "purify the soul of religion,"

---

[91] Cf. Augustine, *De civitate Dei*, discussed above, ch. 4 at nn. 83–91; Thomas, ST I II q. 99 a. 3, 7.201 (with Cajetan's commentary in idem, cited above, n. 13): "Human laws did not bother to institute anything regarding God's cult unless it served in an orderly way human common good; it is for this reason that they also invented many things concerning sacred matters, according to what seemed to be expedient in shaping human mores, as we see in the practice (*ritus*) of the pagans."

[92] For the reception of the work, see Jan Assmann, "Äegypten als Argument. Rekonstruktion der Vergangenheit und Religionskritik im 17. und 18. Jahrhundert," *HZ* 264 (1997): 561–85, at 577–79, and idem, *Moses*, 96f.

[93] *Divine Legation* 3.6, 2d ed. (London: 1738–42), 1.453–54: "As in a sovereign remedy the application of the *Drug*, though vitiated, is greatly to be preferred in desperate disorders to the doing of nothing, though it may produce evil liability in the constitution it preserves, which the sound *Ingredient* would have prevented." Cf. Etienne de la Boétie, *Discours sur la servitude volontaire*, ed. François Hincker, *La Boétie. Oeuvres politiques* (Paris: 1971), 65: "Theatres, games, plays, spectacles, marvellous beasts, medals, *tableaux*, and other such drugs were for the people of Antiquity the allurements of serfdom, the price for their freedom, the tools of tyranny." The pages that immediately follow, invoking such emblematic figures of political religion as Numa Pompilius, make clear that La Boétie thinks as well of religious sanctions to kingship.

had used "national rites and ceremonies" to "constitute the body of it."[94]
These lawmakers had not been some "species of dry, cold-headed cheats,"
but sincerely believed that insofar as their ideas produced the public good
they had to be supernaturally inspired.[95] Warburton also wanted to defend
against the idea that superstition is more socially useful than true religion.
Consequently, like Richard Hooker and Hugo Grotius, he attributed the
function of curbing disorder to the part of truth every religion contains.[96]

For Warburton, the pagan sages, caught in the double-doctrine model,
had taught publicly one thing they thought false but politically useful—the
existence of rewards and punishments in another life—and shared in secret
a different belief. But the dissociation of utility from truth was an essentially pagan misconception.[97] The future bishop saw a link between (1) this
dissociation, (2) the general primacy of the political, and (3) the fundamentally ritualistic nature of ancient religions. First, paganism's focus on the
collective went hand in hand with outward religion:

> In ancient Paganism, Religion ... had for its subject not only each individual,
> the natural man, but likewise the artificial man, society, from whom and by
> whom all the public rites and ceremonies of it were instituted and performed.[98]

[94] *Divine Legation* 3.6, 1.470.
[95] Ibid., 1.454–55.
[96] Ibid., 1.452–53. Compare Hooker, *Laws* 5.1.3–5, ed. W. Speed Hill, George Edelen,
P. G. Stanwood et al., 4 vols. (Cambridge, Mass.: 1977–82) 2.19–22, arguing that the positive
political consequences of pagan superstitions are owed to their sharing in the true religion;
Hugo Grotius, *De imperio summorum potestatum circa sacra commentarius posthumus* 1 (Paris:
1647), 11: "But even though a false religion also contributes something to outward peace
(whence we see here and there a great efficacy for ruling the multitude attributed to superstition), nevertheless the truer a religion is, the more fully it provides this [peace]" (through
both *dogmata et ritus*); and Bonald, below ch. 6, 211–12. Montesquieu, *Esprit des Lois* 24.19
(cited below ch. 6 n. 45), denies the obvious character of a fit between truth and social order.
[97] *Divine Legation* 3.2, 1.323–24 (with reference to Augustine, *De civitate dei* 4.10; cf. ch. 4
n. 85). Warburton seized the opportunity to demonstrate the truth of religion, see 3.6, 1.452:
"General utility and all truth necessarily coincide. For truth is nothing but that relation of
things, whose observance is attended with universal benefit. We may therefore as certainly
conclude that *general utility* is always founded on *truth*, as that *truth* is always productive of
general utility. Take then this concession of the atheist for granted, *that religion is productive of
public good*, and the very contrary to his inference ... MUST follow, namely, that religion is
true." Bonald may have borrowed this neoscholastic reasoning; cf. Bonald, *Théorie du Pouvoir
Politique et Religieux* 2.1.5 (ed. Paris: 1843; repr. Geneva: 1982), 13.45 (the dogmas necessary
for the conservation of society are *eo ipso* true). One finds it, with an inverted subject, later in
Durkheim, FE, 3, trans. Fields, 2: "A human institution cannot rest upon error and falsehood.
If it did, it could not endure.... All religions are true. All are true after their own fashion.
All fulfill given conditions of human existence, though in different ways."
[98] *Divine Legation* 2.1, 1.96–97; cf. 2.5, 1.274 (cited above, n. 76). The true religion focuses
instead on each individual in the human species. Compare Durkheim, FE, 599, trans. Fields,
421: "[T]he idea of society is the soul of religion," and of course the famous note, FE, 630,
trans. Fields, 443, equating "the concepts of totality, society, and deity," as well as 294–95,

Consequently, Warburton's pagan lawmakers considered the part of religion directed at the individual to be instrumental and subordinate to social order, and they did not hesitate to teach what they did not believe in, the immortality of the soul and rewards and punishments in the afterlife. Second, this inability to consider public religion outside the category of utility was owed to the lack of a dogma that might have put, as in Christianity, the accent on truth.[99] In Warburton's view, paganism was purely ceremonial, hence crassly political. In medieval terms, it had only letter, not spirit.[100] Through Hegel and others, we have inherited this model for (at least) Roman religion.[101]

Warburton was far from being alone in accepting that invented double-doctrine religions—associated with legislators such as Numa Pompilius, Orpheus, Zoroaster, or Zalmoxis—succeeded in stabilizing the polity. Thus André du Chesne (1584–1640), in a 1609 work dedicated to the future Louis XIII, approved of the general principle to educate royal children in their religion's "ceremonies and mysteries." The Persian royalty understood that the sublunar world is a replica and image of the Ideas and exemplars hidden in Heaven. And so it knew

> that in order to shape felicitously the organization of a polity the organization of their religion had to be drawn on the image of heavenly realities,[a] and, following this, that the political state had to be a second portrait, drawn according to the image,[b] and following the lines of the picture of religion.[102]

---

trans. Fields 208, identifying the totemic god of the clan as "the clan transfigured" or 350, trans. Fields, 351: "society, of which the gods are only the symbolic expression." The "artificial man" may be a reference to Hobbes's theory of the State in *Leviathan*.

[99] Cf. *Divine Legation* 2.6, 1.288: "[the Christians'] dogmatic theology teaching them that Truth was the end of religion, [where]as the pagans, who had only public rites and ceremonies, thought public utility to be."

[100] As a result of this, paradoxically, a pagan religion could not be a religious society; cf. *Divine Legation* 2.5., 1.274–75: "In reality, Pagan religion did not constitute any society at all. For it is to be observed, that the unity of the object of faith and conformity to a formulary of dogmatic theology, as the terms of communion, are the great foundation and bond of a religious society. Now these the several national religions of Paganism wanted, in which there was only a conformity in public ceremonies. The national Pagan religion therefore did not properly compose a society; nor do we find throughout all the writings of Antiquity that it was ever considered under that idea, but only as part of the State; and as such [the national Pagan religion] had, indeed, its particular societies and companies, as were their colleges of priests and augurs."

[101] Cf. John Scheid, "L'impossible polythéisme. Les raisons d'un vide dans l'histoire de la religion romaine," in Francis Schmidt, *L'impensable polythéisme: Etudes d'historiographie religieuse* (Paris: 1988), 425–457.

[102] André Du Chesne, *Antiquitez et recherches de la grandeur et Maiesté des Roys de France . . . à monseigneur le Dauphin* (Paris: Jean Petit-Pas, 1609), 166: "*Ce qui estoit peut estre aussi le but où visoient les Roys de Perse, qui ne permettoient iamais que leurs enfans fussent appelez à la conduite de leur Royaume, qu'ils n'eussent premierement appris en l'ecole des Mages les ceremonies et les myst-*

These fictions were efficient and appreciated as such.[103] For the Christian critique, it was enough to inveigh against the dangers an instrumentalized faith posed to souls. At times, an author could actually move from a discussion of pagan "ideology" to an apology of a specific Christian polity, as in this (to us) extraordinary passage owed to the same Du Chesne:

> In truth, religion belongs so essentially to the human being and to human society that since the human being who lacks it cannot be human, one cannot find a nation, no matter how barbarous, which lives without some shadow of religion. And one has even employed a false money for those who owing to their defects could not use a "good currency" in this matter. All legislators made use of this means, and there was never any polity to which there was not admixed some degree either of vain ceremonies or of deceptive beliefs that served as a bridle to hold the people in its position.[a] For this reason, most have at their origins fabulous beginnings and a wealth of supernatural mysteries. This is how bastard religions received credit . . . Thus . . . every polity has been headed by a God, in falsehood all other polities, in reality the polity Clovis built for the Frankish people when it came out of Germania.[104]

eres de leur Religion. Instruits qu'ils estoient en ce secret, que comme l'harmonie du second monde suit l'harmonie du premier, et que toutes les actions et les effets de la nature ne sont que portraits et lineamens qu'elle a tiré sur les vrays exemplaires cachez dans le Ciel: Il falloit aussi, pour former l'heureuse Oeconomie d'une Police, que l'Oeconomie de leur Religion fust tirée sur l'image des choses celestes: et que l'estat politic [sic] en apres fust un second portrait tiré sur l'image et sur les traits du Tableau de la Religion."

(a) In the margin: Harmonie du Ciel premier patron de la Religion.
(b) In the margin: Religion premier pourtrait de l'Estat.

[103] It would be worthwhile to follow the figure of Numa. See, e.g., Wolfgang Lazius, Fragmenta quaedam Caroli Magni imp. rom. aliorumque incerti nominis de veteris ecclesiae ritibus ac ceremoniis (Anvers: Ioannes Bellerus, 1560), 14–15 ("divine cult" accounts for the long-lastingness of Roman power); Onuphrio Panvinio (or Panunphio), De ludis circensibus, libri II, [et] de triumphis liber unus (Paris: Claudius Morellus, 1601), Aiii(v)–Aiiii(r), with the same thesis; Montesquieu, Dissertation, 1.116; Gabriel de Mably, Parallele des Romains et des François par rapport au Gouvernement 1.5, 2 vols. (Paris: 1740; repr. Den Haag: Jean [sic] van Duren, 1741), 8: "Numa's wisdom prevented that Rome give its enemies a revenge by destroying itself by itself, and this philosopher established a police all the more useful as he knew how to bring in religion; he gave mores to his people by teaching them how to respect the Gods," countered by Charles-François Dupuis, Origine de tous les cultes, ou Religion universelle, 4 vols. (Paris: An III [1795]), 2.110.

[104] André du Chesne, Antiquitez, "De la Religion des Rois de France," 14–15: "Et à la verité la Religion est si propre à l'homme, et à la societé des hommes, que comme l'homme sans elle ne peut être homme, aussi ne se trouve il peuple tant barbare soit-il qui ne vive sans quelque ombre d'icelle. Mesme ceux qui par leur insuffisance ne se sont peu assez payer d'une bonne monnoye en cet endroit, on leur a emploié encore la fausse. Ce moyen a esté pratiqué par tous les legislateurs, et n'a esté police ou n'y ait eu quelque meslange, ou de vanité ceremonieuse, ou d'opinion mensongere, qui ayt servy de bride à tenir le peuple en office. C'est pour cela que le plus part ont en leurs origines et commencemens fabuleux, et enrichis de mysteres supernaturels. C'est cela qui a donné credit aux Religions bastardes, et les a fait fournir aux gens d'entendement. Et pour cela que Numa et Sertorius, pour rendre les

Alluding to the Augustinian idea that without true religion a state is nothing more than a band of thieves, Du Chesne then went on to explain how the marauding Franks, impressed by the "spectacle of Clovis's baptism," had converted and been shaped into a people. From this moment on, religion more than fear of laws and punishments governed the kingdom, providing "the bond and the stability (*firmament*) of the State."[105]

The relationship between the two tiers of the religious system in the two-doctrine model points forward to Marxism and functionalism. Paganism is conceived of as a deceptive ideological sham; Christianity provides a true, consensual social glue. If the pagan elites keep for themselves and to themselves the true knowledge, they cloak it in public for the masses' eyes under symbols, allegories, and mysteries. Part of this illusionary complex includes the idea that there is a connection, epistemological and ontological, between the two levels where in fact there is not any. After all, the commons have to believe they share a single creed with the elites. External religion, including its ritual aspects, thus masks the true nature of reality and serves social order. In this model, exoteric is to esoteric what external religion is to internal religion, what political order is to knowledge, what vain ceremonies are to actual cognition.[106]

In true Christianity, however, there exists a two-way road between external and internal. The one cannot be conceived without the other. While faith and rites do foster order, the symbols of the liturgy (and for some apologists of the monarchy like André Du Chesne, the monarchy's ceremonies) do refer to Truth. Fundamentally, symbols are either generated by the higher, inner reality, or fashioned after its pattern by worthy humans who are not, therefore, inventors, but vectors of a revelation. Unlike the

---

hommes de meilleure creance, les paissoient de cette sottise, l'un que la Nymphe Egeria, l'autre que sa Biche blanche, luy apportoit de la part des Dieux tous les conseils qu'il prenoit. Et l'authorité que Numa donna à ses Loix, sous titre du patronage de ceste Deesse, Zoroastre legislateur des Bactrians et des Perses, la donna aux siennes souz le nom du Dieu Oromazi: [In the margin: *Dieux mensongers patrons et tutelaires des polices anciennes*] *Trismegiste des Egyptiens, de Mercure: Zalmoxis des Scythes, de Vesta: Charondas des Chalcides, de Saturne: Minos des Candiots, de Jupiter: Licurgus des Lacedemoniens, d'Apollo: Dracon et Solon des Atheniens, de Minerve. Et toute Police a eu un Dieu a sa teste: Faussement les autres, veritablement celle que Clovis a dressee au peuple François sorti de Germanie."* Immediately after the lines quoted at the note above, Du Chesne passed as well to Clovis and France as an exceptionalist counterpoint: *"Mais tout cela se faisoit souz une autre banniere que la nostre: Car nos Roys ayant receu les glorieuses qualitez de premiers Chrestiens, et fils aisnez de l'Eglise, par le sainct caractere de la vraye Religion, que Dieu voulut comme imprimer de son doigt sur la face du grand Clovis."*
(a) In the margin: *Religions nouvelles et fausses inventees pour tenir les peuples en bride* ("novel and false religions invented to hold the people in rein").

[105] Du Chesne, *Antiquitez*, 16–17.

[106] For modern anthropological parallels, the best example is Maurice Bloch, "Symbols, songs, dance," who insists that rituals produce a false cognition.

symbols of false religions, which are mystifying for the immense majority, Christian symbols can lead more than a narrow elite back to the Truth. They have (as for Weber and Durkheim) cognitive roles. They are thus both constitutive of social cohesion (secondarily) and (primarily) the instruments of an emotional and noetic link to God. Catholics and Protestants agreed at least on this: The sacraments both foster the external *politia* of the Church and, being visual signs, excite the faithful to religious devotion and understanding.[107]

In the debates of the early modern era, then, key ideas foreshadowing, on the one hand, Marxist anthropology, and, on the other, functionalist anthropology, coexisted in tight discursive union (coconstruction, to use the current jargon) within the Christian notion of religion. As in late antique and medieval conceptions, there were two ways to relate ritual and politics, one manipulative (and cognitively deceptive) and the other constructive (and cognitively enlightening). Authors sometimes explicitly contrasted one scheme with the other; they shared similar structural elements, but the relations between these parts were either perverse or sane. (One's own faith, needless to say, always represented the healthy exception; all others were twisted). These similarities help to explain the ease with which, historically, the eighteenth-century Philosophes were able to extend the critique of paganism to all of Christianity, just as Protestants had applied it to Roman Catholicism. They help apprehend as well why depictions of "rituals" that we can easily read using a functionalist grid are hospitable to certain Marxist interpretations, and vice versa.[108]

The Warburtonian equation of religious truth and religious utility points to the later sociological approach—to focus on religion's efficiency rather than its veracity, and to identify its reality not with God's existence but with its function.[109] The movement from theology to the social sciences proceeded, understandably, on tracks defined in part by theology's progressively greater willingness to see religion as an integrated facet of society.

Sociology is the heir of theology.[110] The idea that ritual has an inherent ability to constitute, maintain, and disrupt order depends genetically on a

---

[107] Cf. above, at nn. 16–21.

[108] See, e.g., Maurice Bloch, *Ritual, History, and Power*.

[109] Cf. above, *Divine Legation* 3.6, 1.452. Despite Durkheim's shrill attempt to deny comparability in FE, 605, trans. Fields, 426, the similarities between Marxism and French functionalism are not superficial. See Evans-Pritchard, *Theories*, 76–77; and Raymond Firth, "The Sceptical Anthropologist? Social Anthropology and Marxist Views on Society," in Maurice Bloch, *Marxist Analyses and Social Anthropology* (London: 1975), 29–60 at 31–32.

[110] As Emile Durkheim was himself aware, FE, 613, trans. Fields, 431: "The essential notions of scientific logic are of religious origin . . . scientific thought is only a more perfected form of religious thought." Cf. as well the analysis in Nisbet, *Sociological Tradition*, which one

specific conceptualization of the relationship between "religion" and "society"—a configuration in which the two are essentially coinherent. Here the immediate neo-Catholic predecessor of early sociology, while it approximates one medieval formulation, differs in significant ways from the model dominant in the Middle Ages. All the way to, and including the sixteenth century, often in the same circles and often enough even in a single author's thought, two schemes coexisted. In the one, religion is seen as the soul of a body, the commonwealth.[111] In the other, the Church stands next to the *res publica* as one sociation (*societas*) next to another.[112] We may think we are comparing apples and oranges here, but one has to remember that while modern historians distinguish between the Christian religion and the Church as an institution, medieval vocabulary and notions did not necessarily do so.[113] And it is precisely because the Church was seen for so long as a *societas* and a *religio* that ideas developed within ecclesiology concerning the role of rites could be transferred to society. The first model, which one might term "monistic," comes closer to the early sociological understanding of society as an integral whole, where such terms as politics and religion do not designate ontologically independent entities but avatars or functions of this unit. The second is more dualistic; while religion performs important and even critical services for society (and vice versa), the model emphasizes the essential autonomy of the two spheres, materialized in distinct if coordinated institutions.[114] Roughly speaking (for the *longue durée* trend differs from short-term effects of the Reformation), between the Middle Ages and the mid–nineteenth century, the two-societies model waned, leaving its erstwhile companion model alone to rule the field. In the former, religion had fostered order from outside civil society. In the latter, rituals maintained it from inside civil society. In the early modern

---

can push further into the past of European intellectual history, as does Milbank, *Theology and Social Theory.*

[111] Cf. John of Salisbury, *Policraticus* 5.2, ed. Clemens C. I. Webb, 2 vols. (London: 1909), 1.282:11–17: "*Est autem respublica . . . corpus quoddam quod divini muneris beneficio animatur et summae aequitatis agitur nutu et regitur quodam moderamine rationis. Ea vero quae cultum religionis in nobis instituunt et informant et Dei . . . cerimonias tradunt, vicem animae in corpore rei publicae obtinent.*"

[112] See G. B. Ladner, "The Concepts of *Ecclesia* and *Christianitas* . . ." *Miscellanea Historiae Pontificiae* 18 (1954): 49–77.

[113] John of Salisbury, *Policraticus* 5.2, passes directly from the sentence quoted n. 111 to the following, 1.282:17–22: "*Illos vero, qui religionis cultui praesunt, quasi animam corporis suscipere et venerari oportet. . . . Porro, sicut anima totius habet corporis principatum, ita et hii, quos ille religionis praefectos vocat, toti corporis praesunt.*"

[114] To give one example for each in the modern sociological tradition, the former looks more like the main thrust of Talcott Parsons's *The Social System* (London: 1951) and the latter like S. N. Eisenstadt's *Political Systems of Empires* (London: 1963).

era still, depending on the political situation, either scheme could hog the limelight. For example, Gallican thinkers might brandish the latter to fend off aggressive papal claims; they might equally turn to the former when arguing for the role of the clergy in the kingdom or that of the king for the national church. In 1796, in his critique of the Philosophers' individualism and contractualism, Louis de Bonald would turn to the monist model: His civil society has two similarly structured and in the last analysis essentially identical faces, religious society and political society.[115] But the early modern version of the monistic model was not at home only in late eighteenth-century France. We find it on the rise earlier, among Gallican thinkers such as André du Chesne, who could state in 1609 that "Religion and the State are as it were the first and oldest columns of human society, two full brothers sharing one blood and one nature."[116] We find it at about the same time across the channel. The Anglican Richard Hooker's influential *On the Laws of Ecclesiastical Polity* (1593–1604) used a geometric analogy to express the fundamental identity—in a soundly organized human community like England—of commonwealth and church:

> As in a triangular figure its base differs from its sides, and yet one and the selfsame line is both a base and also a side ([it is] a side simply, [or] a base of the triangle if it chances to be the bottom and underlie the rest), so albeit properties and actions of one kind do cause the name of a Commonwealth, [and] qualities and functions of an other sort [cause] the name of a Church to be given to a multitude, yet one and the same multitude may in such sort be both, and it is so with us [in the Church of England and the English commonwealth], that no person appertaining to the one can be denied to be also of the other.[117]

Church and commonwealth correspond to, as it were, two angles of vision on the same human group. They differ only insofar as they consider different aspects of human activity. Or, to put it in Hooker's Aristotelian vocabulary, in the optimal configuration (that of Ancient Israel and England) the two terms point to real differences, but differences that are accidents belonging to a single substance.[118]

---

[115] For what I call Bonald's monism, see David Klinck, *The French Counterrevolutionary Theorist Louis de Bonald* (New York: 1996), 41. I use "monism" and "dualism" in a different sense than Klinck or than Robert Nisbet, "De Bonald and the concept of the social group," *Journal of the History of Ideas* 5 (1944): 315–31 at 324.

[116] Du Chesne, *Antiquitez*, 165–66.

[117] Richard Hooker, *Of the Laws of Ecclesiastical Polity* 8.1.2, ed. Speed Hill et al., 3.319:19–27 (I simplified the early modern English); cf. Helmut Kressner, *Schweizer Ursprünge des anglikanischen Staatskirchentums*, Schriften des Vereins für Reformationsgeschichte 170 (Gütersloh: 1953), 11.

[118] Hooker, *Laws* 8.1.5, 3.325:1–5: "The *Church* and the *Commonwealth* are names that import things really different. But those things are accidents and such accidents as may and should always lovingly dwell together in one subject."

Hooker, Bonald, and others, because they worked in a theological framework, considered that only their own society and a few providential exemplars exhibited this perfect structure.[119] We shall call this "exceptionalism." The Englishman saw in the Catholic Church and in Israel's situation under gentile rule, the Frenchman in contemporary Protestant polities, corrupt variants of the exceptional best. Dualism, in fact, might characterize the defective societies. Early sociology made the normative ideal of monism, once realized only in exceptional and often single instances, into the general model for all human groups. Religion is now an expression of the social; the traces of the original theological discourse are evident in Durkheim's famous formulas defining a society unified by religious beliefs and practices as a Church, or the "idea of society" as "the soul of religion."[120]

Over the course of the several centuries separating the Reformation from Durkheim, thinkers explored the connection between religion and social order in multifarious ways. One finds in the Enlightenment the position that religion provides a brittle and ultimately inefficient cohesive force, and that reason, instead, should serve as the *vinculum sociale*. But this stance did not predominate; far from it. We shall examine in the following pages the eighteenth-century debates on religion's contribution to social cohesion and to the formation and maintenance of social groups.

Most thinkers would have agreed that every society has a religion. Lactantius and Augustine had taught, disapprovingly, that whereas God Himself had instituted Christianity, pagan elites had invented *religiones* for the sake of domination.[121] Enlightenment thinkers tended to extend the theme of imposture to Christianity itself. One detects Augustinian accents in Charles-François Dupuis's statement that the use of religion is a "political fallacy (*erreur politique*) that may have favored despots but never helped a society to be happy," or in his saying that "all those who wish to govern have a mania, they seek to delude."[122] Rousseau himself hesitates. Only religion could have convinced originally unwise individuals to accept the legislator's ideas, which, once the social contract struck, rendered them wise.[123] He approves of primitive Christianity's values, but this a-ritual and unworldly *religion de l'homme*, unlike "civic religions" (*religion du citoyen*),

---

[119] Hooker actually thought that ancient pagan nations, while endowed with different laws and offices for spiritual and temporal matters, were monistic societies as well, but since their religion was false he did not elaborate; cf. *Laws* 8.1.4, 3.321:19–21.

[120] FE, 60, 65, 599; trans. Fields, 41, 43, 421. As noticed fifty years ago by Nisbet, "De Bonald," 322.

[121] Discussed above, ch. 4, 143–45.

[122] Dupuis, *Origines*, 2.109. Compare *De civitate Dei* 4.32, 126:5–15.

[123] *Du contrat social* 2.7, in *Oeuvres complètes*, vol. 3, ed. Bernard Gagnebin and Marcel Raymond (Paris: 1985), 381–84; cf. 4.8, 464: "Never was a state founded without religion as its basis."

not only fails to provide a social bond but is actually antisocial. The other kind of religion, which Rousseau automatically assumes to employ ceremonial, may foster "*sentiments de sociabilité*," the law, patriotism, and capital punishment, yet it "is founded on error and lie, deceives human beings, makes them credulous, and drowns the true cult of the deity in a vain ceremonial." When writing, however, to propose a reorganization of Poland to make it into a strong state and nation, Rousseau unabashedly called for a civic religion, rites, feasts, monuments, and commemorations, on the pagan model of those "religious ceremonies which in their nature were always exclusivistic and national."[124] Among other authors, the Augustinian comparison was reconfigured in another way: While orthodox Christianity contributed optimally to social order, so did invented religions.[125]

But if false or partly false religions contributed to society, did all religions contribute equally? For Rousseau, "Christian law is fundamentally more noxious than useful to the strong constitution of the State." The French revolutionaries would take to the letter his positive words on civic religion, disencumbered of the accompanying doubts.[126] Montesquieu, another giant of early sociology, and fellow *maître à penser* of the revolutionaries, did not merely dissociate the truth of a religion from its social utility. He also sought to examine the fit between types of sociopolitical constitutions and religions, starting a tradition that blossomed in the twentieth century.[127] Rousseau and Montesquieu's avid reader, the counterrevolutionary Louis de Bonald, followed in their steps. In the following century, the young Marx had the revelation that religion did not constitute some spirit of brotherhood but was an avatar of social divisions.[128] But his turn from the consideration of the truth value of religion to the analysis of its social function was far from unprecedented.

By the eighteenth century, many saw religion as constitutive of the group. While not dealing with rites, Nicolas-Antoine Boulanger thought that in their origins, groups had been formed by religious laws, which had fathered alone morality and police. The "first religious families" had undergone a process of "secularization" that had transformed them into nations. In these nations, however, the originally religious modes of thinking

---

[124] *Contrat social* 4.8, 464–65; *Considérations sur le gouvernement de Pologne* 2–3, ed. Jean Fabre, in Rousseau, *Oeuvres complètes*, vol. 3, 957–65. See the comments in Albert Mathiez, *Les origines des cultes révolutionnaires (1789–1792)* (Paris: 1904), 17–20.

[125] Cf. above at n. 96, *Divine legation* 3.6, 1.452–53.

[126] *Contrat social* 4.8, 465. It is also (but on other grounds) Hume's position, who thinks polytheism more conducive to liberty than monotheism.

[127] Cf. *Esprit des Lois* 24.3–5, 2.133–36. The most famous progeny is of course Max Weber. See as well Guy Swanson, *Religion and Regime: A Sociological Account of the Reformation* (Ann Arbor: 1967).

[128] See Chadwick, *Secularization*, 52–57.

and institutions partly remained.[129] Some underlined the role of festive assemblies. According to Dupuis, to maintain social order the Egyptians had
invented "these great national solemnities that draw a whole people to a
single place to celebrate mysteries in common," from whom the Hebrews
had then borrowed. One detects similar proto-Durkheimian tones with
Bishop Warburton, who underlined the role of festivals in making a people's unity, "so that the body politic seems, as it were, one great assembly,
constantly kept together for the celebration of some sacred mysteries." In
the preceding century, Richard Hooker had held to the distinction between
a society and an assembly, the former being constant, the other ephemeral
and "for the performance of public actions."[130] For many thinkers, it was
specifically rites that made the group. Enlightenment thinkers might protest that to make religion rather than reason the bond of society was erroneous and dangerous; Jansenists might see in the fear of death, the wheel
and the gallows the true *vinculum sociale*; and Protestants might remain true
to the sixteenth-century refusal to equate Church unity and uniformity in
external rites.[131] But despite variations there was a degree of convergence
on the relationship between rites and group.

We saw how most sixteenth-century Reformers attributed to the sacraments the secondary—and only secondary—role of marking off the religious group in its aspect of *societas externa*. Most theologians, being theologians, would have been hard put to give the sacraments a primarily social
role. So it comes as no surprise to find Suarez arguing that while religion
unites human beings (as it were providing the *vinculum sociale*), this function
is ancillary to, and derivative from, religion's role in uniting God to each
believer.[132] Durkheimian social science would invert the priority: Individuals bind themselves in ritual to the divine, but the divine is a cypher, to
which effectively humans link in order to create bonds to one another, and,
as a consequence, engender and maintain society. Suarez does take one
important step toward the sociological understanding of religious rites.
Commenting on Thomas Aquinas, he considers that public *cultus* or external worship, including especially rites, would have been necessary in the

[129] *L'antiquité dévoilée par ses mythes*, 2 vols., reed. (Paris: 1978), 1.305–307.

[130] Dupuis, *Origine*, 2.10; Warburton, *Divine Legation*, 1.192–93; Hooker, *Laws* 3.1.14,
1.205.

[131] See Dupuis, *Abrégé* (An VI), 414f., esp. 465–66; Pierre Nicole, "De la charité et de
l'amour-propre" 2, ed. Charles Jourdain, *Oeuvres . . . de Nicole* (Paris: 1845; reed. Hildesheim:
1970); cf. also Holbach's position as described by Manuel, *Eighteenth Century*, 240–41.

[132] *Opus de virtute et statu religionis, Disputatio* 1.1.1.1–7, esp. 1.1.1.6, in *Opera Omnia*, 13,
5: "Before all, religion unites us to God, and as a consequence of this it follows that those
who worship (*colere*) the same God remain in some manner bound to one another—this more
or less according to the kind of worship (*rationem cultus*)." This is as well Thomas's starting
point in ST I II q. 99 a. 3, 7.201.

state of innocence.[133] He is far from certain that the same applies to the sacraments; it is likely that they would not have been necessary had the Fall not happened. Rites are a necessary consequence of the human being's social nature and of the nature of society: Humans would have formed a civil society no matter whether the Serpent had succeeded or not, and any commonwealth has to have a unitary and unifying religion. So while protesting against the Protestant "politicization" and quasi secularization of ceremonies, Suarez accepts a distinction with comparable implications. Sacraments' existence depend on providential history, but rites, albeit religious, are understood to be a consequence of sociability. Suarez's rites belong to the realm of religion, but exist only as a factor, and for the sake of human society's existence. In many ways, the Durkheimian inversion is *en germe* here, especially once one removes from the picture the uncreated God and the vertical dimension of outward religion.[134] In what was much more a sign of this possibility rather than a representative expression of the seventeenth-century zeitgeist, Spinoza wrote in his *Tractatus Theologico-Politicus* (1670) that:

> [T]he ceremonies . . . in the Old Testament . . . had reference merely to the government of the Jews, and merely temporal advantages. As for the Christian rites, such as baptism, the Lord's Supper, festivals, public prayers . . . they were instituted as external signs of the universal church, and not as having anything to do with blessedness, or possessing any sanctity in themselves. Therefore, though such ceremonies were not ordained for the sake of upholding a government [as in Judaism], they were ordained for the preservation of society, and accordingly he who lives alone is not bound by them.[135]

Inward religion alone saves souls; outward religion pertains to political or social salvation.

Catholics were not alone in assuming the general rule of a connection between rite and social group. We just saw that Spinoza did—but this lapsed Jew cannot typify any mainstream religious group. We are less in the world of marginality (if still within the world of religious exiles

---

[133] The whole discussion is in Suarez, commentary on Thomas, ST III, qq. lx–lxi, *Opera Omnia* 20.18–63. Compare seventeenth-century jurists such as Hugo Grotius and Pufendorf, as recently discussed in Daniel Gordon, *Citizens without Sovereignty: Equality and Sociability in French Thought, 1670–1789* (Princeton: 1994), 77–78.

[134] No sacrament would have been necessary had the Fall not occurred and had the Logos not been destined to be incarnated. Had there been no Fall yet had Christ been incarnated, it is likely that the Eucharist would have been instituted. But as for other sacraments (including baptism), only marriage (in part) and especially ordination (owing to its relation to the Eucharist) would have had some probability of having been instituted. Suarez, *Disputatio* 3.3.8–11, *Opera Omnia* 20.62–63, commenting on Thomas, ST III, q. lxi, a. 2.

[135] Benedict de Spinoza, *Tractatus Theologico-Politicus* 5, E. trans. R. H. M. Elwes, *A Theologico-Political Treatise* (New York: 1951), 76.

to the Low Countries), with the French Calvinist pastor Pierre Jurieu (1637–1713). Considering the age before Moses, Jurieu cannot see then any constituted ecclesiastical body besides separate, scattered, and mutually independent families that made as many microchurches. He connects this situation to the absence of sacraments and of a shared cult:

> There was not at that time any confederation between families, any solemn assemblies, any ecclesiastical body endowed with form (*corps d'Eglise formé*). For . . . Augustine has very well remarked that human beings cannot form an ecclesiastical body (*corps d'Eglise*) under the name of a religion, be it false or true, if they are not united together by the bonds of some seals and of some visible sacraments.

Having less "form," the pre-Mosaic Church depended on another power: "to conserve a church in this form, or rather in this absence of external form, the Spirit had to be present in greater amount."[136] Jurieu aims his argument explicitly at the Catholics, who claim that a constituted ecclesiastical body with solemn assemblies, hierarchical ministers, ecclesiastical institutions, and excommunication had always existed. Having proven that they were unknown prior to Moses, Jurieu can conclude that the "essence of the Church" cannot consist in them. Yet, for him, each family, while independent from every other family in matters of worship, was still "united [within itself] by the external bonds of a same cult"—very much like the archaic Greco-Roman family in Fustel de Coulanges's *Cité Antique* (1864).[137] In many ways, while denying the absolute necessity of shared rites, the Reformed minister affirms it for the unit that matters according to his sectarian lights—the godly family. Furthermore, the age before Moses had been an exception. When sacred history did produce the greater unit, the sacraments appeared.[138] Circumcision had been at first only the seal of a promise specific to Abraham's family. But when the Abrahamide "clan" multiplied and became a great people, and idolatry engulfed all other groups, God transformed circumcision into a sacrament, to which He added a second one, Passover. Now Jurieu does not exactly consider, as Fustel de Coulanges will, the emergence of the suprafamilial social unit as

---

[136] Pierre Jurieu, *Histoire des dogmes et des cultes depuis Adam jusqu'à Jésus-Christ* 1.17 (Amsterdam, 1704), 124. The reference is to Augustine, *Contra Faustum* 19.11 (discussed above, ch. 4, 146).

[137] Jurieu, *Histoire* 1.17, 139 and 127–28. Compare Numa-Denys Fustel de Coulanges, *La Cité antique. Etude sur le culte, le droit, les institutions de la Grèce et de Rome* [henceforth CA] 2.5 (repr. Paris: 1984), 58: "la religion domestique . . . constituait la parenté."

[138] Cf. as well *Histoire*, 1.17.5, 139–40: Now the Church, owing to its size, cannot "do without the bonds necessary in great societies;" it must now, "to persist, be united by these external bonds that bind [together] its external limbs: government, profession of faith, and sacraments."

the result of, cause of, or correlate to the appearance of a wholly new cult binding together families. In Fustel's *La Cité Antique*, the plurality of originally independent familial groups, when they draw together to create a larger social unit, effectively come to believe that some of their deities, belonging to the category of nature gods, are identical and common to all; they create a shared cult as "the bond of the new association." Shared meals and banquets provide a central element for any social unit.[139] In the *Histoire des dogmes et des cultes*, faith expands with Abraham's clan while idolatry spreads outside this growing unit; once faith, grace, and the clan have become fully coextensive, God transforms the Abrahamide sign of identity, circumcision, into a sacrament. Prior to the institution of Passover, banquets held after sacrifices are not such a bond between families, for only a given family and a few guests partake in them.

By the late eighteenth century, then, it was a commonplace that religion and social unit were in some way congruent. As a consequence, a change in religion, even rites, was supposed to lead to a transformation in society.[140] No wonder that the monistic equation and its dynamic corollary were put into action with the French Revolution. The attempt to establish revolutionary cults, and its perceived failure (discovered after the fall of the Jacobins) determined the intellectual history of religion and ritual in the nineteenth century. To it we now turn.

---

[139] CA 3.1–3, 132–43.

[140] Hugo Grotius, *De imperio* 1, 21: "A transformation in religion, I say, even in rites, if it is not done with the consent [of all?] or does not involve an evident emendation, in itself shakes the commonwealth and often leads it into the greatest perils." If it is not restrained, a *mutatio rei publicae* will ensue. Montesquieu, *Esprit des Lois* 25.11, 2.162, warns against changes in religion since it is "tied to the State's constitution."

Chapter Six

MEDIEVAL HISTORY AND THE SOCIAL
SCIENCES, CA. 1800–CA. 1970

MONISM TRIUMPHANT: LOUIS DE BONALD

Like the Reformation, the French Revolution is a watershed for the notion of ritual. First, the revolutionaries and their immediate successors in the Directoire agonized much about the relationship of the State to the Church; second, in the aftermath of the Revolution, French and European thinkers debated whether religion might not help to soothe the disruptions of the age. The most articulate intermediary form between theology and the early social sciences, Louis de Bonald's 1796 *Théorie du pouvoir politique et religieux*, can only be understood against this background.

The debates on the place of the clergy in the nation's constitution, the Convention's attempt to introduce revolutionary festivals and cults, culminating in the Cult of Reason of 1793, and the related abolition of public Catholic worship show that for the revolutionaries the social importance of outward religion was self-evident.[1] Disagreements over the necessity of ceremonies (be they Catholic or invented) show that the ideas developed through the Reformation and Counter-Reformation had been routinized. Edgar Quinet, true to the position of Enlightenment thinkers like Charles-François Dupuis, would later reproach the Jacobins for having followed the "medieval" model—to give a cult to the people to maintain its morality, while not believing in it.[2] The revolutionaries drew on commonplaces ex-

---

[1] For these festivals, see Mona Ozouf, *La fête révolutionnaire, 1789–1799* (Paris: 1976)—where one cannot always tell whether the author is Durkheimian or her sources are proto-Durkheimian (see e.g., 16–17, 332–33). Ozouf's predecessor Albert Mathiez, *Les origines* (1904), directly called on Durkheim and made these festivals the ceremonial half of the "revolutionary religion"; Durkheim, in turn, used him in EF, 305–306, trans. Fields, 215–16, to develop the idea of society's creation of its gods. The convergence between event and theory seems easy enough, since Mathiez's sources employ notions Durkheim will inherit. As a cultural analysis, Mathiez's conclusions ring true—which does not necessarily entail that they are true as sociological analysis. F.-A. Aulard, *Le culte de la Raison et le culte de l'Etre Suprême* (Paris: 1892), 35, 54–55, documents how self-consciously some revolutionaries, in pleading for a cult of the motherland, embraced the idea that ancient pagans had worshiped their State.

[2] Edgar Quinet, *La Révolution*, 2 vols. (Paris: 1865), 1.178–87. Cf. Dupuis, *Origine de tous les cultes ou religion universelle*, 4 vols. (Paris: an III [1794/5]), 2.109ff.

pressed in such works as Diderot's *Encyclopédie* or Gabriel de Mably's 1776 *De la législation*. In the entry devoted to "ceremonies," the *Encyclopedia* insisted that, while philosophers did not need sensible signs to remember the objects of Faith, the ordinary people required ceremonies:

> Sensible representations of every nature have a miraculous impact on the commons' imagination, [for as] Saint Gregory the Great says, "An image provides the uneducated with what [Holy] Writings gives to the literate."[3]

The deep-seated analogy between rite and image—which tempts historians to consider rituals as pictures or theatrical scenes to be deciphered and interpreted—received authority from the standard Thomistic position, mediated by the Catholic liturgicists.[4] The Abbé de Mably (1709–85) grounded his defense of cultic practices on a commonplace of scholasticism: The mutual influence of body and soul mandates religion's two aspects.[5] It must comprise as much "spiritual ideas" as "a cult and . . . corporeal ceremonies." The latter "unite citizens to one another through actions belonging to the realm of the senses, and make them prone to only have a single spirit and to fulfil their mutual duties." Thus, religion provides "the bond among citizens."[6] Consequently, and in terms borrowed from early modern scholasticism, Mably underlined that even if a society could owe its creation to nature, it would need "a regular and public cult to make its happiness lasting."[7]

Mably's ideas were well received both by the revolutionaries and in some Catholic milieus. Right at the beginning of the Directoire, in 1794/5, a Parisian publisher reprinted the complete *De la législation*. In the same "Year Three of the Republic," an excerpt of the work was put into circulation. Its editor underlined in his endnotes the superiority of the Catholic cult with a traditional reminder: "Other cults" were "purely human in their institution," but God had instituted the "substance" of Catholic rites and

---

[3] *Encyclopédie ou dictionnaire raisonné des sciences, des arts et des métiers* (Paris, 1751–80; reed. Stuttgart: 1966), 2.839. The *Encyclopédie*'s contributions by Jean-Louis de Cahusac, in their insistence on the equation of feasts, the people in its totality, and the public sphere, were representative of eighteenth-century arguments all the way to the Revolution. See Werner Oechslin, "Fest und Öeffentlichkeit," in Fritz Reckow, *Die Inszenierung des Absolutismus* (Erlangen: 1992), 9–49, at 15–22. For the *Encyclopédie*'s varied positions on religion's function for society, see Gordon, *Citizens*, 81–83.

[4] Cf. above, ch. 5, 170–71, and Asad, "Discipline," 129.

[5] Cf. Trent, session 22, ch. 5, ed. and trans. Norman P. Tanner, *Decrees of the Ecumenical Councils*, 2 vols. (London and Washington: 1990) 2.734:22–30; Martène, *De antiquis ecclesiae ritibus*, 4 vols. (1699; reed. Anvers: 1736), preface, quoting Cardinal Bona.

[6] *De la Législation, ou Principe des Loix* 2.4.3, in *Collection complète des oeuvres de l'abbé de Mably* IX (Paris: Ch. Desbriere, an III [1794/5]), 426, 430. For Mably's influence, see Aulard, *Culte*, 10–12.

[7] *De la Législation* 2.4.3, 426–27; compare Suarez, above, ch. 5, 199–200.

ceremonies, even if the Church had authored their accidental details. In another note that reminds the modern reader of Durkheim's collective effervescence, the anonymous editor expanded on Mably's description of rites' effects:

> [Christian religion] does not limit itself to uniting together those who profess it through the inward bonds of a same faith and mutual charity; it gives them the opportunity to gather, to draw closer, to bind themselves together through the pomp of its solemnities, through the communication of their thoughts and feelings . . . To sum up, it contributes to make them more apt to political and social life (*à les policer et à les rendre sociables*).[8]

Such themes were in the air and were echoed on all sides: The organizers of Republican festivals expected shared happiness, emotionality, and exaltation—as Rousseau had advised in his *Considérations sur le gouvernement de Pologne*.[9] Chateaubriand did not agree with, far from it, his fellow conservative Bonald's belief in the primacy of society over the individual, or his scientific and nonromantic approach to the reconstruction of France.[10] But in 1802 he too denounced the Revolution's invented civic feasts as cold failures, extolling instead the social virtues of a Catholic religion "of the human heart," with "its ecstasies, its flames, its sighs, its joys, its tears, its loves for the world and the desert."[11] In this sentimentalist vein Chateaubriand described the ancient legislators' first institutions as nothing else but "a beautiful music called law, dances, canticles, a few consecrated trees, old men leading children, a love shaped near the sepulcher, and religion and God everywhere"—a social miracle the Jesuits had renewed in their Paraguayan Republic.[12] Despite Chateaubriand's philosophical individualism, he too shared in the general Romantic insistence on emotionality in solemnities and the power of assemblies, an aspect of "ritual" the Durkheimian school and especially Victor Turner would bring to the analytical fore.[13]

Seven years after the An III edition of Mably's works, a priest pleading for the reestablishment of public Catholic cult could find no better argument for his cause than the re-publication of the approximately same fifty-

---

[8] *Principes de Mably, Sur la nécessité de la RELIGION et d'un Culte public (Extraits du Traité de la Législation)* (Paris, An III), 51–52. Compare Monsieur Poyet's *Projet de cirque national et de fêtes annuelles* (Paris, 1792), cited by Mathiez, *Origines*, 132, justifying festivals as "rassemblements" and moments of imaginative binding to one's fellow citizens, which allow moral change and foster love for the commonwealth.

[9] Cf. Rousseau, *Gouvernement de Pologne* 2–3, 958, 964.

[10] Cf. Klinck, *Bonald*, 131–34 and passim.

[11] Cf. Mathiez, *Origines*, passim; François-René de Chateaubriand, *Génie du Christianisme*, ed. Pierre Reboul, 2 vols. (Paris: 1966), passim, quotes at 2.2.1 & 2.3.8, 1.245 & 1.302–303.

[12] Chateaubriand, *Génie* 1.1.8, 1.83; 4.4.4–5, 2.151 and 2.157–58.

[13] Cf. Victor Turner, *The Ritual Process* (1969, reed. Ithaca: 1979); idem, *Drama, Fields, and Metaphors* (Ithaca: 1974).

page excerpt. According to the apologetic preface, allowing public Catholic worship would "strengthen the springs [of political organization], impress upon them a new force and double their energy, not only by demonstrating the submission to civil laws that derives from divine authority, source of all power, but by uniting to one another all consciences and by binding them to the government through a persuasive inward feeling."[14] The booklet concluded with the following commonplaces: (1) There cannot be any true cult without it being public; (2) There cannot be any religion without cult (3) Society cannot be preserved without religion.[15]

Mably (and his editors) anticipates themes much more developed in Bonald. Bonald too will insist on the maintenance (as opposed to production) of society.[16] But his model is dynamic. Religion is normally the strongest force binding together society, yet in certain circumstances (for Mably, if it turns fanatical) it will without fail be destructive of social harmony. Since Bonald posits a tight correlation between perfect (or imperfect) constitutions and perfect (or imperfect) religions, a transformation in either of these spheres entails a transformation in the other.[17] It is to Bonald's understanding of this dynamic relationship, and its consequences for ritual, that we now turn.

Owing to his ultraconservative and fervently Catholic opinions, owing as well to the theological tenor of his reflections on society, Louis, vicomte de Bonald, is no longer read for political guidance.[18] Yet he influenced

---

[14] *De la nécessité d'un culte public. Et des lois propres à établir l'union entre la Religion et le Philosophies; extrait de MABLY, Traité de la Législation liv. II, chap. iii et iv. Publié par F.-B. M*** Ministre du culte Catholique* (Paris: Goujon fils, Oct. 1801), preface, 14 . M*** is probably the Citoyen Mille, from whom one could obtain copies of the work and who lived on the same street as the printer Goujon.

[15] De la nécessité, 50.

[16] Louis G. A. de Bonald, *Théorie du pouvoir politique et religieux* (henceforth TPPR) 2.1.2, in *Oeuvres complètes*, 15 vols. (ed. Paris: 1843; repr. Geneva: 1982), 14.23. Cf. TPPR 2.4.6, 14.213: "[R]eligion is always social, because the human being is always in society, either natural or political, either in *société de production* or in *société de conservation*"; and Joseph de Maistre, *Essai sur le principe générateur des constitutions politiques* 58, in *Oeuvres complètes*, 14 vols. (Lyon: 1884), 1.299: ". . . the religious principle is by essence creative and conservatory." First published in 1810, the *Essai* was reedited at least fifty-three times before 1924.

[17] Gabriel de Mably, *Parallele des Romains et des François par rapport au Gouvernement* 2.16, 2 vols. (Paris: 1740), 1.199: "La religion est le lien le plus fort de la Société quand elle ne dégénère pas en fanatisme. Mais dès qu'elle cesse d'en resserer les parties, elle en romp nécessairement l'harmonie." Compare Bonald, TPPR 2.1.introduction, 14.6: "It is because [political society and religious society] cannot be separated that the revolutions of religious society produced the republics, and that the revolutions of political society produced the sects"; ibidem 2.6.2, 14.310: "*Chaque religion ou secte différente correspond à une forme particulière de gouvernement.*" The idea is already present in Hugo Grotius and Montesquieu; cf. above, ch. 5 n. 140, Hugo Grotius, *De imperio* 1, 21; Montesquieu, *Esprit des Lois* 25.11.

[18] See, however, Robert Spaemann, *Der Ursprung der Soziologie aus dem Geist der Restauration. Studien über L. G. A. de Bonald* (Munich: 1959), and David Klinck, *The French Counterrev-*

generations of thinkers in France and even beyond.[19] His importance for the formation of sociological categories, first underlined in the Anglo-Saxon world by Robert Nisbet, is now a commonplace.[20] We shall look first at Bonald's model of society, both as a structure isomorphic to religion and as an object of change, then at the role of religion for social cohesion, even in its idolatrous variants.

Bonald operates on the principle that the proper unit-object of analysis is society, not the individual human being. The Enlightenment philosophers erred in thinking otherwise; despite what legislators may think, and despite appearances, it is not individuals who make society (especially through a social contract) but the reverse. Simply—and here Bonald follows approvingly his opponent Rousseau—when humans happen to promulgate against the grain of society, they throw it sooner or later into disorder; turmoil lasts until it purges itself violently or until the law is rescinded or changed.[21] One cannot understand history from the standpoint of the individual. For society, "despite the [selfish] efforts of human beings, tends necessarily and invincibly to constitute itself."[22] Events and great trends happen independently of individual action. Perhaps because the Catholic, monarchist, and French patriot Bonald has to account for the French revolution, which drastically modified the best of religions and kingdoms, he does allow for the causative role of human ambition. But in positive political processes at least, the "great man" does not make a difference. If Augustus had not been born, some other Roman would have effected, sooner or later, an essentially identical work of reform involving the establishment of a monarchy.[23] Similarly, it is in relation to society, not to the individual, that religion exists and can be an object of analysis. While human reason is fundamentally handicapped in any attempt to understand God, it can analyze the relationships between God and human beings, which are social in nature. For Bonald, "religion is always social,"[24] and we shall see that as later for Durkheim, it is in a sense society that creates God.[25]

That human beings interact with one another in what Bonald calls political society, and with God (and through God with one another) in religious

olutionary Theorist Louis de Bonald (New York: 1996), with bibliography. I thank Keith Baker for the first reference.

[19] Carl Schmitt read him, along with De Maistre and Donoso Cortes, approvingly—see *Politische Theologie. Vier Kapitel zur Lehre von der Souveränität* (Munich and Leipzig: 1922), 37ff., 49–50.

[20] Cf. Robert Nisbet, "The French Revolution and the Rise of Sociology in France," *American Journal of Sociology* 49 (1943): 156–64.

[21] TPPR 1.1.3, 13.64, with 1.2.1, 13.158–59.

[22] TPPR 2.4.1, 14.127.

[23] Cf. TPPR 1.2.4, 13.177–78, citing Montesquieu.

[24] TPPR 2.4.6, 14.213.

[25] Below, 213.

society makes these two societies "isomorphic" (my expression; Bonald says that they obey the same necessary laws and have the same constitution). For this reason, he applies to each society axioms elaborated in his analysis of the other.[26] This is all the more proper since religious society and political society (as in Hooker's triangle) correspond to two angles of approach to the same entity, civil society. The one considers human beings as "intelligent physical beings," the other shifts accents in looking at them as "physical intelligent beings."[27] In his later *Principe conservateur de la Société*, Bonald anticipates Durkheim even more straightforwardly: Religion is something that must be understood from the standpoint of the human community. "[O]ne can find the rationale for religious beliefs, which the human being cannot find in himself and in individual reason, in the natural and general constitution of society,"[28] understand, in the makeup of respectively the family and political society.

Bonald insists that societies are unlike individual human beings. The latter, being contingent entities, can exist or not exist, and therefore can mistakenly embrace what destroys them. The former necessarily love the elements necessary to their conservation.[29] Bonald borrows here the scholastic opposition between necessary (usually reserved for the divine realm) and contingent. As in twentieth-century Parsonian functionalism, societies maintain in being whatever is a condition for their existence. And as in this tradition of sociology, when perturbed, Bonald's constituted societies have a built-in, homeostatic tendency to return to their original order: "The more a society is constituted, that is, the more its power is one, limited [by such institutions as the *parlements*], and defended [by the nobility], the more it tends to remain in the same state, or return to it."[30] In fact, whereas non-fully constituted societies tend to decrease in constitution owing to disorder (disorder being itself a product of this original defect in constitution), in constituted societies the same turmoil has the opposite effect: It constitutes them more.[31] Ultimately, however, degenerating societies reach a rock-bottom point beyond which they cannot further fall, and a reverse movement leading to greater constitution begins.[32]

---

[26] E.g., TPPR 1.1.1, 13.31.

[27] TPPR, preface, 13.4.

[28] *Essai sur le principe conservateur de la Société* (henceforth: PCS), preface, in *Oeuvres Complètes* (Paris: 1830; reprint, Geneva: 1982), 12.83–84.

[29] TPPR 2.1.2, 14.25 (a proof of the existence of God): "If human society could deceive itself on the object of its feelings, that is hate what can conserve it or love what can destroy it, it could stop conserving itself, and therefore it would not be [a] necessary [entity]."

[30] TPPR 1.2.1, 13.159 (on Egypt).

[31] TPPR 2.6.11, 14.442–44.

[32] Also noteworthy is the functionalist description of the "social body" that opens up the widely read *Du divorce* (1801), in Bonald, *Oeuvres complètes* (repr. 1982), 5.1, as quoted and analyzed by Klinck, *Bonald*, 106–108 and n. 80.

Changes in religion lead to changes in political regimes and vice versa.[33] Bonald relates the historical fate of European states after the Reformation to the faiths they fostered. In this narrative, it is not the individual agent, not even the ruler, who directs the course of social transformation. "The philosophers believed or said that religion does not have any influence on the domestic governance of States nowadays, because it [religion] enters very little in the behavior of those who govern States. The true statesman knows well that religion, because it is the soul of society, is the hidden principle of all events in society."[34]

Indeed, social cohesion owes everything to religion. The human being is composed of body and soul. This explains the primacy of the mental or inward in social matters as well as the necessity of the physical or external. Faithful to the spirit-matter hierarchy prevalent in Western thought, Bonald remarks that minds alone can be actually united; bodies can only be brought into close proximity. For this reason, a social union between human beings is primarily one of minds; hence the heart of social unity is religious.[35]

But Bonald remains true to another tenet of the Catholic tradition—the insistence on the body. Since the human being is also physical, and since nothing can be truly social unless it is public, this union has to effect itself in the physical order through cult (that is, external religion).[36] In the *Théorie de l'éducation sociale*, the 1796 complement to the *Théorie du pouvoir*, Bonald develops the importance of symbols and rituals. They are the necessary outward manifestation of power.[37] This role, far from accidental, is mandated by his theory.

Specifically, the isomorphism and fundamental identity between constituted religious society and constituted political society means that for Bonald cult and political power are essentially equivalent. In the Catholic civil society, created by the coming together of Germanic monarchy and Christianity with the conversion of Clovis and the religious reforms of Pippin and Charlemagne, the ever-present Man-God Christ and the monarch have structurally identical roles. Both are the center of the social circle

---

[33] E.g., TPPR 2.6.2, 14.312.

[34] TPPR 2.6.2, 14.323.

[35] TPPR 2.1.6, 14.46–47: "Civil society is . . . strictly speaking, the reunion of minds and the drawing together of bodies."

[36] TPPR 1.1.4, 13.71: "The intellectual society of God and . . . the social body" can "become general, that is, social, only by becoming exterior and public, and forming the exterior and public cult."

[37] "In a constituted society . . . [power] must manifest itself outwardly for all must share in what belongs to all. The pull (*empire*) that these outward signs have on human beings cannot be resisted, and it need be so, since when general power displays itself to the eyes, one assumes it is accompanied by force, since a power without force isn't a power." Cf. Klinck, *Bonald*, 72–77, drawing on TPPR 3.3 and conclusion, 15:260ff. and 15.353–59.

linking human beings to one another. Both embody (literally) a love—in the one case the mutual love of God and Man, in the other the love between human beings.[38] In Bonald's model love necessarily externalizes itself and makes itself "public." Love in action through force is power (*pouvoir*), and has two faces: in religious society cult, in political society monarchical governance.[39] The one is an embodiment of society's spiritual aspect, the other the spiritual manifestation of society's material aspect. The identification of the ruler with the soul of the social body was not novel; seventeenth-century French authors, for example Moyse Amyraut (a Calvinist) or Jean Filesac, had seen in kingship the spiritual principle warranting the commonwealth's unity.[40]

Bonald, like the vast majority of the thinkers surveyed here, is an exceptionalist. Unsurprisingly, France offers the best configuration: an extremely constituted religious society alloyed to an extremely constituted political society. But Bonald analyzes—not without animus—the non-Catholic or nonmonarchical European polities that have arisen since the Reformation, as well as the particular formations of pre-Constantinian Antiquity. Two cases particularly fascinate him, Egypt and Israel. The one represents for him constituted monarchical power without a constituted religion; the other a constituted religion without constituted political power. The strength of Egypt's monarchical constitution, including its well-regulated ceremonies, explains the longevity and resilience of this polity and its semisurvival as a culture even after its political demise. Even if Egypt ended up being conquered, it (like China vis-à-vis the Mongols) imposed its cus-

---

[38] TPPR 1.1.2, 13.46–47; 1.1.4, 70–71; 2.1.6, 14.47–51; 2.4.2, 14.152–53.

[39] TPPR 2.1.6, 14.48: "This man, called king or monarch, is the general love of society because he represents all humans vis-à-vis each human. He is the principle conserving physical human beings; in acting through the general force of society, he is its conserving power . . . [God] is the general and shared object of the love intelligent beings need have for one another. This intelligence [God] is therefore the general love of society. He is the principle conserving intelligent human beings; in acting through force in outward cult, he is its conserving power."

[40] Moyse Amyraut, *Discours de la Souveraineté des Roys* (Paris: Louis Vendosme, 1668), 177–78: "Their [the kings'] name, then, is in France . . . what was in Minerva's statue the image of Phidias, to which all the junctures and bonds of the work [the statue] ended in such a manner that one could not take it away from [the statue] without the whole statue dismembering itself and falling into pieces . . . It is as if the soul that gives form to the State's body, which gives it life and motion, which holds in harmony all its parts inside [the kingdom] and enables it to act powerfully outside . . ."; Jean Filesac, *De idolatria politica et legitimo principis cultu commentarius* 9 (Paris: 1615), 79, gathered ancient authorities to make the king the soul of his commonwealth—more even, "the common spirit of all his subjects." For ceremonies as the body of an entity (here religion), see Claude Villette, *Les raisons de l'office, et des ceremonies qui se font en l'Eglise Catholique, Apostolique, et Romaine. . . .* (Paris: Guillaume des Ruës, 1611), discussed below, 224–25.

toms on its victors rather than the other way around.[41] Israel is an even
more astonishing phenomenon. It outlasted Egypt and still survives. This
tempts Bonald to make Jewish society a miraculous exception to his system, and as such a demonstration against atheists that the Chosen People's
religious laws were God-given and not man-made, but the bulk of his
reflections places Israel squarely within the global economy of the *Théorie
du Pouvoir*. First, the contrasted cases of the two nations, Egypt and Israel,
show that a civil society can survive without its straightforwardly political
facet, but not without religion. Second, the Jews' case actually gives the
example of a configuration where religion, and religion alone, constitutes
society. "The majesty of cult, the pomp of ceremonies, the establishment
of feasts, the apparatus of sacrifice held the Hebrew people in the Faith
of God"; other precepts reined in its sensuality, yet others its natural feroc-
ity. God aimed at separating Israel from the idolatrous nations, at instilling
in it Faith, temperance, compassion, and humanity, and finally at giving
"it an institution that would withstand time, adversity, and conquerors."[42]
For the Hebrew people, then, it was a religious leadership, the Levites,
and religious symbols and practices that produced its social cohesion. Cen-
trally, an object, the Tabernacle, took the place that the monarch holds in
constituted political societies, that of "external power."[43] Here then, even
if Bonald does not explicitly say so, cult replaces its structural equivalent,
monarchical governance. This Israel looks very much like recent historiography's Latin Europe in the dark centuries, held together, in the absence
of a strong centralizing kingship, by the Church, its personnel, and its
rites and symbols. To quote Karl Leyser's fine book on Ottonian Saxony,
"Sacrality . . . was a substitute for inadequate or failing institutions."[44]

In the latter chapters of the *Théorie*, Bonald turns to a comparison between the different forms of Christianity, where he establishes a correlation

---

[41] TPPR 1.2.1, 13.160–61. Rome owes its own longevity to its severe cult, its religious
respect for the oath, the dignity of established families, and the institution of the dictator that
in times of dire troubles approximates a monarchy; cf. TPPR 1.2.4, 13.186–88.

[42] TPPR 2.3.3, 14.106–107.

[43] TPPR 2.3.3, 14.111–12: "[T]he Tabernacle was in some way the external power of society; one consulted it in all political matters, and the answers that it gave out were orders for
the nation." Cf. 110: "[T]he Tabernacle . . . can be considered as the external power of Jewish
society."

[44] Cf. Leyser, "Ottonian Government," reed. in *Medieval Germany and its Neighbours* (London: 1982), 100; cit. from idem, *Rule and Conflict*, 105. Leyser, however, had lived and fought
through the Second World War. He reminds us constantly of the harsh materiality of early
medieval power, see, e.g., ibidem, 4, on the army as "the most important institution." He
insists as well on the contradictions between "the ritual and sacral role of the Ottonians" and
"day-to-day" rule, ibidem, 101–102. See also Koziol, *Begging Pardon*, 59: "a society riven by
war and possessing few if any permanent institutions . . . hence the supreme importance of
rituals."

or affinity between the degree of presence of the Man-God in the Eucharistic sacrifice and the degree of inherent political stability or "constitution."[45] Where, as in Catholicism, Christ is really and permanently present in the Eucharist, religious society accepts hierarchy, and political society will tend to be at its best, that is, monarchical. Lutheranism, where Christ is present only at the moment of the consecration, has affinities with the government of princes and maintains an episcopal hierarchy. Calvinism, which lacks any form of real presence, fits aristocratic or bourgeois republics lacking in an established priesthood and signs of social preeminence and dignity.[46] As for the French Republic, having abolished all outward cult, it cannot subsist, since without a link to God a mutual union among human beings cannot exist.[47] One is tempted to paraphrase in twentieth-century terms: The degree of ritualization is proportional to the strength and hierarchization of society. Indeed, such a maxim is only one step removed from Bonald's models, insofar as religious society, being intimately coinherent to political society as soul is to body, need fashion itself physically in public cult, whose universal form, present in all societies, is sacrifice, and whose best and unperverted form is the Eucharist.[48] Mediated by the reactionary tradition within Neo-Catholicism, and notably the brilliant if sulphurous Carl Schmitt (d. 1985), the analogy and relationship between, on the one hand, Eucharistic real presence and, on the other hand, the king's presence is currently a staple in German historiography of medieval rituals.[49]

---

[45] Bonald borrows the idea of a fit between forms of religion and governments from Montesquieu, *Esprit des Lois* 24.3–5, 2.133–36; and 24.19, 2.145–46: "The truest and holiest dogmas can have very bad consequences when they are not tied to the society's principles, and, conversely, the falsest dogmas can have wonderful effects when one ensures that they relate to these self-same principles."

[46] TPPR 2.6.1, 14.301–306; 2.6.5, 14.353–54. One is reminded of Swanson, *Religion and Regime*, who correlates the kind of immanence in the world that a society ascribes to the divine with the type of governance this society tends to have.

[47] TPPR 2.1.6, 14.51–52.

[48] TPPR 2.2.1, 14.73–76; 2.2.3, 14.84–85; 2.4.6, 14.204–33; cf. PCS 1.16–1.20, 12.190–235.

[49] See below at nn. 128f. The genealogy can be traced through a string of references, and has been acknowledged. See Thomas Zotz, "Präsenz und Repräsentation. Beobachtungen zur königlichen Herrschaftspraxis im hohen und späten Mittelalter," in *Herrschaft als soziale Praxis: Historische und sozial-anthropologische Studien*, ed. Alf Lüdtke, Veröffentlichungen des Max-Planck-Instituts für Geschichte 91 (Göttingen: 1991), 168–94; Hagen Keller, "Die Investitur. Ein Beitrag zum Problem der 'Staatssymbolik' im Hochmittelalter," *FMSt* 27 (1993): 51–86; Horst Wenzel, "Zur Repräsentation von Herrschaft im Mittelalterlichen Texten," in *Adelsherrschaft und Literatur*, ed. Horst Wenzel (Frankfurt am Main: 1980), 339–75, calling on Hasso Hofmann, *Repräsentation. Studien zur Wort- und Begriffsgeschichte von der Antike bis ins 19. Jahrhundert* (Berlin: 1974), esp. 16–37, for a discussion of Carl Schmitt. To Hofmann's references to the *Verfassungslehre*, one should add Schmitt's splendidly tantalizing pages on the political essence of the Church and the public nature of religious power (*Macht*) in *Römischer Katholizismus und politische Form*, Der katholische Gedanke 13, 2d ed. (Munich: 1925), 10–12,

While God is the ultimate creator of all things, and while Bonald would say that individual humans, despite their delusions, cannot really create anything, humans can produce God in thought, and necessarily strive to conserve this knowledge of the deity. The duality of their nature, which is both physical and spiritual, means that they can do so only if body joins itself to mind, and external religion, that is, cult, to inward religion or inner worship.[50] So God maintains society, but in a sense society maintains God. Durkheim will secularize the latter half of this paradox,[51] but for Bonald it already applies to all religions, true or false.

All societies produce gods—truly constituted societies the true God, deeply flawed societies idols. The latter can be socially useful—as in the polities Bonald considers with greater indulgence, like Rome, which divinized political and community virtues, or Egypt, where "cult deified the productions useful to the human being."[52] But no matter what, the isomorphism between, and normal coinherence of, religious society and political society means that any such fashioning of the divine is essentially connected with power: "Nations cannot exist without a deity, nor societies without power; the senses create Gods for themselves; ambition props up a power."[53] The ancient Jewish understanding of the origins of idolatry, revisited by Christian scholasticism, provides us here with another forerunner of the concept of ideology: "Every human being wants to turn its individual power into the general power of society; every human being wants to make gods out of its passions. The senses give them being and distinguish them though names, designate them by emblems and attribute to them forms; and we have polytheism."[54] Bonald shared Dupuis's position that invented religions fail to prop up society; but we have seen that his favorite imperfect nations, Egypt and Rome, have a greater success than others, like Greece, in maintaining themselves. As in Hooker and Warburton, idolatry admits of degrees in social efficiency.[55] Here again, we meet in an author belonging to the Catholic tradition fundamental components of what will be the functionalist and the Marxist understandings of religion, intimately interlocked but differentiated by the author's value judgments.

26–30, 33, 40–43; trans. G. L. Ulmen, *Roman Catholicism and Political Form* (Westport: 1996), 7–8, 18–21, 24, 29–32.

[50] TPPR 2.1.5, 14.42–43.

[51] FE, 491–97, trans. Fields, 349–52. Cf. Irving M. Zeitlin, *Ideology and the Development of Social Theory*, 2d ed. (Englewood Cliffs: 1981), 54.

[52] TPPR 1.2.2, 13.162.

[53] TPPR 1.1.5, 13.88–89 (on the French Revolution). Power is love in action through force.

[54] TPPR 1.1.5, 13.80–81.

[55] Cf. TPPR 1.2.2, 162: "Here [in Egypt], cult deified the productions useful to the human being; there [in Western Asia], it deified passions harmful to society."

If religion can do so much to stabilize civil society, it is because it stands at the heart of what Bonald calls "national character"—"culture" for later social scientists. Strength of national character allowed Egypt and Rome to last, as civilizations, well beyond their political demise. In discussing Christian society, Bonald does state that it could not have grown and acquired cohesion under the influence of a false religion, but to explain this unsurprising exceptionalist assertion, he puts forward an analysis of the power of religion in general: "[Religion] mingles itself with the laws, the *mores*, the thoughts, the feelings, the deeds, the civil and domestic habits of a whole people, and penetrates, as it were, its whole life." This capacity, next to miracles, may account for the ease with which antiquity's pagans and modern "savage" nations have adopted the Faith: "Even in the most mysterious beliefs, there is something that *assimilates itself* to the thoughts and feelings of social man, even unbeknownst to him, in order to enlighten and direct them, pretty much as alimentary substances *assimilate* themselves to our bodies to feed them."[56] In this, religion according to Bonald was not unlike the medieval Eucharist, which both incorporated and was incorporated by human beings.[57] But Bonald went one step further: He made religion the dynamic essence of the social body and the heart of the cultural system.

RITUAL EFFERVESCENCES IN THE NINETEENTH CENTURY

That other Catholic conservatives should have sung a similar tune will not surprise us. Joseph de Maistre (1753–1821) went as far as to say that all institutions (not simply nations) owed whatever lasting power they had to religion—a religion in which he insisted on cult.[58] Here de Maistre was not simply restating the old idea that God rewarded even pagan nations (like Rome) for the meticulousness with which they cultivated their deities. He spoke "constitution," and this for him was as much a political structure as a biological entity in which religion was an organ coordinated to the body's ends.[59] And religion, while certainly a force he identified with the Roman papacy and Catholic parties, was also a fluid intimately tied to social matter

---

[56] PCS, preface, 12.77–78 and 12.84.

[57] See Philippe Buc, *L'ambiguïté*, 206ff. (overly anthropologized).

[58] See *Considérations sur la France* (1796) 6, ed. Jean Tulard (Paris: 1980) 63, below, note 82, as well as 5, 58: The power and longevity of popular feasts, as compared with revolutionary festivals, is owed to their distant religious origins.

[59] *Essai sur le principe générateur des constitutions politiques et autres institutions humaines* (1810) 32, 1.269: "Empires have always lasted in proportion to the degree of influence that the religious principle had acquired in the constitution of the polity." Elsewhere, *Considérations* 2, ed. Tulard, 43, de Maistre uses organicist vocabulary to explain how "any function" (in this case an essential aspect of French character) "produces a duty."

and able to "divinize" institutions.[60] In the earlier part of his career, Bonald's disciple Félicité-Robert de Lammenais (1782–1852) agreed that "no human society could take form and perpetuate itself unless religion presided over its birth and transferred to it that divine force that is the life of every lasting institution." Given its foundational position, one could readily understand the importance "attached not only to public beliefs but to the smallest ceremonies of worship (culte)."[61] Sociological monism came into its own with the (possibly Herderian) idea of a "national soul," a political faith standing above and beyond individual reason and conserving a government that de Maistre could, in his more lyrical moments, assimilate to a religion, cult and all.[62] In polemics against the Reformers, Catholics had insisted that the priesthood ministered in its liturgical actions for a public community. Bonaldian influences reenergized this understanding and gave it a sociological turn. For the leading French liturgist of the nineteenth century, Prosper Guéranger, liturgy was not mere prayer; it was rather "prayer envisaged at its social state."[63]

The influence of conservative thought on Saint-Simon and Auguste Comte no longer needs to be retraced.[64] Even left-wing historians leaned in the direction of a monist identification of religion and society. If we trust Owen Chadwick, the young Jules Michelet "thought the religious structure not to be entangled with the political structure but to be the same struc-

---

[60] *Considérations sur la France* 5, 56–57: "All the institutions one can imagine are grounded on a religious idea, or are impermanent. They are strong and lasting in proportion to their, so to speak, divinization." And further, on European institutions: "Religion, being mixed to everything, animates and gives support to everything." Cf. idem, *Essai sur le principe générateur* 30, 1.266: "[E]very constitution is in its principle divine," with n. 1: "One can even make this assertion general and lay down, without exception: That no institution whatever it may be can last if it is not founded on religion."

[61] *De la religion considérée dans ses rapports avec l'ordre politique et civil* (1825?) 1, in *Oeuvres complètes*, 12 t. in 6 vols. (Paris: 1836–37), 7.1–2.

[62] Joseph de Maistre, *Etude sur la souveraineté* 10, in *Oeuvres*, 1.375–76: "There need be a religion of the State as well as [there is] a politic of the State. Or rather, religious and political dogmas, mixed and molten into one, must form together a universal or national reason strong enough to repress the errings of individual reason . . . by nature the enemy of any association . . . Government is a true religion; it has its dogmas, its mysteries, its ministers . . . It lives only through national reason, that is, political faith, which is a *symbol*" able to transform individual existence into a common existence. For Herder on religion, see Manuel, *Eighteenth Century*, 291–99.

[63] Prosper Guéranger, *Institutions liturgiques* 1.1, 4 vols., Paris: 1878), 1.1: "La liturgie n'est donc pas simplement la prière, mais bien la prière considérée à l'état social"; cf. ibidem, 1.1, 1.2: The private recitation of liturgical formulas by the clergy "is not a work of private devotion; it is an act of social religion."

[64] See, e.g., Nisbet, *Sociological Tradition*. Nice critique in Milbank, *Theology and Social Theory*, 52–61.

ture."[65] At the end of his career, Hippolyte Taine sang the emotive and
poetic power of religion, able to convey "ideas . . . in pictures" to the people
owing to its "rites, legends, and ceremonies," and make the individual tran-
scend egotism for the common good. In a vein reminiscent of the *Encyclopédie* and Catholic liturgists,[66] he distinguished between the "tiny elite" and
the commons, for whom (in incarnational vocabulary), "truth, to be felt,
must put on a body." Taine like De Maistre saw in it an "organ" critical for
every society; and alluding to the Revolution and to contemporary disputes, he added in a telling development of the biological metaphor that
one could not cut off religion from the social body, for "it will grow up
again like flesh after a bloody operation."[67] Edgar Quinet (1803–75) argued
forcefully, on the background of contemporary discussions concerning the
relationship of government and established cults, that the revolutionaries
should have radically suppressed the Church. They should have known
better than to try to create a new religion at one stroke, "a bundle of rites
and ceremonies," imitating Catholicism while they repudiated it.[68] But
even Quinet's criticism of the Jacobins' indecisive attitudes and half-mea-
sures reveals that he held a similar notion of the centrality of religion in
the polity:

> [The Jacobins hoped that] the great Revolution would happen without the
> Church noticing it; that all the relationships be changed, but without religion
> (which is the reunion and soul of all relationships) suffering from any of these
> changes; one was to take away from the [Catholic] cult all civic actions, without
> the cult knowing it; the nation was to be regenerated without religion (which
> is the moral consciousness of a nation) being made aware of it; [one would]
> make all the laws anew, without religion (which is the very substance of the
> laws) being altered in the least from this.[69]

In fact, Quinet had sought to prove how every society had been "instituted"
by religion. In an earlier romanticizing work entitled *Du génie des religions*,
he had waxed lyrical on the moment when, by inventing God, primitive
human beings had given its beginnings to society. The worship of a single

---

[65] Chadwick, *Secularization*, 199–200, with reference to Michelet, *French Revolution*, introduction 1.1.2.

[66] Cf. above, 204. Saint-Simon had already transferred this model to science; its truths
would be imparted to the less intelligent through rituals and cults. Cf. Zeitlin, *Ideology*, 64.

[67] Chadwick, *Secularization*, 210–11, citing Taine, *Ancient Régime* (trans. 1876), 209–10. For
a splendid discussion of the grammar of organicist analogies, easily superior to any in the
field of medieval studies, see Judith Schlanger, *Métaphores de l'organisme* (Paris: 1971).

[68] Edgar Quinet, *Le Christianisme et la Révolution française* (Paris: 1984), 237–39.

[69] Edgar Quinet, *La Révolution*, 2 vols. (Paris: 1865), 1.157.

Spirit allowed a communion of individual souls or minds into a single Spirit, and the birth of society from the idea of God.[70]

The influence of theological notions reached beyond such generalities. No less than Bonald, his contemporary Benjamin Constant—a Protestant—believed he lived in an age of crisis and looked for a solution in religion.[71] For the emergence of sociology, the common ground they shared is as revealing as the differences between Catholic conservative and liberal Protestant. Like Bonald, Constant envisaged a tight causal nexus between religion and society, so that "each revolution that occurs in humankind's situation produces one in religious ideas."[72] Religion's own transformations derive from a dialectic between religious feeling (*sentiment religieux*) and religious forms. For Constant, "dogmas, beliefs, practices, ceremonies, are forms that religious feeling takes and that it later shatters."[73] Religious feeling creates institutions, which it renders obsolete by its own evolution and must then destroy, starting the cycle anew. The prime example is the reaction of early Christianity to the religious institutions (symbols, practices, and hierarchies) of the Roman world, and Christianity's subsequent ossification into Catholicism.[74] While Constant in his original definition of "form" includes on a par both the more intellectual aspects of religion (dogmas and beliefs) and its more physical aspects (practices and ceremonies), in the remainder of the book the category comprises mostly the latter. So he is not too far from presenting, unsurprisingly for a Protestant, a model in which history is moved by a dialectic of the Spirit. The Spirit in its becoming creates rituals that over time, as it keeps pro-

---

[70] Edgar Quinet, *Du Génie des religions* (Paris: 1842), here ch. 1.4, "De l'institution religieuse de la société," 29: "At that critical moment the State succeeded to the family and humankind to human being. A shared life began among the minds (*esprits*), which all recognized and worshipped the same Spirit. Heretofore scattered individuals joined into a same mind (*pensée*). Still infant intelligences were for the first time given the milk of the same substance . . . The tribe gathered around the fetish; a national god founded the nation; religious unity founded political unity; and from the idea of God society sprang forth, already alive." The book's thesis appears in the "Warning to the reader," (v). Right before putting forward this story of beginnings, Quinet assails Rousseau, who (according to him) made primitive man an eighteenth-century philosopher, forgetting "imagination, poetry, religion, and instincts [for the] sacred" (27).

[71] Cf. Benjamin Constant, *De la Religion, considérée dans sa source, ses formes et ses développements*, 5 vols (Paris: 1830–31), preface, 1.xxxxix–xl; ibidem 5.7, 2.484–85.

[72] Constant, *Religion* 12.1, 4.345–46. Cf. for example 12.2–3, 4.354ff., where Constant discusses archaic Greece, "the contradictions characteristic of that era of polytheism, and the manner in which these contradictions disappear." Specifically, he sees in Hesiod's poems the "contradictions which the social state . . . introduced in religious notions" (4.366–69) as the values attached to older gods clash with the newer personifications, fetishism with the new community, the jealous Zeus with Zeus who warrants justice.

[73] Constant, *Religion* 1.1, 1.12.

[74] Constant, *Religion* 1.2, 1.49–50.

gressing, turn into its own shackles. The contradiction provokes a revolution. Perhaps equally unsurprisingly, Constant strongly decries a philosophical tradition that he considers typically French and to a lesser degree,
English: to look at religion primarily in terms of its utility for individuals
and society.[75] These traditions want religion "as a kind of police force, to
warrant their property, protect their life, discipline their children, maintain
order in their domestic life."[76] Here they approximate incriminatingly the
pagan societies that Constant analyzes. In all, considerations of interest
contribute to religious formalism.[77] Indeed, the stability that religious forms
create, and which humans value, hinders the march of spiritual progress.

Yet the Protestant at times lapses into an appreciation for the constitutive
force of religion. Even among the savages, the primitive stage of fetishism
brings in some morality, fosters the association of human beings, and sanctions the oath, all-important for regulated human interaction. Religious
tabou is the basis of "laws and the whole maintenance of order (*police*)."[78]
At the following stage of religious evolution, the priests take the fetishes
belonging to individuals and fashion a "generic divinity" to "conciliate the
exigencies of superstition with society's needs."[79] The *De la Religion* dwells
at length on fetishism. For Constant, this is warranted, since "this religion
contains the seeds of all the notions that make up later beliefs."[80] One is
reminded, of course, of Emile Durkheim's justification of his own concentration on the "elementary forms of religious life." The following considerations also anticipate Durkheim and before him Fustel de Coulanges:

> The isolation in which the fetishes dwelled no longer fits the gods of people
> gathered in society. Human beings united in a body need to unite in their
> feelings. They enjoy seeing these feelings shared. They share their gods (*met-
> tent leurs dieux en commun*). This reunion of the gods happens necessarily as
> soon as that of human beings occurs. As human society forms itself, a celestial
> society forms itself. The objects of worship organize themselves into a Pan-
> theon (*un Olympe*) as soon as worshipers organize themselves into a people.[81]

[75] Cf. Constant, *Religion* 4.12, 274 (on the political use of religion in China); 12.12ff.,
4.492f.

[76] Constant, *Religion* 1.6, 1.80.

[77] Constant, *Religion* 2.2, 1.168–70. Cf. 2.2, 1.175: "Where there isn't any more profit, cult
stops."

[78] Constant, *Religion* 2.3, 1.185–88.

[79] Constant, *Religion* 6.2, 3.9–10. Quinet may have borrowed this evolutionary scheme, see
Génie 1.4, quoted above n. 70.

[80] Constant, *Religion* 2.8, 1.149.

[81] Constant, *Religion* 3.2, 2.6–7. Compare Fustel, CA 3.3, 132: "At the very moment at
which these families united [into a *phratria*], they conceived of a divinity superior to their
domestic deities, common to them all, and which watched over the entire group," or 3.3, 143:
"The bond of the new association [the City] was again a cult."

Almost against his original intent, Constant attributes a positive socially constitutive role to religious forms and, among them, to "ceremonies":

The influences of fetishism and polytheism differ in that the one isolates individuals and the other unites them in making it their duty to worship together (*en commun*) the same gods. Thus what had been a consequence becomes a cause: polytheism, the result of savage hordes drawing close to one another, consolidates this movement. Religion institutes festivals where the different tribes meet and accustom themselves to live with one another.[82]

Festivals played an equally critical role in Fustel de Coulanges's *Ancient City*. This work's importance for the sociological models of religion and ritual no longer needs demonstration.[83] Here is a historian who borrowed from contemporary sociological understandings and wrote history using them, to be in turn co-opted by the social sciences. Fustel (1830–89) divided ancient history into two overlapping phases: In the one, social groups derived their unity from religious ritual; in the other, they did not. The transformation, which began at the end of the archaic period (in Greece the sixth century B.C.E.), had been capped by the triumph of Christianity. With it, the Spirit began its reign, the once essentially fused spheres of religion and politics gained independent existence, and energies now invested in faith no longer fueled patriotism.[84] The scheme's debt to age-old Christian opposition between Old Testament (or pagan) ritualism and New Testament spirituality is evident.[85] So is the convergence with Benjamin

---

[82] Constant, *Religion* 7.10, 3.405. For De Maistre as well, the founding moment of a society involves religious festivals, in the origins identical with the new institutions themselves, *Considérations* 6, ed. Tulard, 63: "Ces législateurs même, avec leur puissance extraordinaire, ne font jamais que rassembler des élémens préexistants dans les coutumes et le caractère des peuples; mais ce rassemblement, cette formation rapide qui ne tiennent que de la création, ne s'exécutent qu'au nom de la Divinité. La politique et la religion se fondent ensemble: on distingue à peine le législateur du prêtre; et ses institutions publiques consistent principalement *en cérémonies et vacations religieuses*."

[83] Nisbet, *Sociological Tradition*, 238f., and Arnaldo Momigliano, "The Ancient City of Fustel de Coulanges" (1970), repr. in idem, *Essays in Ancient and Modern Historiography* (Middletown and Oxford: 1977), 325–43. See also Hartog's preface to the 1984 edition of the *Cité Antique*, and his *Le XIXe siècle et l'histoire. Le cas Fustel de Coulanges* (Paris: 1988). But I have benefited mostly from the articles by François Héran, "De la Cité Antique à la Sociologie des institutions," *Revue de Synthèse* 4th s., 3 (1989), 363–90; idem., "Le rite et la croyance," *Revue française de Sociologie* 27 (1986), 231–63; idem, "L'institution démotivée." The influence of Fustel on Durkheim was not always direct and is complicated to trace owing to the latter's occasional misrepresentation of his predecessor's thought.

[84] CA 5.3, 458–62; cf. idem, *Histoire des institutions politiques de l'ancienne France*, 2d ed. (Paris: 1877), 319–20 (henceforth HIPAF 1877). This discussion was added to the first edition of Paris, 1875 (HIPAF 1875). Interesting variants between the first, second, and third (Paris: 1891) editions shall be noted.

[85] CA 5.3, 458–59: "Au lieu qu'autrefois la religion ... n'était guère autre chose qu'un ensemble de pratiques, une série de rites que l'on répétait sans y voir aucun sens, une suite

Constant: In the course of Fustel's great transformation, "religious feeling" progressively abandons cult; it becomes a set of "vain ceremonies," "no longer vivified by a faith," whose meaning one has forgotten.[86] More interesting perhaps is Fustel's evolutionary transition from ritual to law as the prime *vinculum sociale*. Thus, before Solon's reforms, "[public] interest was not the supreme rule from which social order derived, rather, it was religion. The duty to accomplish cultic rites had been the social bond."[87] Since at least the seventeenth century, one had considered religion and law as alternative *liens sociaux*. Fustel simply posited a passage from one vector of solidarity to another. From ritual to spirit, from religion to law: These two evolutionary schemes, heavily indebted to Christian Theology even when inverting its terms, still inhabit some of the more influential twentieth-century conceptualizations of change. In Ernst Kantorowicz's *The King's Two Bodies*, kingship, once understood and legitimized through the language of liturgy, starting with the High Middle Ages becomes "law-centered."[88] For George Duby, echoed by Brian Stock, the transition from the early to the High Middle Ages is characterized, among other phenomena, by the "passage from a ritualistic and liturgical religion . . . to a religion of action that incarnates itself."[89] And for Peter Brown, the waning of trial by ordeal across the same divide is symptomatic of a fundamental change. Social solidarity, once maintained by communitarian rituals (such as trial by water and fire), is now imposed from the outside by state institutions and law. It is probably not an accident that Brown belongs to the first generation to have adapted functionalist anthropology to medieval history—an anthropology that owes much to Fustel de Coulanges.[90]

---

de formules que souvent on ne comprenait plus, parce que la langue en avait vieilli, une tradition qui se transmettait d'âge en âge et ne tenait son caractère sacré que de son antiquité, au lieu de cela, la religion fut un ensemble de dogmes et un grand objet proposé à la foi. Elle ne fut plus extérieure; elle siégea surtout dans la pensée de l'homme. elle ne fut plus matière; elle devint esprit." Cf. Héran, "De *la Cité Antique*," 384–85; idem, "L'institution démotivée," 86.

[86] CA 5.1, 417. But for Fustel the new religion does not ossify itself into ritualism, CA 5.3, 458. Cf. Constant, *Religion* 1.1, at n. 73 above.

[87] CA 4.9, 376.

[88] I owe this reminder to Gerard Caspary.

[89] George Duby, *L'an mil* (Paris: 1980), 226. See as well Brian Stock, *Implications of Literacy: Written Language and Models of Interpretation in the Eleventh and Twelfth Centuries* (Princeton: 1983), 91, 141, 472. This may be to take too seriously the polemics of the new orders against the old, couched in terms of the opposition between Old and New dispensation, ritual and spirit. See most eloquently Nicolas of Clairvaux, *Ep.* 8, PL 196:1603bc: "*De veteri testamento et umbra Cluniasensium ad Cistersiensium evolavimus puritatem*" (We fled away from the Old Testament and the shadow of the Cluniacs to the purity of the Cistercians).

[90] See Peter Brown, "Society and the Supernatural: A Medieval Change," repr. in his *Society and the Holy in Late Antiquity* (Berkeley: 1982), 302–32. Cf. as well Michael Clanchy, *From Memory to Written Record* (1st ed., London: 1979; cf. 2d ed. 1993), 23–28, 202–30: With the High Middle Ages, writing progressively becomes legally dispositive; in the preceding era, it

The revolutionaries had felt that they were focusing back public worship onto its rightful object, society.[91] Fustel, born in 1830, could not have known this revolutionary ideal directly. But in his history of the Ancient Régime's political institutions he reiterated the idea, expressed by Montesquieu and others, that the Greeks and Romans, or pagans in general, had effectively rendered a cult to Society or the State:

> [The emperor] was a god because he was emperor. Regardless of whether he was good or bad, great or puny, in worshipping him [through the Imperial Cult], it was political authority one worshipped. Indeed, this religion was not anything else but a remarkable conception of the State. . . . These generations did not suffer a monarchy, they wanted it. The feeling they expressed for it was neither resignation nor fear, it was piety. They had a religious enthusiasm (*fanatisme*) for the power of a single man just as other generations have had the *fanatisme* of republican institutions. It belongs to the human being's nature to make a religion out of any idea that fills its soul. In some eras it renders a cult to freedom; in other times it worships the principle of authority.[92]

The same relation between rituals, power, and identity applied to the two other fundamental political groupings in the Empire, the *civitas* and the province. The *provincia* seemed to Fustel "all at once a kind of religious and political confederation." He insisted on the annual cult the provincial assembly rendered to the emperor. It "marked [the province's] unity and simultaneously its submission to the Empire"; all members were represented and "performed the sacrifice together and shared out in a sacred meal the victim's flesh."[93] The civic games similarly animated the Ancient City. As in the case of the imperial cult, Fustel emphasized the ritual component; he noticed as well the ordering of the audience according to status, and the interactive communication between people and magistrate. Far from being "vain ceremonies," civic rites fostered identity and freedom,

---

had had a commemorative function thanks to the rituals that fixed its messages in collective memory.

[91] See the sources cited in Aulard, *Culte* (above, n. 1), proclaiming "Liberty . . . the goddess of the French" or "the fatherland, mother and public Deity (*divinité commune*)."

[92] HIPAF 1875, 95–96; 1877, 104–105. Fustel had read Montesquieu and took issue with his idea that Roman religion was "political"; cf. CA 3.7, 194, and above, ch. 5 n. 76.

[93] HIPAF 1875, 109; 1877, 118: "La province était une sorte de confédération religieuse et politique à la fois. Elle marquait son unité et en même temps sa soumission à l'empire par un culte. Il fallait qu'aux cérémonies annuelles de ce culte tous les membres de la confédération fussent représentés; ils faisaient ensemble le sacrifice et se partageaient la chair de la victime dans un repas sacré." Cf. HIPAF 1875, 122; 1877, 131: "Par elles [les assemblées], les peuples étaient en communication incessante avec le pouvoir. Ne nous figurons pas cette société muette et résignée; c'est sous un tout autre aspect que les documents nous la montrent. Tantôt elle remercie et adule, tantôt elle récrimine et accuse; toujours elle parle; elle est, pour ainsi dire, en perpétuel dialogue avec un gouvernement qui ne peut jamais ignorer ses opinions et ses besoins . . ."

and "the City gathered around its altar drew from it a precise idea of its unity, of its own existence, of its perpetuity, of its independence vis-à-vis [imperial] power."[94] Indeed, before the great transformation finalized by Christianity, the City, like every active and live social organ (*organisme*) "took on the form of a religion."[95] Religion had been "the inspiring and organizing spirit (*souffle*) of society"; it animated the City from the inside, "maintaining the feeling of life without which the most beautiful institutions are vain and powerless."[96] Here the French historian sounds like the twelfth-century schoolman John of Salisbury, who had made religion the soul of the social body,[97] but Fustel has displaced the accent to the benefit of rites. While the ancients worship an "idea" like political authority, and while Fustel does speak of "belief," for him, the *lien social* of any group in Antiquity is *un culte*, meaning a form of worship with both spiritual and material aspects, and it is the latter's ceremonial apparatus that he most details.

The scheme was not without posterity. A good century after the *Histoire des institutions politiques de l'Ancienne France* (1875), Peter Brown would revisit the scheme of an empire held together by a religion's rites. Like Bonald's Israel, Egypt, and Rome, which lasted as cultures or societies beyond loss of political strength thanks to their original constitution, Fustel's Rome had survived the barbarians through the lingering shadow of its cults.[98] Brown's "cult," now "of the saints," identity figures for a new faith, allows the survival of a community beyond (and owing to) Fustel's great revolution—the triumph of Christianity. Locally, the "cult of the saints" enacts a civic identity and, like the synthetic cults of Fustel's archaic Mediterranean world, integrates subgroups—in Brown's model the urban poor,

---

[94] HIPAF 1875, 130; 1877, 140–41. The theme of civic liberties is attenuated in the third edition (Paris: 1891), but not that of social identity and cult; see the addition in HIPAF 1891, 163 (for the Ancients, "the State or the City had always been a holy thing and the object of cult. The State had had its gods and was itself a kind of God"). HIPAF 1891, 178–79 elaborates on 1875, 86–87. Key passages such as HIPAF 1875, 95–96 and 106 ("a kind of political religion whose supreme deity was the emperor"), 106–11 remained unchanged; HIPAF 1875, 129–30 was made less lively in HIPAF 1891, 245–46.

[95] HIPAF 1875, 130; 1877, 140: "Cet organisme municipal, comme tout ce qui était actif et vivant en ce temps-là, revêtait la forme d'une religion." This passage drops out from the 1891 edition, 245–46. Compare CA 3.18, 265 and 5.1, 415, identifying the polity to "a Church" or "a religion."

[96] CA 3.3, 150; HIPAF 1877, 141 (follows immediately the text cited at n. 94).

[97] Compare John of Salisbury, *Policraticus* 5.2 (as ch. 5 n. 111): "Those things that institute and give form to respect for religious worship among us and . . . transmit God's ceremonies hold the place of the soul in the commonwealth's body."

[98] See above, ch. 6, 210–11; HIPAF 1891, 327 (part of a new conclusion, and as such absent in 1875 and 1877): During the barbarian invasions, it may have been the "community of prayers, vows, and thoughts," which the provincial assemblies had engendered, that contributed the most to the preservation of Gallic unity.

women, and barbarians, formerly excluded from the ancient city.[99] Supralo-
cally, all over Europe, the new leaders of the cities, the bishops, control the
holy bodies and exchange their relics. Displayed in ceremonial advents,
and ritually circulated, these fragments "condensed the solidarity" of
Christendom, thus maintaining—at least among the rising episcopal
elites—the unity of the Roman world.[100]

FROM LETTER AND SPIRIT TO LETTER AND FUNCTION: DURKHEIM

Between Fustel de Coulanges and Peter Brown stands Emile Durkheim, a
man more concerned with the French society of his age than with ancient
and late antique polities. I shall not provide yet another exposition of Durkheim's sociology of religion; it would be superfluous.[101] The same principle
of economy applies, to a lesser extent, to other thinkers who influenced
medieval studies, especially anthropologists in the indirect orbit of the
Durkheimian school such as Gluckman, Douglas, and Turner, or the self-
styled Weberian but (at times) very Parsonian Clifford Geertz. At the risk
of being allusive, I eschew an exhaustive and exhausting presentation, and
elect instead to effect a triangular confrontation involving the models of
some of these social scientists, those of some historians influenced by them,
and those of medieval authors.[102]

---

[99] Fustel, CA 3.14, 239, had insisted on the immense difficulty of establishing a social confederation above the cities, but saw little hindrances to such phenomena at lesser levels of
sociogenesis (between families and between phratries). Brown transfers the problématique to
different sociological groupings (classes, genders, ethnicities).

[100] Peter Brown, The Cult of the Saints (Chicago: 1981), esp. 41–42, 89–90, 94, 96, 100.
Brown does not refer to Fustel's works. See as well Hegel, Phänomenologie des Geistes, in
Gesammelte Werke, vol. 9, ed. Wolfgang Bonsiepen and Reinhard Heede (Hamburg: 1980),
240ff., whose ideas on the religious opposition between family (gendered feminine and "private") and commonwealth (masculine and "public") Brown parallels in explaining the conflict
between Roman families and the bishops. Brown himself, in his "The Saint As Exemplar,"
Representation 2 (1983), 11–14, "revisited" the functionalism of his early studies on sanctity.

[101] Three standard works and critiques, Raymond Aron, Les étapes de la pensée sociologique
(Paris: 1967), 345–61; W. S. F. Pickering, Durkheim's Sociology of Religion (London: 1984);
Stephen Lukes, Emile Durkheim (London: 1973).

[102] Sarah Beckwith, "Ritual, Church and Theatre: Medieval Dramas of the Sacramental
Body," in Culture and History 1350–1600, ed. David Aers (Detroit: 1992), 65–89, at 79, nicely
criticizes the importation of Durkheimian notions into the explanation of late medieval Corpus
Christi plays, but still embraces utilization of twentieth-century understandings of ritual. For
a critique of Van Gennep and Turner's notion of "rites of passage," see Milbank, Theology and
Social Theory, 122–23, 131. For the lack of adaptability of Victor Turner's model to a late
medieval context, see Gabriela Signori, "Ritual und Ereignis. Die Strassburger Bittgänge zur
Zeit der Burgunderkriege," HJ 264,2 (1997): 324–25. Turner himself admits in The Ritual
Process: Structure and Anti-Structure (Chicago, 1969; Ithaca, 1977), 107, that "the reader will
have noticed immediately that many of these properties [of communitas] constitute what we
would think of as characteristic of the religious life in the Christian tradition." His wording

The relationship between exegesis and social scientific discourse, which Talal Asad rightly insists upon, constitutes a first factor of continuity and distortion. Already with Leibniz one finds an explicit statement of this continuum. Discussing the Jesuits and the Chinese Rites Controversy, the German philosopher asserts the superiority of the outsider over the autochthonous interpreter as well as that of the trained technician over the conceptually ill-equipped native, and parallels them with the Christian exegete's providential authority over the Jewish Old Testament (and its Jewish commentators).[103] Between 1500 and the birth of the social sciences, what changed was the "reality" or "truth" (res, veritas) that the interpreter sought to access behind the "letter" of the rites. To quote the early seventeenth-century liturgist Charles Villette, "the ceremonies of the Church are the mirrors of the Holy Spirit . . . the ceremony's action is its body, and its signification, its soul."[104] But, for Villette as for the Middle Ages East and West, the interpretation consists in accessing a preexistent, supernatural, and eternal reality, and establishing, noetically and ontologically, a connection to it.[105] Such a link is a necessary prerequisite for salvation. Exegetes construe the process of interpretation as an unveiling of the real text, which stands hidden under, yet hinted at by the letter, through tell-tale signals such as discordances, absurdities, or paradoxes.[106] To quote Villette again, "[T]he Holy Ceremonies are the bark (escorce) of the Catholic Religion"— a metaphor that authorizes exegesis to find the marrow, but also points to the critical role of the ceremonial "letter" in protecting the spirit within it.[107] For Durkheim too, the social scientist's intellectual labor leads to a

---

can indeed be rather theological. See, e.g., *The Ritual Process*, 103: During the rites of passage, the initiates "have to be shown that in themselves they are clay or dust, mere matter, whose form is impressed upon them by society." Turner then gives the example of the medieval knight's vigil—but to what extent is this merely an illustration and not an expression of the fundamental theology at work in his anthropology? Janet Nelson's recourse to Arnold Van Gennep's rites of passage to explain the royal anointing in her "Rulers' Inauguration Rituals," repr. in her *Politics and Ritual*, 259–81, at 270, seems to me unnecessary since Van Gennep created this concept on the analogy of the Christian sacrament of baptism, itself the theological basis for the medieval royal anointing.

[103] Cf. Leibniz, *On the Civil Cult of Confucius*, discussed above ch. 5, 183–84. See as well the excellent pages in Asad, "Towards a Genealogy," 58–62.

[104] Claude Villette, *Les raisons de l'office, et des ceremonies* (Paris, 1611), prefatory epistle to the Queen Mother Marie de Médicis, iii, developed in ibidem, 2.2 ("*L'ame de la Ceremonie est en l'intelligence d'icelle*"), 10.

[105] See above, chapter 1, Liudprand on Otto's prayer at Birten and the Holy Lance, and, for Byzantium, Sabine MacCormack, "Christ and Empire, Time and Ceremonial in Sixth-Century Byzantium," *Byzantion* 52 (1982): 287–309.

[106] See, e.g., Gerard Caspary, *Politics and Exegesis* (Berkeley: 1979), 65f.

[107] Villette, *Raisons*, prefatory epistle, ii, as well as 1.2, 4. Compare Durkheim: The rites are "but the outer envelope in which mental operations lie hidden" (FE, 599; Fields, 422).

"truth" or reality, a *res*. It is hidden under a veil; as for Villette, the rite is its envelope.[108] Absurdities in the natives' accounts of their own religion, rituals, and beliefs, point to the presence of this true meaning and to its contents.[109] Durkheim's formulation is still theological:

> When all we do is consider the letter (*lettre*) of the formulas, these religious beliefs and practices appear disconcerting, and our inclination might be to write them off to some kind of inborn aberration. But we must know how to reach beneath the symbol to grasp the reality of which it is a figure (*réalité qu'il figure*) and that gives the symbol its true signification (*signification véritable*).[110]

Like many a theologian Durkheim identifies the *res* or reality to be discovered with truth. However, for the social scientist, the "real" consists in elements that serve the conservation of society—if we translate back into a theological vocabulary, its physical "salvation."

Such is the efficient, true meaning of rites. In a nutshell, we have moved from the exegetical pair letter-spirit to the social scientific pair appearance-function. This means that the social scientist can access the rite's efficiency and meaningfulness only at the cost of a displacement of native belief. Like Augustine, Durkheim thinks of religion in terms of two components, beliefs (which he also calls "representations") and rites.[111] But just as the African Father did when dealing with Jewish ceremonies, the French sociologist dismisses native belief. For the immense majorities of the societies that the social scientist observes, current autochthonous interpretations stand at an unbridgeable distance from the "original feelings" that accompanied the birth of religion, and which were, in the beginnings, visibly correlated to religion's social function.[112] This dismissal owes much to William Robertson-Smith, and before him, to the double-doctrine model.[113] It allows Durkheim to displace native beliefs and substitute, in the structural role this category held in theological models, an ersatz: collective representa-

---

For the dyad inner-outer in exegesis, see Caspary, *Politics*, 113–14, followed by Buc, *L'ambiguïté*, 188.

[108] Compare Durkheim's "to pull aside the veil (*voile*)" to get at the realities behind religion (FE, 612; Fields, 431) with the exegesis of Matthew 27.51 (at the crucifixion, the veil of the temple is rent, and all the Jewish mysteries made clear). See as well FE, 529, trans. Fields, 374: "an interpretation that hides their fundamental reason for being."

[109] See the reference ch. 5 n. 70. "[The rite's] profound causes can be glimpsed through the very manner in which the faithful explain it" (FE, 530, trans. Fields, 375).

[110] Durkheim, FE, 3, trans. Fields, 2 (here modified to emphasize the exegetical vocabulary).

[111] FE, 50, trans. Fields, 34.

[112] FE, 9–10, trans. Fields, 6–7; examples 581–82, 583, Fields 410, 411.

[113] Cf. William Robertson-Smith, *Lectures on the religion of the Semites* (Edinburgh: 1889), 17–18, 399.

tions.[114] Thus he can simultaneously dismiss "the feelings of the faithful" as nonprivileged intuitions and state that "a society is . . . constituted . . . above all by the idea it has of itself."[115] Expressed in rites, these collective representations unify the social group.[116] So when one considers closely the economy of the *Elementary Forms of Religious Life*, one realizes that Durkheim is effecting a two-step operation around the object of "belief." First, he evacuates the religious culture that natives actually profess by arguing that it is irrelevant for the way a society functions. The social scientist thus dismisses culture (at least as it might exist in the consciousness of social agents) from the essential workings of the social machinery. Second, he renders history irrelevant: Transformations in beliefs over time are nothing more than an overgrowth that cannot change the eternal social-structural soil that bears it. In a second step, however, Durkheim re-creates another culture, "collective culture" or "collective consciousness," and places it in the heads of the natives. Time does not modify it. But can a historian accept the term "consciousness"? It is unclear how any native would be "conscious" of it. Like the Jews of the Old Testament, Durkheim's natives, collectively seen, hold a critical truth without being quite aware of it.

Intellectuals have a disposition toward fancy collages and castles in the air. The theological inheritance has cast a mantle of legitimacy on this propensity, empowering anthropologists and historians to tinker, cut, and paste, and imagine mentalities that do not actually recoup native culture. True, natives themselves practice bricolage. But while the social scientist should make this practice an object for study, he or she is not thereby authorized to imitate it.[117] In mathematical terms, an analytical function and the objects it operates on do not belong to the same logical order. Native cultural practices both invite us to follow their syllogisms and force us to caution: We should not supplement their ideas with ours. One should retrace the natives' bricolage but not tinker in their stead. One should

---

[114] FE, 13, trans. Fields, 13: "Religious representations are collective representations that express collective realites. Rites . . ."

[115] Within eight pages of the French edition, FE, 597, 604, trans. Fields, 420, 425. Compare the seductive elaboration in terms of symbolic representation of integration by Peter Berger and Thomas Luckmann, *The social construction of reality: a treatise on the sociology of knowledge*, repr. (London: 1971), 82, 92–96 and notes, whose truth value, however, is not the concern of this book.

[116] FE, 60, trans. Fields, 41.

[117] Hence this scholar's unease when reading a sentence such as the following: "If, in this play, Christ's body is quite literally pulled apart in what Bakhtin called a 'comical operation of dismemberment,' if the host is quite literally taken from its immolation in the church, if it is felt, pricked, cooked, trodden on, then we too are surely critically licensed to 'finger it familiarly on all sides, turn it upside down, inside out, peer at it from above and below, break open its external shell, look into its centre, doubt it, take it apart' " (Beckwith, "Ritual, Church and Theatre," at 66).

master a culture's grammar, but not think thoughts none of its members ever thought. The master of "Interpretation of Cultures" rightly cautioned his reader against carefree readings and loose method: They are nothing but "cabalism" and "subjectivism."[118] Unfortunately, disciples have been less clear headed than their mentor—and unaware of how much Geertz's own model stands on a distorted hermeneutical continuum with the medieval European past.

Repräsentation: The Real Presence of the State in Ritual

Clifford Geertz's model has seduced medievalists, and not without reason. Many have been enthralled by the anthropologist's tantalizing analysis of the Balinese "theater state":

> [M]ass ritual was not a device to shore up the state, but rather the state ... was a device for the enactment of mass ritual. Power served pomp, not pomp power.[119]

For Geertz, however, ceremony also shaped society, and actualized the "ontology" it presented, because ceremony stood on a continuum with the practice of power. To quote Geertz again, "the ceremonial forms that the Negara [theater state] celebrates in ritual and the institutional ones that it takes in society are the same forms."[120] A recent study of early medieval French political culture has suggested that tenth-century princely rituals

---

[118] Clifford Geertz, "Thick Description," in his *Interpretation of Cultures* (n.p.: 1973), 3–30, here 27, 29–30.

[119] Clifford Geertz, *Negara: The Theatre State in Nineteenth-Century Bali* (Princeton: 1980), 13 (Nicholas B. Dirks, *The Hollow Crown: Ethnohistory of an Indian Kingdom* [Cambridge [UK]: 1987], is an especially engaging Marxian revision of Geertz's model). See the reflections, starting with this text, on the adaptability of Geertz to Ottonian Germany, by Timothy Reuter, "Ottonian ruler representation in synchronic and diachronic comparison," in Gerd Althoff and Ernst Schubert, eds., *Herrschaftsrepräsentation im ottonischen Sachsen*, VuF 46 (Sigmaringen: 1998), 366–67, 379–80. Recent uses of Geertz include Peter Arnade, *Realms of Ritual*; David Warner, "Henry II at Magdeburg: Kingship, ritual and the cult of the saints," *Early Medieval Europe* 3,2 (1994): 135–66; John Bernhardt, *Itinerant kingship and royal monasteries in early medieval Germany, c. 936–1075* (Cambridge [UK]: 1993), 45–50; and Gordon Kipling, *Enter the King: Theatre, Liturgy, and Ritual in the Late Medieval Civic Triumph* (Oxford: 1998), 47. See also the authors inventoried in Peter Arnade, "Crowds, Banners, and the Marketplace: Symbols of Defiance and Defeat during the Ghent War of 1452–1453," *Journal for Medieval and Renaissance Studies* 24, 3 (1994): n. 3. Geoffrey Koziol, *Begging Pardon and Favor: Ritual amd Political Order in Early Medieval France* (Ithaca: 1992), does not quote Geertz; but it is clear that, despite the last, theoretical chapter, it is Geertzian anthropology that informs the whole of *Begging Pardon*. See the verbal echoes, e.g., the title of chapter 5: "Toward an Iconic Kingship," compared with Geertz, *Negara*, 136: "iconic kingship," or *Negara*, 131, for the king as a "ritual object," or 130, for the king as icon of kingship.

[120] Geertz, *Negara*, 104, 108.

functioned analogously: They displayed the ruler's subjection, humility, and penitential posture before the Supreme Judge, while in institutional practice aristocrats ritually begged their political betters for "pardon and favor."[121] Equally seductive has been Geertz's notion of iconicity. An "icon" is an image of a higher reality endowed with the creative power to reproduce downward this superior essence in which it participates. This notion in turn relates to Geertz's understanding of ritual as being simultaneously "model of" (reflective) and "model for" (active)—what the German language would call *Abbild* and *Vorbild*. The king, especially in ceremonial, is not only the king but as well the primary image of essential kingship; as an icon, it induces among subordinate holders of power the production of lesser replicas of royalty's essence.[122] Finally, this theater of power can by no means be equated to a puppet play where actors and roles are dissociated.[123] It does not "represent" but makes present—a notion German medievalists such as Hagen Keller have fully embraced.[124]

The attractiveness of the Geertzian model for medievalists is owed to its remarkably strong affinities with early medieval understandings. First, the liturgy did make present the foundational, hence eternal, events of Christian sacred history.[125] We underlined the critical importance of this notion in the economy of Liudprand's *Antapodosis*: This narrative relates the Ottonian liturgy of war to the Biblical figures of King David and Thomas the Apostle along with their theological meanings. Second, if we assume an easy transfer of clerical models of ecclesiastical *potestas* to the royal sphere, kingly power could be conceived of as a creative image of the divinity,

---

[121] Koziol, *Begging Pardon*. The book's focus on prostration should be applauded, for the medievalist can hardly find a ritual that was as frequent in regular political life (at least in our sources) as self-humiliation, one that took place on stages of so many different scales, or one that seems so well to straddle and challenge the boundaries between religious and political act.

[122] Geertz, *Negara*, 108–109; idem, "Religion As a Cultural System," repr. in *Interpretation of Cultures*, 87–125, at 93–94, 112–14; cf. Victor Turner, *The Ritual process*, 117: "All rituals have this exemplary, model-displaying character; in a sense, they might be said to 'create' society, in much the same way as Oscar Wilde held life to be 'an imitation of art.' " See, for an application, Koziol, *Begging Pardon*, 170–73. This idea has entered the mainstream of late antique studies, see, e.g., Jas Elsner, *Imperial Rome and Christian Triumph: The Art of the Roman Empire*, A.D. *100–450* (Oxford History of Art, Oxford: 1998), 81.

[123] See, e.g., Koziol, *Begging Pardon*, 305.

[124] Geertz, "Religion," 118; Keller, "Investitur," *passim*, esp. 51–52 and n. 2. See above, n. 49.

[125] See MacCormack, "Christ and Empire," at 299, 302–305, on how Byzantine "dramatic homilies" (297ff.) that insist that the sacred story they tell happens "today" are a key to imperial ceremonies. Thus, at Pentecost, also the day of the giving of the Tables of the Law, Constantine VII's *Book of Ceremonies* provides for a reaffirmation of the emperor's election and a recoronation. The idea was not merely East Roman, see Leo the Great, *Tractatus* 26.2, CCSL 138, 126:24–32.

emanating downward to be shared by lesser princes.[126] Third, the theater state's ability to make present furiously reminds the medievalist of the "real presence" in the Eucharist—a theological notion Geertz may be winking at when he compares Balinese rituals to "a high mass."[127]

Geertz contraposes the Balinese conception—power serves theater— against the early modern European notion of the primacy of power politics, exemplified by Machiavelli and Hobbes. The relative ease with which one can transpose Negara iconicity to the Middle Ages might then derive from the structural affinities between an extra-European world still suffused, putatively, with religiosity and the lost world of archaic medieval political culture. But the medievalist should note that the transfer is written from the onset in the anthropologist's model.[128] The parallels are not coincidental. Geertz warmly mentions, in one of these scholarly notes publishers force us to bury in the back of our books, his debt to the work of a German medievalist in exile, Ernst Kantorowicz's *The King's Two Bodies* (1957).[129] Upon closer scrutiny, ideas of liturgical kingship, Eucharistic lore, and social bodies all converged in the German tradition, and then traveled to the New World, to return to Europe through Geertz and further gild German conceptions. It is to this process that we now turn.

In effect, several generations of thinkers borrowed from the same conservative family, finding support for familiar ideas from slightly distant cousins or uncles. When German medievalists use the notion of "pres-

---

[126] See Olivier Guillot, "Une *ordinatio* méconnue: le Capitulaire de 823–825," in *Charlemagne's Heir: New Perspectives on the Reign of Louis the Pious*, ed. Peter Godman and Roger Collins (Oxford: 1990), 455–86; Hincmar of Reims, *De divortio*, 110:9–13 ("*reges . . . quos deus ideo in tam excellentissimo loco posuit, ut a subiectis omnibus conspici et ad speculi vicem haberi*"), with further references in Böhringer's note 23, and Devisse, *Hincmar* 1.683–84. This notion was most at home, however, in the conception of the episcopate, or of the papal office. See Cyprian of Carthage, *De ecclesiae catholicae unitate* 5, CCSL 3, 252–53; Jerome, Ep. 60, CCSL 54, 14: "*In te omnium oculi diriguntur, domus tua et conuersatio quasi in specula constituta magistra est publicae disciplinae*"; Leo the Great, *Sermones* 3–5, ed. Antoine Chavasse, CCSL 138 (Turnhout: 1973), 10–25. See Morrison, "Ex Multis" (as above, ch. 2, n. 51).

[127] Geertz, "Religion as a Cultural System," 116. A whole cottage industry links the Eucharist, theater, ritual, and social order (or its simple logical obverse, subversion), the most intelligent of which is possibly Beckwith, "Ritual, Church and Theatre." Suggested in the ninth century, the real presence imposed itself as a dogma only in the High Middle Ages. Its key elements, however, already existed in the ideas of the presence of the emperor in his icons.

[128] For some of these early exchanges between anthropology and history, see (cursorily) Buc, "Political ritual: medieval and modern interpretations," in Hans-Werner Goetz, ed., *Die Aktualität des Mittelalters* (Bochum: 2000), 255–72.

[129] *Negara*, 236. Cf. as well the reference in his earlier "Centers, Kings, and Charisma: Reflections on the Symbolics of Power," reed. in Geertz, *Local Knowledge* (New York: 1983), at 123. Wolfgang Ernst, "Kantorowicz: New Historicism avant la lettre?" in *Geschichtskörper. Zur Aktualität von Ernst H. Kantorowicz*, ed. Wolfgang Ernst and Cornelia Visman (Munich: 1998), 187–205 at 192, has also noticed the connection.

ence," Geertz provides them with an apparently extra-European reinforcement to an inheritance elaborated in Europe between the two World Wars. For Germany, 1918 had meant defeat, the abdication of the Kaiser, and the establishment of parliamentary democracy with the Weimar regime. The shock compares to the one France had undergone, a century earlier, with the Revolution. Like their postrevolutionary French counterparts, German scholars from all disciplines focused on the remaking of a political community in the context, and within the constraints, of mass participation in politics. The same concern with unity—the desire to overcome all dichotomies, be they metaphysical (e.g., the Kantian disjunction between things and thought) or political—dominated the agenda.[130] And as in the French nineteenth century, one had recourse to an imaginary organic Middle Ages.[131] Not unsurprisingly, some of these thinkers drew on the French reactionary tradition and specifically on Bonald and Maistre. To conceptualize and re-create unity, they called on the isomorphism between religious and political societies dear to Bonald. No wonder then that a number of German theories parallel those of the great reactionary's unreactionary French descendant, Durkheim.[132] Thus, the jurist Rudolf Smend underlined the similarities between the "integrative" bond to the State and the bond to the Divinity, a line of thought that recalls Bonald's isomorphism between the monarch and Christ the Man-God,[133] as well as Durkheim's famous equation of Society, Totality, and God.[134] In general, like the French

---

[130] Cf., e.g., a proponent of the unity of body, spirit, and soul, Helmuth Plessner, *Grenzen der Gemeinschaft. Eine Kritik des sozialen Radikalismus* (Bonn: 1924), repr. in *Gesammelte Schriften*, ed. Günter Dux, Odo Marquart and Elisabeth Ströker (Frankfurt: 1980–85), vol. 5, 14: "Radikalismus heisst Dualismus"; cf. as well 130: The necessity of power (which includes ordering Ceremonial) can be denied only on the ground of utopian "dualistic idealism." The philosopher Arnold Gehlen and the jurists Gerhard Leibholz and Rudolf Smend called (often superficially) on phenomenology—Husserl but also Theodor Litt, *Individuum und Gemeinschaft. Grundlegung der Kulturphilosophie*, 2d rev. ed. (Leipzig and Berlin: 1924).

[131] See Otto Gerhard Oexle, "Die Moderne und ihr Mittelalter. Eine folgenreiche Problemgeschichte," in *Mittelalter und Moderne. Entdeckung und Rekonstruktion der mittelalterlichen Welt*, ed. Peter Segl (Sigmaringen: 1997), 307–64.

[132] Cf. Alain Boureau, *Histoires d'un historien. Kantorowicz* (Paris: 1990), 158–62, for an excellent analysis of the inter-war-era cultural convergences between right and left on community cohesion. See as well Carlo Ginzburg, "Mythologie germanique et Nazisme: sur un ancien livre de George Dumézil," reed. in Ginzburg, *Mythes, emblèmes, traces. Morphologie et Histoire* (Paris: 1989), 181–208 at 202–207.

[133] Cf. above, n. 38.

[134] Smend, *Verfassung und Verfassungsrecht* (Munich and Leipzig: 1928), 50 n. 2, referring to Georg Simmel; cf. Durkheim, FE, 630–31 n. 2; Fields, 443 n. 18. Durkheim as well as Smend concentrated on ritual as an agent for social cohesion, not for political agendas. The Durkheimian model tempts to a similar depoliticization Janet Nelson, "Ritual and Reality in the Early Medieval *Ordines*" (1975), reed. in *Politics and Ritual*, ed. Nelson, 329–39, at 338: "[T]he early medieval *ordines* . . . are better approached as patterns of symbols expressing the continuity and integration of society through kingship, than as juristic texts in which conflict-

reactionaries, many German thinkers, regardless of their religious commitment and of its intensity, turned to religion, the Church, and ritual as a model for the reintegration of the State. In this sense, then, and insofar as Nazi culture was rooted in a wider German reactionary ambience, it is possible to argue that NSDAP totalitarianism purposefully approximated a "religion" (as the early twentieth century understood the term).[135] It forces us as well to consider the current interest in rituals in the light of the greatest crisis of the twentieth century.

The greatest of the German conservative thinkers in that era was Carl Schmitt. His thought, unequaled in clarity, sharpness, and passion, still haunts German sociology. Whether the intellectual historian takes him as illustrative of the interwar climate or as one of its main shapers, it remains that his works provoked sharp discussions and reaction. In agreement or disagreement, his ideas were repeatedly quoted and alluded to. And as this century is brought to its close, scholars still endeavor to separate what in his theories was bound to the times and what can be salvaged for the social sciences. Schmitt's ideas also inform—directly and indirectly—current Mediaevistik. Schmitt's attractiveness to medievalists is understandable. Schmitt, himself indebted to Bonald and Maistre, explicitly reclaimed medieval theology and Catholic ecclesiology in elaborating his "political theology."[136] One of its key concepts was political *"Repräsentation,"* which Schmitt developed, on the one hand, in opposition to liberal ideas of parliamentary representation (which catered only to the proctoring of segmentary and often private interests) and, on the other, by reflecting on the Catholic Church. The *ecclesia* "represents" the absent person of Christ as well as the providentially redeemed human community (*civitas humana*).[137]

---

ing hierocratic or theocratic claims are clearly spelled out," with her note 36 quoting Douglas, *Natural Symbols*, reed. (London: 1970), herself "recalling Durkheim's premise 'that society and God can be equated.' "

[135] See the ferocious contemporary critiques by Erich Voegelin, *Die politischen Religionen* (Stockholm: 1939).

[136] As discussed with great savvy in one of the earliest critical discussions of his work, Hugo Ball, "Carl Schmitts Politische Theologie," *Hochland* 21:2 (1924), 261–86, repr. in Jacob Taubes, *Der Fürst dieser Welt. Carl Schmitt und die Folge*, Religionstheorie und politische Theologie 1, 2d ed. (Munich: 1985), 100–15, here at 104–105. Clear introductions to, and discussions of Schmitt, Smend, and other inter-war-era German thinkers in Oliver Lepsius, *Die gegensatzaufhebende Begriffsbildung* (Munich: 1994) and in the essays edited by Gerhard Göhler, *Institution-Macht-Repräsentation: Wofür politische Institutionen stehen und wie sie wirken* (Baden-Baden: 1997), esp. Lutz Berthold, "Die beiden Grundbedeutungen des Repräsentationsbegriffs, dargestellt an Autoren aus dem Umfeld der Weimarer Staatslehre," 363–75.

[137] Carl Schmitt, *Römischer Katholizismus und politische Form* (Munich: 1923, 1925), 24–26, 43–44; trans. G. L. Ulmen, *Roman Catholicism and Political Form* (Westport: 1996), 17–19, 31–32. Milbank, *Theology and Social Theory*, 16, shows himself quite Catholic in refusing, in a similar vein, the depoliticization of the Church.

Truly to "represent" is to make present an in-itself invisible, preexisting "totality" that is both here and not here.[138] In Schmitt's *Verfassungslehre*, the parallel to the Catholic Eucharist (already explicit in Bonald) was implicit, but other German thinkers of the 1920s, whether in agreement or in disagreement, spelled it out.[139] Schmitt's most intelligent critic, Hans Julius Wolff, actually compared the different eucharistic lores that the different Christian sects propounded with different types of representation.[140]

Other thinkers would develop the ideal of group representation. For Schmitt, however, one cannot represent subparts of the social totality, but only the supreme unit itself. To be "represented" is, for power, essential. Any polity needs form (in the Platonic sense); the essence of any such form comprises necessarily the depiction (*Darstellung*) of political unity.[141] As representative, the ruler makes the unity of the *Volk* visible to itself.[142] At one extreme of the political spectrum—that is, absolute monarchy—*Repräsentation* is not simply passive "form" or image, but form as formative, the agent creative of the polity. Absolute monarchy "is nothing else than absolute *Repräsentation*, and is based on the idea that political unity is first produced through *Repräsentation*, through depiction (*Darstellung*)."[143] Schmitt considers monarchical absolutism a limit case, but it is also an ideal type: For any polity, the creative role of *Repräsentation* will be pro-

---

[138] Carl Schmitt, *Verfassungslehre* (1928; reed. Berlin: 1965), 209–10. The expression of simultaneous presence and absence may derive from early modern Catholicism, see Pascal, *Pensées* 248, ed. Michel Le Guen (Paris: 1977), 183: "Figure porte absence et présence." One finds it also, owing to Paul, Col. 2.5 and I Cor. 5.3, in medieval epistolography.

[139] See, e.g., Gerhard Leibholz, *Das Wesen der Repräsentation, unter besonderer Berücksichtigung des Repräsentativsystems* (Berlin: 1929; cf. the reed., 1973), 26, 28, 29 nn. 1–2. Cf. Boureau, "Les cérémonies," 1255.

[140] Hans J. Wolff, *Organschaft und juristische Person. II: Theorie der Vertretung* (Berlin: 1934; reed. Aalen: 1962), cited from the partial reed. in *Zur Theorie und Geschichte der Repräsentation und Repräsentativverfassung*, Wege der Forschung 184, ed. Heinz Rausch (Darmstadt: 1968), 119 n. 3.

[141] Schmitt, *Verfassungslehre*, 207.

[142] Schmitt, *Verfassungslehre*, 210, with *Römischer Katholizismus*, 29, trans. Ulmen, 21. Cf. Lutz Berthold, "Bedeutungen des Repräsentationsbegriffs," 370–71. The theme of unity is picked up, with explicit reference to Schramm, Otto Brunner, and Schmitt, by Horst Wenzel, "Zur Repräsentation von Herrschaft im Mittelalterlichen Texten," in *Adelsherrschaft und Literatur*, Beiträge zur Älteren deutschen Literaturgeschichte 6, ed. Horst Wenzel (Frankfurt am Main: 1980), 339–75, esp. at 345, 351, 355.

[143] Schmitt, *Verfassungslehre*, 205; echoed in 207: "It is possible that the political unity is itself effected first through the depiction. This is the case in proportion to the proximity of a state form to absolute *Repräsentation*." The discussion concludes on the assertion that while political unity can owe its origin to another *method* than depiction, only *Darstellung-Repräsentation* endows the polity with form. Representation being political, an entity able to represent is essentially public and political, see Schmitt, *Römischer Katholizismus*, 26, 40, on the Catholic Church, and the discussion by Ball, "Carl Schmitts Politische Theologie," 113–15.

portional to the degree to which the constitution approximates absolute monarchy.[144]

Schmitt's thought influenced, and continues to influence, German historians. It also crossed the Atlantic. While not uncomplicated, Kantorowicz's debt to the German jurists is clear.[145] Along with the romantic Stefan George—whose politics stood behind Kantorowicz's passionate exaltation of the prophetic leader in *Kaiser Friedrich der Zweite* (1927)—they had shaped his intellectual and professional milieu. The subtitle of *The King's Two Bodies, A Study in Political Theology*, was a direct allusion to Schmitt's *Political Theology*. But—and here the full complexity of Kantorowicz's relation to the German past emerges—it alluded simultaneously to Erik Peterson's principled denial that orthodox Christian theology, unperverted, might ever provide a ratification of the this-worldly order.[146] Kantorowicz, after the war, rejected the far right's politics and the nationalism that had presided to the writing of his *Frederick II*. This conversion, however, manifested itself through silences, not through engagement. Peterson was explicitly quoted—but as a secondary source for late antique theology, not as a theorist of modern politics. As for Schmitt, he never appears.[147] Yet the *King's Two Bodies* is, fundamentally, a historical illustration of Schmitt's dictum that "all the key concepts of the modern theory of the State are secularized theological concepts."[148] Kantorowicz's narrative, in an exploration of key dualities in medieval political thought that paved the road to the notion of the ruler as embodiment of the political community, moves from liturgy to law to corporation theory—the Schmittian itinerary from religion to sociology. In retracing the transfer from Church to State of the notion that the community is a mystical body, it parallels Schmitt's own transfer, the conceptual reshaping of the secular polity on the model of the Catholic Church. For the jurist, two political forms were *Repräsentation* par excellence, the Church and absolute monarchy. The historian made them the bookends of his study. But in exploring these historical transfers, *The King's Two Bodies* offered its reader a subtle reminder of the existence of another

---

[144] Cf. the general discussion, *Verfassungslehre*, 204–208, pitting against one another two ideal types, the Nation (total primacy of the principle of identity) and the absolute monarchy (total primacy of *Repräsentation*).

[145] Cf. Boureau, *Histoires*, 156–67.

[146] Erik Peterson, *Der Monotheismus als politisches Problem* (Leipzig: 1935), repr. in his *Theologische Traktate* (Munich: 1951), 41–105. Cf. Friethard Scholz, "Die Theologie Carl Schmitt," in Alfred Schindler, ed., *Monotheismus als politisches Problem* (Gütersloh: 1978), repr. in *Der Fürst dieser Welt. Carl Schmitt und die Folge*, ed. Jacob Taubes, Religionstheorie und politische Theologie 1, 2d ed. (Munich: 1985), 153–73.

[147] The only track I have found is in Kantorowicz, "Mysteries of State" (1955), reed. in his *Selected Studies* (Locust Valley: 1965), 381–98, at 382 n. 6.

[148] Schmitt, *Politische Theologie*, 37.

political model. Parliamentarism, much maligned by Schmitt, who had argued it was unable to truly represent the community, becomes in Kantorowicz's narrative an alternate and positive road. In a silent rebuke to Schmitt, two late medieval and early modern political theologies stand face-to-face. The English Parliament's resistance to the king and absolutist France's cult of the royal State reenact Germany's alternatives during the 1920s and 1930s. Kantorowicz knew that they had been his as well.

Of the great figures that defined German historiography after the Second World War, not all left even such subtle traces of recantation. Percy Ernst Schramm (1898–1970), possibly the leading twentieth-century German historian of royal ceremonial, drew directly on Schmitt's metaphysics of power. We should not reduce the relationship between two subsets of the same intellectual milieu, interwar jurists and historians, to a simple genealogy between two thinkers, even if it is emblematic. Indeed, Schramm's work echoes other contemporary conservatives than Schmitt. The Berlin jurist Rudolf Smend had argued in his *Verfassung und Verfassungsrecht* (1928) that the State had to create itself permanently and could do so no better than through symbols and forms. More than statutes and laws, more than rational legislative formulations of the substantial contents of politics, symbols and practices such as flags, emblems, national hymns, marches, and demonstrative parades allowed the "representation" and "embodiment" or "incarnation" (*Verkörperung*) of State unity, and the "integration" of the individual into the political body, from whom he or she should have been alienated owing to the State's hugeness and to its radical distance from the individual.[149] We have met this distrust for reason before, in the pages of Taine: "[T]ruth, to be felt, must put on a body." Listen now to Percy Ernst Schramm. In the concluding pages to his *History of the English Coronation* (1937), Schramm praised the festivals of Fascist Italy and those of Nazi Germany "behind the *Hakenkreuz*." Such parades were necessary, he argued, because:

> the essence of a State is something more than its constitution, its system of laws, and its theory. It must demonstrate (*beweisen*) its life; it must likewise have a body (*Leib*) that everyone can assimilate into himself (*in sich aufnehmen*) with his senses. This is the deepest meaning of State feasts: they call the people to the awareness that it constitutes a body (*Körper*) of which each individual is a member ... States [e.g., Fascist Italy and Nazi Germany] that have been renewed have new forms of public life in which the specificity of a people expresses itself more clearly than in the paragraphs of their legislation.[150]

---

[149] Smend, *Verfassung*, esp. 13, 16–18, 28–29, 32–33, 46–50.

[150] Percy Ernst Schramm, *Geschichte des englischen Königtums im Lichte der Krönung* (Weimar: 1937), 230–31; trans. *A history of the English coronation* (Oxford: 1937), 230–31 (slightly modified to foreground Schramm's ontology). The conceptual and verbal parallels seem to

These metaphysics of power continued to inform scholarship after 1945. In his book on the feasts at the Bavarian court in the baroque age, Schramm's contemporary Eberhard Straub called explicitly on Schmitt.[151] The prince's office is a "recapitulation" of all social and political forces; his pomp and the representation of his majesty provide an exemplary symbol (*Sinnbild*) of hierarchical order, making "visible the moral Ideas that give life to the State." The prince himself is an image (*Abbild*) of a God identified with order. Princely festivals simultaneously depict, actualize, and embody order:

> [In the age of the Baroque], the whole social order was shot through with the Idea of Representation; [order] first made its visible appearance through the depiction (*Darstellung*) of its ranks. The totality of the social members found its *Darstellung* in Majesty; Majesty recapitulated into a unity the plurality of [social] organs.[152]

Straub's disquisitions culminate in the assertion, shared with the French counterrevolutionaries of the preceding century, that the modern democratic state, based on the sovereignty of the individual, cannot but fail to truly represent itself and outwardly display its essence. After the French revolution, all political displays have become arbitrary and ornamental; appearances and inward reality no longer match one another. Unlike in the previous era, feasts cannot be generated by the Ideas that are depicted in them. Worse, the new State finds itself forced to resort to a new kind of theatrical politics, in which "Führers" offer their disoriented and jaded people such bloody plays as Stalinist show trials and *Kristallnacht*.[153] The disjunction of essence and outer form, characteristic of democracy, leads straight to the perverted aesthetics and to the violence of totalitarian regimes. The Schmittian critique of the parliamentary constitution, elabo-

---

me very strong, and owing to them I would tend to disagree with Keller, "Investitur," 51–52 n. 2, for whom the influence of the jurists on the historians was indirect and passed through the 1930s public debate on the Weimar order. For Taine, see above, n. 67. Strong echoes as well in Schramm of the Romantic tradition; cp. Johann Wolfgang von Goethe, [Italienische Reise.] *Reise-Tagebuch, 1786* (16 September), Konrad Scheurmann and Jochen Golz, eds. (Mainz: 1997), 56, cited above, for the sake of showing *longue durée* continuities, as an epigram to chapter 4.

[151] Eberhard Straub, *Repraesentatio Maiestatis oder churbayerische Freudenfeste. Die höfischen Feste in der Münchner Residenz vom 16. bis zum Ende des 18. Jahrhunderts* (Munich: 1969), esp. 1–13, 334–37. Straub uses Lünig, but forgets Lünig's power-political cynicism, to transform him into a political theologian. *Repraesentatio Maiestatis* belongs to Clifford Geertz's bibliography, see "Centers, Kings, and Charisma," 123.

[152] Straub, *Repraesentatio Maiestatis*, 8.

[153] Straub, *Repraesentatio Maiestatis*, 9, 336–37: "Schauprozessen, Sportfesten, Parteitagen, Revolutionsfeiern, Kameradschaftsabenden, Erstürmung von Kirchen, Synagogen, und Hochschulen".

rated in the context of Weimar, has been extended to the latest failure of
German politics, Nazi Germany—1918 and 1933 are on a continuum. So
are, in the aftermath of the Marshall Plan, fascism and bolshevism.

Straub provides a brutal but unsurprising avatar of neo-Catholic political
metaphysics. Rituals constitute order; when they lose their religious referent they lose constitutive power. Schramm's work stands in the same tradition, but with much more subtlety. Wafts of Eucharistic theology tickle the
reader's nostrils when Schramm quotes Goethe in the introduction to his
collected studies: "The symbol is the thing without being the thing, and
still it is the thing, an image brought together in the spiritual mirror and
still identical with the object [itself]."[154] The notion of symbolism is put to
the service of an interrogation on the history of power. Schramm ponders:
How can the "State" exist before the term denoting it is invented? The
word is absent, "still [and here Schramm waxes theological] the word is not
lacking, for it could not be lacking; rather, it is 'acted' (agiert) and 'played
forth' (vorgespielt)" in such scenes as the festive banquet closing the 936
Aachen coronation.[155] Mutatis mutandis, the function of such rituals is an
eternal one: They allow the people to become a political body and to inte-
grate into their very substance something of the State.[156] In the early and
high Middle Ages, the king, as well as his "signs of lordship" and rituals,
"depicted (darstellte) the State"; they "embodied the State, which was 'present' in them." Schramm justifies this in Schmittian tones: "[I]t belongs
quite obviously to the authority of any government to make itself 'present.'" Among others, Arno Borst echoes this model: Ceremonies "work in
a formative manner on reality, for they make something sensible which
one would otherwise not even be able to give a name to," the State, or
sovereignty.[157] As in the world of Louis de Bonald, the ruler and rituals
manifest power; even more, as in Bonald's neo-Catholic metaphysics, they
make it be.

This dynamic, "performative" theme present in the German intellectual
tradition—that a social unit creates or "forms" itself through self-presenta-
tion in ritual—came to influence through Kantorowicz and/or Geertz a

---

[154] Percy Ernst Schramm, "Zur wissenschaftlichen Terminologie," in Kaiser, Könige und
Päpste. Gesammelte Aufsätze, 4 t. in 5 vols. (Stuttgart: 1968–71), 1.19–29, at 21; Herrschaftszeichen und Staatssymbolik, 3 vols. (Stuttgart: 1954–56), l.v.

[155] Schramm, "Die 'Herrschaftszeichen,' die 'Staatssymbolik' und die 'Staatspräsentation'
des Mittelalters," in Kaiser, 1.30–58, at 31–32.

[156] Schramm, Geschichte des englischen Königtums, 230–31, cited above, 234.

[157] Schramm, Kaiser, 1.43. See also the conclusion to Herrschaftszeichen und Staatssymbolik,
3.1067: "Der König ist das 'Zeichen' des Staates"—as Peter is the sign of the whole Church
or Rupert of the archbishopric of Salzburg. See as well his introduction, 1.1, on the "signs
that the rulers, as the embodiment of the medieval 'State' have deployed to make their lordship visible." The king employs signal objects, gestures (Gesten) and customs (Brauche) to
make kingship visible. Cf. Borst, Lebensformen im Mittelalter (Frankfurt: 1973), 487. See as

generation of Anglo-American medievalists.[158] Richard Trexler's fifteenth-century Florence provides a first example. The city, an originally plebeian republic, auto-generated its public honor through carefully orchestrated ceremonies that enabled it to capture the aura of visiting princes. Trexler had made this model explicit in his introduction to a Florentine source, published a year earlier. It applied as well to a northern principality like Valois Burgundy. Not only the historian but contemporary observers were aware of this method of generation of the political unit: "By the 1420s astute travelers like the Florentines understood that Burgundian ritual was literally creating that state's [Burgundy's] identity."[159] At the other book-end of the Christian Middle Ages, with a remarkably ecumenical flair for spirituality and social-scientific inspiration, Peter Brown advanced that the unity of early medieval Christendom might have been created by a plurality of acts of saintly *repraesentatio Christi*. The holy man, Brown suggested, by bearing "in his own person the central paradigm of the Christian community . . . was Christianity in his region."[160] Representation, after a journey through sacral kingship and Bali, had returned to Christendom and its saints.

To Forget the Devil[161]

The genealogies just delineated raise a troublesome issue. Is the social-scientific "reading" of texts generated by a culture from which the social sciences themselves descend eo ipso invalid? In a recent book, John Milbank has examined a similar issue—the applicability of social scientific models to religion. He sternly warns that:

Sociology is only able to explain, or even illuminate religion, to the extent that it conceals its own theological borrowings and its quasi-religious status . . .

---

well Heinrich Fichtenau, *Lebensordnungen*, 1.76 (in a section entitled *Repräsentation*): "Ehre ist Ehrung, sie muss fortwährend 'aktualisiert' werden, um zu bestehen."

[158] See Alain Boureau's pointed critique of those he calls the American "Neo-Ceremonialist school" (Jackson, Hanley, Bryant, Giesey) in his *Le simple corps du roi* (Paris: 1999), conveniently summarized in his "Ritualité politique et modernité monarchique," in *L'Etat ou le roi*, ed. Neithard Bulst et al. (Paris: 1996), 11–14, and "Les cérémonies royales entre performance juridique et compétence liturgique," *Annales E.S.C.* 46,6 (1991): 1253–64.

[159] Richard Trexler, introduction to the *Libro Cerimoniale of the Florentine Republic by Francesco Filarete and Angelo Manfidi* (Geneva: 1978), 10. See as well Trexler, *Public Life in Renaissance Florence* (New York: 1980), calling on Geertz, "Centers, Kings, and Charisma" (as n. 129), and on Victor Turner, "The Center Out There," *History of Religion* 12 (1972), 191–230.

[160] Peter Brown, "The Saint As Exemplar," in *Persons in Groups*, ed. Richard Trexler (Binghamton, NY: 1985), 192, drawing, like Trexler, on Geertz.

[161] Cf. Philippe Buc, "Political rituals and political imagination in the medieval West, 4th–11th centuries," forthcoming in Janet Nelson and Peter Linehan, *The Medieval World* (London 2001).

"scientific" social theories are themselves theologies or anti-theologies in disguise. Contemporary theologies which forge alliances with such theories are often unwittingly rediscovering concealed affinities between positions that partake of the same historical origins.[162]

But whether and how the historian can use a given social-scientific model to approach specific medieval documents is more complicated. It depends on at least three factors. First, on the specific issues he or she is researching. Second, on the nature of the continuities between the modern model and the mentalities that shaped the data. Third, on the degree to which the historian takes into account the "concealed affinities"—the twisted continuities and half-ruptures between theology and social science.

Obviously, the historian can employ a modern economic model to analyze medieval domanial records even though the people who redacted the latter were unaware of anything approaching this theory. The results will stand or fall on the quality and quantity of the available data, at least as long as the historian only looks to reconstruct strictly economic processes, such as production or consumption. Problems arise when he or she expands analysis to economic mentalities and assumes, for example, that rational choice governed medieval agents' behavior, or that the authors of the sources shared, however faintly, in some version of modern economic thought. The historian can legitimately draw connections that his or her subjects themselves would never have made.[163] But he or she should not build syllogisms whose terms are all cultural when the natives could have produced these syllogisms themselves (and should have produced themselves given that they had all the terms at their disposal) but never did produce them. Effectively, the danger zone begins where there are *longue-durée* cultural continuities, or where such continuities are assumed and simplified.

Indeed, for the anthropological theories that we have been considering, the problem may not be that they do not dovetail with the medieval world vision. Rather, it lies in the misapprehension of this world vision, and in its forced harmonization with the social-scientific model. In other words, there exist, as we have seen, significant continuities between, on the one hand, medieval political culture, and, on the other, the historiographical avatars of anthropology. Yet the latter lop off an equally significant aspect of the former. The quest for order in the world—a recurrent and ever-heightened concern since the Protestant Reformation—was pursued within different theological parameters in the the early Middle Ages. To forget them is, among other amnesias, to forget the devil, to forget dualities

---

[162] John Milbank, *Theology and Social Theory: Beyond Secular Reason* (Oxford: 1990), 3, 52.
[163] My thanks to Dan Gordon for raising the issue in these terms.

coexisting with monism in medieval political culture, to forget the textual and argumentative nature of our documents, and finally to forget that medieval culture was a culture of hermeneutics. Since all these blind spots are related to one another, we shall review them together.

Totality was both one and not one. Kingship could be envisaged in a plurality of ways. One could see it as an "institution" within a monistic *ecclesia* or as one half of a duality, as a *potestas extera* standing outside the *ecclesia*. Some thinkers might even adhere simultaneously to these two conceptions, which to a modern mind seem so antithetical to one another.[164] As in the Balinese model, royal *potestas* might be an image of God's power, and royal solemnities might refer to the heavenly liturgies. But authors could also reject kingship in another sphere, at a significant distance from God. The antagonism of the age of persecutions long remained alive. Immediately after the Constantinian peace, Lactantius pointedly concluded his *Divine Institutes* with a reminder that neither wealth, nor office, nor even royal power could be trusted to confer immortality. It was the height of unreason, then, as well as a form of apostasy, to "seek the [imperial] presence and prostrate oneself in the dirt."[165] Two generations later, Ambrose of Milan refused to accept the hug-and-kiss of imperial *salutatio* because he, as bishop, represented a power at least equal to the *imperium*, understand, God.[166] This oppositional stance never died. One of Ambrose's successors, an archbishop of Milan invoked (so we are told) the local exemplary figure to justify his own refusal to prostrate himself before Emperor Lothar. In the words attributed to the prelate, Lothar was "not the Lord God."[167] *Regnum* stood against *regnum*. Exhorted to come to communion

---

[164] The subtlest discussions of this coexistence are Morrison, *The Two Kingdoms: Ecclesiology in Carolingian Political Thought* (Princeton: 1964), and Caspary, *Politics and Exegesis*.

[165] Lactantius, *Divine Institutes* 7.27.15, CSEL 19, 671:20–24: "*Nemo divitiis, nemo fascibus, nemo etiam regia potestate confidat; inmortalem ista non faciunt. Nam quicumque rationem hominis abiecerit ac praesentia secutus in humum se prostraverit, tamquam desertor domini et imperatoris et patris sui punietur.*"

[166] Ambrose, *Epistola* 30.3, ed. Otto Faller, CSEL 72:10 (Vienna: 1967), 209. See much earlier the early third-century *Encratite Acts of Thomas* 11.138, ed. by Wilhelm Schneemelcher and trans. by R. McL. Wilson in Edgar Heenecke, *New Testament Apocrypha* (Philadelphia: 1963), vol. 2, 442–531 at 515: "King Misdaeus and his kinsman Charisius both went away to the house of Siphor the Captain, and found Judas [Thomas] sitting and teaching. Now all who were there stood up for the king, but Judas did not rise." Furious, Misdaeus overturns Thomas's chair.

[167] Andrew of Bergamo, *Historiola* 7, SS rer. Lang., 225:24–29: "*Tunc temporis aecclesie Mediolanensi Angelbertus archiepiscopus regebat. Volebat imperator* [Lothar] *dicere, quod ille in ipso consilio* [contra Juditham] *fuisset* [sic], *et venientes nobiles eum in gratia miserunt. Sed dum ante imperatore* [sic] *ducerent, ille vero tantum caput inclinavit et verba salutatoria dixit; ad pedes vero noluit venire propter reverentiae honorem aecclesiarum. Tunc imperator dixit: 'Sic contenis te, quasi sanctus Ambrosius sis!' Archiepiscopus respondit: 'Nec ego sanctus Ambrosius, nec te dominus Deus.'* " See as well Buc, "Les débuts de Sauxillanges: à propos d'un acte de 927," *Bibliothèque de l'Ecole des*

with the heretical emperor Valens "who held the kingdom (*regnum*)," the Nicene Eulogius retorted derisively to the Arian magistrate, "I have a share in the Kingdom (*regnum*) and in the Priesthood (*sacerdotium*)"—an allusion to the "royal priesthood" promised to Christians. Much against imperial will, ceremonial honors verified the holy man's assertion. On the road to exile, Eulogius and his followers were repeatedly granted solemnities reserved by law to the emperor and his representatives: "[C]ities and towns gave them *occursus*, and honored the victorious athletes [of God]."[168] True *basileia* and its trappings belonged to the confessors. The ruler, in fact, could be situated so far from God as to be the icon of the "prince of this world." Gregory of Tours conveniently dreamt that three bishops enthroned King Chilperic into Hell.[169] Like Satan, who had literally fallen to his infernal throne, the evil Frankish ruler received simultaneously punishment and status in his appointed seat. In another influential late antique source, the devil appeared to Martin as Christ, but in imperial garb, to obtain the saint's obeisance.[170] For Sulpicius Severus, the Lord was the true emperor, but an emperor who would not bedeck himself with the ornaments of dubious secular princedom. Such reverse mimesis pertained to the prince of this world, who "transfigures himself into an angel of Light" (cf. 2 Cor. 11.14). In contradistinction to the Balinese model, medieval thinkers were well aware of the possibility of power politics; unlike Machiavelli or Hobbes, they considered any instrumentalization of religion, even outward, a devilish perversion. But its likelihood made the interpretation of the spirit behind a ceremony critically important.

Late antique and medieval Christianity, even in the Byzantine East, had a strong dualistic component. The model of the Negara, however, like most influential postmedieval sociologies, is monistic. As in De Bonald, religion (or its cultural ersatz) and society are isomorphic; even more, they are essentially one. But a monistic model cannot apprehend (and indeed, to be fair, the Negara never intended to apprehend) a medieval mentality in which the oppositions between *sacerdotium* and *regnum*, *ecclesia* and *saeculum*, God and the devil, maintained a fundamental fracture within totality.[171] The fracture is perhaps best revealed in the great crisis which, for

---

chartes 156, 2 (1998): 537–45, for a founder's provision that the clergy attached to his minster would bow before anyone but Christ.

[168] Cassiodorus, *Historia ecclesiastica tripartita* 7.33.4–5:17–19 and 25–27, ed. Walter Jacob and Rudolph Hanslik, CSEL 71 (Vienna: 1952), 434.

[169] See above, chapter 3, 116, Gregory of Tours, *LH* 8.5.

[170] Sulpicius Severus, *Vita Martini* 24.4–8, ed. Jacques Fontaine, SC 133 (Paris: 1967), 306–308. Cf. Jacques Fontaine, "Hagiographie et politique," 113–40. This text (and the devil) is rightly noticed by Brown, "Saint as Exemplar," 190–91.

[171] Sharpest, although already determined by Henry III's deposition of contending popes at Sutri in 1046, the anonymous *De ordinando pontifice*, ed. Erwin Frauenknecht, MGH Stu-

German historiography at least ushered in the High Middle Ages: the conflict between Pope Gregory VII and the Salian king and emperor Henry IV.[172] From epistolary exchange to epistolary exchange, and even within a single letter, the pope hesitates. Shall he place the king in the positive or negative register of providential history? One can do no better than quote Gerard Caspary:

> For Origen and for most of the Fathers, as for most of the Early Middle Ages, theology of politics did not consist of an isolated, distinctive, and somehow frozen political stance. Origen could hold at one and the same time a theology of politics that saw the Roman Empire as having a christological dimension, as being a purely secular good established by God essentially for the sake of non-Christians, and yet as also being an instrument of the Devil. Similarly Gregory VII, in a single letter, saw kingship as being so worldly that it could be conceived as essentially an invention of the Devil, and yet at the same time as capable of functioning as an ecclesiastical office.[173]

Gregory's correspondence reveals a mind genuinely and honestly struggling to understand and categorize a king and his behavior.[174] For the pope, as for many observers of the famous "ritual" that might have reconciled him to the king, Henry's penance and absolution at Canossa (1077), the

---

dien und Texte 5 (Hannover: 1992), 96–97:291–96: "*Ubi enim inveniuntur imperatores locum Christi obtinentes? Si verius liceat nobis dicere potius officio diaboli funguntur in gladio et sanguine, ut, dum per penitentiam* [episcopi] *eruantur vitia spirituali resecatione, ipsi insaniant vel in cede vel in membrorum obtruncatione; quod secundum gratiam apud Deum omnino est abhominabile.*" Historians commonly relate this text to Anselm of Liège's contemporary statement, attributed to bishop Wazo in the context of a dispute with Henry III over seating, *Gesta episcoporum Leodiensum* 66, ed. Georg H. Pertz, MGH SS 7 (Hannover: 1846) 230:4–7, that bishops are anointed "to give life" but the emperor "to kill": "*Alia . . . est et longe a sacerdotali differens vestra quam asseritis unctio, quia per eam vos ad mortificandum, nos autem Deo ad vivificandum ornati sumus; unde quantum vita morte praestantior, tantum nostra vestra unctione sine dubio est excellentior.*" But it is not an eleventh-century invention; cf. Morrison, *Two Kingdoms*, 120, citing Alcuin as well as the fragmentary letter of Hrabanus Maurus to Brunward of Hersfeld, ed. Ernst Dümmler, MGH Epistolae 5 = Karolini aevi 3 (Berlin: 1899), 528:4–7: "*Duae dignitates atque potestates inter homines constitutae reperiuntur. Una ex humana inventione reperta, hoc est imperialis atque regalis. Altera vero ex divina auctoritate instituta, hoc est sacerdotalis. Quarum una hominum corpora parat ad mortem, altera animas nutrit ad vitam.*" The first antithesis was borrowed by Gregory VII, *Registrum* 4.2, ed. Erich Caspar, MGH epistolae selectae 2, 2 vols. (Berlin: 1955), 1.295:22–23: "*illam* [regiam dignitatem] *superbia humana repperit, hanc* [episcopalem] *divina pietas instituit.*" Twelfth-century reformers adopted it; cf. Buc, *L'ambiguïté*, 254 n. 43. For the Byzantine East, see Dagron, *Empereur et prêtre*, esp. 192–200, revisiting a common prejudice.

[172] Cf. the essays collected in Hellmut Kämpf, ed., *Canossa als Wende*, Wege der Forschung 12 (Darmstadt: 1963).

[173] Caspary, *Politics and Exegesis*, 189, focusing on *Registrum* 8.21.

[174] See as well Christian Schneider, *Prophetisches Sacerdotium und Heilsgeschichtlisches Regnum im Dialog 1073–1077* (Munich: 1972).

issue was one of interpretation.[175] In the rewritings of the event, the letter of the event morphed to fit the spirit that authors felt had animated the participants.

The devilish opposition between inner spirit and outward "performance" leads us to another key deficit in social-scientific modeling of medieval political culture: It commonly assumes that the medieval political agent trusted ceremonial appearances. Facile oppositions between modernity and the Middle Ages have left some scholars with the impression that a disjunction between public behavior and inner feelings first arose in the world of the Renaissance courtier.[176] Another wedge, then, in the overly tempting projection of Java into Francia stems from medieval political culture's deep attention to hypocrisy.[177] This again relates to the presence of the devil, whom Liudprand, following Tertullian, portrayed as the perverse interpreter par excellence.[178] Devilish (or pagan or Jewish) is the disjunction between appearances and reality, letter and spirit—a chasm rupturing the road to salvation and to apprehension of the true *mysterium*. While early modern authors may have underlined in an unprecedented manner the split "between public forms of behavior and private thoughts and feelings,"[179] this split was quite conceivable in early medieval political culture. When comparing faiths, Christian authors underlined that only the *exception*, the true religion, overcame it; when engaging in polemics within Christendom, they produced narratives in which only the *exception*, that is, the author's favored camp, established a smooth vertical link between ceremonies' letter and their spirit. For Cardinal Beno, one of the few authors who describe Canossa in a light favorable to Henry IV, the king, in accepting the humiliating, harsh, and excessive penance that Gregory VII had enjoined upon him, had "made himself for three days a spectacle (*spectaculum*) to angels and human beings, and a derisive play (*ludibrium*) to" Gregory. The reference to martyrdom (cf. 1 Cor. 4.9: *morti destinatos quia spectaculum . . .*

---

[175] Recent historiography in Monika Suchan, *Königsherrschaft im Streit. Konfliktaustragung in der Regierungszeit Heinrichs IV.* (Stuttgart: 1997), 112–20. The key study is Harald Zimmermann, *Der Canossagang von 1077. Wirkungen und Wirklichkeit* (Mainz: 1975). Typically, given his despiritualizing approach, Althoff argues that what happened at Canossa was a ritual of negotiated surrender, *deditio*, not of penance. See his "Demonstration und Inszenierung," repr. in *Spielregeln der Politik*, 229–57 at 240–43.

[176] The key offender is Stephen Greenblatt, *Renaissance Self-Fashioning: From More to Shakespeare* (Chicago: 1980), still followed by Talal Asad in his excellent article, "Towards a Genealogy," 65f., despite a welcome *caveat* (68). For a recent critique, see David Aers, "A Whisper in the Ear of Early Modernists," in *Culture and History 1350–1600*, ed. David Aers (Detroit: 1992), 191–92, 195–96.

[177] See Kurt-Ulrich Jäschke, review of *Begging Pardon*, by Koziol, *Francia* 23:1 (1996): 278–82, with Koziol, *Begging Pardon*, 316–21.

[178] Liudprand, *Antapodosis* 4.7, 99:140–55.

[179] Asad, "Towards a Genealogy," 67–70.

angelis et hominibus) simultaneously indicted the pope's manipulation of the rites of penance, which he had turned into carnal theater, and pointed to Henry's greater spirituality.[180] But according to Henry's enemies, the king had stage-managed his penance, disguising his fierceness under the garb of dovelike simplicity. Aptly, therefore, he had been absolved by the pope only "as to his outward appearance" and as to "the exterior man." Hugh of Flavigny, to whom we owe this distinction, felt duty bound to expose the king's devil-inspired deception.[181] So did Gregory's other partisans. In a number of narratives, the celebration of the mass of reconciliation after Henry's penance becomes the occasion for a form of Eucharistic ordeal. The pope tested, according to Bonizo of Sutri (circa 1085/86), "whether Henry believed that Gregory was legitimately pope, whether Henry had been [justly] excommunicated . . . and whether Henry could be absolved" by the pope. Participation in the Eucharist would verify as well "whether Henry had humbled himself in the mind (*mente*) as [he had humbled himself] corporally (*ut corpore*)."[182] In most versions, incriminatingly, the king refuses to partake of the sacrament. For Berthold of Reichenau, writing circa 1080, Henry's refusal allowed the pope to see through the king's instrumentalization of the penance: "From this, the pope, thanks to the Spirit's revelation, wisely perceived as if some evidence of moral impurity [in the king] and as if a testimony of some hypocrisy hidden in him."[183]

Hypocrisy was not born with the polemics of the papal revolution. Already at the turn of the second century, Tertullian could attack the imperial cult by pointing to the participants' inward reservations. The Roman elites

---

[180] Beno, *Gesta Romanae ecclesiae contra Hildebrandum* 2, ed. Kuno Franke, MGH Libelli de Lite, vol. 2 (Hannover: 1892), 374:13–16: "*qui perverse iudicatus perversoris iudicis iniuriam et violentiam patienter et publice et cum lacrimabili afflictione, nudis pedibus in laneis vestibus, hieme preter solitum aspera, apud Canusium spectaculum angelorum factus et hominum et Hildebrandi ludibrium, triduo pertulit.*"

[181] Hugh of Flavigny, *Chronicon*, ed. Georg H. Pertz, MGH SS 8 (Hannover: 1848), 444:52–445:4, introducing Gregory's letter to the German princes recounting Canossa: "*Verum nos, quibus Christus fides, Christus refugium, Christus est solatium, nenias eius [regis Henrici] diabolico ab ore ructatas, iniquitatis calamo dictatas, confusionis atramento signatas, a memoria bonorum omnium repellentes, quid egerit, quomodo absolutionem, quantum ad exterioris hominis habitudinem, optinuerit, cum sacra scriptura testetur, quia 'Qui ficte deum querunt nunquam invenire merentur,' ex verbis patris nostri sepe facti* [Gregorii papae] *audiamus . . .*"

[182] Bonizo of Sutri, *Liber ad amicum* 8, ed. Ernst Dümmler, MGH *Libelli de Lite* 1 (Hannover: 1891), 610:22–27: "*Nam divinae mensae . . . hoc modo fecit esse participem, ut, si se mente ut corpore fecisset humiliatum et si se iure crederet pontificem, seque vero excommunicatum . . . et per hoc crederet posse absolvi, sacramentum . . . illi fieret in salutem; sin vero aliter, ut Iude post bucellam intraret in illum Satanas.*"

[183] Berthold of Reichenau, *Annales* ad an. 1077, ed. Georg H. Pertz, MGH SS 5 (Hannover: 1844), 290:16–18: "*Unde mox apostolicus quasi quoddam indicium inpuritatis et quasi testimonium latentis in eo cuislibet ypocrisis, spiritu revelante, non inprudenter capiebat.*" Henry's "deceitful and simulatory circumlocutions and promises" thematically dominates the narrative.

honored the ruling emperor through rites (*religio*) involving decoration, lighting, and banquets in the streets. However, theirs was a perverse spirit:

> They performed sacred [rites] for the emperor's prosperity and swore by his Genius . . . yet not in order to celebrate public rejoicings, but rather, changing the name of the ruler in their heart, to learn to perform public vows for themselves within the ceremonial of another man, and to consecrate an exemplar and an icon of their own hope [to rule].[184]

The cult of the emperor schooled hopeful usurpers in the worship that they hoped one day to receive themselves. Hypocrisy—the split between inner disposition and outward participation in the solemnities—went hand in hand with ambition. As we have seen, medieval authors shared sophisticated late antique Christian Carthage's ability to imagine hypocrisy at solemnities.[185] Hugh's murderous *adventus* and Chilperic's prostration constitute only two among many possible examples. Hincmar of Reims shows us the fifteen-year-old Charles, son of Charles the Bald, pretending submission to his father, probably with a bow, but "erect in a stubborn spirit."[186] But one of the more striking literary renditions of hypocrisy in ceremonial may be Radulphus Glaber's eleventh-century account of King Charles the Simple's betrayal in 923. Intending to make their king prisoner, Herbert of Vermandois and his young son visited him. Charles had been warned, but as they entered, a chance combination of the father's dissimulation and of the son's artlessness obliterated his suspicions:

> The king rose up and offered Herbert his kiss. But Herbert threw his body to the ground and received the king's kiss [in this posture]. Then as his son was kissed, the youth, albeit aware of the [planned] deceit, being new to deception, remained standing and did not prostrate himself before the king. Seeing this, his father, who stood close to him, struck powerfully the youth's neck, and said: "Know that one must never meet with an erect body one's lord and king when he is about to give his kiss."[187]

---

[184] Tertullian, *Apologeticum* 35.10–12, ed. Jean-Pierre Waltzing (Paris: 1929), 76–77: ". . . *sacra faciebant pro salute imperatoris et Genium eius deierabant . . . non ut gaudia publica celebrarent, sed ut vota publica propria iam ediscerent in aliena solemnitate et exemplum atque imaginem spei suae inaugurarent, nomen principis in corde mutantes.*"

[185] One should not forget who transmitted these late antique texts. For example, a large collection of Tertullian's works belonged to Agobard of Lyons, Paris BNF 1622.

[186] *AB ad an.* 862, 91: "[Karolo filio Karoli regis] *quasi subdito* [regi Karolo], *sed voce submissa et animo contumaci erecto . . .*"

[187] Radulphus Glaber, *Historiarum libri quinque* 1.5, ed. John Frances (Oxford: 1989), 12: "*Surgens itaque rex osculum ei porrexit; ille vero toto se humilians corpore, osculum regis suscepit. Deinde cum eius filium osculatus fuisset, stansque iuvenis quamvis conscius fraudis, novus tamen calliditatis, regi minime semet supplicaret, pater cernens qui propter astabat valenter alapam collo iuvenis intulit, 'Seniorem' inquiens 'et regem erecto corpore osculaturum non debere suscipere quandoque scito.'* "

The monistic "iconic" framework explodes. To texts that, read literally, suggest that prostrations before one's lord or king mirrored gestures of respect before God and His saints, one can oppose others that, just as literally, point to the theater of power as a potential stage for deception and hypocrisy. Even the good ruler, in fact, could put up a facade during ceremonial. For like the martyrs, God's elects rightfully sent deceptive signals if it served the higher good. Thus Henry II according to Thietmar of Merseburg: While laughing with his entourage during a festive Easter 1003 at Quedlinburg, he dissimulated his enmity against the rebellious Boleslav of Poland and Henry margrave of the Nordgau.[188] The Balinese may have bought lock and key the model of the Negara; medieval authors, and one must therefore suspect, medieval agents, stood too far from monism for "political rituals" to be simply integrative, either through action or belief. Doubts about any performance in the "theater of power" prevented that.

Yet the conclusion shouldn't be fully postmodern. Ruptured or contended ceremonies and fear of hypocrisy do not bespeak a culturally widespread, radical doubt vis-à-vis solemnities.[189] Late twentieth-century agnosticism and the psychoanalytical mantra of anxiety and destabilization cannot be projected back into the Middle Ages. The devil's existence maintains dualism; but it also makes the cultural ensemble cohere.[190] Indeed, the devil's existence accounts for the hypocrisy, deception, manipulativeness, and grasping contentiousness of one's enemies and renders necessary one's own exposition and subversion, through the pen or through violence, of these enemies' solemnities. Furthermore, it is truth that evil perverts. Thus, perversion itself testifies to the reality and validity of what it perverts.

Hypocrisy and devilish deception account, in part, for the attention medieval authors gave to the deciphering of ritual events. But more generally, owing to the basic Christian dialectic between the Old and the New Testament, early medieval political culture was a culture of interpretation. Ritual studies have long stood in the shadow of William Robertson-Smith. In his famous *Lectures on the religion of the Semites*, the grandfather of social anthropology decried "our modern habit . . . to look at religion from the side of belief rather than of [ritual and customary] practice" even though

---

[188] Thietmar, *Chronicon* 5.31, 257:4–9.

[189] See, e.g., Beckwith, "Ritual, Church and Theatre," 68: "The play [the *Croxton* play of Corpus Christi] can do nothing but intensify that doubt [in the real presence] in the very act of alleviating it."

[190] Cf. Carol Straw, *Gregory the Great* (Berkeley: 1988), 50, 62–65, 257, for the devil as God's jester and enforcer. Articulation of this idea owes much to conversations with Brad Gregory as well as to a seminar I gave in 1997 at the Historisches Seminar der Universität Münster.

"the antique religions had for the most part no creed [and] consisted entirely of institutions and practices." When applying anthropological theories to the medieval evidence, however, historians should be careful and
remember the explanation Smith gave for the prevalent prioritization of
opiniones over rites: "All parts of Christendom are agreed that ritual is important only in connection with its interpretation."[191] When analyzing a
medieval world dominated by Christianity, can we make the reverse of the
mistake Smith criticized—force upon the documents a grid that downplays
belief and ignores the centrality of interpretation for medieval culture? We
cannot, like Brian Stock, invent an early medieval world devoid of "spirit"
and characterized by unreflective "letter."[192] Already in late antiquity,
Christian groups watched, and partook in solemnities, their own as well as
those of the pagans, with an eye to the mystery to which these ceremonies
pointed. In polemics that reveal as much "orthodox" as "heretical" practice,
Hippolytus of Rome criticized the Naassenes, a Gnostic group, for "attending the [pagan] Mysteries of the Great Mother." Magna Mater's priests
were castrated, and the Naassenes watched her festivals in the belief "that
by means of what is enacted there, they perceive their [own] whole mystery." In other words, they read through the eunuch-priests' mutilated flesh
their own castration according to the spirit, that is, the sexual abstinence
that they advocated.[193] Were the Naassenes heretical and therefore exceptional? The spirit hidden in ceremonial letter is exactly what Perpetua (or
her hagiographer) found in the arena, and what Ambrose found in the
spatial organization that he imposed on the Jews and in the psalms that
they sang as he dug up their graveyard in Bologna.[194] It was a true spirit—
not the carnal ambition that Tertullian saw hidden behind the Roman
elites' participation in the imperial cult. In being a culture of interpretation,
whose discourse was dominated by a class of specialists in textual interpre-

---

[191] *Lectures on the religion of the Semites* (Edinburgh: 1889), 17–18. As for mythology, it takes
the place of dogma, but unlike dogma, it isn't binding, can be plural, and is posterior to ritual.

[192] Brian Stock, *Implications of Literacy: Written Language and Models of Interpretation in the
Eleventh and Twelfth Centuries* (Princeton: 1983), 91: "Ritual, too, underwent a transformation
[in the eleventh century]. Archaic ritualism needed no interpretation; the meaning arose from
the acting and performing of events. This sort of ritual was replaced by a complex set of
interactions between members of groups which were in large part structured by texts, or, at
the very least, by individuals' interpretations of them."

[193] Cf. Hippolytus, *Refutatio omnium haeresium* 5.9.7, ed. Miroslav Marcovich, Patristische
Texte und Studien 25 (Berlin: 1986), 166:33–40. Cf. ibidem 5.8.1, 154:1–4.

[194] See above, chapter 4, at n. 124. The elitism and secrecy inherent in mystery religions
probably ensured the loss of many *pagan* allegories. In Augustine's discussion of the double-
doctrine model we get a glimpse of pagan interpretation. See *De civitate Dei* 7.5, 190:3–7:
"*Primum eas interpretationes sic Varro commendat, ut dicat antiquos simulacra deorum et insignia
ornatusque finxisse, quae cum oculis animadvertissent hi qui adissent doctrinae mysteria, possent animam mundi ac partes eius, id est deos veros, animo videre . . .*"

tation,[195] early medieval political culture stands at an uncommensurable distance from many of the societies on which social scientists have based their theories.

In a debate with Claude Lévi-Strauss, Paul Ricoeur politely underlined the limits of the structural anthropologist's *pensée sauvage*. Lévi-Strauss's model, Ricoeur argued, yields decreasing results when applied to more complicated cultures with an autochthonous tradition of religious hermeneutics, cultures, that is, in which thought conceives of itself in relation to a past that has to be worked through in interpretation.[196] The Christian Middle Ages were such a world, and we should renounce, once and for all, importing into them the reductionist, too-often vague, and essentially alien concept of "ritual." Time has come to forget this dangerous word.

---

[195] Cf. Dan Sperber, *Du symbolisme en général* (Paris: 1974), 29–32, 60–61.

[196] Paul Ricoeur, "Structure et herméneutique," *Esprit* 322 = 31:11 (Nov. 1963), 596–627; reworked in idem, *Le conflit des interprétations. Essais d'herméneutique* (Paris: 1969), 31–63.

Chapter Seven

EPILOGUE

THE PREVIOUS CHAPTER ends on a negative note. "Ritual," it suggests, leads the historian into reductionist explanations of the medieval evidence. Is there a way to salvage the concept? A good recent analysis owed to Catherine Bell deconstructs "ritual" on philosophical grounds (ours are historical). Her critique convinces. But Bell then moves on to suggest an alternate concept, that of "ritualization." As astute reviewers have suggested, the product of her reformulation is very much open to the same criticisms that she levies against ritual.[1] We shall not travel this road. Like "feudalism," ritual carries within itself too much baggage to be conducive to clear thinking, at least as far as my own is concerned.[2] The call to the concept, moreover, too often legitimizes dubious scholarship, or at least tries to do so. Ironically, in the late twentieth century, validation through scholarly reference to the social sciences (or "theory" in general) has replaced the medieval typological reference to sacred scriptures.

The objections put forward in the preceding chapters against the concept and a number of its uses should now be reviewed. They have much to do with the conditions of possibility and validity of historical inquiry. The medieval data will bear certain questions and approaches, but not others.

For the early Middle Ages and most of late antiquity, simple access to a ritual as historical fact is impossible, if by "fact" one understands "event." This is not only because we do not have access to ritual practices, but only to texts depicting them (a given that renders impossible from the very start the use of certain kinds of anthropological models).[3] Nor is it a factor of the low density of surviving documents, which prevents the cross-checking

---

[1] See Philip Smith, review of *Ritual Theory, Ritual Practice*, by Catherine Bell [Oxford: 1992], *American Journal of Sociology* 98,1 (1992): 420–22.

[2] See E. A. R. Brown, "The Tyranny of a Construct: Feudalism and the Historians of Medieval Europe," *AHR* 79,2 (1974): 1063–88.

[3] This renders difficult, and my opinion impossible, the application of the "logic of practice" developed by Pierre Bourdieu. Bourdieu vehemently denies that one is allowed to treat a practice as text. A text is already modelized (and often a model); furthermore, it obfuscates systematically the practice it purports to report as well as the microlocal circumstances that would allow, for Bourdieu, apprehension of this practice. See Bourdieu, *Le sens pratique* (Paris: 1980), e.g., 34–35, 135–42, 162–63. For an attempt, see Stephen D. White, "Proposing the Ordeal and Avoiding It: Strategy and Power in Western French Litigation, 1050–1110," in *Cultures of Power*, ed. Thomas N. Bisson, 89–123.

of information and the reaching of truth at the intersection of plural evidence.[4] The impossibility is also a product of the specificities of medieval political culture and of its structures of communication. Even the rare cases in which there exist multiple documents bearing on the same single event can be hard to reconstruct. Indeed, the plurality may be itself an index of high contentiousness over this event, as the narratives focusing on A.D. 864 have shown. One fights over matters of importance. One forges events endowed with a high charge of meaningfulness. Historians have long known that medieval authors wrote with higher Truth, identified with the Good (what ought to have happened), rather than fact (what actually happened) in mind.[5] For what mattered truly (as they understood it), distortion (as we understand it) was more often than not the order of the day. This is especially the rule for many of the practices historiography has considered rituals par excellence—coronations, anointings, funerals. These events were too momentous for authors not to recraft them or invent them out of whole cloth if necessary. Often, indeed, the most detailed depictions of ceremonial come from outright forgeries.[6] It was not simply power politics, oriented to the struggles of the moment, that generated invented solemnities in texts. Ecclesiastical institutions wrapped their honor, prestige, rights, and properties in the halo of legendary past kings and imagined ceremonial.[7]

Structures of communication fed this tendency to imagine rituals. When those men and women whose opinion mattered did not constitute a face-to-face community but were spatially (or temporally) scattered (as for example the Carolingian imperial aristocracy), reporting (writing and telling) became more important than performance. If one must speculate on the dynamics of ritual in early medieval society and risk (despite my lachrymose warnings) an analysis, one must distinguish between compact and dispersed audiences. Owing to the different structures of the contexts of reception, an ordeal in a village and Theutberga's ordeal must have functioned in

---

[4] As in the early modern English world of libels, recently analyzed by Alastair Bellany, "Libels in Action: Ritual, Subversion and the English Literary Underground, 1603–1642," in *Politics of the Excluded*, ed. Tim Harris (New York: forthcoming); or in the early modern world of martyrdom reconstituted by Brad Gregory, *Salvation at Stake* (Cambridge, Mass.: 1999).

[5] See recently the articles in Horst Fuhrmann, *Fälschungen im Mittelalter*, 6 vols., Schriften der MGH 33:1–6 (Hannover: 1988–90), and above, introduction, 3.

[6] See, e.g., a forged charter for Saint-Maixent, recounting the reception of, and liturgical clamor to, Pippin of Aquitaine in the monastery. Léon Levillain, *Recueil des actes de Pépin Ier et de Pépin II rois d'Aquitaine* (Paris: 1926), 248–68 at 262, with Buc, "Political rituals and political imagination."

[7] See Buc, "Conversion of Objects: Suger of Saint-Denis and Meinwerk of Paderborn," *Viator* 28 (1997): 99–143; fundamental are Amy G. Remensnyder, *Remembering Kings Past: Monastic Foundation Legends in Medieval Southern France* (Ithaca: 1995), and eadem, "Legendary Treasure: Reliquaries and Imaginative Memory," *Speculum* 71, 4 (1996): 884–906.

markedly dissimilar fashion.[8] They need have been prepared differently, performed differently, and discussed differently (preparation, performance, and interpretation no doubt working on one another since, for agents, each presupposed the other). Perhaps, as Peter Brown proposed, the local ordeal produced social consensus (and, relatedly, few documents).[9] Ordeals undertaken by queens seem rather to have engendered disputes and strife (and more documents).[10] The fungibility of human perceptions and memory means that individual members of compact audiences might witness and remember differently an event. But the potential for divergence in interpretation was much greater for dispersed audiences, since many received their information secondhand and were not as constrained by local memory not to forge anew the report that they had received.

Yet a different structure for reception did not constitute a barrier to imaginings. The late medieval chronicler Jean Chastellain depicted the Duke of Burgundy as the sole coronator of the French king, and the initiator of the acclamation "Vivat Rex," much to the surprise of a twentieth-century specialist in the coronation. Chastellain's narrative does not correspond to the normal blueprint, in which the archbishop of Reims places the crown on the king's head and the peers shout the clamor of approval. "What would be otherwise a most vexing novelty" is explained by Chastellain's "poor observation point" during the actual ceremony.[11] But it is much more likely that he was not so badly informed, and purposefully claimed for his Burgundian master an exceptional rank materialized by an exceptional role in the accession solemnities. He may also have sought to place the duke's rival the king of France in the Burgundian's debt (and paint him as an ungrateful person in the light of later conflicts). In early modern Europe, with a political culture conditioned by much wider audiences and the existence of the printing press, some organizers of solemnities openly articulated their quandaries. One explains the need to produce brochures propounding the authoritative meaning of an event to correct already published misinterpretations. Another explains how the Rouen city council sought another road to avoid misinterpretation. In 1540, preparing

---

[8] As suggested to me by Amy Remensnyder.

[9] For the ordeal as an agent of consensus, see Peter Brown, "Society and the Supernatural: A Medieval Change," repr. in Brown, *Society and the Holy in Late Antiquity* (Berkeley: 1982), 302–32. But see the sharp rebuke in White, "Proposing the Ordeal," 104–105.

[10] See Steven D. White, "Imaginary Justice: The End of the Ordeal and the Survival of the Duel." Medieval Perspectives 13 (1998): 32–55." Geneviève Bührer-Thierry, "La reine adultère," *Cahiers de civilisation médiévale* 35, 4 (1992): 301–312, inventories a number of the sources.

[11] Cf. Richard A. Jackson, *"Vive le Roi": A History of the French Coronation from Charles V to Charles X* (Chapel Hill: 1984), 38–41.

the reception for a meeting in the city of the French king Francis I and Emperor Charles V, the Rouen magistrates avoided placing on the pictorial sets that decorated the way, "any writings or slogans because one or another prince or their subjects could have glossed on them or come up with inventive things (*deviner choses*) that would have not pleased one or another prince." Misinterpretations, oral or written, after or during a ceremony, created trouble.[12]

This discussion serves to remind us of a self-evident principle. The historian, being a historian, must apprehend any practice through an approach that is site specific and contextual. The cultural anthropology that he or she might develop should be local as well. But far from being fruitless, the elucidation of the places in which the social sciences and early medieval cultural practices converge or diverge helps to put the finger on what is specific to the latter. We are, then, not reduced to an apparently vacuous realm, interpretation. Interpretation itself points to "facts," facts of culture.

Chapter 6 has identified some of the places where there exists either a divergence or a false fit between modern social scientific models and the thought world that informs medieval documents. It has underlined the difference in the ultimate objective that they attribute to rite (the conservation of society or religious salvation) as well as the simplification entailed in looking monistically at a world where monism and dualism coexisted in a complex fashion; following the examination begun in chapter 5, it could have drawn as well the consequences of the origins of the modern opposition between ritual and ceremony.

The opposition between practices empty of any spirit and those that have a transcendental content or referent is a root dichotomy in European political culture. In its more extreme form, it is simply a dichotomy between pure, spiritless practice and pure spirit unencumbered with material form. Originally, as we saw, the opposition served claims to superiority. It was harnessed to successive theological causes, first to establish Christianity's superiority over Judaism, then to evacuate paganism of its religious substance, then in the age of the Gregorian Reform to the benefit of newer religious orders and movements, and finally during the sixteenth-century Reformation for the Protestant critique of Roman Catholicism. Simultaneously, and precisely because of this theological valence, the dichotomy could be employed in the service of nonecclesiastical entities and persons, such as the Ottonians or good King Guntram, by highlighting *mysterium* in friends' practices and denying it to opponents.

[12] See Buc, "Ritual and interpretation," 199–200. See also Peter Arnade, *Realms of Ritual,* 194, who suggests that the ability of early modern courts to enforce through the printing press an "authorized interpretation" of urban ceremonies gave them "a new and important advantage." But, as we saw, the importance of interpretive writing was not completely new.

Insofar as the dichotomy was founded on the hinge of sacred history—the transvaluation of ceremonious Judaism into spirit-indwelled Christianity—it could transport itself from *Geschichtstheologie* to history proper. In the nineteenth century, it became a category for historical discourse and analysis. Historical schemes could posit a movement from societies held together by vain ceremonial or empty ritual to societies animated by truth—be it the older truth of spiritual religion or the newer truths of law and scientific knowledge. The Enlightenment ideologized the latter evolution (from ceremony to science) in what Koselleck would call a future-looking historical concept (*Zukunftsbegriff* or *Erwartungsbegriff*).

In a related and probably slightly anterior appropriation, with the secularization of the notion of religious *societas* into "Society," the dichotomy was taken up by the still inchoate social sciences, in the service of typologies of nations and societies. Its originary normative valence often lingered, but not only in the direct transposition, which equated the better society with less ceremonial. Thinkers like Rousseau hesitated: Did reason and civic religion provide the better social bond? Indeed, a simple logical inversion of the value attached to the dichotomy's two terms produced schemes in which a more ceremonious society was seen as more cohesive. This latter configuration received a boost with the conscious reinvention of ritual by European states in an age of conservative reaction to the French Revolution and Enlightenment rationalism.[13] In a mutant replay of Catholic (and Evangelical) retorts to Reformed Protestantism, one doubted whether one could have a national spirit without external forms. In the distance between the social scientific dichotomy and its theological ancestry (to which it is now oblivious), we capture how medieval authors wrote about solemnities.

Indeed, that the authors who described solemnities usually did so with the aim to establish some superiority, and not to classify actions in an ostensibly value-neutral way, shaped narration. The first part of the essay has shown how late antique and medieval authors, when depicting actual or invented solemnities, employed a number of strategies. They might: (1) emphasize the *mysterium*, the vertical axis connecting the event to providential history and scriptural antetypes. To use the expression common to both Liudprand and Hincmar, the aim was to show how a "miracle of the ancients was being renewed" (*renovatum antiquum miraculum*) in the present. Authors might, inversely, (2) deemphasize the *mysterium* when dealing with a world they considered as hopelessly secular or with enemies to whom they wanted to deny sacrality (unless reference could be made to

[13] See, e.g., David Cannadine, "The Context, Performance and Meaning of Ritual: The British Monarchy and the 'Invention of Tradition,' c. 1820–1977," in *The Invention of Tradition*, ed. Terence Ranger and Eric Hobsbawm (Cambridge [UK]: 1983), 101–64.

providential condemnation).[14] Since writers anticipated struggles over interpretation, and no doubt had experience or report of real clashes, they (3) papered over and hid the presence of alternate readings of the solemnity, or of actual challenges to it during its performance, and suggested that it had proceeded smoothly; or, alternately, they (4) underlined disruptions, ambiguities, and alternate understandings when the solemnity, real or imagined, served their enemies. Obviously, often enough, they (5) combined these strategies.[15]

One can assume that social agents had recourse to liturgification in action as well as in writing (even if, given the crafted nature of the sources, it is difficult to ascertain when it actually was employed).[16] *Mysterium*, when present in a source, was purposefully and demonstratively evident as such. This visibility accounts in part for the attractiveness for medievalists of certain strands of anthropology, and (in part also) for the success with which they are employed.

Such places in which social scientific models and medieval documents seem to cohere are as instructive as the places where they do not, as soon as one identifies the grounds for convergence. This takes us back to Clifford Geertz's Negara, already discussed in chapter 6. In a recent book, Renato Rosaldo has distinguished between two scholarly conceptions of ritual. According to him, they correspond to two really existent kinds of rituals. Rosaldo characterizes the two scholarly approaches as, respectively, the "microcosmic view" of ritual (he cites Durkheim and Geertz as examples), and ritual seen "as a busy intersection." The first kind of ritual "encapsulates a culture's wisdom." The second kind acts as a "catalyst"; it "precipitates processes" that unfold over a long time.[17] In dealing with the Middle Ages, historians have preferred the microcospic view. In this model, the performance constitutes a microcosm, in which a macrocosm, namely, a culture's essence, values, or structures, stand condensed. Through an interpretation of the performance, one can gain access to the greater cultural whole. This preference is not necessarily always the product of laziness—the temptation to divine in a single sacrificial victim's liver the makeup of

[14] As in the case of Charles the Bald's death, above, chapter 2, 85–87.

[15] For examples, see Buc, "Ritual and interpretation."

[16] The dynamics receive a further dose of complexity with the onset of systemwide conflicts between kings and the Church after the Gregorian Revolution. Liturgification had always provided a wedge through which clerics might assert authority. But in the High and late Middle Ages, when the distinction between *regnum* and *sacerdotium* was actualized in a radical degree, systematic claims to clerical preeminence could derive from liturgification. See Buc, *L'Ambiguité*, 318–19 and nn. 18–19; Marc Bloch, *Les rois thaumaturges*, reed. (Paris: 1983), 216 n. 1. Correspondingly, independent-minded laymen sought a sacred history without a clergy central to it.

[17] Renato Rosaldo, *Culture and Truth: The Remaking of Social Analysis*, rev. ed. (London: 1993), 15–17.

the whole.[18] The propensity owes much to the liturgification of the sources. It is also a factor of the theological origins of anthropology. In the liturgy, the really real, Truth, is present and whole. The Mass commemorates and reenacts Christ's sacrifice, *sub specie eternitatis*. The Man-God's death is itself a recapitulation of all of sacred history, contains within itself the cosmos in its totality, and explains the essence of the human being in its fallen and redeemed state.[19] In exploring medieval Christian political culture, then, one can legitimately start with the hypothesis that a liturgical or liturgified ceremony, for instance, the investiture, miniaturizes key conceptions, beliefs, and values.[20]

But solemnities did not miniaturize an unproblematic conception of order. As argued in the previous chapter, this is why medievalists cannot apply to medieval Christendom Geertz's model of "religion as a cultural system" without fundamental revisions. Christian self-understanding would have rejected the continuum between "culture" and "religion." The relationship between Church (*ecclesia*) and world (*mundus, saeculum*) was anything but straightforward. In early medieval Christianity, there coexisted simultaneously two contradictory urges, which Gerd Tellenbach has labeled the sacramental and the ascetic, and which were related to what this essay labeled the monist and dualist models. The one strove to fully extend the Church into the world; the other to keep the *saeculum* at bay.[21] This second strand of Christian thought was self-consciously "countercultural" and vociferously spoke of separation from the ways of the *saeculum*. Anthropologists, reacting to the illegitimate extension of Western categories, have underlined rightly how the sacred-profane dichotomy dear to Durkheim is far from a general attribute of all cultural ensembles. But

---

[18] See Ginzburg (as in introduction, n. 31).

[19] Other key moments of Christ's life recapitulated sacred history in the same way. See Leo, *Tractatus* 26.2, CCSL 138, 126:24–30, on Christ's Nativity: "Even though childhood, which the Son of God's majesty did not spurn, has been transported, through an increment of age, to maturity, and even though through undergoing fully the Passion and the triumph of the Resurrection all the deeds (*actiones*) of the humble state that He took on for our sake have passed away, nevertheless, today's feast of Jesus born from the Virgin Mary renovates for us these sacred beginnings. And when we worship the birth of our Lord and Savior, we are found to celebrate our own beginnings. Indeed, Christ's engendering is the origin of the Christian people, and the birthday of the Head is the birthday of the body." Leo moves on to state that humans may be different in orders and in time, but all baptized are reborn in Christ's birth, just as His crucifixion, resurrection, and ascent are the crucifixion, resurrection, and ascent of all (126:32–37).

[20] As argued by Keller, "Die Investitur," especially 58–59, 72–74.

[21] See Gerd Tellenbach, *Libertas: Kirche und Weltordnung im Zeitalter des Investiturstreites* (Leipzig: 1936), partial trans. as *Church, State, and Christian Society at the Time of the Investiture Contest* (Oxford: 1940; reed. Toronto: 1991).

the dichotomy is certainly present in that medieval Christian West that generated it, and from which the early social sciences borrowed it.[22] Let us accept, hypothetically, that the common social-scientific axiom is true, that medieval religion was an integral subset of the medieval cultural complex. It is, in this case, susceptible to social-scientific analysis just as any other cultural data. But the terms of this analysis have to respect the specificities of the religion considered. For medieval religion's key symbols and its grid of meanings speak not only of continuities, but as well of deep reversals and hard-to-bridge chasms. The oppositional self-understanding must be taken into account in any approach to medieval religion as a cultural system.

The coexistence of "good" (consensual) and "bad" (contested or manipulated) rituals is symptomatic of the paradoxical complexity of early medieval understandings. One of the key values liturgy conveyed is consensus. Made into an axiom thanks to the meeting of oligarchic Roman political culture and early Christian values, the *consensus omnium* is both a medieval Catholic sine qua non for the liturgy and a modern social-scientific object. Historically speaking, the one determined the other. This inheritance explains the connection posited between ritual, consensus, order, and social cohesion. But not every culture associates religious ceremonies with consensus, order, and community. And not every society makes consensus into a key value. If one trusts Inga Clendinnen's evocative reconstruction of the world of the Mexica, Aztec ritual was fundamentally violent, individual centered, and competitive, and Aztec discourse did not connect religious practices and community formation.[23] While (as seen with martyrdom and other prophetic modes of action) medieval political culture had a place for transgression and violence, it was with a view to the consensus ideally and ultimately to be achieved.

To see how these contradictions played themselves out outside the texts, I must turn to speculation. I emphasize that this is *speculation*. We do not have the data that would warrant firm conclusions about social action without calling on universalizing models of society and human behavior—precisely what I have tried to avoid. The following paragraphs, then, are fully *tentative* and should not be employed to build further historiographical syllogisms.

---

[22] See the discussion in François-André Isambert, *Le sens du sacré. Fête et religion populaire* (Paris: 1982), 215–97 (a book that has faced similar aporias as this one). My thanks to Jean-Claude Schmitt for the reference.

[23] Inga Clendinnen, *Aztecs: an interpretation* (Cambridge [UK]: 1991). Laura Nader, *Harmony Ideology* (Stanford: 1990), explains how anthropologists and natives alike came to consensualize Mesoamerican indigenous cultures. I am grateful to Nancy Kollmann for this reference.

The centrality of certain ceremonial practices to narratives suggests that they were extremely important in reality.[24] For while it is a priori possible that the literary tradition autonomously replicated certain tropes that no longer corresponded to living values and actual contemporary behavior, it is much more likely that one finds these solemnities in the sources because of the weight the ambient culture attached to them. For instance, processions (litanies and *occursus*) seem to have been a favorite means in the ninth-century Carolingian world for expressing the quality of a political relationship. The high value the sources placed on consensus must have been shared by medieval social agents, at the very least by those in the higher spheres who were the audience of clerical narrative and from whose family circles the upper clergy were recruited. Beliefs and ideas must have had an impact on behavior and on the functioning of ceremonies. Experience and expectation feed back into action. If a culture upholds that certain practices express consensus, the performance of such practices is likely to generate a degree of consensus (since consensus is first and foremost a thing of the mind).[25] But here again, the belief in evil and manipulation must have interjected doubt, opened a window for interpretation and even dissent, and rendered problematic the generation of consensus. For in an early medieval political culture that believed in the devil, not all consensus was good.[26]

The sources, correspondingly, do not merely show the importance attached to consensus. They suggest also that social actors cheated and manipulated what Althoff calls the "rules by which one plays politics."[27] Far from being governed by irrefragable *Spielregeln*, solemnities could be disrupted. We should not think of such oppositional acts of violence as

---

[24] See Koziol, *Begging*, 323.

[25] The reasoning's abstracted structure is: "The belief that A expresses/generates B entails that the performance of A expresses/generates B." The validity of the syllogism depends on the categories that B belongs to. Compare: "The belief that certain magical practices make yams grow engenders the growth of yams." The proposition is false since yams are not things of the mind. A more interesting, for less clear-cut, proposition is: "The belief that certain practices express consensus means that the performance of such practices must generate a degree of social cohesion." But here one does not have simply A and B, but A, B (consensus), and B' (social cohesion), and therefore the implicit idea that B expresses B' or B generates B'. Is this principle that consensus expresses/generates social cohesion a belief of the natives or is the principle a theorem of the social scientist?

[26] E.g., Thietmar, *Chronicon* 6.6, 280:14–16: "*Longobardorum vero mens hactenus in malo unanimis divinae pietatis instinctu dividitur, et ab iniusto supplantatore disiuncta ...*" See also above, ch. 3, n. 123.

[27] One fine example being Hugh of Lusignan's *Conventum*, recently studied by Dominique Barthélemy, "Du nouveau sur le *Conventum Hugonis?*" *Bibliothèque de l'Ecole des chartes* 153 (1995): 483–95, and by Stephen D. White, "Politics of Fidelity: Hugh of Lusignan and William of Aquitaine," *Georges Duby. L'écriture de l'Histoire*, ed. Claudie Duhamel-Amado and Guy Lobrichon (Bruxelles: 1996), 223–30, who takes an approach diametrically opposed to Althoff's.

exceptions that confirm the rule that normally one played according to the rules, and therefore assume that, being transgressions, they were savagely punished, hence extremely rare. First, that ceremonies proceeded according to a rough blueprint allowed opponents to act at the most judicious moment. In Liudprand of Cremona's *Antapodosis* the word *mos*, ritual custom, regularly flags and announce political plots made possible by the regularity of solemnities.[28] Second, and more fundamentally, these disruptions could be rationalized as serving the higher good. One does not have to wait for the chilling late medieval world of Philippe de Commynes, putatively the age of incipient reason of state and Machiavellianism, *avant la lettre*, for murders during peace parleys. A Frankish source recounting frontier warfare will not blame the use of *calliditas* against pagan enemies—even when recently converted. Inviting a Norman chieftain to a colloquium on an island, a standard locus for peacemaking, to slaughter him seems to have been considered fair game.[29] Similar transgressive behavior against fellow Christians, planned or executed, was considered, no doubt, as impiety and even blasphemy by the perpetrators' opponents.[30] But as for the perpetrators, they could rationalize their deeds by downplaying the Christian morality of their opponents (hence bringing them closer to pagans and apostates) and by adopting the stance of service to higher ends transmitted by the cultural memory of martyrdom. Whether transgression was ultimately punished or legitimized depended greatly on the balance of force on the ground.

Consequently, contemporaries were starkly aware that danger inhered in ceremonies. The possibility that violence might occur diverted the pen of the early eleventh-century chronicler Thietmar of Merseburg, and perhaps the attention of Otto I himself in 961, away from the liturgical meaning of the imperial coronation toward down-to-earth considerations. On the eve of the 961 ceremony in Rome, Thietmar reports, Otto ordered his swordbearer Ansfrid not to pray while the liturgy was under way, but to hold tight the sword of state above his head. The Saxon ruler suspected that the Romans might make an attempt on his own life while he lay prostrate in prayer.[31] Here, far from symbolizing the God-given imperial ministry

---

[28] See above, ch. 1. And, as recently suggested, the ceremony might be chosen as the date for violence so as to have the greatest symbolic impact. See Robert Jacob, "Le meurtre du seigneur dans la société féodale," *Annales ESC* 45, 2 (1990): 247–63.

[29] Commynes, *Mémoires* 3.11–12, ed. Joseph Calmette, reed. 3 vols. (Paris: 1981), 1.248–49; *Reginonis Chronicon ad an.* 885, 124. *Colloquia* belong to the rituals regulated by Althoff's rules, see his "Colloquium familiare—colloquium secretum—colloquium publicum," repr. in idem, *Spielregeln der Politik*, 157–84.

[30] Compare William Longsword's 942 assassination (Philippe Lauer, *Louis d'Outre-Mer* [Paris: 1889], 87f., 276–84; nicely analyzed in Koziol, *Begging*, 155–56).

[31] Thietmar, *Chronicon* 4.32, 169–71.

(Romans 13.1–7), the *gladium* was rematerialized as the only weapon allowed in Saint-Peter, and potentially the sole barrier between the emperor
and the hidden blade of a would-be assassin. Obviously, one should not
naively use this text as if it reported faithfully the Saxon king's intimate
fears in 961. This story, rather, cloaked the figure of Ansfrid, later bishop
of Utrecht (995–1010) in a dramatic aura, for the benefit of his see and his
family's ecclesiastical foundations, sometime between 961 and its reception
in the *Chronicle*, circa 1013.[32] Still, it points to a fact of culture: Thietmar
or his source found danger, rather than smooth performance, the most
fitting mood to attach to the emperor-making liturgy.

The feeling of danger that hovers in many sources suggests that even
when undisrupted solemnities did not necessarily produce for all participants and observers a seamless icon of order. Furthermore, as argued in
chapter 6, the smoothest performances could be interpreted *mala parte* as
deceptive shows reflecting less heavenly kingship than devilish ambition.
Paradoxically, then, when one reinscribes medieval solemnities within the
medieval thought world in its full complexity, and not in the medieval
thought world as simplified by social-scientific monism, one is led to suspect that participants could have a hard-nosed attitude. When one identifies medieval political culture to its monist strand, it is logical to argue, for
instance, that a royal coronation such as Otto I's in 936 played out the
ideal structure of the German kingdom.[33] But if one also takes dualism into
account, in any reconstruction of the event, dissent, pious dissimulation,
and divergent interpretations have to be imagined as well.[34] Yet this did not
disrupt incommensurably people's willingness to participate in solemnities
or the trust that they were necessary. The dialectic between monism and
dualism allowed good and bad rituals, confidence and doubt, to coexist
without cognitive dissonance. Just as the conviction that some false saints
trod the earth and that some pseudo-relics lay enshrined in churches did
not shatter a general belief in sanctity, solemnities were all at once (individ-

---

[32] For the date of Book 4, see Holzmann's introduction, xxix; for Ansfrid, see Herbert
Grundmann, "Bemerkungen zur Kaiserkrönung Ottos I.," repr. in *Otto der Grosse*, ed. Harald
Zimmermann (Darmstadt: 1976), 214–16.

[33] Schramm, "Die 'Herrschaftszeichen,' die 'Staatssymbolik' und die 'Staatspräsentation'
des Mittelalters," in *Kaiser*, 1.30–58, at 31–32.

[34] All the more as, while our principal source, Widukind of Corvey, makes the 936 coronation the seamless beginning both of the second book of his *Deeds of the Saxons* and of Otto's
rule, other sources suggest that Otto had to struggle with his brothers for the *regnum*, and
that his brother Henry had to be kept under guard by a Saxon faithful away from the ceremony. See Flodoard, *Annales ad an.* 936 (cited above ch. 1 n. 5). That Henry was being
watched in Saxony by one of Otto's closest allies is reported by Widukind himself, *Deeds* 2.2,
67:6–10.

ually) objects of doubt and (as a genre) a central part of the accepted order.[35] The devil's existence, and the dualism whose principle he was, accounted for manipulation of rituals and for evil consensus; that, according to the monist framework, he was ultimately God's agent and subject to His will may have allowed many a social agent to tolerate suspected disjunctions between solemnities' letter and spirit. But since paradoxes have two terms that cannot be completely collapsed together, this historian wonders how complete this resolution was. The individual voices that refused prostration before king and magnates as well as those that considered it the order of things should be allowed to stand without synthesis.

Finally, texts were forces in the practice of power. They should not be decrypted for (elusive) facts about rituals and then set aside. Documents such as the Lothariangian archbishops' chain letter of protest against Nicholas I, the *Annals of Saint-Bertin*, martyrs' *Acta* and *Passiones*, the *Antapodosis*, or Gregory's *Ten Books of Histories* were instruments of power. Their authors sought to impact directly the present. If, in the words of Geoffrey Koziol, "ritual was part of political reality,"[36] so were—and perhaps even more so for all that we know—texts depicting "rituals" or announcing their performance.

First, a solemnity reported in a text might have an impact as report. In a letter, all the more significant as it was preserved in an early medieval formulary and hence considered a potential blueprint for other such actions, the brethren of a minster beseeched their colleagues from another institution for help. The king had taken away from them the privilege "to receive a rector" taken from their own community. To reverse this decision, they would pray God, they said, but also asked a favor of their fellows, "that these coming three days you implore God's mercy both in psalmodies and in masses that the clement and merciful God deign to infuse in the hearts of the lord king such and such and of the lady queen and of their magnates and of the rulers (*rectores*) of the palace that" the king rights this wrong.[37] For a secular historian, God and the saints, aroused by this translocal liturgical network, could not change the king's heart. He or she must, however, assume that contemporaries believed the contrary. It was the imaginative knowledge that such a liturgy, with its tinge of protest,

---

[35] Cf. Klaus Schreiner, "*Discrimen veri ac falsi*. Ansatz und Formen der Kritik in der Heiligen- und Reliquienverehrung des Mittelalters," *Archiv für Kulturgeschichte* 48, 1 (1966): 1–53.

[36] Koziol, *Begging Pardon*, 305, 307.

[37] Ed. Karl Zeumer, *Formulae merowingici et karolini aevi*, MGH Leges 5 (Hannover: 1886), 262:11–25, to be read in conjunction with the text copied right before it in the collection, a clamor to the king in which the minsters' brethren request him, "as if we all lay down prostrate at your most glorious feet," to right this very wrong.

had been performed, not the performance itself and whichever emotions it might directly generate, that would (God helping) influence the king to give back the right of election to the brethrens.

Second, solemnities engendered texts, often at a distance from their very performance, that took on a life of their own. Exegetical culture taught that there existed a disjunction between the seeming and the real. This gap called forth interpretation. Contemporaries cannot have experienced political solemnities without wondering how to understand the message. They would have tried to resolve any polysemy apparent in the performance.[38] But the interests of persons and groups taking part in, witnessing, or receiving reports concerning it could diverge and had the potential to create divergent versions. This could happen over time. The 754 meeting between Stephen II (r. 752–57) and Pippin I (r. 751–68) at Ponthion, preface to the anointing by the pope of the Frankish ruler and his two sons, may have been polysemic in itself; the divergence between Frankish and papal interests generated even more polysemy. For the *Liber Pontificalis*, Pippin sent his son Charles with some magnates at a hundred miles' distance from the palace, then went out himself for a distance of three miles with his wife, other children, and magnates, descended from his horse, prostrated himself before the pope, and served as his groom for some of the way. In the version provided by the *Chronicle of Aniane*, Pippin does not participate in the *occursus*, does not perform groom service, and it is the pope who prostrates himself to the ground "along with his clergy, covered with ashes, and dressed in a hair-shirt," to ask for help against the encroaching Lombards.[39] This inferiority of the pope in ceremonial dovetails well with the chronicler's interest, in the first years of Louis the Pious's reign, to downplay papal authority, an interest that itself testifies to the debates over Frankish emperorship that Charlemagne's 800 coronation had provoked. Circa 818/19, looking back at a foundational moment for the Carolingian dynasty, texts were produced or recycled that argued, through ceremonial, one position or the other.[40] It was the present these narratives sought to shape, not the past in which they often located their highly charged solemnities.[41] As ever, the historian's task is to identify the relevant context for a text.

[38] Compare Koziol, *Begging Pardon*, 307–11.

[39] *Vita Stephani II* 25, in *LP*, 1.447:10–15. Noble, *Republic of St. Peter*, 80, remarks on the divergence with the *Chronicle of Aniane* ad an. 754, MGH SS 1, 292:43–293:9. Compare the readings in Fichtenau, *Lebensordnungen*, 1.50, tr. Geary, 32, and the discussion in Koziol, *Begging*, 309–10. See now Rosamond McKitterick, "The Illusion of Royal Power in the Carolingian Annals", *EHR* 460 (2000): 1–20, casting doubt on the reliability of the Carolingian renditions of papal involvement in the dynastic change of 751–54.

[40] See Buc, "Political rituals and political imagination."

[41] See Johannes Fried, "Die Königserhebung Heinrichs I.," with Hagen Keller, "Widukinds Bericht."

Yet a scholar should not confuse the intensity of his or her interest in an object (here "ritual") and the degree of centrality of this object for a past society. "Ritual in text" was one of several nodes of meaningfulness in narratives, and one of several vectors for competition. The best way for the historian to deal with it, then, may be to use it as an indicator of conflict. Prowess (or abject defeat) in warfare, "sacred virtues" (or the lack thereof), and the sexual propriety of women (or their misbehavior) constituted other markers of legitimacy or illegitimacy. Outside the realm of texts, brute force and such seldom mentioned factors as economic and social resources made the power of kings and princes.[42] Oftentimes, ceremonies may have been feeble dross. If this essay has focused on "ritual," as defined by historiography, it is because only this focus could bring out its place in medieval political culture and invalidate some of the claims of this historiography. Another book, by another historian, may well build on this secure sense of limits. Humbly, I close mine here.

---

[42] This is why, in my opinion, Gerd Althoff's *Verwändte, Freunde und Getreue* (Darmstadt: 1990) succeeds as a book much better than his *Spielregeln*: More dimensions of aristocratic action are taken into account and so "ritual" is less of an autonomous force.

Index

absolutism, 234
Abyssinia, ceremonies in, 178
acclamations, 129, 132, 141–42, 151, 154.
  See also clamor, slogans
Adalbert, king of Italy, 17, 20, 27, 51
Adalbert, margrave of Tuscany, 80–82, 87
Adelheid, queen of the Saxons, 36, 49
Adventius, bishop of Metz, 57, 64–65
adventus, 5, 37, 39–42, 44, 74–76, 98–99,
  113–14, 176; of the martyr, 151. See also
  occursus
Albinus, governor of Marseilles, 116
Alcuin, 24
Aleonissa, J.-F., 183n.67
Althoff, Gerd, 1, 8, 19, 26, 31, 256
Ambrose, bishop of Milan, 61, 91–92, 114,
  154, 239, 246; as model, 120–22, 239
amicitia, 24–28, 146
amphitheater, symbolic of secular power,
  152–53. *See also* circus games, 97
Amyraut, Moyse, 210
Andernach, battle of, 46, 48
Andreas of Bergamo, 85, 239
anger, 100n.52, 141; royal, 70, 75, 115, 117
Angilbert, archbishop of Milan, 239
Angiltrud, empress, 25, 54
animals, submissive, 23, 134
Annals of Fulda, 55, 67–70, 80–81, 86
Annals of Fulda, Regensburg Continuation
  of, 51, 53–54
Annals of Lorsch, 108
Annals of Saint-Bertin, 58, 67, 70, 72, 75, 79.
  See also Hincmar of Reims
anointing, 46, 249
Ansfrid, count, 257–58
Antapodosis. See Liutprand of Cremona
anthropological readings, 4; and medieval
  history, 229
antiquarianism, 176–77
appearances and reality, 23–24
Apuleius, 129
Aquinas, Thomas, 164, 166
arms, forbidden in churches, 111
Arnulf of Bavaria, 35, 45

Arnulf of Carinthia, emperor, 19, 40–42,
  51–55, 62, 76
Asad, Talal, 3n.7, 161n.3, 171n.20, 224
assassination of kings, 27, 94, 105, 110–11,
  258
assemblies, 88, 131–32, 140–41, 199, 201,
  205; provincial, 221n.98. *See also* festivals
asylum, 99. *See also* sanctuary
Augustine of Hippo, 3, 10, 20, 22, 91, 118,
  120, 144–47, 171, 185, 188–89, 197, 201
autocracy, 96
Auxerre, 61
Aztecs. *See* Mexica

bad ritual, 97; defined, 8, 10; and good rituals, 255; invalidating, 72; role of, 78; *See
  also* good rituals; manipulation
banners, 54, 72, 76, 77. *See also* flags
banquet, 5, 6, 29–30, 44, 52, 93, 98n.41,
  113–16, 138, 167; role for group, 202
baptism, 5–6, 45, 84, 89n.3, 103, 139, 148–
  49, 165, 167, 176, 200; of Clovis, 107,
  193
Barcelona, 39
Bavaria, 17–19, 34, 51–52, 54, 83
Bede, 148
beginnings, 144, 182–84, 225
Begriffsgeschichte, 5, 162–63
belief, 256; devalued or displaced, 161, 225–
  26
Bell, Catherine, 248
Beno of Osnabrück, 242–43
Berengar I, king of Italy, 20, 25–27, 41
Berengar II, king of Italy, 16–20, 23–24,
  26–27, 30–31, 33–34, 36, 40, 46, 51
Bergamo, 41–43
Bernard, Jean-Frédéric, 178–79
Bertramm, bishop of Bordeaux, 103–4
Bidenbach, Balthasar, 171–72
Birma, ceremonies in. *See* Pegu
Birten, battle of, 22, 47–50
bishops, powers of, 92
blindness, 7, 79, 80, 100, 137–39, 142, 155
Bloch, Maurice, 142n.78, 171n.21

Lightning Source UK Ltd.
Milton Keynes UK
17 February 2011
167693UK00001B/33/P